Praise for *Practical Augmen*

"A valuable addition to the library of anyone setting out on their virtual journey."

—Dr Rab Scott

Head of VR, Nuclear AMRC

"A well-presented introduction to advanced visualization technologies, which will provide readers with an informed overview of this fast-paced, high-tech industry."

—Chris Freeman

Augmented Reality Technical Fellow, University of Sheffield AMRC

"Filled with excellent, imaginative information that will inform both experienced and first-time readers alike. *Practical Augmented Reality* is worth reading not only for its wealth of data and research, but also for its insights into the markets and opportunities ahead of us. If you have an interest in this exciting new technology, this is a must-have resource and an enjoyable exploration into this brave new world."

—Roy Taylor

Corporate Vice President for Content and Technology, AMD (Advanced Micro Devices)

"Steven Aukstakalnis stands on the ever-changing edge of the virtual and augmented reality world. Drawing from a rich history in the industry, he is able to share a clear understanding of the technologies, products, and ideas that will reshape the way we work and play. May the knowledge he shares empower you to help create a truly fantastic new future!"

—Brent Baier

Creator of the Peregrine Glove

"Mixed or augmented reality is a grand frontier not only for computation, but for how people experience their world and each other. This book sets a frame around that which isn't framed. Read it in order to understand our new world."

—Jaron Lanier

Author of *Who Owns the Future* and *You Are Not A Gadget*

Practical
Augmented Reality

Practical
Augmented Reality

A Guide to the Technologies, Applications, and Human Factors for AR and VR

Steve Aukstakalnis

✦✦Addison-Wesley

Boston • Columbus • Indianapolis • New York • San Francisco
Amsterdam • Cape Town • Dubai • London • Madrid • Milan
Munich • Paris • Montreal • Toronto • Delhi • Mexico City
São Paulo • Sydney • Hong Kong • Seoul • Singapore • Taipei • Tokyo

Library of Congress Control Number: 2016946688

ISBN-13: 978-0-13-409423-6
ISBN-10: 0-13-409423-9

Text printed in the United States on recycled paper at RR Donnelley in Crawfordsville, Indiana

1   16

Publisher
Mark L. Taub

Executive Editor
Laura Lewin

Development Editor
Songlin Qiu

Marketing Manager
Stephane Nakib

Managing Editor
Sandra Schroeder

Senior Project Editor
Lori Lyons

Production Manager
Dhayanidhi

Copy Editor
Gill Editorial Services

Indexer
Tim Wright

Proofreader
H. Muthukumaran

Technical Reviewers
Yuval Boger
Victor Luo
Eric Maslowski
Carl Wakeman

Editorial Assistant
Olivia Basegio

Cover Designer
Chuti Prasertsith

Compositor
codeMantra

In memory of my mother and elder brother,
both of whom passed away in the course of writing this book.
You left us way too early and are deeply missed.

Contents

FOREWORD

After months of electrical, mechanical, Zero-G, underwater, and network certification, we had finally launched two Microsoft HoloLens mixed-reality devices to the International Space Station (ISS). On the morning of February 20th, 2016, our team, stationed at NASA Johnson Space Center's Mission Control, successfully made the first holographic call to space. Astronaut Scott Kelly picked up and proceeded to take us on a tour of his home for the past year. At one point, he guided us to the cupola (observation module), slowly lowered the solar shields, and showed us the curvature of the Earth as it floated into our view. As if that was not enough, Scott then drew annotations on top of the various ISS modules and talked about their importance in the discovery of science and the maintenance of life-support for the crew. This unforgettable moment was my affirmation in the future of virtual and augmented reality.

Back on Earth, we are using similar technologies at NASA to bring our scientists to Mars, provide CAD-level design visualizations to our spacecraft engineers, and enhance the capabilities of our robot operators. By providing better contextual awareness of the distant environments, we are dissolving the physical barriers between the operators and the robots they are expected to operate. By resolving issues earlier in the design, we can reduce the cost of building our spacecraft, which ultimately allows us to build more spacecraft.

Our fascination with this industry started many years ago as we investigated various hardware and software platforms. We have used many of the technologies that are discussed in this book and are excited for the many yet to come. Developing for this platform is unique and we often run into unforeseen challenges. Let this be a guidebook for understanding the expanding field of virtual and augmented reality as this technology becomes ubiquitous like the television and the internet. Start with an open mind and a clean slate and you can avoid some of the common misconceptions for new users.

At NASA, building spacecraft requires the right set of materials and resources, just as building an application in the world of VR/AR. As a developer, use this book as an index of equipment in your tool belt and make sure to pick the right tool for the right job, even if that means not using VR or AR at all.

Every spacecraft we build has various scientific instruments installed inside. To maximize science and reduce risk, we must be extremely selective in what payloads to ship. As a content creator, use the anecdotes in this book to help you choose the right experience for your target audience.

One of NASA's core missions is to inspire the next generation of explorers: the astronauts that will take humanity to the asteroids, Mars, and beyond. When the first representatives of Earth step foot on Mars, we will all be virtually present. We will welcome their arrival and explore alongside them. Together, we will make discoveries that will forever change our reality.

—Victor Luo
Senior Technical Lead, Software Systems Engineering
NASA Jet Propulsion Laboratory
California Institute of Technology
Pasadena, California
July 2016

PREFACE

Despite the public fascination with augmented reality (AR) and virtual reality (VR), few within the broader audience understand how these systems actually function. AR and VR are seen as cool technologies for better gaming and entertainment experiences, but beyond that point, the general understanding of the topic is vague. Since the initial wave of interest in the early 1990s, a new generation of tech-savvy youth, college aged individuals, and professionals has emerged with the same interest and fascination as two decades prior, but with relatively few up-to-date resources clearly explaining the enabling technologies, how they are intended to harness the strengths of the human perceptual system, or which show the variety of existing, problem-solving applications outside of gaming. This book attempts to fill that void.

Readers should recognize that, although the latest generation of products at the heart of this field come from highly talented individuals, the true pioneers of augmented and virtual reality can be found in the scientific literature, tech briefs, conference proceedings, and patents filings of the 1980s and 1990s. Those like Tom Furness, Mark Bolas, Stephen R. Ellis, Scott Fisher, Warren Robinett, Nathaniel Durlach, Ian McDowall, Fred Brooks, Henry Fuchs, Elizabeth Wenzel, Scott Foster, Jaron Lanier, and Tom DeFanti quietly worked in their labs solving the big problems, developing innovative hardware and software solutions, exploring the relevant human perception and performance issues, and in general, laying the groundwork for the current reemergence of this field.

It is upon their shoulders that I stand.

Who Should Read This Book

This book is intended as a supplementary text for undergraduate and graduate courses in computer science, engineering, architecture, and other fields that make use of standard computer visualization techniques as well as AR and VR systems.

If you are in business, engineering, or science, this book will detail a host of applications where these technologies are having a strong impact on design quality, cost control, more efficient collaboration and manufacturing workflows, and increased data understanding.

If you are a gamer or general AR/VR enthusiast, this book is ideal for providing a solid grounding in perceptual mechanics and the underlying enabling technologies of head-mounted displays, spatial sound solutions, sensors, and a range of tactile and force feedback devices.

Although there are no specific prerequisites, the author presumes an understanding of basic computing principles and human biology.

How This Book Is Organized

This book is organized in a manner that explains augmented and virtual reality systems from the inside out. As opposed to diving right into the various enabling technologies, it first looks at the mechanics of sight, hearing, and touch, each of which is immediately followed with respective explanations of wearable displays, 3D audio systems, and tactile/force feedback devices. The objective is helping you, the reader, gain an understanding and appreciation of how our extraordinary perceptual mechanisms directly dictate the design and application of relevant enabling technologies and the ranges of performance they attempt to achieve.

This book is separated into four parts:

- Part I, composed of two chapters, introduces basic concepts such as a clear delineation between augmenting and immersive displays and their respective histories, explanations of visual space and content, position and orientation in three dimensions, commonly used coordinate systems, and general navigation approaches.

- Part II, composed of ten chapters, explores the mechanics of our senses of sight, hearing, and touch, each followed by explanations of the key respective enabling technologies of visual, audio, and tactile displays, as well as sensors and input devices.

- Part III, composed of eight chapters, provides case studies and descriptions of a wide range of existing applications for these technologies in areas such as entertainment, architecture and construction, science and engineering, healthcare and medicine, education and training, telerobotics, and more.

- Part IV, composed of three chapters, explains the key human factors issues associated with the use of augmenting and immersive displays, legal and social considerations, as well as an outlook on what the future holds for key enabling hardware and software technologies.

The following is a detailed description of each chapter:

Part I, "Introduction to Augmented and Virtual Reality," spans Chapters 1 and 2.

- Chapter 1, "Computer-Generated Worlds," gives a general introduction to augmenting and immersive display systems, including optical and video see-through variants as well as a history of each.

- Chapter 2, "Understanding Virtual Space," provides a basic overview of the concept of virtual space, including the similarities and differences with physical space, the conventions used to define, characterize, and organize space, as well as approaches for navigation.

Part II, "Understanding the Human Senses and Their Relationship to Output / Input Devices," spans Chapters 3 through 12.

- Chapter 3, "The Mechanics of Sight," explores the physiological processes enabling us to visually perceive real and virtual worlds, including a review of the visual pathway, spatial vision, and monocular and stereo depth cues.

- Chapter 4, "Component Technologies of Head-Mounted Displays," examines ocularity, display types, imaging and display technologies, and optical architectures.

- Chapter 5, "Augmenting Displays," explores numerous monocular and binocular augmenting displays currently available on the market, highlighting their key functional and design differences as well as the initial uses for which they are intended.

- Chapter 6, "Fully Immersive Displays," presents the details of the latest generation of commercially available, fully immersive head-mounted displays across several classes ranging from PC and console-driven devices to lower end systems based on modern smartphones.

- Chapter 7, "The Mechanics of Hearing," explains how our ears convert rapid variations in the average density of air molecules into what we perceive as sound, how our brain localizes and separates sound sources, and how sound cues contribute to an overall sense of immersion within virtual environments.

- Chapter 8, "Audio Displays," details the various types of audio displays and spatial sound solutions used in augmented and virtual reality systems, examining their functional differences and the types of application settings within which each is most beneficial.

- Chapter 9, "The Mechanics of Feeling," explores the mechanisms enabling our sense of touch, including the anatomy of the skin, the functionality and range of capabilities of the various mechanoceptors and proprioceptors, and how tactile and kinesthetic cues can supplement visual and audio displays.

- Chapter 10, "Tactile and Force Feedback Devices," examines a number of technologies and product solutions used to produce tactile and kinesthetic cues, as well as the challenges in leveraging the power of our sense of touch.

- Chapter 11, "Sensors for Tracking Position, Orientation, and Motion," covers a variety of key sensor technologies used to track position, orientation, and motion of users, head-mounted displays, and input devices.

- Chapter 12, "Devices to Enable Navigation and Interaction," covers a number of the current and emerging technology solutions enabling navigation through and interaction with virtual environments and the objects contained therein.

Part III, "Applications of Augmented and Virtual Reality," spans Chapters 13 to 20.

- Chapter 13, "Gaming and Entertainment," digs in to some of the unique applications for augmenting and immersive systems in the areas of art and entertainment, including multiplayer first-person games (MFPG), location-based entertainment, and cinematic virtual reality. The chapter also highlights strengths and challenges posed in harnessing these new technologies within this application area.

■ Chapter 14, "Architecture and Construction," presents case studies that illustrate the widely varying ways in which augmenting and immersive displays are being used to solve design visualization, communication, and project management challenges.

■ Chapter 15, "Science and Engineering," explores actual ongoing application of these technologies in such widely varying areas as space systems, naval architecture, and automotive, marine, and nuclear engineering.

■ Chapter 16, "Health and Medicine," looks at the application of augmenting and immersive displays in such areas as the training of physicians, treatment of post traumatic stress disorder (PTSD) and phobias, vascular imaging, and healthcare informatics, highlighting the strengths and benefits of the solutions compared to methods traditionally employed.

■ Chapter 17, "Aerospace and Defense," presents case studies within which augmenting and immersive displays, spatial audio, and tactile and force feedback systems are used to leverage strengths of the human perceptual system in the control of complex machines such as jet aircraft to train astronauts and help refine skill sets and situational awareness of soldiers on the battlefield.

■ Chapter 18, "Education," explores some of the existing, high-impact applications for augmenting and immersive systems in tangible skills training, aiding students in learning abstract concepts in complex fields such as architecture, and experiential learning for children.

■ Chapter 19, "Information Control and Big Data Visualization," looks at the applications of immersive displays in the visualization, manipulation, and interrogation of massive data sets that are now generated by many scientific studies and business operations.

■ Chapter 20, "Telerobotics and Telepresence," explores several examples of the application of these advanced visualization and control technologies in the operation of semi-autonomous robotic systems at a distance.

Part IV, "Human Factors, Legal, and Social Considerations," spans Chapters 21 through 23.

■ Chapter 21, "Human Factors Considerations" looks at some of the more pressing complications and physical side effects resulting from the use of these advanced visualization tools, including such problems as visually induced motion sickness and vergence–accommodation conflicts. It also highlights steps that can be taken to minimize their impact.

■ Chapter 22, "Legal and Social Considerations," examines some of the profound legal, social, and ethical issues resulting from the rise of commercially available augmenting and immersive display technologies, including product safety, potential courtroom applications and the presentation of evidence, the increasing violence and realism of first-person games, and more.

- Chapter 23, "The Future," explores some of the next major advances for key enabling component technologies, highlighting the short- and long-term outlook and the benefits that the changes will enable.

In addition, this book includes two appendixes:

- Appendix A, "Bibliography," contains bibliographic citations for the parenthetical references found in the text of each chapter.
- Appendix B, "Resources," provides a consolidated list of dozens of visual displays, spatial audio solutions, tactile and force feedback devices, position/orientation sensors, and the web addresses for each of their manufacturers. Also included is a listing of a variety of DIY resources for those inclined to develop or tinker with their own system, and a list of product trademarks.

Conventions Used in This Book

The following typographical conventions are used in this book:

- *Italicized text* indicates emphasis on a word or phrase.
- **Bold** *text* indicates an important term or phrase.
- Parenthetical citations in the form (Doucet et al., 2012) are used extensively in this book and denote references to other works. In each instance, the full bibliographic citation can be found within Appendix A.

> note
>
> A note highlights useful or interesting information and facts.

Companion Website

The companion website to the book can be found at **PracticalAR.com**. This site provides regular updates on new products, sensors and applications, hyperlinks to important papers and presentations, an author blog, and more.

> Register your copy of *Practical Augmented Reality: A Guide to the Technologies, Applications, and Human Factors for AR and VR* at informit.com for convenient access to downloads, updates, and corrections as they become available. To start the registration process, go to informit.com/register and log in or create an account. Enter the product ISBN (9780134094236) and click Submit.

ACKNOWLEDGMENTS

Writing a book of any type takes time, research, and assistance from a variety of sources. From those who support and encourage you in the effort to those who beat you like a rented mule when the gears are not turning, each plays a critical role in arriving at a finished product. To this end, initial thanks go to God Almighty for the grace and wisdom provided over the course of the project. Next, my deepest thanks go to Laura Lewin, executive editor with Pearson Technology Group and Addison-Wesley Professional, who provided the opportunity and oversight. Laura pushed me hard to keep the effort on track and at a high standard. Heartfelt thanks also go to the editorial and production teams. Songlin Qiu was the detail-oriented development editor, and Olivia Basegio, editorial assistant, provided crucial support across all activities leading to publication.

This book has also been heavily influenced by a technical review panel; Victor Luo from NASA's Jet Propulsion Laboratory, Yuval Boger of Sensics, Inc., Eric Maslowski of the University of Michigan's UM3D Lab, and Carl Wakeland, a Fellow at Advanced Micro Devices, Inc… Your insights, recommendations, corrections, and willingness to share your time and expertise are graciously appreciated.

To my friends and colaborers, including Steven "1234" Harris, Peter and Sonya, John and Stacy, Bernie and Naomi, as well as the rest of my friends at HCBC, thank you for your encouragement and prayers.

And to my family: it has been said that gratitude is when memory is stored in the heart and not the mind. Know that you have filled both.

ABOUT THE AUTHOR

Steven Aukstakalnis (Awk-sta-call-niss) is the former Director of the Virtual Environment and Interactive Systems Program at the National Science Foundation Engineering Research Center for Computational Field Simulation. He has served on the professional research staff at the University of Washington and the faculty of Mississippi State University. He is the author of two previous books about virtual reality and interactive systems. The second, *Silicon Mirage*, was published in six languages and adopted as a text in schools around the world. He is an invited lecturer and researcher for a host of universities, corporations, and government agencies. Steven lives in South Florida and is an avid kayaker and sailor.

CHAPTER 1

COMPUTER-GENERATED WORLDS

Augmented and virtual reality are often part of the same conversation, though there are significant differences between the two technologies. One provides textual, symbolic, or graphical information that holds a real-time relationship with a situation or surroundings, and the other provides a complete replacement to our visual world. In this chapter we explore the basic foundations of augmented reality (AR) and virtual reality (VR), drawing clear distinctions between the differing capabilities of these systems and laying the foundation for a study of the enabling technologies and the host of problem-solving applications they enable.

What Is Augmented Reality?

The phrase *augmented reality* is a general term applied to a variety of display technologies capable of overlaying or combining alphanumeric, symbolic, or graphical information with a user's view of the real world. In the purest sense, and using the phrase in the manner for which it was originally coined, these alphanumeric or graphical enhancements would be aligned, correlated, and stabilized within the user's real-world view in a spatially contextual and intelligent manner.

Although the phrase *"augmented reality"* is itself a modern creation, coined in the early 1990s by Boeing research scientist Tom Caudell (Caudell and Mizell, 1992), the first technological developments enabling modern augmented reality devices can be traced back to the early 1900s and a patent filed by Irish telescope maker Sir Howard Grubb. His invention (patent No.12108), titled "A New Collimating-Telescope Gun-Sight for Large and Small Ordnance," describes a device intended for use in helping aim projectile firing weapons.

Grubb's description of the invention published in the 1901 Scientific Transactions of the Royal Dublin Society was of profound vision to say the least:

> *"It would be possible to conceive an arrangement by which a fine beam of light like that from a search light would be projected from a gun in the direction of its axis and so adjusted as to correspond with the line of fire so that wherever the beam of light impinged upon an object the shot would hit. This arrangement would be of course equally impracticable for obvious reasons but it is instanced to show that a beam of light has the necessary qualifications for our purposes."*

> *"Now the sight which forms the subject of this Paper attains a similar result not by projecting an actual spot of light or an image on the object but by projecting what is called in optical language a virtual image upon it." (Grubb, 1901)*

This invention solved a fundamental challenge presented by the human eye only being able to focus on one depth of field at a time. You're either focusing on something close up, or something in the distance, such as is illustrated in Figure 1.1. The design of the human eye makes it impossible to focus on both simultaneously. This makes aiming a rifle or pistol outfitted with only iron sights particularly challenging and a skill which, to this day, requires regular practice to master.

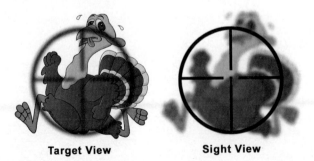

Target View   **Sight View**

Figure 1.1 This image illustrates one of the grand challenges in shooting posed by the human eye only being able to focus on one depth of field at a time.

Credit: Running turkey by dagadu / Depositphotos.com

Formally referred to as a reflector sight or reflex sight, Grubb's invention, the basic function of which is illustrated in Figure 1.2, used a series of optical elements to overlay a targeting reticle, focused at optical infinity, on a distant target.

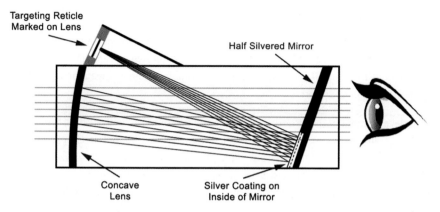

Figure 1.2 Adaptation of a 1901 patent diagram illustrating a version of Howard Grubb's collimating reflector sight suitable for firearms and small devices.

Grubb's innovation directly inspired the development of more advanced gun sights for use in military aircraft. The first known use of the technology for this purpose came in 1918 when the German optics manufacturer Optische Anstalt Oigee developed what was known as the Oigee Reflector Sight shown in Figure 1.3. The system was based on a semi-transparent mirror mounted on a 45-degree angle and a small electric lamp to create a targeting reticle. Aligned correctly with the aircraft's gun, the device enabled pilots to achieve considerably greater weapons accuracy (Wallace, 1994).

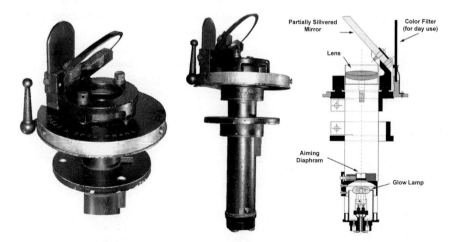

Figure 1.3 The 1918 Oigee Reflector Sight built by the German optics manufacturer Optische Anstalt Oigee used an electric lamp and collimating to create a virtual targeting reticle on a partially reflecting glass element. The system was deployed in German Albatross and Fokker DS1 aircraft.
Credit: Images and illustration courtesy of Erwin Wiedmer

Head-Up Displays

As the onboard systems of fighter aircraft and helicopters grew in complexity, the information processing tasks required of pilots also increased dramatically. The sizeable array of sensors, weapons, avionics systems, and flight controls increasingly resulted in pilots spending more time focusing on dials and displays inside of the cockpit instead of what was happening outside of the aircraft, often with tragic results. These developments forced scientists and engineers in the United States and several other countries to undertake extensive research into more intuitive and effective methods of communicating critical flight, sensor, and weapons systems information to the human operators.

Following the development of the airborne electronic analog computer in the 1950s, these research efforts resulted in the introduction of the first modern head-up (or heads-up) display (HUDs), a transparent display mounted in front of the pilot that enables viewing with the head positioned "up" and looking forward, instead of angled down, looking at instruments lower in the cockpit. Because the information projected onto the HUD is collimated (parallel light rays) and focused on infinity, the pilot's eyes do not need to refocus to view the scene beyond the display outside of the aircraft.

A typical HUD contains three primary components: a projector unit, a combiner (the viewing glass), and a video generation computer (also known as a symbol generator) (Previc and Ercoline, 2004). As shown in Figure 1.4, information is projected onto the combiner at optical infinity to provide pilots of both military and commercial aircraft with a variety of data and symbology necessary to increase situational awareness, particularly in low visibility landing and taxiing operations, without having to look down into the cockpit at the more traditional information displays.

The first combat aircraft to deploy with an operational HUD was a British low-level strike aircraft known as the *Blackburn Buccaneer* in 1958 (Nijboer, 2016). To this day, all HUDs incorporate a number of the basic concepts embodied in Grubb's original inventions.

The same principles of keeping a human operator focused on the task at hand have also resulted in the integration of these heads-up technologies into an increasing number of new automobile designs (Newcomb, 2014).

Figure 1.4 This image shows the basic flight data and symbology displayed in the HUD of a U.S. Marine Corps AV-8B Harrier ground-attack aircraft. Information shown on the display includes altitude, speed, and level of the aircraft to aid in flight control and navigation and help pilots keep their eyes on the environment.

Credit: Image courtesy of DoD

Helmet-Mounted Sights and Displays

Through the 1960s, as cockpit avionics, sensors, and weapons systems continued to advance, scientists and engineers in military labs around the world similarly continued efforts at easing a pilot's information processing burden and improving the control of sensors and weapons. The next logical step was moving the display of some of this information from the HUD to the pilot's helmet.

The first major step in this evolution was the development of a helmet-mounted sight (HMS) in the late 1960s by the South African Air Force (SAAF). The HMS aided pilots in the targeting of heat-seeking missiles (Lord, 2008). To this point, pilots had been required to maneuver an aircraft so the target fell within view of the HUD.

In the early 1970s, the U.S. Army deployed a head-tracked sight for the *AH-1G Huey Cobra* helicopter to direct the fire of a gimbaled gun. This was followed by the U.S. Navy deploying the first version of the Visual Target Acquisition System (VTAS) in the *F-4 Phantom II* aircraft to exploit the lock-on capabilities of the AIM-9G Sidewinder air-to-air missile. In operation, the Sidewinder seeker or the aircraft radar was "slaved" to the position of the pilot's head. The pilot steered the missile using the sight picture displayed on his single-eye 'Granny Glass' (VTAS I) or on the inside of his visor (VTAS II), along with a sensor to track head movements.

In the ensuing years, dozens of different helmet-mounted displays have been designed and come in a wide variety of forms, including monocular (single image to one eye), biocular (single image to both eyes), binocular (separate viewpoint-corrected images to each eye), visor projections, and more. The key feature with each is the ability to overlay information onto a pilot's real-world view. This information takes a variety of forms, including standard avionics and weapons information, as well as sensor data such as that provided by Forward Looking Infrared Radar (FLIR). These systems are explored in greater detail within Chapter 5, "Augmenting Displays," and Chapter 17, "Aerospace and Defense."

Smart Glasses and Augmenting Displays

During the past several years, augmenting display technologies have transitioned from purely defense and specialty application areas into commercially available products, with many more on the way. As you progress through this book, a number of these new displays are presented along with a host of innovative application overviews.

At the time of this book's preparation, there were two general categories of wearable augmenting displays, both of which are illustrated in Figure 1.5.

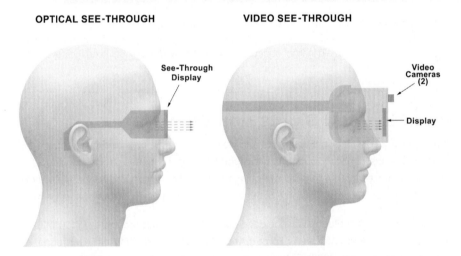

OPTICAL SEE-THROUGH   **VIDEO SEE-THROUGH**

Figure 1.5 This image illustrates the core differences between the two primary types of head-worn augmented reality displays. On the left, an optical see-through display overlays symbology and graphics directly on a user's real-world view. On the right, a video see-through display combines imagery gathered from outward-facing video cameras with computer-generated graphics. These combined images are presented to the user on display elements within the headset.
Credit: Head by decade3d / Depositphotos.com

Optical See-Through

With Optical See-Through displays, the user views the real world by *looking directly through* monocular or binocular optical elements such as holographic wave guides or other system that enables the overlay of graphic, video, and symbology onto real-world surroundings.

Video See-Through

With a video see-through head-mounted display (HMD), the real-world view is first captured by one or two video cameras mounted on the front of the display. These images are combined with computer-generated imagery and then presented to the user.

Handheld/Mobile AR Devices

Although the emphasis of this book focuses on traditional *wearable* AR and VR technologies, it is important to note the existence of handheld augmented display devices based on tablet computers and smartphones such as that shown in Figure 1.6. Because all the systems use the onboard cameras to merge a real-world scene with computer-generated imagery, they would be classified as video see-through devices.

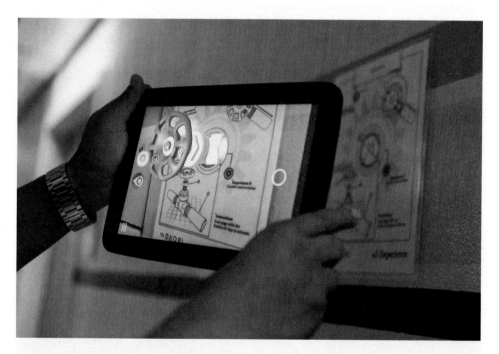

Figure 1.6 Handheld augmented reality systems based on smartphones and tablets display information overlays and digital content tied to physical objects and locations. In the example shown, the tablet app is able to recognize an AR icon embedded in the wall-mounted illustration to reveal a 3D model of a valve handle, which remains stable as the user moves the tablet.
Credit: Image courtesy of Office of Naval Research

Another key attribute of some augmented reality displays is the analysis of camera imagery by the host system. An example of such a system is provided in Chapter 17, within which camera imagery is analyzed to detect where a cockpit ends and window begins to insert virtual aircraft into a pilots view.

What Is Virtual Reality?

The phrase *virtual reality* has been extraordinarily difficult to define for a variety of reasons, not the least of which is the problem caused by the conflicting meaning and intent of the words *virtual* and *reality*.

Increasingly, it seems that any display technology even remotely associated with the words *"three dimensional"* is being hoisted onto the "us too" bandwagon by lazy marketers and others wishing to get caught up in the wave of hype. This general lack of specificity and broad application of the term has opened the doors to tremendous confusion.

For the purposes of this book, we prefer to rely on the original use of the phrase, which refers to display technologies, both worn and fixed placement, that provide the user a highly compelling visual sensation of *presence*, or *immersion*, within a 3D computer model or simulation such as depicted in Figure 1.7. This is accomplished via two primary methods: the use of stereoscopic head-mounted (or head-coupled) displays, as well as large fully and semi-immersive projection-based systems such as computer-assisted virtual environments (CAVEs) and domes.

Figure 1.7 This staged image is intended to illustrate the basic concept of immersive virtual reality. As opposed to looking at a desktop monitor, which is essentially a 2D window on a 3D world, an immersive virtual reality system provides the user the visual sensation of actual presence inside the 3D model or simulation.
Credit: Composite Image courtesy of NASA and innovatedcaptures © 123RF.com

Many virtual reality systems and applications also incorporate one of several 3D audio solutions to supplement the visual display. These systems are covered in greater detail within Chapter 8, "Audio Displays."

Although the phrase *virtual reality* was first popularized in 1987 by Jaron Lanier, former founder and CEO of VPL Research, Inc., a manufacturer of the first commercially available VR products, the development of the core concepts and enabling technologies of virtual reality began decades earlier.

Of particular note is the work of American computer scientist and graphics pioneer Ivan Sutherland. In the mid-1960s while serving as an associate professor of electrical engineering at Harvard University, Sutherland visited the Bell Helicopter company, where he saw a stereoscopic head-mounted display slaved to an infrared camera that was to be mounted below a helicopter to assist in difficult night landings. As Sutherland explains:

> "We got a copy of that head-mounted display with its two CRTs. The leap of idea that we had was "wouldn't it be interesting if the computer generated the picture instead of the infrared camera?"" (Sutherland, 2005).

As shown in Figure 1.8, the Bell Helicopter HMD used by Sutherland was based on two CRTs, one mounted on each side of the user's head. Images from the CRTs were steered around and into the user's eyes using a series of lenses and half-silvered mirrors. Sutherland and a colleague developed an armature suspended from the ceiling that tracked movement of the user's head. The visual effect provided by the system was to overlay simple wireframe geometric shapes on top of the user's view of the real world. By virtue of the tracking armature suspended from the ceiling and attached to the display, transformations could be calculated and the view of the wireframe images updated to reflect these physical changes of viewpoints.

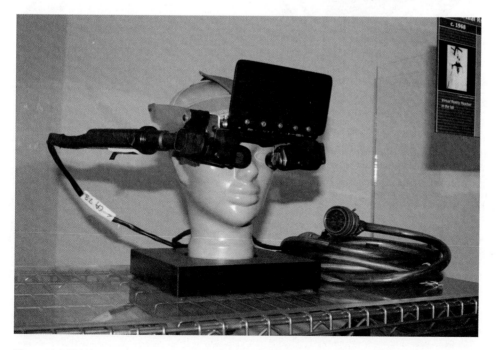

Figure 1.8 This image shows the head-mounted display developed by Bell Helicopter and used by computer scientist Ivan Sutherland and students to conduct early augmented and virtual reality research.

Credit: Image courtesy of Pargon via Flickr and distributed under a CC 2.0 license.

Parallel to Sutherland's work in the 1960s and 1970s in civilian research labs, the U.S. Air Force was involved in its own development efforts. Of particular note was work carried out at Wright-Patterson Air Force Base in Ohio under the direction of Dr. Thomas Furness. One of these projects focused on development of virtual interfaces for flight control. In 1982, Furness demonstrated a system known as VCASS (Visually Coupled Airborne Systems Simulator) shown in Figure 1.9.

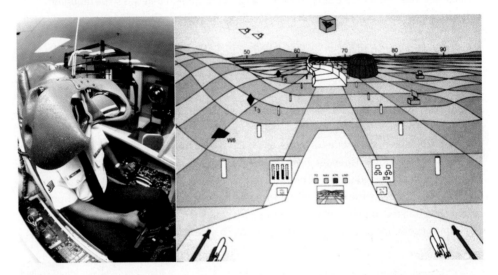

Figure 1.9 The image on the left shows an engineer wearing the U.S. Air Force Visually Coupled Airborne Systems Simulator (VCASS) helmet while seated in a laboratory cockpit (circa 1982). The terrain scene, symbology, and avionics data on the right are representative of the imagery displayed to the user.
Credit: Images courtesy of DoD

The VCASS system used high-resolution CRTs to display visual information such as computer-generated 3D maps, sensor imagery, and avionics data to the simulator operator. The helmet's tracking system, voice-actuated controls, and other sensors enabled the pilot to operate the aircraft simulator with gestures, utterances, and eye movements, translating immersion in a data-filled virtual space into control modalities (Lowood, 2016).

Between these early systems and today, a multitude of fully immersive stereoscopic head-mounted displays have been developed, albeit a majority for the high-end simulation and training market. It is only in the past couple of years that commercially available versions of these systems have entered the marketplace. Many of these displays will be described in greater detail in Chapter 6, "Fully Immersive Displays."

Conclusion

In this chapter we have explored the basic foundations of virtual and augmented reality systems, drawing clear distinctions between their differing capabilities as well as their varied, though related, pathways to existence. Despite the enormous hype associated with virtual reality, it is near certain that augmented reality will ultimately be the more widely adopted of the two technologies.

Keep in mind that the most successful products in any market are those that fulfill an important need or solve real problems. To this end, there are innumerable applications areas for general consumers and enterprise users where a personal data display would be highly useful while going about daily life or in the course of one's work. The widespread prevalence of smartphones, apps, and the overall "mobile lifestyle" already proves this.

In contrast, fully immersive virtual reality is spatially restricting and largely isolates the user from the real world. Once the user dons a head-mounted display, the loss of reference to one's surroundings severely limits mobility. Beyond gaming and entertainment for the mass market, virtual reality will find expansion into a myriad of specialty application markets detailed throughout this book. But realistically, is immersive virtual reality something that a dominant portion of the population will want or need as a standalone product? This is unlikely.

As the reader progresses through this book, it will become readily apparent that current implementations of pixel-based LCD, OLED, and AMOLED virtual reality displays will ultimately give way to dual-use augmenting headsets or even contact lenses. Efforts at developing such systems are already well underway.

CHAPTER 2

UNDERSTANDING VIRTUAL SPACE

The concept of virtual space is confusing given the widespread hype, new age philosophical musings, and creative use of terminology. In this second of two introductory chapters, we explore a basic overview of the concept of a virtual space, including the similarities and differences with physical space, the conventions used to define, characterize, and organize the space, as well as tools and techniques for navigation.

Defining Visual Space and Content

Viewpoints and definitions on the concept and nature of space vary widely depending on your field of study or profession. From a historical perspective, the topic has been the focus of some of the greatest debates among philosophers and scientists dating back to the period of antiquity. The Greek philosopher and mathematician Plato (428–348 BC) addressed the subject in his dialogue titled *Timaeus*, within which space is described as the womb and the receptacle in which creation takes place, and in the *Parmenides*, saying that if one is somewhere, it is *in something* (Jowett, 1901). Aristotle (384–322 BC) postulated in *Physics* (Book IV) that space, or place, is the inner limit of a containing body (Mendell, 1987).

More recent definitions from the broader scientific and mathematics communities clarify the concept of *physical* space as a boundless, three-dimensional extent within which objects and events occur and have relative position and direction (Merriam-Webster 2016). Physicists typically consider physical space, along with time, to be part of a four-dimensional continuum known as *spacetime*.

In the field of computer science, the word *space* is used more as an analogy or metaphor as foundational concepts and scientifically validated truths about physical space, time, and matter are stood on their heads. In this context, spaces and worlds are characterized and defined purely by mathematics. They do not exist in physical form, but rather as bits and bytes stored within silicon-based transistors found in semiconductor memory or on secondary storage devices. Governed only by those properties specified by a programmer or designer, infinite flexibility is available in how these virtual spaces, worlds, or environments appear, are organized, and behave.

As virtual and augmented reality developers work to accurately simulate the visual and acoustic properties of these digital spaces, it is important to explore some of the key foundational concepts used in their creation.

Visual and Object Space

As applied within the field of virtual and augmented reality, the phrase **visual space** can be defined as the perceived space, or visual scene, of the virtual environment being experienced by a user or participant. Visual space is unique because the scene perceived by the user is actually the result of light entering the eye, passing through the cornea and lens, and ultimately falling on the rods and cones of the retina, where it is converted into electrical impulses and sent onto the brain for interpretation (a process discussed in greater detail in Chapter 3, "The Mechanics of Sight"). In other words, what we perceive as the location of objects in the world around us is actually a *reconstruction* of light patterns bathing the retinas of both eyes.

The optical pathway of the eye and various sensory cues such as the perception of depth, size, shape, distance, direction, and motion weigh heavily on exactly what is ultimately "seen" by the user, but equally important are the specifics of the manner in which stereo imagery is presented. Is the visual scene distorted by optics? Are perspective, and thus the size and position of objects, distorted by projection onto a curved surface such as a hemispherical display or other large-scale immersive viewing system? Each eye often sees a different representation of the space.

Given this multitude of variables in play, visual space can be considered the subjective counterpart of virtual **object space**, within which the location and shape of entities in the 3D model can be precisely defined using one of multiple coordinate systems and simple geometry.

Content

In most cases the content contained within a virtual space/world/environment is created using any of dozens of commercially available 3D CAD and geometric modeling programs, such as Autodesk 3ds MAX, AutoCAD, Maya, and Dassault Systèmes CATIA, such as shown in Figure 2.1. The individual objects, or complex, highly detailed models such as the airframe of a modern aircraft or piping layout of an oil refinery, are then imported into a simulation engine for viewing with a chosen display.

Figure 2.1 Sophisticated 3D models, or simple individual objects, can be created using any number of CAD and geometric modeling programs.
Credit: Image courtesy of i.love.marimilk via Flickr under a CC 2.0 license

Even in the case of scientific visualization applications such as that shown in Figure 2.2, where large datasets of unpredictable size and structure are fed into a system for viewing, the individual primitive elements used to create the visual representation—such as points, straight lines, circles, curves, triangles, and polygons—to solids—such as cubes, cylinders, spheres, and cones, as well as the infinite variety of complex surfaces—are the product of mathematical predefinition by an engineer or software designer. Beyond the actual geometric representation, there are other features and attributes of these models, including textures, light reflection properties and transparency, sound reflection properties, and strength properties (for tactile / force feedback interactions). Nothing in a virtual world just comes into existence. Everything therein is created with intent.

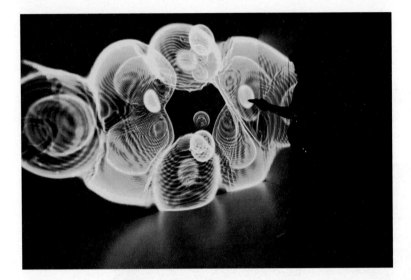

Figure 2.2 Researchers at Idaho National Laboratory's Center for Advanced Energy Studies the Earth and Environmental Sciences use immersive virtual reality systems such as the computer-assisted virtual environment (CAVE) to display complex scientific data for visualization and analysis.
Credit: Image courtesy of Idaho National Laboratory via Flickr under a CC 2.0 license

Finally, the visual content within a majority of virtual and augmented reality applications that readers are likely to encounter outside of research environments will be based on 2D and 3D analytic geometry (also called Cartesian geometry) principles described in the next section.

Defining Position and Orientation in Three Dimensions

Humans are spatial beings. We see, hear, interact with, and move through our physical surroundings in three dimensions. As will be seen throughout this book, our perceptual mechanisms are clearly optimized to process information in this form. In fact, the leveraging of these perceptual strengths is one of the core rationales for the ongoing design, development, and fundamental research of these advanced human-computer interfaces in the first place. As a result, most virtual environments are themselves defined using 3D coordinate systems in which are placed 2D and 3D geometric elements.

Defining Position

There are three primary coordinate systems used in the layout and programming of virtual and augmented reality applications; the Cartesian rectilinear system, an angular method known as spherical polar, and cylindrical. Although a general user will rarely encounter the need to work with these systems, an understanding of their basic function and application is useful.

Cartesian Coordinates

Out of familiarity, accuracy, and simplicity, most virtual spaces are defined using a standard Cartesian coordinate system, such as is represented in Figure 2.3. Within this system, each point is uniquely specified using three numerical coordinates (x,y,z) representing specific distances (measured in the same unit of length) from three mutually perpendicular planes. It is in this form the geometry of objects, the interrelationships between multiple objects, and their locations within object space are precisely defined and stored.

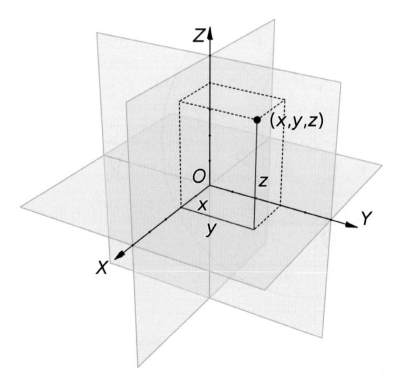

Figure 2.3 Every point in a 3D Cartesian coordinate system is identified by unique x, y, and z values.
Credit: Illustration by Jorge Stolfi via Wikimedia

In addition to serving as the most commonly utilized approach for mathematically mapping actual, theoretical, and creative virtual spaces, the Cartesian system is also used to define a user's position and viewpoint within that space.

Spherical Polar Coordinates

Although the positions of points, lines, planes, and complete objects within a virtual space will typically be defined using standard Cartesian coordinates, the location of objects and features relative to the user's position, such as that of a virtual sound source, or in the mapping of spherical video (also known as 360° video) will often be defined using a different system known as *spherical polar* coordinates. As shown in Figure 2.4, this coordinate system is based on fundamental planes bisecting a sphere and is composed of three elements: azimuth, elevation, and the distance (magnitude or range). This system and its application in the localization of sound sources are covered in additional detail in Chapter 7, "The Mechanics of Hearing."

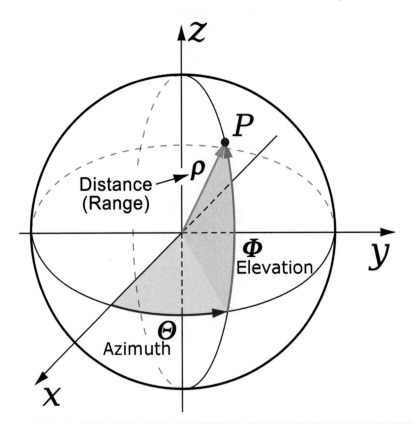

Figure 2.4 A diagram of spherical coordinates, defining a point (*P*) by azimuth (*Θ*), distance/range (*ρ*), and elevation (*Φ*).

Credit: Illustration by Andeggs via Wikimedia

Cylindrical Coordinates

The third coordinate system commonly applied within virtual reality applications, and a holdover from Apple's QuickTime VR of the 1990's, is the cylindrical method. Used extensively in the creation of still image mosaics for 360° × 180° "immersive" panoramas or 360° video backgrounds, the mathematical techniques enabled by this coordinate system allow for the precise mapping and alignment of multiple images for overlap and edge stitching, with all points being the same distance from a central reference axis.

As shown in Figure 2.5, this central reference axis (L), also called the cylindrical or longitudinal axis, serves as the origin (O) for defining a radial distance (ρ). The angular coordinate is defined by (φ) and the height by (z).

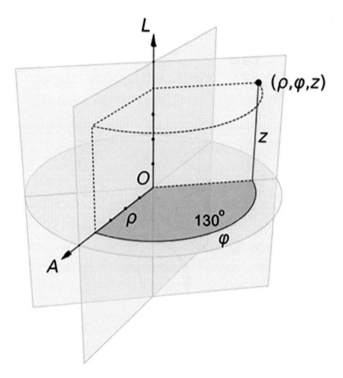

Figure 2.5 A cylindrical coordinate system with origin O, polar axis A, and longitudinal axis L. Noting the hash marks along A and L, the dot is the point with radial distance (ρ) = 4, angular coordinate (φ) = 130°, and height (z) = 4.
Credit: Illustration by Jorge Stolfi via Wikimedia

Although cylindrical coordinates are useful in those settings requiring rotational symmetry about the longitudinal axis, it is important to point out that this method is limited in terms of its vertical field of view, such as with 360° × 180° panorama applications.

Defining Orientation and Rotation

In addition to defining an object's location (or position), it is frequently necessary to both define and track the *orientation* and the rotation of objects and user viewpoints in relation to the coordinate system of the object space. Some simple examples include defining movements of objects such as a virtual hand or tracking the direction a user is looking while wearing a head-mounted display.

In two dimensions, there is only one degree of freedom with rotation taking place about a single axis, resulting in a single numeric value.

In three dimensions, orientation is defined similar to that of a physical, rigid body and requires at least three independent values. As shown in Figure 2.6, it is most common to use what are referred to as Tait-Bryan angles, more accurately expressed as roll, pitch, and yaw.

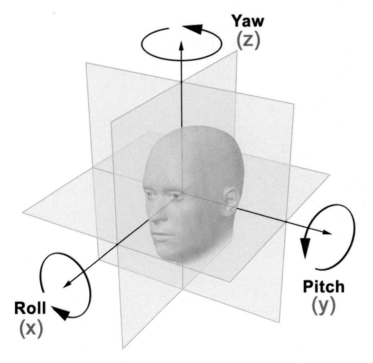

Figure 2.6 This image illustrates the three types of rotation: roll, pitch, and yaw.
Credit: Illustration by S. Aukstakalnis

It is common within the virtual and augmented reality arena to see position (x,y,z) and orientation (roll, pitch, and yaw) generically referred to as **six degrees of freedom** (frequently abbreviated as 6 DOF).

Defining object rotation and orbits within 3D computer simulations is slightly more complicated. Referring back to Figure 2.6, if you wanted to reorient the head from facing the lower left of the image to the upper right, you essentially have two choices: sequentially rotate the head along individual axes until the desired position is achieved, or carry out the repositioning in a single smooth motion.

In the first option, you would use Euler angles, which are based on combinations of single rotations by a given angle about a fixed axis, although gimbal lock and jerky motion become issues. The second option is to use **quaternions,** which, as shown in Figure 2.7, is a normalized 4-coordinate system that provides a way to interpolate smoothly between orientations in space and is faster than combining rotations expressed in matrix form.

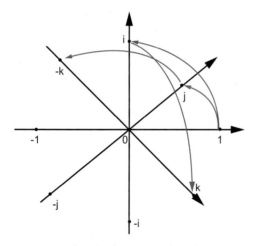

Graphical representation of
quaternion units product as
90°-rotation in 4D-space

$$ij = k$$
$$ji = -k$$
$$ij = -ji$$

Figure 2.7 This image shows a graphical representation of quaternion units in 4D-space. Used to represent rotations, quaternions are compact, don't suffer from gimbal lock, and can easily be interpolated.
Credit: Illustration by Prokop Hapala via Wikimedia

In addition to defining object position, orientation, and rotation within a simulation, several of these techniques are used in calculating position and orientation of an actual user's head and hands. The technologies enabling this capability are given a detailed treatment in Chapter 11, "Sensors for Tracking Position, Orientation, and Motion."

Navigation

Although on the surface the topics of navigation and wayfinding in a virtual environment might seem to be relatively simple concepts, they are in fact two of the most complex, and unsettled, in the entire field. Areas under intense investigation include navigational interface design, studies on spatial cognition and comparisons with real-world findings, human factors considerations, and more.

In general, navigation within most virtual environments is handled in two ways: by physical movement for close-in tasks and via the use of manual interfaces for traversing greater virtual distances (Slater et al., 1995). In a simplistic example, imagine standing in a virtual room with a beautifully rendered sports car in the center. It is unlikely you will use any type of manual interface to maneuver your viewpoint, but rather will physically walk around the model of the automobile to take in the sleek design, perhaps stick your head in one of the window, and so on.

Now consider standing within a virtual model of the Forbidden City in Beijing, China, and you want to go exploring. If you are wearing a head-mounted display, the range of your physical movement will be limited by the length of the cabling or the effective range of the tracking technology employed. If you are in a large-scale immersive display facility such as a CAVE, your physical movement will be limited to the effective display area of that system (10-12 square feet on average).

So what are your options?

Quite literally, there have been dozens of manual interfaces introduced over the years, including 3D mice, wands, game controllers, gesture recognition gloves, motion detecting rings, joy sticks, steering wheels, omnidirectional treadmills, eye tracking navigation, and a host of others devices providing myriad options to suit various needs. Each has provided some mechanism such as a button, toggle, or miniature joystick to facilitate translation of one's viewpoint through the object space.

Beyond the manual interfaces are larger systems enabling users to effectively walk in place, extending the normal intuitive means of locomotion. These include omnidirectional treadmills and, as shown in Figure 2.8, a 10-foot diameter hamster ball-like device known as the VirtuSphere. Details of many of the current commercial iterations of controllers facilitating navigation through a virtual environment can be found in Chapter 12, " Devices to Enable Navigation and Interaction."

Figure 2.8 The VirtuSphere is a 10-foot diameter device that rolls in place to provide an infinite spherical plane upon which a user can walk in any direction.
Credit: Illustration by Paul Monday via Wikimedia under a GNU GFDL license

As would be expected, there is not yet, nor is it expected that there will ever be, a single universal interface solution. Invariably, the means of locomotion, navigation through, and interaction with objects in a virtual environment will be a function of the task at hand. For instance, the navigational needs of a gamer are significantly different from those of an architect or aerospace engineer performing design reviews.

Conclusion

As can be seen within this chapter, virtual spaces (virtual environments, virtual worlds) are nothing more than mathematically defined 3D representations of real or imagined objects, locations, or phenomena. There is nothing mystical or spiritual about it. They can be explained with precise, easily understood language without the need of distracting, confusing, terminology such as *hyper-realities*, *cyber-modalities*, or *computer-mediated alternate universe*. The basic concepts contained within this chapter will be greatly expanded upon throughout the remainder of this book.

CHAPTER 3

THE MECHANICS OF SIGHT

The amazing human eye is a marvel of engineering. Seventy percent of all of the body's sensory receptors are located in the eyes. Forty percent of the cerebral cortex is thought to be involved in some aspect of processing visual information. To fully understand the key technologies behind augmented and virtual reality, it is important to understand the primary sensory mechanism these systems address. In this chapter we will explore the mechanics of human sight, highlighting the physiological processes enabling us to visually perceive real and virtual worlds.

The Visual Pathway

Everything starts with light. It is the key underlying stimulus for human sight. Light is a form of electromagnetic radiation that is capable of exciting the retina and producing a visual sensation. Light moves through space as waves move over the surface of a pond. Science classifies electromagnetic radiation by a measure of its wavelength, which is the distance between two consecutive crests of a wave. The entirety of the electromagnetic spectrum includes radio waves, infrared, visible light, ultraviolet, x-rays, and gamma rays. As shown in Figure 3.1, the human eye is only sensitive to a narrow band within the electromagnetic spectrum falling between wavelengths roughly measuring 380 nanometers and 740 nanometers in length. A nanometer (nm) is one billionth of a meter.

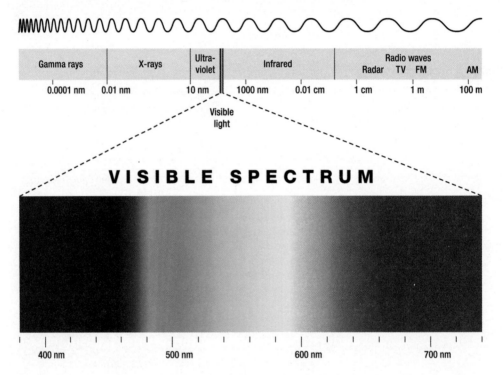

Figure 3.1 This diagram shows all the regions within the electromagnetic spectrum. The color callout shows the small portion to which the retinas of the eyes have natural sensitivity.

Credit: Illustration by Peter Hermes Furian / Depositphotos.com

For clarity, there are no precisely defined boundaries between the bands of the electromagnetic spectrum; rather, they fade into each other like the bands in a rainbow. Gamma ray wavelengths blend into x-rays, which blend into ultra-violet, and so on. The longest wavelengths perceptible by humans correspond to light we see as red, and the shortest wavelengths correspond to light that we see as violet. However, the spectrum does not contain all the colors that a healthy human eye can distinguish. For instance, unsaturated colors such as pinks, purples, and magentas are a mix of multiple wavelengths.

In the real world, an object's visible color is determined by the wavelengths of light it absorbs or reflects. Known as spectral reflectance, only the reflected wavelengths reach our eyes and are discerned as color. As a simple example, the leaves of many common plants reflect green wavelengths while absorbing red, orange, blue, and violet.

Entering the Eye

The human eye is a complex optical sensor but relatively easy to understand when thought of as functionally similar to a camera. Light enters through a series of optical elements, where it is refracted and focused. A diaphragm is adjusted to control the amount of light passing through an aperture, which ultimately falls onto an image plane. As shown in Figure 3.2, the human eyes performs the same basic functions, with the cornea and crystalline lens providing focus while the iris serves as the diaphragm, adjusting appropriately to allow just the right amount of light to pass through the aperture. Instead of coming to rest on film, the inverted light field falls onto the extremely sensitive retina.

The Cornea

Light from all directions within the visual field initially enters the eye through the cornea, a transparent, dome-shaped structure, the surface which is composed of highly organized cells and proteins. Most of the refraction of light by the eye (~80%) takes place at the air-cornea interface because of its curvature and the large difference in the indexes of refraction. Set behind the cornea is another transparent structure called the crystalline lens, which is a fine focus mechanism because its shape can be changed, thus providing variability to the effective focal length of the optical system (Delamere, 2005). The space between the two optical elements, known as the anterior chamber, is filled by a clear, watery fluid called the aqueous humor, which is produced by the ciliary body. The aqueous humor provides nutrients (notably amino acids and glucose) for the central cornea and lens because they do not have their own blood supply. The front of the cornea receives the same nutrients via tears spread across the surface as a person blinks.

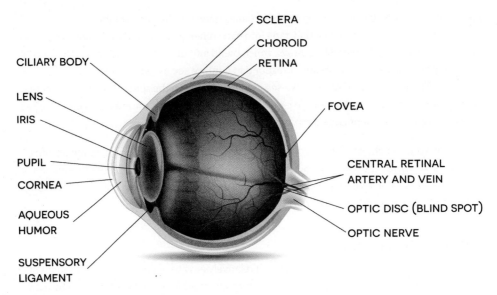

Figure 3.2 This illustration shows a vertical cross section through the human eye revealing major structures and chambers.
Credit: Illustration by guniita © 123RF.com

Pupil

After light passes through the cornea and the aqueous-filled anterior chamber, a portion of that light then passes through a hole located in the center of the colored structure of the eye known as the iris. This hole, known as the pupil, allows the light to strike the retina. The pupil is black in appearance because most of the light entering through the hole is absorbed by the interior of the eye with little if any reflectance.

As described earlier, similar to the aperture of a camera diaphragm, the size of the pupil can be varied to account for changes in visual stimulus, resulting in dilation of the iris as shown in Figure 3.3. In low light situations, the pupil will expand to allow more light to enter. In brightly lit conditions, the pupil contracts in size. This involuntary reaction is called the pupillary reflex.

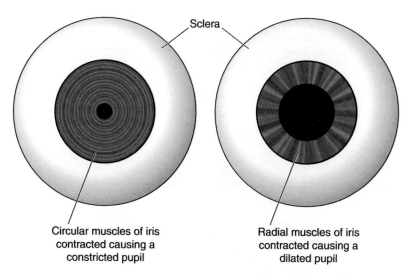

Circular muscles of iris
contracted causing a
constricted pupil

Radial muscles of iris
contracted causing a
dilated pupil

Figure 3.3 Similar to the aperture of a camera diaphragm, the size of the pupil constricts to account for changes in visual stimulus and focus.
Credit: Illustration by hfsimaging © 123RF.com

Crystalline Lens

Light passing through the pupil immediately enters a new optical element known as the crystalline lens. This is an almost perfectly transparent, flexible structure and is composed of concentrically arranged shells of fiber cells. The most superficial fibers are metabolically active and, similar to the cornea, the crystalline lens receives all its nutrition from the fluids that surround it.

Accommodation

The crystalline lens is held in position by the ciliary muscles and delicate suspensory ligaments around its outer circumference. As shown in Figure 3.4, when the eye is at a relaxed state, such as when you are simply looking off in the distance, the crystalline lens assumes a flattened shape, thus providing the maximum focal length for distance viewing. To assume this shape, the ciliary muscle that encircles the crystalline lens, like all radial muscles, transitions from a constricted state to an enlarged, open state. In doing so, this exerts outward tension on the suspensory ligaments (zonules) connecting the muscle and lens, which in turn pulls the lens flat. When the eye focuses on near-field objects, the process is reversed. The ciliary muscle that encircles the crystalline lens constricts, thereby relieving tension on the suspensory ligaments and allowing the lens to naturally reassume a more rounded, biconvex (convex on both sides) shape, thus increasing its refractive power needed to clearly focus on the near-field object. This variable process by which the optical power of the eye is changed to allow an observer to rapidly switch focus between objects at different depths of field is referred to as **accommodation**.

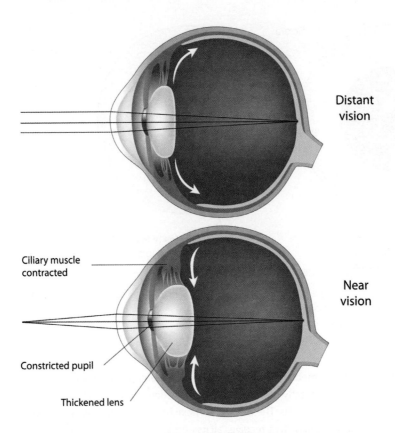

Distant
vision

Ciliary muscle
contracted

Near
vision

Constricted pupil

Thickened lens

Figure 3.4 This illustration shows the process of accommodation in which the optical power of the eye is changed to allow an observer to rapidly switch focus between objects.
Credit: Illustration by alila © 123RF.com

It is widely believed that blurring on the retina is the stimulus for accommodation, although the process is also strongly linked to vergence, discussed later in this chapter (Leigh and Zee, 2015, 524).

As will be seen in Chapter 21, "Human Factors Considerations," this extraordinary reflex action, although perfect for viewing our real-world surroundings, is highly problematic when using most current 3D display technologies. One of these challenges is the fact that current 3D displays present images on a 2D surface. Thus, focus cues such as vergence, as well as blur in the retinal image, specify the depth of the display surface rather than the depths in the depicted scene. Additionally, the uncoupling of vergence and accommodation required by 3D displays frequently reduces your ability to fuse the binocular stimulus and causes discomfort and fatigue for the viewer (Lambooij et al., 2009).

It is interesting to note that the crystalline lens is highly deformable up to about 40 years of age, at which point it progressively begins losing elasticity. As a result of increasing stiffness due to metabolic activity in the outer shell, by the mid-fifties, ciliary muscle contraction is no longer able to change the shape of the lens (Atchison, 1995; Duane, 1912).

Image Inversion

Thus far we have seen that the eye is equipped with a compound lens system. Light enters the eye by passing between mediums, passing from air into a denser medium (the cornea), which performs ~80% of the refraction for focusing, with the crystalline lens performing the remaining 20%. Although the cornea is a strong fixed lens, the crystalline lens is a variable, double convex lens. Following the refraction rules for converging lens, light rays will pass through the focal point on the opposite side. As shown in Figure 3.5 (although not at proper scale), the result is that the light field entering the eye is optically inverted before reaching the retina.

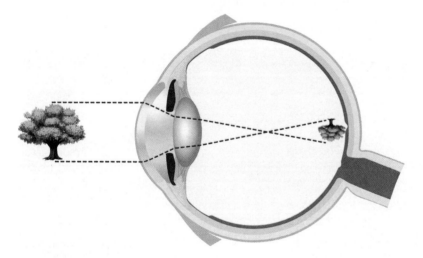

Figure 3.5 The double convex shape of the crystalline lens results in the inversion of the light field entering the eye.
Credit: Illustration by peterhermesfurian © 123RF.com

Vitreous Body

After passing through the crystalline lens, light then enters the interior chamber of the eye, which is filled with a clear gel-like substance known as vitreous humor. As you would expect, this liquid has the perfect properties to enable the easy passage of light. Vitreous is 98% water, along with hyaluronic acid, which increases viscosity, a network of fine collagen fibrils that provides its jelly-like properties, as well as various salts and sugars (Suri and Banerjee, 2006). The substance is essentially stagnant, is not actively regenerated, and is not served by any blood vessels.

Image Formation and Detection

We have finally reached the point where light begins the process of being converted from waves deriving from a small detectable sliver of the electromagnetic spectrum into a form that allows us to actually "see." The mechanisms enabling this conversion operate under conditions ranging from starlight to sunlight, recognize the positioning of objects in space, and enable us to discern shape, size, color, textures, and other dimensional aspects to interpret and derive meaning from our surroundings.

The Retina

Visual perception begins as the optical components of the eye focus light onto the **retina** (from the Latin, *rete*, meaning *net*), a multilayered sensory tissue that covers about 65 percent of its interior surface of the eye and serves a similar function as the film (or a CMOS/CCD image sensor) in a camera. The thickness of the retina ranges from 0.15 mm to 0.320 mm (Kolb et al., 1995). As shown in Figure 3.6, near the middle of the retina is a feature called the macula, and the center of the macula contains the fovea. The fovea is naturally centered on objects when we fixate on them and is the point on the retina with the greatest acuity. The entire intricate superstructure of the eye exists in the interests of the retina (Hubel, 1995).

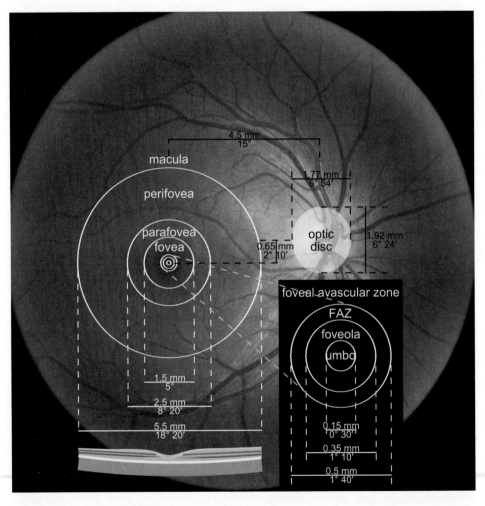

Figure 3.6 This image shows the major features of the retina as viewed through an ophthalmoscope.
Credit: Illustration by Zyxwv99 via Wikimedia under a CC BY 2.0 license

An amazing aspect of the retina is the fact that it is near completely transparent (Huang et al., 1991; Slater and Usoh, 1993; D'Amico, 1994). As light falls upon the retina, it actually passes straight through until it comes into focus on the outermost, or deepest, layer known as the **pigment epithelium**, as shown in Figure 3.7. That image is then reflected back into the immediately adjacent layer where the photoreceptor neurons are located.

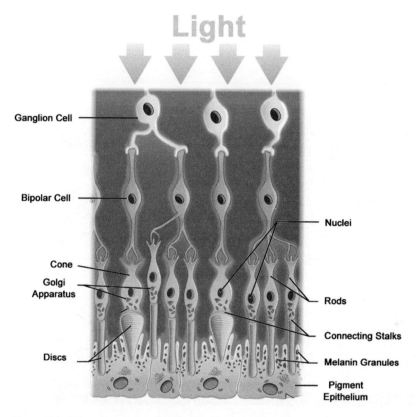

Figure 3.7 This cross-sectional illustration shows the complex structure of the human retina.
Credit: Illustration by OpenStax College via Wikimedia under a CC 3.0 license

Rods and Cones

The photoreceptors of the eye, referred to as rods and cones due to their shapes, actually face away from the incoming light. Rods are more numerous, responsible for vision at low light levels, and are highly sensitive motion detectors. Rods are found mostly in the peripheral regions of the retina and are responsible for our peripheral views. Cones are active at higher light levels, have a high spatial acuity, and are responsible for our color sensitivity.

Light reflected from the pigmented epithelium results in a chemical reaction with two photopigments: **iodopsin** in cones (activated in photopic or bright conditions) and **rhodopsin** in rods (activated in scotopic or dark conditions). This reaction, known as isomerization, results in changes in the electrical properties of the photoreceptors and the release of neurotransmitters (chemical transmitters/transmitter substances). These neurotransmitters stimulate neighboring neurons, thus enabling impulses to be passed from one cell to the next.

Based on their measured response curves shown in Figure 3.8, individual cones are sensitive to one of three light conditions; red (the most numerous) shows peak sensitivity at a wavelength of 564 nm, green at 533 nm, and blue at 437 nm. Rods show a peak sensitivity to wavelengths around 498 nm (green-blue) (FAA, 2016).

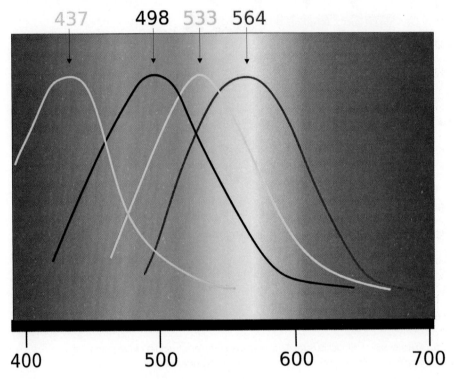

Figure 3.8 This graph shows the spectral sensitivity curves of short (437), medium (533), and long (564) wavelength cones compared to that of rods (498).
Credit: Illustration by Pancrat via Wikimedia under a CC BY 3.0 license

Impulses from the rods and cones stimulate bipolar cells, which in turn stimulate ganglion cells. These impulses continue into the axons of the ganglion cells, through the optic nerve and disk, and to the visual centers in the brain.

Rod and Cone Density

There are approximately 100–120 million rod and 7–8 million cone photoreceptors in each retina (Riggs, 1971). As shown in the distribution graph in Figure 3.9, most cones are concentrated in the fovea, while rods are absent there but dense elsewhere. Despite the fact that perception in typical daytime light levels is dominated by cone-mediated vision, the total number of rods in the human retina far exceeds the number of cones (Purves et al., 2001).

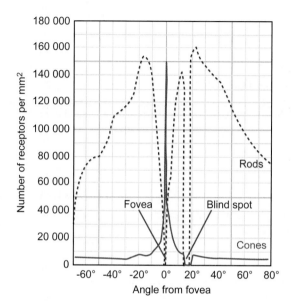

Figure 3.9 This graph shows why we see color (photopic vision) most clearly in our direct line of sight. The peak number of cones occurs in the fovea, where it reaches approximately 150,000 cones per square millimeter.
Credit: Illustration by Cmglee via Wikimedia under a CC 3.0 license

It is important to note that there are no photoreceptors in the optic disk, more accurately known as the optic nerve head. This lack of photoreceptors means there is no light detected in this area, resulting in a blind spot for each eye. The blind spot for the left eye is located to the left of the center of vision and vice versa for the right eye. With both eyes open, we do not perceive the blind spots because the field of view of each eye overlaps with the other, although they still can be experienced. Follow the instructions in the caption of Figure 3.10 to find your blind spots.

Figure 3.10 To find the blind spot for each eye, start by placing this book flat on a table. Cover your left eye and look at the dot on the left side of this image. Remain aware of the cross on the right without looking directly at it. Slowly move your face closer to the image. At some point, you will see the cross disappear. Reverse the process to find the blind spot for the right eye.
Credit: Illustration by S. Aukstakalnis

Spatial Vision and Depth Cues

Based on the visual processes described in the previous section, there are, quite literally, billions of pieces of information being sent to the cerebral cortex every second for analysis. This stream of information undergoes repeated refinement, with each level in the hierarchy representing an increase in organizational complexity. At each level, neurons are organized according to highly specific stimulus preferences, with the cortical destinations of impulses differentiating content and cues. Theoretically, the nature of the representations (patterns of nerve impulses) is thought to shift from analogue to symbolic (Mather, 2009).

In this section, we will explore many of the specific triggers, or cues, that are believed to enable the brain to perceive depth in the visual stimuli entering the eyes.

Extraretinal Cues

Extraretinal depth cues are those triggers or pieces of information that are not derived from light patterns entering the eye and bathing the retina, but from other physiological processes. In this section we explore the two most dominant of these cues.

Accommodation

As described in the previous section, when the human eye is at a relaxed state, such as when you are simply looking off in the distance, the crystalline lens of the eye is flattened, thereby providing the maximum focal length for distance viewing. As shown in Figure 3.11, when the eye focuses on near-field objects, the process is reversed. The ciliary muscle that encircles the crystalline lens constricts, thereby relieving tension on the suspensory ligaments and allowing the lens to snap into a more rounded, biconvex shape, thus increasing its refractive power needed to clearly focus on the near-field object.

Accommodation is an involuntary physiological process by which the optical power of the eye lens changes to focus light entering the eye and falling on the retina. It is widely believed that blurring on the retina is the stimulus for accommodation, although the process is also strongly linked to vergence (Leigh and Zee, 2015, 524). It is also theorized that movement of the ciliary muscles themselves contributes to this cue (Helmholtz et al., 1944).

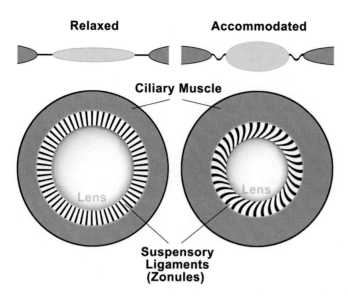

Figure 3.11 Accommodation is the process by which an observer's eye changes optical power to obtain a clear image or focus on an object on a different focal plane. In this illustration, constriction and relaxation of the radial ciliary muscle affects the focal length of the crystalline lens.
Credit: Illustration by S. Aukstakalnis

Vergence

One of the most powerful depth cues and an oculomotor function that is at the foundation of binocular vision is that of *vergence eye movements*, which is the pointing of the fovea of both eyes at an object in the near field. As shown in Figure 3.12, this process entails the eyes simultaneously rotating about their vertical axis in opposite directions to the degree necessary so that when looking at a nearby object, the projected image of that object is aligned with the center of the retina of both eyes. When looking at an object in the near field, the eyes rotate toward each other, or *converge*. When looking at an object in a far field, the eyes rotate away from each other, or *diverge*.

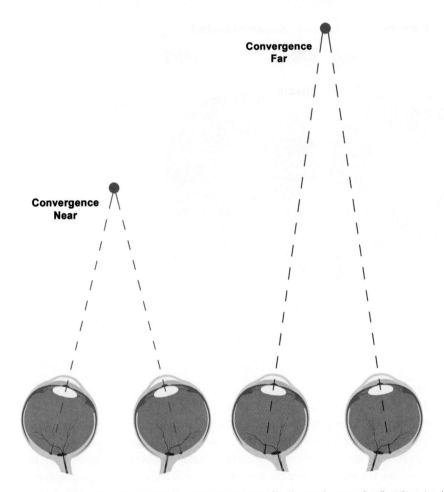

Figure 3.12 Vergence is the simultaneous movement of both eyes in opposite directions to obtain or maintain binocular vision.
Credit: Eye illustration by Ginko / Depositphotos.com

When the eyes rotate in opposite directions, this is known as *disconjugate* movement. Literally all other eye movements are together, or *conjugate*.

Accommodation and vergence are normally tightly coupled physiological processes. As an example, when focusing your eyes on something in the distance and then shifting your attention to an object closer to you, that process starts with your eyes converging on that object in the near field. This results in the image of that object appearing larger on the retina and out of focus. That blurriness in turn triggers the accommodation reflex, which results in a change in the focal power of the crystalline lens bringing the image on the retina into sharp focus.

The vergence and accommodation processes are extremely important for virtual and augmented reality enthusiasts to understand. As pointed out in Chapter 21, users of flat panel-based stereoscopic head-mounted displays often complain of headaches and eye strain. That side effect is caused by the eyes having to remain focused on a flat plane (the display surface) that is within inches of the eye. Even if you are paying attention to and accommodating for objects at what appear to be differing focal planes within the virtual space, the depth of field is just simulated. The imagery presented to each eye is portrayed on a 2D display surface, and that is where the eye remains focused. Ultimately, this constant focusing in the near field on the surface of the display elements, which is made possible by the constricting of the ciliary muscle surrounding the edge of the lens, greatly contributes to such discomfort. Further, there is a mismatch, or decoupling, in the sensory cues provided to the brain by the vergence and accommodation processes.

An additional aspect to the vergence cue just described comes in the form of tension in the six extraocular muscles shown in Figure 3.13 that control eye movement (Jung et al., 2010).

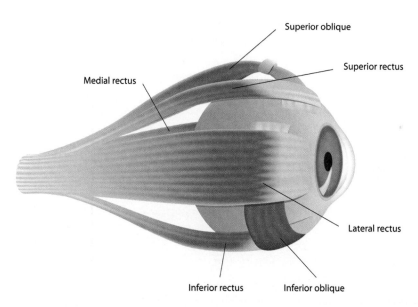

Figure 3.13 This illustration shows the six muscles used in movement of the eyeball. The lateral rectus and media rectus (opposite side, not shown) are the primary muscles controlling vergence.
Credit: Illustration by alila © 123RF.com

Binocular Cues

Binocular depth cues are those triggers or pieces of information that are detected as a result of viewing a scene with two eyes, each from a slightly different vantage point. These two scenes are integrated by our brain to construct a 3D interpretation of our real or virtual surroundings.

Stereopsis

Binocular vision is sight with two eyes. The primary depth cue for binocular vision is known as stereopsis, which is a direct result of retinal or horizontal disparity. We have two eyes laterally separated by an average distance of about 2.5 inches (63 mm) (Dodgson, 2004), with each eye capturing the scene from a slightly different angle. As shown in Figure 3.14, stereopsis is the perception of depth gained by the slight offset from those two scenes that is constructed by the brain based on the differences between these two retinal images.

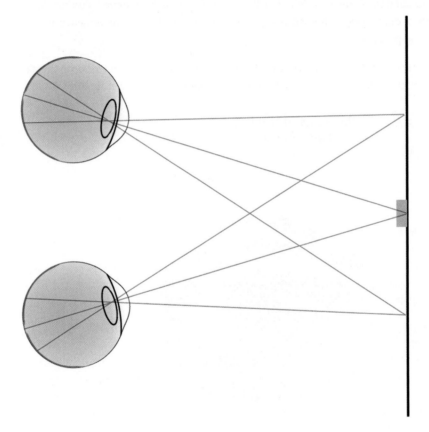

Figure 3.14 Stereopsis is the perception of depth and 3D structure obtained on the basis of visual information deriving from two eyes.
Credit: Illustration by S. Aukstakalnis

Within a binocular view, each point in one retina is said to have a corresponding point in the other retina (Howard and Rogers, 2012, 150). These retinal corresponding points correlate to an area before the observer called the "horopter," such as is shown in Figure 3.15. The term *horopter* (meaning the horizon of vision) was introduced in 1613 by François d'Aguilon, a Belgian Jesuit mathematician, physicist, and architect. The term defines the locus of all object points that are imaged on corresponding retinal elements at a given fixation distance. Thus, a line can be drawn through an object of regard such that all the points on the line correspond to the same point on the retinas of both eyes. This allows the object to be seen as a single point. Theoretically, the horopter is the locus space in which each point produces images that fall on corresponding points for a given point of binocular fixation (Howard and Rogers, 2012, 150).

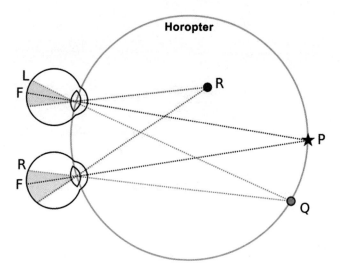

Figure 3.15 This illustration depicts the concept of a horopter, which is the locus of points in space having the same disparity as fixation. This can be defined theoretically as the points in space that project on anatomically identical or corresponding points, in the two retinas. Note how points R, P, and Q map to identical positions on both retinas.
Credit: Illustration by Vlcekmi3 via Wikimedia under a CC 3.0 license

According to this model, if corresponding points have a regular horizontal distance from the retina, the horopter would be a circle passing through the center of rotation of the two eyes and the fixation point. Thus, as the point of fixation gets closer, this circle would become smaller (Bhola, 2006).

This simple concept of binocular disparity leading to stereopsis can be demonstrated using the stereo pair shown in Figure 3.16. This print form of stereo images can be viewed using what is known as the cross-eyed viewing method. For those who have never tried, it may take a few minutes to master, but the effort is worth it. To get started, position this book approximately two feet in front of you and, while looking at the image pair straight on, slowly cross your eyes. You will then begin to perceive a third image in the center. Vary the degree to which your eyes are crossed until you can form a stable middle image and watch as the astronaut floats above the moon surface.

Figure 3.16 The stereoscopic disparity of the two images in a 3D pair is a strong indicator of distance. To view this stereo pair, slowly cross your eyes and attempt to fuse together a third, combined image.
Credit: Image courtesy of NASA

As a side note, once you have successfully fused the two images and can perceive depth, slowly tilt your head to the left and right. The progressive vertical separation of the images is the result of a loss of stereopsis as the images on the two retinas are displaced.

Finally, as is seen elsewhere in this chapter, neurons in the visual cortex of the brain have been identified that assist in the creation of stereopsis from binocular disparity.

Monocular Cues

Monocular depth cues are those triggers or pieces of information that are derived from light patterns on the retinas but are not dependent on both eyes. As will be seen in this section, monocular cues are divided between those requiring movement of light patterns across the retina (that is, viewer motion) and those that can be discerned from a fixed viewing position.

Motion Parallax

Motion parallax is a strong, relative motion cue within which objects that are closer to a moving observer appear themselves to move faster than objects that are farther away (Gibson et al., 1959; Ono et al., 1986). Figure 3.17 illustrates this phenomenon. From a physiological perspective, this perceptual phenomenon is the result of the speed at which an image moves across the retinas of the eyes. Objects closer to the observer will pass into, through, and out of your field of view considerably faster than objects off in the distance.

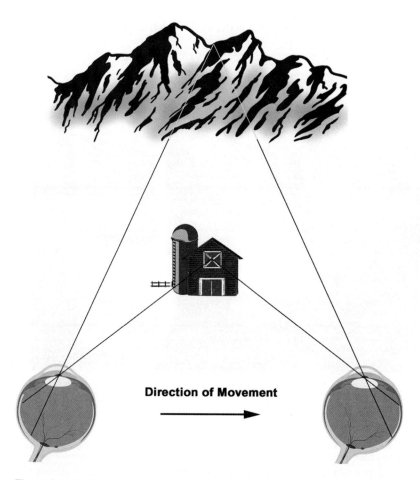

Direction of Movement

Figure 3.17 Motion parallax is the perception that nearby objects appear to move more rapidly in relation to your own motion than background features.
Credit: Illustration elements by sergeiminsk and Ginko © 123RF.com

This visual cue provides important information about relative depth differences and can reliably provide 3D scene layout and help enable navigation in the environment (Helmholtz, 1925). This retinal image motion results in two types of motion boundaries: those that are parallel to the direction of observer movement and provides shear, and those that are at right angles to the direction of observer movement and provide dynamic occlusion, in which objects in the near field dynamically cover and uncover objects in the far field (Yoonessi and Baker, 2013).

Occlusion

Also known as interposition, occlusion cues are generated when one object blocks an observer's view of another object. In such a situation, the blocking object is perceived as being closer to the observer. This is clearly shown in Figure 3.18, within which the progressive interposition of cars provides a strong indication of depth. Occlusion indicates relative (as opposed to absolute) distance.

Figure 3.18 Occlusion, or interposition, is a simple but powerful depth cue within which one object partially blocks another.
Credit: Illustration by joyfull / Depositphotos.com

Recent investigations have reinforced the potential importance of these cues in stereoscopic depth perception (Harris & Wilcox, 2009). Some research suggests that the primary function of monocular cues in stereoscopic depth perception is to define depth discontinuities and the boundaries of the occluding objects (Anderson, 1994; Gillam and Borsting, 1988; Nakayama and Shimojo, 1990).

Deletion and Accretion

Two components of the occlusion phenomenon are known as deletion (hiding) and accretion (revealing) and refer to the degree that an object or surface in the near field reveals or covers objects or surfaces in the far field as your viewpoint translates past their position. In both real and virtual environments, if an object or surface in the near field is significantly closer to the observer than that in the far field, the deletion or accretion of the distant object will occur at a faster rate as you move by, such as shown in Figure 3.19. Alternatively, if two objects are in the far field but in close proximity to each other, the rate at which deletion or accretion will occur is much slower.

If it is not already apparent, the deletion and accretion phenomenon applies regardless of the direction of an observer's movement.

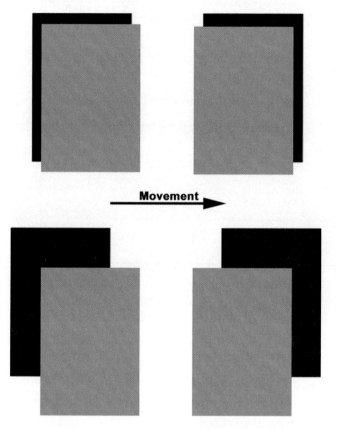

Figure 3.19 The human visual system produces the perception of depth even when the only useful visual structural information comes from motion.
Credit: Illustration by S. Aukstakalnis

This cue is extremely important to remember when designing virtual environment simulations. Under the right circumstances, these cues can be heavily leveraged to produce a variety of interesting effects.

Linear Perspective
Linear perspective is the monocular depth cue provided by the convergence of lines toward a single point in the distance (Khatoon, 2011, 98). As shown in Figure 3.20, looking down this image of a Hong Kong skyway, we know that the walls do not converge but remain parallel along the entire length.

Figure 3.20 Linear perspective is a depth cue within which parallel lines recede into the distance, giving the appearance of drawing closer together. The more the lines converge, the farther away they appear.
Credit: Image by Warren R.M. Stuart via Flickr under a CC 2.0 license

Kinetic Depth Effect (Structure from Motion)

Kinetic depth effect is perception of an object's complex, 3D structure from that object's motion. Although challenging to explain and demonstrate without moving media, consider a cube suspended between a light and a wall. If motionless, the cube could appear as any of the random silhouettes shown in Figure 3.21. Even the square shape in the upper left would be recognized as just that—a square. But rotated through the remaining views, most observers would quickly recognize the source of the silhouettes as a cube, even in the absence of other depth information or surface details.

Figure 3.21 The kinetic depth effect demonstrates the ability to perceive 3D structure from moving 2D views and silhouettes.
Credit: Illustration by S. Aukstakalnis

This phenomenon first appeared in scientific literature in the 1950s based on experiments performed by research scientists Hans Wallach and D. N. O'Connell (Wallach and O'Connell, 1953). Widely studied since, there are two key theories as to how the 3D forms are perceived. The first is the result of changes in the pattern of stimulation on the retina as the object moves, and the second is related to previous experience. In most situations, the kinetic depth effect is experienced along with other depth cues, such as that of motion parallax described earlier.

Familiar Size

As the name of this cue indicates, if we know how large an object is at a distant location, our brain can use that understanding to estimate absolute distances, such as shown in Figure 3.22. Some studies speculate that this cue can be recharacterized as the awareness of the relationship between the size of one's body and the size of an object as knowing the size of an object must be anchored to some relative metric, and the body is really the only relevant thing we have to which sizes can be compared (Linkenauger et al., 2013).

Figure 3.22 The familiar size cue draws upon existing observer knowledge of an object in view to help estimate absolute distances.
Credit: Image by Anoldent via Flickr under a CC 2.0 license

Relative Size

As shown in Figure 3.23, if two objects are similar in size but offset in terms of their distances from the position of the observer, we perceive the one that casts a smaller image on the retina as being farther away, and the one with the larger image as being closer. This depth cue is heavily weighted based upon personal experience.

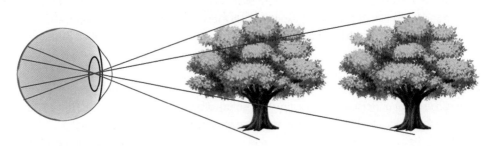

Figure 3.23 If two objects are of equal size, then if one is farther away, it will occupy a smaller area on the retina. A larger retinal image makes something appear closer.
Credit: Illustration by S. Aukstakalnis

Aerial Perspective

Aerial perspective (also known as atmospheric perspective) refers to the effect of light being scattered by particles in the atmosphere, such as water vapor and smoke between an observer and a distant object or scene. As shown in Figure 3.24, as this distance increases, the contrast between the object or scene feature and its background decreases. This is also the case with markings and details of the object. As can be seen in the photograph, the mountains in the distance become progressively less saturated and shift toward the background color. Leonardo da Vinci referred to this cue as "the perspective of disappearance."

Figure 3.24 This photo shows loss of color saturation, contrast, and detail as distance increases from the observer.
Credit: Image by WSilver via Flickr under a CC 2.0 license

This atmospheric effect comes about as visible blue light has a short wavelength in the range of about 475 nm. Thus, it is scattered more efficiently by the molecules in the atmosphere, which is why the sky usually appears blue. At sunrise and sunset, orange (590 nm) and red (650 nm) colors would dominate the scene as the associated wavelengths are longer and less efficiently scattered by the atmosphere.

Texture Gradient
Texture gradient is a strong depth cue within which there is a gradual change in the appearance of textures and patterns of objects from coarse to fine (or less distinct) as distance from the observer increases. As shown in Figure 3.25, the individually defined cobblestones progressively become less and less distinguishable as distance increases from the observer until they appear to blend into a continuous surface.

Three key features can be identified in this cue (Mather, 2006):

- **Perspective gradient**—Separation of texture elements perpendicular to the surface slant or angle of viewing appears to decrease with distance.

- **Compression gradient**—The apparent height of texture elements decreases with increasing distance.

- **Density gradient**—Density, or number of elements per unit area, increases with increasing distance.

Figure 3.25 This photograph shows a wonderful example of texture gradient, within which there is a gradual change in the appearance of textures and patterns of objects from course to fine as distance from the observer increases.

Credit: Image by Jeremy Keith via Flickr under a CC 2.0 license

Lighting/Shading/Shadows

Lighting, shading, and shadows are powerful cues in the perception of scene depth and object geometry, and their effects vary widely. The angle and sharpness of shadows influence perceived depth. Shadows and reflections cast by one object on another provide information about distances and positioning. Smaller, more clearly defined shadows typically indicate a close proximity of an object to the surface or object upon which the shadow is cast. Similarly, the perception of greater depth can be influenced by enlarging a shadow and the blurring of edges. The manner in which light interacts with an irregular surface reveals significant information about geometry and texture. A number of these effects are shown in Figure 3.26.

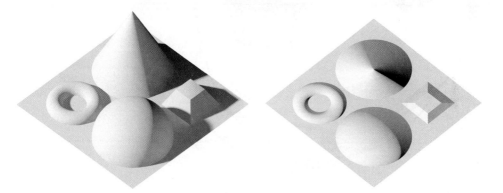

Figure 3.26 This photograph illustrates how shading and shadows can significantly impact the perception of depth in a closed space.
Credit: Illustration by Julian Herzog via Wikimedia under a CC 4.0 license

Optical Expansion

Extend your arm straight out, palm up, and slowly move your hand towards your face. As you hand moves closer, the image projected on your retina also grows in size isotropically and increasingly occludes the background. Known as optical expansion, this cue not only allows an observer to perceive an object as moving, but the distance of the object as well (Ittelson, 1951). Sensitivity to this dynamic stimulus develops at a young age and has been observed in infants who show a coordinated defensive response to an object approaching straight on (Bower et al., 1970). A still-frame example of this cue is shown in Figure 3.27. Not only does the object grow larger as distance decreases, but background cues increasing disappear.

Figure 3.27 Within the optical expansion cue, the visual image increases size on the retina as an object comes toward us, causing the background to be increasingly occluded.
Credit: Illustration by S. Aukstakalnis

Relative Height

In a normal viewing situation, objects on a common plane in the near field of your vision are projected onto a lower portion of the retinal field than objects that are farther away. This phenomenon can be seen in the simple example shown in the left side of Figure 3.28. The key is your height relative to the objects in your field of view. Conversely, if objects being viewed are on a common plane above your viewpoint, such as a line of ceiling lanterns, objects closest to you will appear in a higher portion of the retinal field than objects that are farther away. Artists have used this technique for centuries in order to depict depth in 2D drawings and paintings.

Figure 3.28 Relative height is a concept where distant objects are seen or portrayed as being smaller and higher in relation to items that are closer.
Credit: Image by Naomi / Mitch Altman via Flickr under a CC 2.0 licenses

Conclusion

As has been shown throughout this chapter, the human visual system is a remarkable sensory and interpretation mechanism capable of a high dynamic range of performance. Many of the capabilities explored have direct relevance to the overall subject matter of this book. For instance, the processes of vergence and accommodation have direct implications on the design of both fully immersive as well as augmented head-mounted displays. Understanding the various cues used by our visual system to perceive depth can contribute significantly to the actual design of virtual environments.

Throughout the remainder of this book are numerous instances where we refer back to the content of this chapter, solidifying the importance of understanding the mechanics of how our primary sensory mechanism functions. Beyond this chapter, enthusiasts and practitioners alike are strongly encouraged to build upon their knowledge in this area by digging into the papers and others resources provided in Appendix A, "Bibliography," at the end of this book.

CHAPTER 4

COMPONENT TECHNOLOGIES OF HEAD-MOUNTED DISPLAYS

Head-mounted displays for virtual and augmented reality come in a variety of forms, from single eye information displays to fully occluding stereoscopic headsets such as the HTC Vive and Oculus Rift. At the heart of each are two primary component assemblies; image displays and optics. In this chapter we explore the diverse range of these core enabling technologies, identifying the strengths and limitations of each solution.

Display Fundamentals

All head-mounted displays for virtual and augmented reality incorporate the same basic subsystems, although in widely varying sizes and configurations. In their simplest form, these displays consist of at least one image source and optics in a head mount (Melzer, 1997). Depending on the specific display design and intended application, this basic definition will expand to include a variety of different attributes and features, such as second visual display channel, sensors for tracking gaze direction and duration, and more. As will be seen throughout this book, head-mounted displays come in a variety of form factors and sizes and are rarely identical in terms of performance, even when employing the same basic components.

In this chapter, our primary emphasis will be to build foundational concepts concerning the technical performance of these basic subsystems. To this end, we begin with defining basic display categories, followed by reviewing the most common image displays and optical systems.

Ocularity

Head-mounted displays can be categorized by their ocularity, or the specification of their design in serving one or two eyes. To this end, there are three types: monocular, biocular, and binocular. Figure 4.1 illustrates the differences.

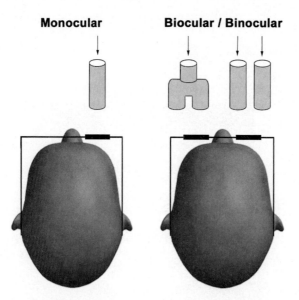

Figure 4.1 All head-mounted displays fall into one of three optical and display configurations: monocular, biocular, and binocular. These designations define a display's ocularity.
Credit: Illustration by S. Aukstakalnis

Monocular

A monocular display provides a single viewing channel via a small display element and optics positioned in front of one eye, with the other eye free to view the normal, real-world surroundings. Typically these devices are of a small form factor and are used as information displays. Examples include various military aviation implementations and devices such as Google Glass or the Vuzix M-100 Smart Glasses (detailed in Chapter 5, "Augmenting Displays").

Biocular

A biocular display provides a single viewing channel to both eyes. This type of display is most common with head-mounted cinematic viewers as well as those applications in which an immersive capability is needed, but without stereopsis. Generally this type of application is in relation to close proximity tasks. An example of such an implementation is an arc welding training system detailed in Chapter 18, "Education."

Binocular

The third display category is binocular, where each eye receives its own separate viewing channel with slightly offset viewpoints mimicking the human visual system to create a stereoscopic view.

A summary of these display categories and the primary advantages and disadvantages of each is shown in Table 4.1.

Table 4.1   Ocular Design Advantages and Disadvantages

Ocularity	Advantages	Disadvantages
Monocular	Low weight, small form factor, least distracting, easiest integration, least computational overhead, easiest alignment.	Possibility of binocular rivalry and eye-dominance issues, small field of view (FOV), no stereo depth cues, asymmetric mass loading, reduced perception of low-contrast objects, no immersion.
Biocular	Less weight than binocular, no visual rivalry, useful for close proximity training tasks requiring immersion, symmetric mass loading.	Increased weight, limited FOV and peripheral cues, no stereo depth cues, often lens is larger to accommodate larger eye box.
Binocular	Stereo images, binocular overlap, larger FOV, most depth cues, sense of immersion	Heaviest, most complex, most expensive, sensitive to alignment, computationally intensive operation.

Display Types

Building on the concept of ocularity, there are three general categories for head-mounted displays. The first provides a computer-generated replacement to your true visual surroundings, and the second two provide an enhanced view of the real environment.

Fully Immersive

Fully immersive displays completely occlude the user's view to the outside world. Fully immersive stereoscopic head-mounted displays (that is, classic virtual reality) combined with sensors to track position and orientation of the user's head provide the visual sensation of actual presence within a computer-generated environment.

Video See-Through

Video see-through displays are invariably fully immersive as a baseline design, but with the key difference being that the primary imagery displayed within the device comes from either front-facing video cameras or those set in a remote location (telepresence). Depending on the specific application for which the device was designed, those video signals can be combined with computer-generated imagery and output from other sensors. As an example, within the case studies presented in Chapter 17, "Aerospace and Defense," we look at an application for a video see-through display within which a pilot is able to practice aerial refueling operations with a virtual tanker seen flying outside of their aircraft while using such a display.

Optical See-Through

Optical see-through displays are the key enabling technology underpinning the phrase *augmented reality*. These systems are designed to overlay, supplement, or combine graphics, symbology, and textual data with the user's real-world view seen through the optical elements.

Imaging and Display Technologies

The imaging and display technologies employed within head-mounted viewing devices for virtual and augmented systems have made considerable advances over the past two decades. What was once a realm completely dominated at the high end by CRTs has been all but completely replaced by four key imaging and display technologies, each providing a vastly improved, lightweight, and easier to implement solution. In the following sections we will explore the basic functionality of each display type, highlighting the benefits and trade-offs within this application setting.

Liquid Crystal Displays Panels

Liquid Crystal Displays (LCDs) are a relatively mature technology originally used in near-eye displays for virtual and augmented reality as far back as the 1980s by groups such as NASA (Fisher et al., 1986), the University of North Carolina (Chung et al., 1989), companies such as VPL Research (Conn et al., 1989), and others. LCDs are now used in many HDTVs, desktop and laptop monitors, and tablet and cell phone displays.

As shown in Figure 4.2, an LCD is an electronically modulated transmissive display device composed of two sheets of polarizing material, the axes of which are aligned perpendicular to each other. Between the polarizing sheets is an array of cells arranged in rows and columns containing liquid crystal molecules. These cells are enclosed on each side by thin glass substrates, upon one of which are printed millions of precisely positioned tiny transistors. Electrical current passed through the liquid crystal in each cell causes the crystals to come into and out of alignment. Varying the current passing through the liquid crystal material allows each cell in the array to serve as a shutter modulating the passage of light.

1	Glass plates	6	Command lines
2	Polarizer	7	Rubbed polymer layer
3	Polarizer	8	Spacers
4	RGB color mask	9	Thin-film transistors
5	Command lines	10	Front electrode
		11	Rear electrodes

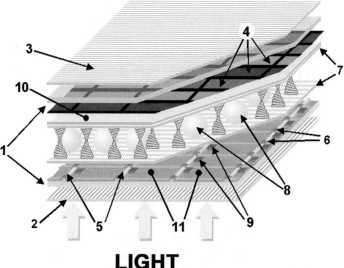

LIGHT

Figure 4.2 This illustration details the complex structure of an active matrix liquid crystal display. Note that light is provided by an external source.
Credit: Illustration by Lozère via Wikimedia

For color LCDs, an additional substrate is added to the stack containing red, green, and blue filters, or masks, each of which is precisely positioned over an individual cell. Three RGB liquid crystal cells (known as subpixels) form one pixel. When an electrical current is applied, each cell modulates the passage of light based on the intensity of the signal. The combined output from the three subpixels produces the color of the light seen by the observer. If all three subpixels are fully open, the result is a white dot, the color of the backlighting, which is explained next.

Because liquid crystal materials do not emit their own light, the light must be provided by a separate source. Although small LCDs such as those in watches often use reflected ambient light, modern color LCD panels such as those found in some head-mounted displays typically rely upon illumination provided by blue LEDs at the edge of the display panel, which is filtered through a yellow phosphor, and then spread via a diffuser to create a pseudo white light. This light is, in turn, further filtered into different colors by the color mask layer of the liquid crystal elements.

Organic Light Emitting Diode Panels

Organic Light-Emitting Diode (OLED) is a solid-state display technology based on organic (carbon and hydrogen bonded) materials that will emit light when electric current is applied. As shown in Figure 4.3, the base layer of an OLED is a thin glass substrate upon which are stacked a series of organic films sandwiched between two electrodes (a metallic cathode and transparent anode). As electrical current travels through the organic layers between the cathode (a conductor) to the anode (an emitter), electrons are given to the emissive organic layer and removed from the conductive layer. The removal of electrons from the conductive layer results in "holes" that need to be filled by other electrons. As these holes migrate to the emissive layer and recombine with electrons (a bound state known as an exciton), energy is released in the form of light, a process referred to as **electroluminescence**. Although colors can be controlled through the careful crafting of the organic emissive materials used within the OLED, most manufacturers opt for adding red, green, and blue plastic films within the OLED stack.

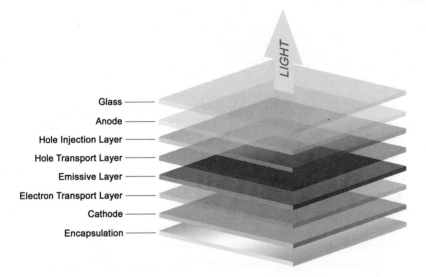

Figure 4.3 This illustration shows the basic architecture of an Organic Light-Emitting Diode (OLED).
Credit: Illustration by S. Aukstakalnis

There are two main types of OLED displays: Passive Matrix OLED (PMOLED) and Active Matrix OLED (AMOLED). The difference is in the electronics used to drive the display. A PMOLED display uses a complex electronic grid to sequentially control individual pixels in each row (or line) in the display and does not contain storage capacitors. Thus, update rates are slow and the power draw is high to maintain a pixel's state. In general, PMOLED are used for simple character and iconic displays.

Most applicable to near-eye virtual and augmented reality displays is the AMOLED, a basic design for which is shown in Figure 4.4. Similar to the control of an Active Matrix LCD, an AMOLED is driven by a thin film transistor (TFT) layer that contains a storage capacitor to maintain each subpixel's state. This provides a significant level of control over individual pixels, including the ability to completely switch them off allowing for deep blacks and high contrast.

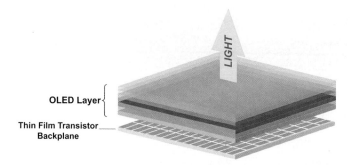

Figure 4.4 Similar to an active matrix LCD, an Active Matrix OLED (AMOLED) uses a thin film transistor layer that contains a storage capacitor to maintain each subpixel's state.
Credit: Illustration by S. Aukstakalnis

In many ways, AMOLEDs are far superior to LCDs. These advantages include the fact that AMOLEDs can be very thin because there is no need for backlighting (they produce their own light), and they have lower power consumption, fast refresh rates, low persistence, excellent color reproduction, and high resolutions. As will be see in Chapter 6, "Fully Immersive Displays," most commercially available head-mounted displays on the market at the time this book was prepared utilize AMOLED modules as their image sources.

Digital Light Projector Microdisplay

A Texas Instruments **digital light projector** (DLP) chip, technically referred to as a **digital micromirror device** (DMD), is a class of micro-electro-mechanical systems (MEMS) known as spatial light modulators. As shown in Figure 4.5, on the surface of this chip is an array of up to two million individually controlled micromirrors measuring ~5.4μ (microns) in size, each of which can be used to represent a single pixel in a projected image (Bhakta et al., 2014). Images are generated by directing an RGB light source to shine on the mirror array while simultaneously sending a video or graphics signal to the DLP chipset, which activates an electrode beneath each DMD mirror. When the appropriate red, green, or blue image channel is to be displayed (a technique known as field sequential color), controllers load a memory cell underlying each mirror cell with a 1 or a 0, causing each mirror to tilt toward or away from a light source with an orientation of ±17°. Tilted toward the light source (+17°), the reflected point of light appears ON. Tilted away from the light source (−17°), the point appears OFF (or dark). As each mirror can be reoriented thousands of times per second, in turn varying the duration that each mirror spends in either the ON or OFF position, different shades of a reflected color can be produced. Used in conjunction with any of a variety of light sources and optics, the DMD device can project efficient patterns of light at high speeds.

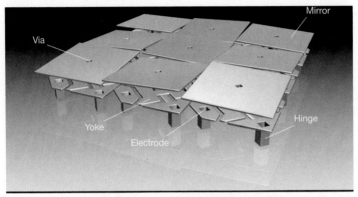

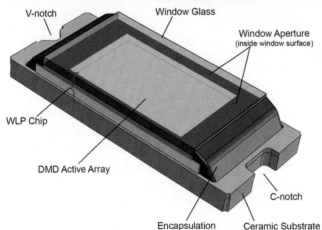

Figure 4.5 This illustration shows the basic architecture of a DLP digital micromirror device. Each highly reflective pivoting aluminum mirror in the DMD chip serves as an independent light switch. *Credit: Illustrations courtesy of Texas Instruments*

As shown in Figure 4.6, the DLP DMD chip architecture and small size enables considerable flexibility in their integration within near-eye displays for both virtual and augmented reality. In one orientation, the DMD micromirror array is positioned directly in front of the user's eyes. The array is then illuminated from either the side or the bottom by low power 3-in-1 RGB LEDs, with the light then transferred via optics into the user's eye to form an image on the retina. A second orientation places the DMD chip off to the side, with the reflected light transferred via waveguide (see the next section) into the user's eye. In either configuration, the eye itself serves as the last element in the optical chain, with the retina serving as the display surface (Bhakta et al., 2014).

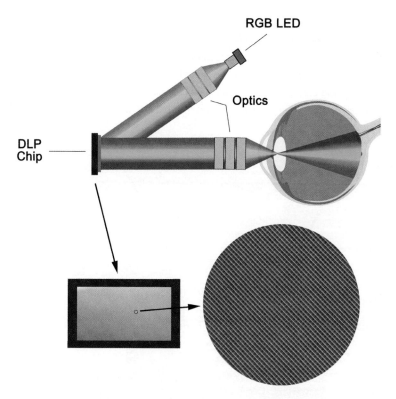

RGB LED

Optics

DLP
Chip

Figure 4.6 A Texas Instrument DLP digital micromirror device uses the retina of the human eye as the last element in the optical chain of a head-mounted display.
Credit: Illustration by S. Aukstakalnis

DMDs represent one of the fastest display technologies in existence. The speed of color refresh and low latency, the high resolution for such a small form factor (a 0.3-inch array diagonal enables a 1280 × 720 image), flexible illumination direction, and low power requirements make DMD an ideal imaging solution for head-mounted displays

Liquid Crystal on Silicon Microdisplay

Liquid Crystal on Silicon (LCoS) imaging technology is a cross between LCD and DLP technologies. As explained earlier in this section, an LCD is composed of an array of cells containing liquid crystal molecules sandwiched between two sheets of polarizing material with one cell (subdivided into red, green, and blue sections) representing one pixel. The state of each pixel is modulated by controlling the phase of the liquid crystal molecules and thus, the passage of light. This makes the LCD a "transmissive" technology. In comparison, DLP displays use an array of individually controlled micromirrors (each representing one pixel) that reflect sequentially projected light from an RGB source. The state of each pixel is modulated by tilting the mirror, making this a "reflective" technology.

As shown in Figure 4.7, an LCoS device is a combination of both transmissive and reflective technologies. Constructed on a silicon wafer overlaid with a highly reflective coating, LCoS uses nematic or ferroelectric liquid crystal to modulate field sequential colored light reflected off this backplane. Because control circuits are beneath the reflective surface behind each pixel (as opposed to surrounding each pixel as in traditional LCD architectures), there are no obstructions in the light pathway, enabling the generation of substantially clearer images.

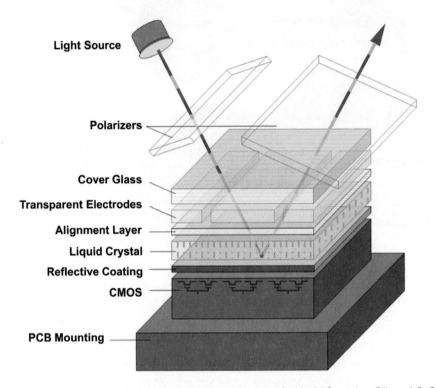

Figure 4.7 This illustration details the basic architecture of a Liquid Crystal on Silicon (LCoS) chip. Note that an LCoS chip modulates light from an external source to produce an image.
Credit: Illustration by Aesopus via Wikimedia under a CC 3.0 license

Similar to the DLP DMD solution covered earlier, the LCoS chip architecture and small size enable considerable flexibility in their integration within small form factor near-eye displays for both virtual and augmented reality. A powerful example of one such implementation is the Google Glass monocular head-mounted display.

As shown in Figure 4.8, a side-projecting red, green, and blue (RGB) micro-LED array is used to produce field-sequential color illumination. This light is steered through a wedge fly-eye microlens element (shown in Figure 4.9), where it illuminates the reflective inner surface of an LCoS chip. Upon exiting the chip, the resulting modulated light (for each color channel) is reflected off a polarizing beamsplitter and further down the optical path of the display, where it is ultimately steered into the user's eye.

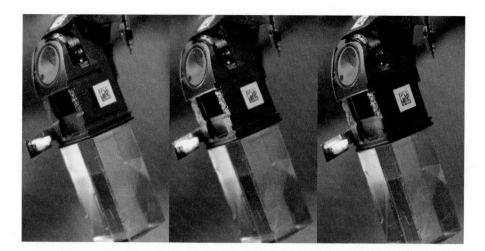

Figure 4.8 This image sequence shows the side-projecting red, green, and blue (RGB) LED array used in Google Glass to create field sequential colored light for generation of the appropriate image channels.

Credit: Image courtesy of Sid Hazra

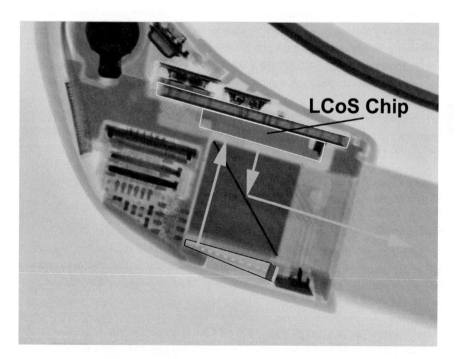

Figure 4.9 This annotated x-ray of a Google Glass display shows a simplified path that a field of sequential light from an RGB LED takes through a wedge fly-eye microlens, into an LCoS chip, off a polarizing beamsplitter, and further down the optical path of the display.

Credit: Image courtesy of Andrew Vanden Heuvel, AGL Initiatives

Related Terminology and Concepts

When evaluating display technologies for virtual and augmented reality systems, the lexicon (or jargon) of the field can often be confusing, and perhaps no more so than when dealing with the properties of light. In this section we cover some basic terminology and concepts essential to a solid foundation of understanding concerning the technical performance of displays.

About Light

Light is radiant energy capable of exciting photoreceptors in the human eye. As discussed in Chapter 3, "The Mechanics of Sight," the human eye is only sensitive to a narrow band within the electromagnetic spectrum falling between wavelengths roughly measuring 380 nanometers and 740 nanometers in length.

Lumen—A lumen (lm) is the unit of measure for quantifying luminous flux (defined next), the total quantity of visible light energy emitted by a source. Most light measurements are expressed in lumens. You will frequently see this unit of measure used in relation to displays based on projection technologies.

Luminous flux—Luminous flux is a quantitative expression of light energy per unit of time radiated from a source over wavelengths to which the human eye is sensitive (380 nm–740 nm). The unit of measure for luminous flux is the Lumen (lm). One watt of radiant power at 555 nm, the wavelength to which a healthy human eye is most sensitive (a yellowish green color), is equivalent to a luminous flux of 680 lumens (Meyer-Arendt, 1968).

Luminous intensity—Luminous intensity is the luminous flux per solid angle emitted or reflected from a point. The unit of measure for expressing luminous intensity is the lumen per steradian, or candela (cd).

Candela—A candela is the unit of measure for quantifying luminous power per unit solid angle emitted by a point light source in a particular direction.

Luminance—Luminance is the measure of luminous intensity per unit area projected in a given direction. Luminance describes the amount of light that passes through, is emitted or reflected from a particular area, and falls within a given solid angle. The unit of measure for expressing luminance is candela per square meter (cd/m^2). Readers will also frequently see luminance expressed in "nits" or footlamberts (fL). 1 fL = 3.426 cd/m^2.

Illuminance—Illuminance is the luminous flux incident on a surface per unit area. The unit of measure is the lux (lx), or lm/m^2 (lumen per square meter). For a given luminous flux, the illuminance decreases as the illuminated area increases.

Brightness—Brightness is purely a subjective attribute or property used to express the luminance of a display. Brightness is perceived, not measured. From a technical standpoint, the words *brightness* and *luminance* should not be interchanged (although they frequently are). Brightness is not a measurable quantity.

Display Properties and Characteristics

There are a wide variety of properties and characteristics to consider in relation to head-mounted displays for augmented and virtual reality systems. Each of the following properties and characteristics directly impacts the quality and performance of such displays.

Spatial resolution—The term *spatial resolution* refers to the number of individual pixel elements of a display and is presented as numerical values for both the vertical and the horizontal directions. For instance, the spatial resolution of the Oculus Rift CV1 is 1200×1080 resolution per eye.

Pixel pitch—Pixel pitch refers to the distance from the center of one pixel (RGB triad, LED cluster, and so on) to the center of the next pixel measured in millimeters. This concept is illustrated in Figure 4.10.

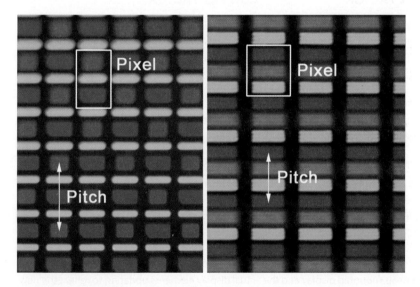

Figure 4.10 This image illustrates the concept of pixel pitch, which is the distance from the center of one pixel (RGB triad, LED cluster, and so on) to the center of the next pixel and which is expressed in millimeters.
Credit: Illustration by S. Aukstakalnis

Fill factor—When referring to pixel-based visual displays, regardless of type, the phrase *fill factor* refers to the amount of black space between individual pixel elements. Because these types of displays are typically composed of a precision array, an excessive black area between pixels can give the visual effect of a fine grid overlay or "screen door" effect when the display surface is viewed close up.

When expressing the phenomenon, the phrase *high fill factor* refers to minimal black spacing between pixels. A *low fill factor* would be an expression of excessive black spacing between pixels. This phenomenon is illustrated in Figure 4.11.

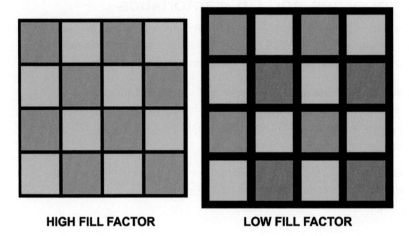

HIGH FILL FACTOR   **LOW FILL FACTOR**

Figure 4.11 This image illustrates the concept of the phrase fill factor, which refers to the amount of black space between individual pixel elements. A low fill factor results in a strong "screen door" effect in near-eye displays.
Credit: Illustration by S. Aukstakalnis

Of the four primary imaging technologies covered in this chapter (LCD, AMOLED, DLP, and LCoS), DLP has the least perceptible spacing between pixels (or the highest fill factor) due to the exceedingly small size of the individual mirrors comprising the reflecting surface of the chip.

Persistence—The term *persistence* refers to the length of time a pixel remains illuminated. Full persistence refers to when pixels remain illuminated for the time span of an entire frame. Low persistence refers to when pixels remain illuminated for only a fraction of the time span of an entire frame. Increasing refresh rate decreases persistence time. Persistence is typically represented in percentages.

Latency—The term *latency* refers to the elapsed time (measured in milliseconds) between the movement of a head-mounted display and the actual display elements updating to reflect the new scene view. Latency is by no means just a display issue, but the totality of time required for all system components to complete their processing tasks and updated imagery to be displayed.

Response time—The term *response time* refers to the measure of time a pixel takes to change. Measured in milliseconds, the longer the response time, the more pronounced are the visible image artifacts. Low response times are crucial for head-mounted viewing devices.

Color gamut—The *color gamut* of a display defines a specific range of colors a device is capable of producing. Although there are a variety of methods used to express a display's color gamut, the most common are the xy chromaticity diagram of the XYZ color system established by the International Commission on Illumination (CIE), as well as the percentage of the NTSC (RGB) color space.

Contrast—*Contrast* is a measure of the relative difference between light and dark areas of a display. LCDs tend to be low contrast display, whereas AMOLEDs are high contrast.

Optical Architectures

Optics within a head-mounted display serve three general purposes:

Collimation of light such that an image source appears at a distance greater than its physical distance from the wearer's eyes;

Magnification of the image source such that an image appears larger than the actual source;

Relay of light patterns from an image source, sometimes located off axis, to the wearer's eyes (Melzer et al., 2009).

As detailed in the previous section, there are a variety of imaging and display technologies employed within head-mounted viewing devices. Each separate implementation requires its own specific optical design, whether it is to enable users to focus on a flat panel array positioned within inches of their eyes or to relay imagery generated by a microdisplay in an off-axis position such as the side of a display device and into their field of view. In many ways optics are the greatest challenge, and often the limiting factor, in the design of head-mounted viewing devices. Each optical element added to a system means an increase in size and mass of the overall display.

Another significant challenge comes as a result of the fact that head-mounted displays are human-centered systems. The complexity and sensitivity of our sensory mechanisms demands precision and accommodation; otherwise, problems arise, including discomfort, nausea, and an overall poor end user experience.

Basic Concepts

There is not now, and it is likely there will never be, a single head-mounted display device that meets all end user needs. That which is necessary or acceptable for gaming and entertainment with general consumers will be unlikely to serve the needs of professional users. Then there is the consideration of costs. Precision systems for professional end uses such as flight simulation or augmentation will invariably be priced well outside of the reach of the average consumer. That said, there are a variety of optical designs, as well as features and considerations common to all head-mounted displays, about which readers should be aware and are covered in this section.

Field of View

A key consideration in all head-mounted displays for virtual and augmented reality applications is the FOV, which is defined as the total angular size of the virtual image visible to both eyes and which is expressed in degrees (Barfield and Furness, 1995). As binocular displays involve variable amounts of left- and right-eye FOV overlap, it is sometimes useful to express both the horizontal binocular FOV and the total FOV as separate values.

As shown in Figure 4.12, for a healthy adult, the average horizontal binocular FOV, which is the foundation for stereopsis and is important for depth perception, is 120°, with a total FOV measuring approximately 200°. Our vertical FOV is approximately 130°.

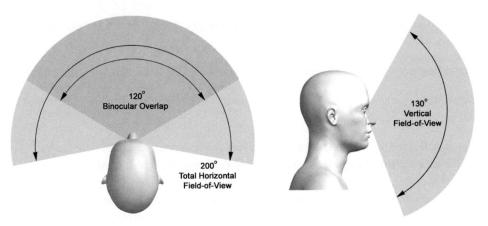

Figure 4.12 This image illustrates the extremes of the average human horizontal and vertical fields of view.
Credit: Illustration by S. Aukstakalnis

Binocular Overlap

The binocular field, also known as the area of binocular overlap, is that part of the total visual field within which the monocular FOV for our two eyes overlap. This feature of human vision is extremely important for perception of depth because the relative angles in which objects in a scene are visible gives an estimate of how far this object is located (Boger, 2013).

Interpupillary Distance

Interpupillary distance (IPD) is the distance between the centers of the pupils of the two eyes. This measurement is extremely important for all binocular viewing systems ranging from standard eyewear to stereoscopic head-mounted displays.

As discussed in greater detail in Chapter 21, "Human Factors Considerations," proper IPD settings are extremely important because poor eye-lens alignment can result in image distortion, the effect of which can be eye strain and headaches and may contribute to the onset of nausea (Ames et al., 2005). Incorrect settings can also impact ocular convergence and incorrect perception of the displayed imagery.

Eye Relief

In a head-mounted display, eye relief is the distance from the cornea of the eye to the surface of the first optical element. Eye relief defines the distance at which the user can obtain the full viewing angle of the display device. This measurement is an extremely important consideration, particularly for those individuals who wear corrective lenses, and in particular, glasses, because eye relief for spectacles alone is approximately 12 mm. As an example, although the HTC Vive (detailed in Chapter 6) allows the user to adjust the eye relief setting to accommodate the use of glasses, the Oculus Rift CV1 (also detailed in Chapter 6) does not. As would be expected, adjusting the eye relief directly impacts the user's actual perceived FOV within the display.

Exit Pupil

The term *exit pupil* refers to the diameter of light transmitted to your eye by an optical system.

Eye Box

The phrase *eye box* refers to the volume within which users can place their pupils and experience the full performance of the device. As shown in Figure 14.13, this volume is dictated by the eye relief and exit pupil.

Pupil Forming and Nonpupil Forming Optics

There are two primary optical system designs, or architectures, used in virtual and augmented reality displays: pupil forming and nonpupil forming (Barfield, 2015). Commercially available fully immersive displays such as HTC Vive, Oculus Rift, and Sony PSVR use nonpupil forming architectures. As shown in Figure 4.13, these three systems use a single magnifier to directly collimate light from the display panel.

Nonpupil Forming Optical Architecture

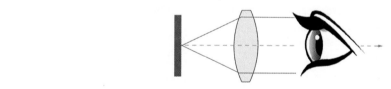

Pupil Forming Optical Architecture

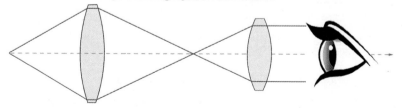

Figure 4.13 This image illustrates the most basic configurations for pupil and nonpupil forming optical architectures.

Credit: Illustration by S. Aukstakalnis

Although single lens, nonpupil forming optical designs result in lighter, more compact displays, with a large eye box, the trade-off is that they impose significant distortion in the process of bending the light field. The effect is known as pincushion distortion and is illustrated in Figure 14.14. To counteract this effect, images displayed within these viewing devices must be rendered with an equal and opposite barrel distortion to cancel out the effect.

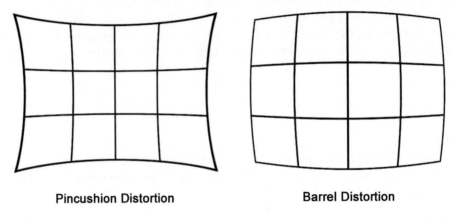

Pincushion Distortion   **Barrel Distortion**

Figure 4.14 This image illustrates pincushion distortion, where optics introduce extreme distortion at the edges of the display. This is typically compensated for by rendering images with an opposite barrel distortion. Failure to accurately correct for this phenomenon results in poor depth perception and contributes to incorrect distance judgements.
Credit: Illustration by S. Aukstakalnis

On the other hand, pupil-forming optical system architectures such as those frequently used in combination with DLP DMD and LCoS microdisplays offer significantly greater flexibility in the overall design of head-mounted viewing devices due to the ability to fold, bend, or otherwise manipulate optical tracks to accommodate different design objectives. Figure 14.15 shows a number of optical elements, beam splitter, and combiner configurations used within these architectures.

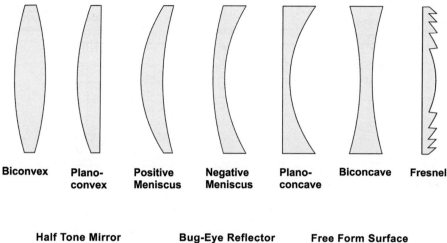

| Biconvex | Plano-convex | Positive Meniscus | Negative Meniscus | Plano-concave | Biconcave | Fresnel |

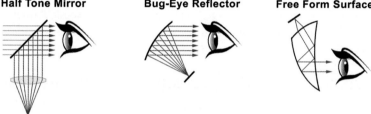

Figure 4.15 This image shows a variety of individual optical elements as well as some of the various combiner technologies and strategies used in the design of optical architectures for head-mounted displays.

Credit: Top optical element illustrations by ElfQrin via Wikimedia under a CC 3.0 license. Combiner illustrations are derivitive works from public domain sources.

Waveguides

A waveguide is a physical structure that enables the propagation of light waves through an optical system by internal reflection. As shown in Figures 14.16 through 14.19, the waveguide constrains the movement of light between two surfaces starting from the point at which the light enters the waveguide through to where it exits.

Although the basic concept of internal reflection is fairly straightforward, from this point the display technology grows in complexity, principally in the means through which light from an image source is introduced into (the in-coupling) and out of (the out-coupling) the waveguide. In general, there are four primary types of waveguides currently employed within existing commercially available augmenting displays:

Holographic Waveguide—Holographic waveguides use holographic optical elements as the in- and out-coupling mechanisms. This technique is currently used within the Sony Smart Eyeglass displays and is illustrated in Figure 4.16.

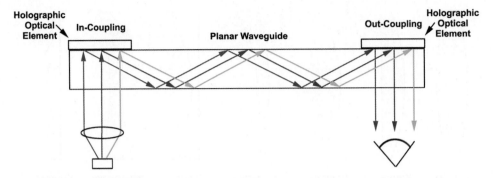

Figure 4.16 This image illustrates the basic functional concept behind a holographic waveguide.
Credit: Illustration by S. Aukstakalnis

Diffractive Waveguide—A detractive waveguide contains surface relief gratings with features sometimes measuring in the nanometer range. Detractive waveguides, a basic illustration for which is shown in Figure 4.17, are currently used within Microsoft HoloLens, various Vuzix displays, and a variety of defense and avionics optical systems.

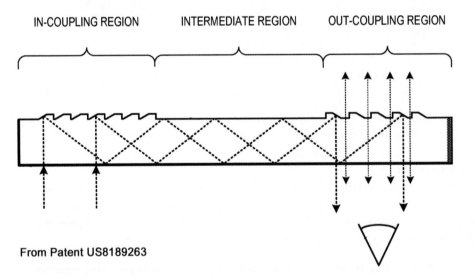

Figure 4.17 This adapted patent image shows an example of a basic detractive waveguide design used within a number of commercial and defense optical systems.

Polarized Waveguide—A polarization waveguide such as shown in Figure 4.18 is a multipart assembly embedding a parallel array of partially reflecting polarized surfaces and multilayer coatings to direct light toward the eye of the viewer. This method was developed by and used within the Lumus DK-50 AR glasses.

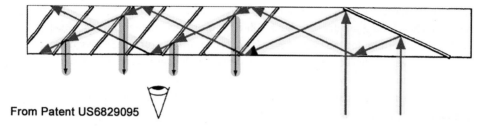

From Patent US6829095

Figure 4.18 This adapted patent image illustrates the basic polarized waveguide technology used within the Lumus DK-50 AR glasses. Arrows highlighted in yellow depict light entering the waveguide and progressing through the various polarized surfaces before exiting (in blue).

Reflective Waveguide—A reflective waveguide such as illustrated in Figure 4.19 uses a single planar light guide with at least one semireflective mirror. This technique is used by Epson in its Moverio product line as well as Google Glass.

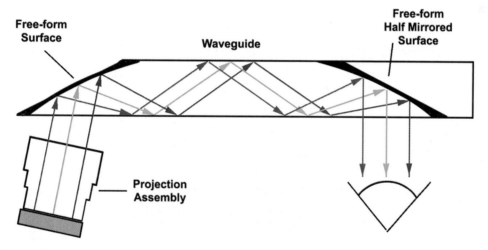

Figure 4.19 This image shows the basic design principle and optical pathway of the Epson Moverio display line.

Conclusion

Each of the image-generation technologies covered in this chapter has been applied to virtual and augmented reality as an afterthought. None were developed with this particular application setting in mind. The result is that hardware developers are forced into compromises and trade-offs, designing from the outside in, as opposed to the inside out. Complex spatial phenomena are simulated on 2D surfaces, squeezed through sometimes laughable optical systems and presented to our eyes in an attempt to fool the users into believing they're someplace else.

But these are necessary steps. It is because of these limitations, compromises, and trade-offs that researchers have spent decades digging into the problems, learning how our visual system functions, and deciphering the best ways to format and present structured light patterns to our eyes. Given the host of new display technologies under development, from depth indexed projections using oscillating optical fibers to holographic imaging technologies, it is abundantly clear that the flat panel-based head-mounted displays capturing the attention of the public today will be considered relics in just a few short years.

CHAPTER 5

AUGMENTING DISPLAYS

With increasingly powerful computing and display technologies, our ability to augment our real-world view with information in the form of graphics, text, and symbology is beginning to unfold. In this chapter, we explore a number of proven and promising augmenting displays currently available on the market, highlighting their key functional and design differences and the initial uses for which they are intended.

Binocular Augmenting Displays

Binocular augmenting displays currently constitute the greater portion of new displays entering the market. As will be seen, few of these displays are intended for general consumers because there currently is a significant void in solid applications with broad market appeal. On the other hand, business, industrial, and defense settings provide ample opportunities for application developers to solve a problem, meet an information need, make workflows more efficient, and so on. In this section we explore a number of these displays, highlighting their particular performance features and the application settings within which they are being targeted.

Epson Moverio BT-300

One of the earliest players in the commercial head-mounted augmented reality display market, Epson's Moverio line was launched in 2011 with the BT-100, the first self-contained, Android-powered, wearable see-through binocular display based on reflective waveguide optics technology. From the day the device was introduced, tech hipsters hammered Epson in public forums and blogs for releasing a thick lens, narrow field of view (FOV) display that couldn't possibly be used with their favorite computer game or worn on the street to find the nearest coffee shop. All the while, Epson was quietly building a sizeable user base within industrial and enterprise application settings where just such a display device was needed.

Fast forward to the present. Epson has introduced the third generation of its Moverio smart glasses known as the BT-300. As shown in Figure 5.1, the new streamlined design features small planer reflective waveguide elements and a proprietary, silicon-based OLED (Si-OLED) digital display technology providing higher resolution, contrast, brightness, and truer black projected tones. As explained in Chapter 4, "Component Technologies of Head-Mounted Displays," LCDs produce black tones by blocking the transmissions of light through reorienting liquid crystal molecules. Because individual OLED pixel elements produce their own light, deeper blacks are achieved by simply turning pixels off. Similarly, OLED display technologies are well known for producing significantly richer colors, enabling a greatly improved image quality overall (Seiko Epson, 2016; Nelson, 2016).

Figure 5.1 This image shows the slim, lightweight design of the Epson Moverio BT-300 augmenting display.
Credit: Images courtesy of Epson America, Inc

Although most other current and forthcoming commercially available augmenting displays emphasize their untethered, wireless designs, the Moverio BT-300, like its predecessors, offloads most of the computing and electronics subsystems to a small hand controller that also includes three programmable buttons and a circular trackpad.

There are a variety of applications for this device for the general consumer, although it is important to reiterate that Epson continues to target the BT-300 toward industrial and other enterprise application settings. Specifications for the BT-300 can be seen in Table 5.1.

Table 5.1   Epson Moverio BT-300 Specifications

Feature	Specification
Ocularity	Binocular
Image Source	Proprietary Silicon OLED (Si-OLED)
Resolution	720p
Frame Rate	30 Hz
Color	NTSC 90%
Display Luminosity	1200 cd/m² (nits)
Contrast	100,000:1
Display Optics	Reflective Waveguide

(Continued)

Table 5.1   (Continued)

Feature	Specification
Field of View	23° (80"@ 5 meters)
Transparency	Full Transparency
Head Tracking	IMU (compass/ accel/ gyro)
Camera(s)	(1) 5 MP
Communications	Wi-Fi 802.11a/b/g/n/ac, 2.4 / 5 GHz Bluetooth Smart Ready USB 2.0
Main Processor	Intel Atom 5 1.44 GHz Quad Core
RAM	2 GB
Onboard Storage	Micro SD (max.2 GB), MicroSDHC (max. 32 GB)
Additional Sensors	Android 5.1-based Controller GPS Microphone Ambient Light
Shield(s)	NA
Development Env.	Android 5.1

(Epson, 2016)

Lumus DK-50 Development Kit

There is a saying in Silicon Valley that "you can mine for gold or you can sell pickaxes." This say-ing refers to supplying the critical tools and components that everyone else needs to provide popular goods and services. In the emerging fields of virtual and augmented reality, this adage is readily apparent with several relatively unknown, but critically positioned, companies provid-ing key enabling technologies. One of those companies is Lumus, Ltd of Rehovot, Israel, and the key component it supplies to several augmented reality display manufacturers is polarization waveguide optics modules.

As described in Chapter 4, and as shown in Figure 5.2, this type of waveguide embeds a parallel array of partially reflecting polarized surfaces within the waveguide substrate to first allow images (light patterns) from a micro-display protector such as an LCoS chip pass into the waveguide substrate (known as the couple-in). After propagating through the waveguide via internal reflection, another array of partially reflecting polarized surfaces directs the light out (the couple-out) and into the user's eye.

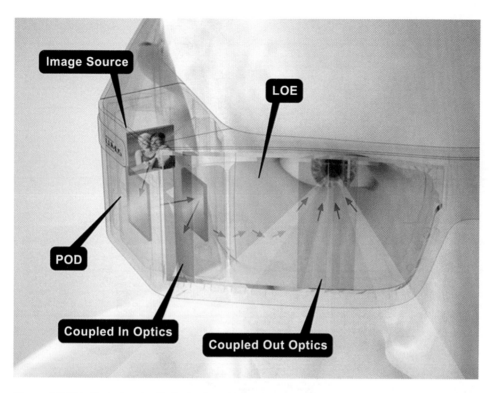

Figure 5.2 This illustration details the basic optical path used in the Lumus waveguide optics modules.
Credit: Image courtesy of Lumus, Ltd

Lumus manufactures and distributes these waveguides as complete display modules with varying levels of performance. The modules are used in a variety of augmenting displays, several of which are detailed next, including their own DK-50 Development Kit shown in Figure 5.3.

Figure 5.3 The Lumus DK-50 developer kit glasses are intended as a reference design and test platform for other manufacturers.
Credit: Image courtesy of Lumus, Ltd

Although not intended as a consumer product, but more as a reference design and test platform for other manufacturers (pickaxes instead of mining for gold), the DK-50 is a comprehensive wireless, standalone binocular display built around the Lumus OE-32 display modules (shown in the inset of Figure 5.3). The device offers 720p resolution and a 40° FOV. The system contains an onboard Snapdragon processor running Android, embedded 9DoF IMU motion sensor, and twin 4MP cameras. The system includes a software development kit (SDK) for applications development and a client program that enables an Android phone to serve as a wireless remote control and mobile network back channel (Lumus, 2016). Specifications for the DK-50 can be seen in Table 5.2.

Table 5.2 Lumus DK-50 Specifications

Feature	Specification
Ocularity	Binocular
Image Source	LCOS micro-display (color seq.)
Resolution	720p
Frame Rate	60 Hz
Color	Full Color
Display Luminosity	4100 cd/m² (nits)
Contrast	>250:1
Display Optics	Lumus Waveguide (thickness <2 mm)
Field of View	37°@ 720p, 40° @ WXGA
Transparency	~80%
Head Tracking	9DoF IMU
Camera(s)	Two 4 MP cameras, 80°
Communications	Wi-Fi 802.11, 2.4 GHz Bluetooth 4.0 PCB integrated antenna
Main Processor	Snapdragon 800
RAM	2 GB
Onboard Storage	16 GB
Additional Sensors	
Shield(s)	
Development Env.	Android

(Lumus, 2016)

AtheerAiR (Augmented interactive Reality) Glasses

Intended for field engineers and deskless workers within the engineering, construction, health-care, and logistics sectors, the AiR (Augmented interactive Reality) glasses from Atheer, Inc of Mountainview, California, shown in Figure 5.4, are a binocular system based on LCoS display modules and Lumus waveguide optics. The system is specifically engineered to facilitate interaction with objects and data presented to the user through natural gestures, voice commands, and motion tracking. Used in combination with the AiR Enterprise Suite, a cloud-based collaboration and task flow interaction solution, an AiR Glasses wearer can team up with other users for collaborative design and task reviews, as well as engage remote experts via video calls, real-time image annotations, and more.

Figure 5.4 The AtheerAiR Glasses are specifically engineered to facilitate interaction with objects and data presented to the user through natural gestures, voice commands, and motion tracking.
Credit: Image courtesy of Atheer, Inc

At the heart of the gesture recognition capability is a robust software application known as Ari, which turns any mobile device with a standard camera into a gesture interface. This capability is particularly important in those usage scenarios in which a worker may be wearing gloves, such as in a surgical suite or industrial setting where a manual interface would be impractical or problematic. Specifications for the AtheerAiR device can be found in Table 5.3.

Table 5.3   AtheerAiR Glasses Specifications

Feature	Specification
Ocularity	Binocular
Image Source	LCOS micro-display (color seq.)
Resolution	720p (1280 × 720) each eye
Frame Rate	60 Hz

Color	Full Color
Display Luminosity	4100 cd/m^2 (nits)
Contrast	>250:1
Display Optics	Lumus Waveguide (thickness <2 mm)
Field of View	50°@ 720p
Transparency	~80%
Head Tracking	9DoF IMU (InvenSense MPU 9250)
Camera(s)	Two 4 MP cameras, 80°
Communications	Wi-Fi 802.11, 2.4 GHz Bluetooth 4.1 Optional 4G Lite PCB integrated antenna
Main Processor	NVIDIA Tegra K1 processor
RAM	2 GB
Onboard Storage	Up to 128 GB
Additional Sensors	Directional microphone
Shield(s)	Front Shield
Development Env.	AiR OS AiR SDK AiR Suite for Enterprise

(Atheer, 2016)

DAQRI Smart Helmet

Although many augmented reality display manufacturers are targeting a consumer or specialty application environment, DAQRI, LLC of Los Angeles, California, is headed in a completely different direction, with its efforts focused on bringing professional-grade wearable augmenting display technologies to the wider architecture, engineering, and construction (AEC) markets.

Currently built around reflective waveguide optics modules from Lumus, Ltd of Rehovot, Israel, the highly instrumented and ruggedized DAQRI Smart Helmet shown in Figure 5.5 is intended to provide companies the ability to supplement a user's view of a work environment with task-specific graphics, symbology, and contextually relevant work instructions, correlated to and stabilized within 3D space. The end goal is using these supplementary information overlays is to increase worker productivity, efficiency, and safety.

Figure 5.5 The sensor-laden DAQRI Smart Helmet is intended to bring augmenting display capabilities to the wider AEC professional market.
Credit: Image reproduced with the permission of DAQRI. © 2016 DAQRI or its affiliates. All rights reserved

Built into a hard hat-like shell with a face shield, the underlying systems include an array of cameras, FLIR thermal infrared, and a 3-camera Intel RealSense R-200 package (forward facing) for IR depth mapping and to track user motion. Connecting the user to an industrial facility's existing information ecosystem is enabled through a range of options, including built-in WiFi, Bluetooth, and cellular capability (DAQRI, 2016).

Because no two worksites are the same, each application setting necessitates some level of customization and integration, which is enabled through DAQRI's 4D Studio authoring environment. At the time of this book's preparation, detailed system specifications had not been publicly released. Those known are summarized in Table 5.4.

Table 5.4   DAQRI Smart Helmet Specifications

Feature	Specification
Ocularity	Binocular
Image Source	LCOS micro-display (color seq.)
Resolution	Undisclosed
Frame Rate	Undisclosed
Color	Full Color

Display Luminosity	Undisclosed
Contrast	Undisclosed
Display Optics	Lumus Waveguide (thickness <2 mm)
Field of View	Undisclosed
Transparency	Undisclosed
Head Tracking	VizNav Camera 10 degrees of freedom (DOF) IMU (2)
Camera(s)	360° Video Camera Array (HD) 13 MP HD Color Camera Absolute Scale FLIR Thermal
Communications	WiFi (undisclosed spec) Bluetooth (undisclosed spec) Cellular (undisclosed spec)
Main Processor	Gen 6 Intel Core M7
RAM	Undisclosed
Onboard Storage	Undisclosed
Additional Sensors	Intel RealSense (forward facing) IR Thermal
Shield(s)	ANSI Compliant Face Shield
Development Env.	DAQRI 4D Studio

(DAQRI, 2016)

Osterhout Design Group R-7 Smartglasses

While some of the largest technology companies in the world are racing to stake out market positions within the augmented and virtual reality arenas, several significantly smaller, lesser known firms have already been here for many years. Quietly solving big problems with the enabling technologies and securing fundamental intellectual property positions, they are turning out highly advanced visualization tools years ahead of their competitors. One of those companies is Osterhout Design Group (ODG) of San Francisco, California.

With roots extending into national security and defense-related projects, ODG has been delivering cutting-edge head-mounted augmenting displays to government and enterprise customers for several years. Osterhout's latest display, a refinement of a device originally intended for defense applications, is the ODG R-7 smartglasses shown in Figure 5.6.

Figure 5.6 The Osterhout Design Group R-7 smartglasses are considered the current state-of-the-art in professional augmenting displays.
Credit: Image courtesy of ODG

Primarily targeting enterprise users, the stereoscopic display is already seeing major traction across key markets including healthcare, energy, transportation, warehouse and logistics, and government. The device delivers the on-board processing power, performance, and connectivity of a tablet computer in a completely untethered design. Software applications for the device have already been developed to assist surgeons, pilots, maintenance inspectors, warehouse and construction workers, and many others. Specifications for the R-7 can be seen in Table 5.5.

Table 5.5   Osterhout Design Group R-7 Smartglasses Specifications

Feature	Specification
Ocularity	Binocular
Image Source	LCOS micro-display (color seq.)
Resolution	720p
Frame Rate	80 fps
Color	Full Color

Display Luminosity	Auto-Adjustment Capable
Display Optics	Undisclosed
Field of View	30°
Transparency	80%
Head Tracking	9 DoF IMU
Camera(s)	Video: 1080p @ 60fps, 720p @ 120fps
Communications	Bluetooth 4.1 (HS, BLE, ANT+) WiFi 802.11ac GNSS (GPS/GLONASS)
Main Processor	Snapdragon 805 2.7 GHz Quad-Core Processor
RAM	3 GB
Onboard Storage	64 GB
Additional Sensors	Altitude Sensor Humidity Sensor Ambient Light Sensor 2 Digital Microphones (User and Environment)
Shield(s)	Magnetic Removable Photochromic Shields
Development Env.	ReticleOS (Android framework + Kit Kat) Qualcomm Vuforia SDK for Digital Eyewear SDK with full API suite and tools Developer Program and Website

(ODG, 2016)

NVIS nVisor ST50

One of the oldest display manufacturers in the augmented and virtual reality industry is NVIS, Inc of Reston, Virginia. Founded in January 2002, the company manufactures some of the highest performance near-eye display systems available on the market. With an emphasis on high-fidelity immersive training and simulation, the company product line includes head-mounted displays, virtual binoculars, and custom embedded displays used in advanced vehicle and weapons simulators.

One of the most widely used of its display offerings is the nVisor ST50 shown in Figure 5.7. Originally designed for the U.S. Army's Research and Development Engineering Command (RDECOM) to support dismounted soldier training programs, the system is now in training, simulation, and research facilities around the world.

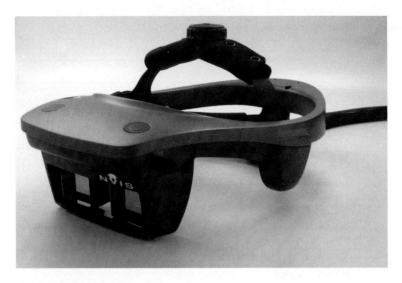

Figure 5.7 The nVisor ST50 is one of the highest performance and precise optical see-through head-mounted displays currently available.
Credit: Image courtesy of NVIS, Inc

At its core, the nVisor ST50 uses Organic Light-Emitting Diode (OLED) microdisplays from EMagin. These microdisplays provide 1280 × 1024 resolution imagery to each eye in a low-power, compact design. Custom optical elements spread the display imagery across a 50° diagonal FOV with < 2% distortion, making this display an ideal solution where absolute precision is needed between real and virtual environments. A removable front cover allows the nVisor ST50 to serve in both augmenting as well as fully immersive applications. More detailed specifications can be found in Table 5.6.

Table 5.6   NVIS nVisor ST50 Specifications

Feature	Specification
Ocularity	Binocular
Image Source	OLED Microdisplay
Resolution	1280 × 1024 (per eye)
Color Depth	24-bit (8 bits per R,G,B)
Refresh Rate	60 Hz
Display Luminosity	23fL
Display Latency	< 0.002 ms
Display Optics	Proprietary optics, <2% distortion
Field of View	40° H × 32° V

Overlap	100%
See-Thru Transm.	44%
Eye Relief	23 mm
Interpupillary Dist.	53–73 mm (Independently Adjustable)
Head Tracking	Supports a variety of external solutions
Microphone	Integrated, shell-mounted
Audio	Integrated Stereo Headphones, 15–25,000 Hz Resp.
Connections	HDMI
Controls	ON/OFF, Brightness, Display Config, Head Sizing
Weight	1050 g (2 lb, 5 oz.)
Shield	Removable front cover to accommodate both AR/VR .

(NVIS, 2016)

Microsoft HoloLens

One of the most widely anticipated display products for this market, the Microsoft HoloLens device shown in Figure 5.8, is a high-definition stereoscopic 3D optical see-through head-mounted display which, in early marketing efforts, is referred to as *holographic computer*. First announced in January 2015, the fully untethered, head-mounted computing system and display uses holographic waveguide elements in front of each eye to present the user with high-definition holograms spatially correlated and stabilized within your physical surroundings.

Made available to developers only a few short months before this book's publication, Microsoft has been intentionally slow at releasing significant detail about the inner workings of this device, although from what is solidly known, the HoloLens is a masterpiece of engineering and capability. For instance, users can interact with holograms via gaze, gestures, and voice recognition. Through spatial mapping capabilities, sound sources can be attached to holographic objects that in turn grow louder and softer as the user move closers or farther away.

Figure 5.8 Microsoft HoloLens is a powerful head-mounted computing and display device that provides users alphanumeric, symbolic, and graphical overlays to their real-world surroundings using holographic waveguide technology.
Credit: Images courtesy of Microsoft Sweden via Flickr under a CC 2.0 license

As will be seen in Chapter 17, "Aerospace and Defense," the capabilities of this device are so promising that it is now in use by astronauts aboard the International Space Station to explore the use of an immersive procedural reference (a manual or guidebook) as well as facilitate providing the crew information and task support from ground-based subject matter and systems experts whenever it is needed.

In the spring of 2016 it was revealed that Microsoft was retargeting the initial release of HoloLens from a consumer gaming and entertainment device to a visualization and productivity tool for enterprise users. Early adopters include Case Western Reserve University, NASA, Saab, and Volvo (Surur, 2016).

More detailed specifications for the HoloLens device can be found in Table 5.7.

Table 5.7   Microsoft HoloLens Specifications

Feature	Specification
Ocularity	Binocular
Image Source	LCoS Microdisplays
Resolution	720p / 2 HD 16:9 light engines Holographic Resolution: 2.3M total light points Holographic Density: >2.5k radiants

Frame Rate	30 FPS
Color	Color Sequential RGB
Display Luminosity	Undisclosed
Contrast	Undisclosed
Display Optics	See-Through Holographic Waveguides
Field of View	~30° (horiz) (Kreylos, 2015)
Transparency	Unspecified at time of publication
Head Tracking	1 IMU 4 Environment Understanding Cameras 1 Depth Camera
Camera(s)	4 Environment Understanding Cameras 1 Depth Camera 2MP Photo / HD Video Camera
Communications	Wi-Fi 802.11ac Micro USB 2.0 Bluetooth 4.1 LE
Main Processor(s)	Intel Atom x5-Z8100 1.04 GHz Intel Airmont (14 nm) Custom Holographic Processing Unit (HPU)
RAM	2 GB
Onboard Storage	64 GB flash
Additional Sensors	4 Microphones 1 Ambient Light Sensor
Shield(s)	Progressive smoke-colored removable shield
Development Env.	Windows 10, 32-bit
Weight	579 g (1 lb, 4 oz.)

(Microsoft, 2016)

Sony SmartEyeglass SED-E1

A recent Sony entry into the augmented reality wearable display marketplace is the SmartEyeglass device shown in Figure 5.9. Intended to serve as platform for developers, the device interfaces with compatible Android-based smartphones to host and drive associated applications. The device uses thin holographic waveguides to superimpose green monochromatic information such as text, symbology, and images into the user's field of view. Operation of the device is enabled through a well designed wired controller that communicates with a host Android mobile device over a Bluetooth or WLAN connection.

Figure 5.9 This images shows the Sony SmaryEyeglass augmenting display with integrated Smart GOLD prescription lenses from Rochester Optical Manufacturing Co. mounted to the back of the device. These prescription lenses are designed to match the shape of the waveguide and are secured by a removable device nosepiece.
Credit: Image courtesy of Rochester Optical Manufacturing Co

Sensors on the device include a 3MP camera, along with an accelerometer, gyroscope, electronic compass, brightness sensor, microphone, and noise suppression submicrophone. This sensor data is passed over the wired connection to the controller, where it is made accessible to the smartphone applications via wireless connection. Specifications for the SmartEyeglass device can be seen in Table 5.8.

Table 5.8   SONY SmartEyeglass SED-E1 Specifications

Feature	Specification
Ocularity	Binocular
Image Source	µDisplay Microdisplay
Resolution	419 × 138
Frame Rate	15fps (WLAN mode), ~10 fps (BT mode)
Color	Monochrome (green) with 8 bit color depth
Display Luminosity	1000 cd/m² (nits)
Display Optics	Holographic waveguide
Field of View	20° Diagonal (19° × 6°)
Transparency	85% Transparency
Head Tracking	IMU (compass/ accel/ gyro)
Camera(s)	(1) 3 MP
Communications	Wi-Fi 802.11b/g Bluetooth 3.0 NFC
Main Processor	Undisclosed

RAM	Undisclosed
Onboard Storage	Undisclosed
Additional Sensors	Brightness sensor Microphone Noise suppression sub mic
Development Env.	Android 4.4 and above

(Sony, 2015)

Monocular Augmenting Displays

Monocular augmenting displays principally serve the role of information devices, superimposing alphanumeric, imagery, and iconic data within the user's field of view without significant impact on overall scene analysis. Applications for these types of devices range from providing medical professionals a convenient way to view medical records, images, and vital sign telemetry to providing technicians with diagrams or other data to aid them in completing specific tasks more efficiently.

In this section we explore several of these devices, noting particular strengths and the fields for which their use is primarily intended.

Vuzix M100 Smart Glasses

Vuzix Corporation of Rochester, New York, is one of the oldest companies operating in the augmented reality arena. Originally founded in 1997 (albeit under a different name), Vuzix has close ties to the defense community and has developed a number of different specialty display devices over the years, including a digital night vision weapon sight widely used by the U.S. military as well as a high-resolution monocular display device for viewing tactical maps and video.

Leveraging capabilities and technologies developed over the years, in January 2013, Vuzix introduced the M100 Smart Glasses, an Android-based wearable computer and monocular display shown in Figure 5.10. The device is now used worldwide within a broad assortment of enterprise applications. These include manufacturing operations, guiding workers through warehouse facilities to increase workflow efficiency in picking tasks, telemedicine and remote assistance, and even by parking enforcement officers who are able to scan license plates with a glance and issue tickets on the spot via a belt-worn printer. The device can be used by apps to take photographs, record and play back video, and track user position (via GPS) and the orientation of the wearer's head. As highlighted by the manufacturer, one of the major strengths of the device is its ability to make use of thousands of existing Android apps. Developer resources are also available to assist in the creation of custom utilities.

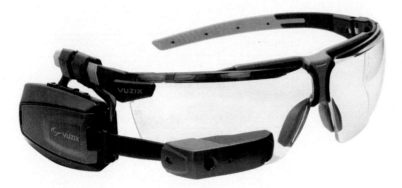

Figure 5.10 The Vuzix M100 Smart Glasses are currently one of the most widely used augmenting displays in existence.
Credit: Image courtesy of Vuzix Corporation

From the user perspective, the device presents the visual sensation of a 4-inch smartphone screen held at a distance of about 14 inches. Along with left or right eye mounting options, the display housing and arm can be adjusted for individual user needs and comfort. Specifications for the M100 can be seen in Table 5.9.

Table 5.9   Vuzix M100 Specifications

Feature	Specification
Ocularity	Monocular
Image Source	Micro LCD
Resolution	420×240 (WQVGA)
Frame Rate	
Color	24-bit Color
Display Luminosity	>2000 cd/m^2 (nits)
Contrast	
Display Optics	Non-See-Thru Combiner
Field of View	15° (diag)
Transparency	NA
Head Tracking	9 DoF IMU
Camera(s)	5 MP Photos 1080p Video
Communications	Wi-Fi-802.11 b/g/n Bluetooth 4.0 LE mUSB: control/power/upgrade

Main Processor	OMAP4460 @ 1.2 GHz
RAM	1 GB
Onboard Storage	4 GB
Additional Sensors	Gesture Sensor (2 axis w/ select) Microphone (2) Ambient Light Proximity Sensor GPS
Shield(s)	NA
Development Env.	Android iOS

(Vuzix, 2016a)

Vuzix M300 Smart Glasses

In early 2015, Intel Corporation made a substantial investment in Vuzix, acquiring approximately one-third of the company and accelerating the development and introduction of the next generation of wearable display products for enterprise, professional, and prosumer users. One of the first new devices to emerge was the M300 Smart Glasses shown in Figure 5.11.

Figure 5.11 The new Vuzix M300 provides most of the features and capabilities of a modern smartphone in a hands-free wearable display device.
Credit: Image courtesy of Vuzix Corporation

Leveraging advances in computing, display, and sensor technologies, the new device includes significantly improved ergonomics, a faster CPU, hot swappable batteries, gesture controls, and most of the features and capabilities of a modern smartphone. Additionally, improved protection against water, dust, and dirt gives the user wide versatility to employ the M300 in almost any working environment. Specifications for the M300 can be seen in Table 5.10.

Table 5.10   Vuzix M300 Specifications

Feature	Specification
Ocularity	Monocular
Image Source	Micro LCD
Resolution	640 × 360 (nHD)
Frame Rate	
Color	24-bit Color
Display Luminosity	>2000 cd/m^2 (nits)
Contrast	
Display Optics	Non-See-Thru Combiner
Field of View	20° (diag)
Transparency	NA
Head Tracking	9 DoF IMU
Camera(s)	13 MP Photos 1080p Video
Communications	Wi-Fi b/g/n/ac – Dual-B 2.4/5 GHz Bluetooth4.1/2.1+EDR MIMO 2x2 imicroUSB 2.0 HS
Main Processor	Intel Atom
RAM	2 GB
Onboard Storage	16 GB
Additional Sensors	Gesture Sensor (2 axis w/ select) Microphone (2) Ambient Light Proximity Sensor GPS
Shield(s)	NA
Development Env.	Android iOS

(Vuzix, 2016b)

Google Glass

Google Glass is a wearable computer with a monocular optical see-through head-mounted display developed by Google, Inc. of Mountainview, California. No single AR/VR display developed to date has stirred more emotion, generated more excitement (and pushback), or triggered more research, development, and application studies than this device. Despite being pulled from availability to the general consumer in early 2015, Google Glass maintains an avid user base within a number of professional application settings including hospitals, warehouses, and remote service industries. Some of the interesting applications for this device include its use with unmanned aerial vehicles (UAVs) by the government of Nepal to track rhinos, tigers, and elephants (Pandey, 2014) and as a sighting tool to enable rifle users to aim their weapon around corners (Wagstaff, 2014). Figure 5.12 shows the baseline external design of the device.

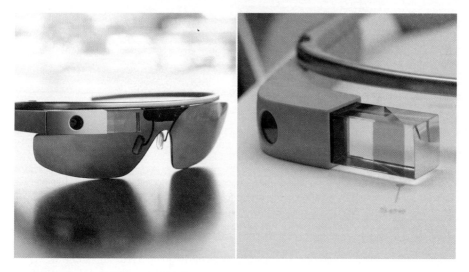

Figure 5.12 This image pair shows close-up detail of the Google Glass display.
Credit: Images by Ted Eytan / Mitch Altman via Flickr under a CC 2.0 license

Google Glass is also a work of art in terms of its engineering. Although few of the enabling technologies contained therein are new or revolutionary, their combination in such a small form factor for this purpose, combined with the creative manner in which they can be leveraged by the user to accomplish a host of tasks, was itself groundbreaking. Figure 5.13 shows an x-ray of the device with detailing of key internal components.

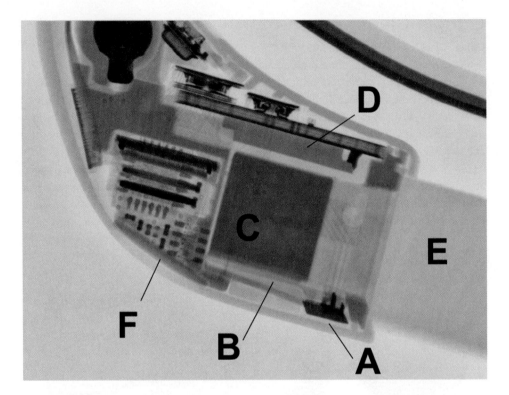

Figure 5.13 This x-ray shows the intricate detail and engineering found within the display assembly of Google Glass. The details of the annotations are as follows: **A**) RGB LED **B**) Wedge Fly Eye Lens **C**) Polarizing Beamsplitter **D**) LCoS Display **E**) Waveguide **F**) Camera.
Credit: Image courtesy of Andrew Vanden Heuvel, AGL Initiatives

At the time of this book's preparation, Google Glass was undergoing a redesign and was anticipated to be released by early 2017. More detailed specifications for the current version can be found in Table 5.10.

Table 5.11 Google Glass Explorer Version 2 Specifications

Feature	Specification
Ocularity	Monocular
Image Source	LCOS micro-display (color seq.)
Resolution	360p (640 × 360)
Frame Rate	NA
Color	Full Color
Display Luminosity	150 cd/m² (nits)
Contrast	NA

Display Optics	Reflective Waveguide
Field of View	~15°
Transparency	NA
Head Tracking	9DoF IMU (Invensense MPU 9250)
Camera(s)	Photos: 5 MP Video: 720p
Communications	Wi-Fi - 802.11 b/g 2.4 GHz Bluetooth 4.0 LE
Main Processor	OMAP 4430 System on a chip, dual-core
RAM	12 GB
Onboard Storage	16 GB Flash
Additional Sensors	Touchpad Microphone Ambient Light Proximity Sensor
Shield(s)	No
Development Env.	Android 4.4, KitKat

(Google, 2014)

Conclusion

In this chapter we have explored a number of existing and most promising augmenting displays currently available on the market, and in doing so, have not even scratched the surface. There are dozens of companies large and small in garage workshops and more formal laboratory settings tinkering, experimenting, and working on innovative display ideas. Some are just squeaking by in terms of financial resources, whereas other efforts have drawn in hundreds of millions in venture capital, such as the mysterious Florida-based Magic Leap.

Although there are increasingly louder calls from technophiles for consumer-level augmented reality displays, a key challenge facing hardware and software manufacturers can be summed up with two simple questions: What specific use do you have in mind? Outside of gaming applications, what is the nature of that killer app you envision?

The challenge answering these questions is the very reason that most augmenting display manufacturers and software houses are initially targeting business and enterprise users over general consumers. Professional applications for these technologies are numerous. From increasing worker and process efficiency to increasing the situational awareness of an emergency room physician or soldier on the battlefield, these problems, challenges, and needs are readily apparent. Until the "gotta have it" application ideas begin to emerge for the general public, developers of augmenting displays will continue to focus attention on those market segments certain to generate revenue.

That said, mobile device-based augmenting displays will likely play a disruptive role in the consumer-level augmented reality market in the very near future. As an example, innovative, low-cost systems such as the SmokeVR headset shown in Figure 5.14 from California-based PhaseSpace Inc. are expected to enter the market in late 2016–2017.

Figure 5.14 This February 2015 photograph from the Stanford VR conference shows a prototype of the highly innovative SmokeVR mobile device-based stereoscopic augmenting display from PhaseSpace Inc.
Credit: Image courtesy of Tracy McSheery of PhaseSpace

Based on work originally carried out in 2007 under contract with the Office of Naval Research, the device uses an innovative wide-area optical design to provide a 100-degree horizontal field of view, no chromatic distortion, and exceptional image quality. By adding a simple clip-on shield to the front, the device instantly converts for use as a fully immersive virtual reality display.

This new paradigm in computer-human interfaces is still relatively young. In many respects, we are still trying to understand how to effectively leverage the strengths of the human perceptual system, and in doing so, come to a better understanding of how to make use of this new medium.

CHAPTER 6

FULLY IMMERSIVE DISPLAYS

Virtual reality is here. No longer limited to university and government labs, major advances in several core enabling technologies have given rise to the first generation of high-quality, mass-produced head-mounted displays that are now available to general consumers. In this chapter we look into the details of the latest generation of commercially available, fully immersive head-mounted displays across several classes ranging from PC and console-driven devices to lower end systems based on modern smartphones.

PC-Console Driven Displays

We are living in an extraordinary time in history. There have been few instances since the introduction of the basic desktop computer mouse that we have experienced a genuine paradigm shift in the manner in which average individuals interact with computers and other complex information systems. Although there has been excitement surrounding the very concept of being able to enter high-fidelity, computer-generated worlds for some time, such experiences have been limited to those facilities and organizations with deep pockets and specific missions to fulfill. But times are changing. In this section we will explore a number of PC and console-driven head-mounted displays currently dominating the general consumer market as well as overall public attention. A basic overview is provided for each highlighting unique characteristics and features, as well as a detailed table of device specifications.

Oculus Rift CV1

What started in 2012 as a crowd-funded product development effort for a small company known as Oculus has resulted in a massive resurgence in the public's awareness of, and excitement for, fully immersive virtual reality systems. Following two prerelease developer models (DK1 and DK2) and the start-up's acquisition by social media giant Facebook, Inc., the first consumer version of the display is now shipping to customers and it is, without a doubt, an impressive piece of engineering.

As shown in Figure 6.1, the Oculus Rift CV1 (Consumer Version-1) is a lightweight stereoscopic wide field of view (FOV) head-mounted display based on two low-latency AMOLED flat panels with a 1080×1200 resolution per eye. Of particular note within this display is the use of highly specialized, free-form hybrid Fresnel lenses, a side view of which is shown in Figure 6.2. In addition to the irregular lens surface, the Fresnel diffraction pattern is extremely tight. This combination of a nonrotationally symmetric surface and Fresnel pattern make these lenses extremely difficult to manufacture, although highly effective at providing the user an immersive $110°$ horizontal FOV with minimal distortion or artifacts.

Figure 6.1 The Oculus Rift CV1 (Consumer Version -1) is the first commercial headset produced by Facebook-owned Oculus VR.
Credit: Image by eVRydayVR via Wikimedia

Figure 6.2 This side view of an optical element from the Oculus Rift CV1 (Consumer Version -1) shows the nonrotationally symmetric inner lens surface.
Credit: Image courtesy of iFixit

The asymmetric optics used in this display also enable partial binocular overlap, which makes the horizontal FOV appear wider at the expense of binocular rivalry.

Position and orientation of the device is tracked using the combination of an internal IMU (accelerometer, gyroscope, and magnetometer) as well as a "constellation" of IR LEDs built into the display housing and support strap that are visible to a separate IR camera, even when the user is turned away from the sensor. The system is designed for use in either a standing or a seated position and has an effective operating area measuring 5×11 feet.

More detailed specifications for the Oculus Rift CV1 display hardware can be found in Table 6.1.

Table 6.1   Oculus Rift CV1 Display Specifications

Feature	Specification
Ocularity	Binocular
Image Source	AMOLED
Resolution	1080 × 1200 per eye (2160 × 1200 combined)
Refresh Rate	90 Hz
Display Optics	Hybrid Fresnel
Field of View	~110°
Eye Relief	Not adjustable
Interpupillary Dist.	58–72 mm (adjustable)
Head Tracking	IMU (compass/ accel/ gyro) Optical tracking of IR LED "Constellation" on headset
Tracking Area	5 × 11 feet
Built-In Camera	No
Microphone	Integrated microphone
Audio	Integrated stereo supra-aural headphones
Connections	(1) HDMI port (2) USB 3.0 ports
Phone Integration	No
Weight	470 g (1 lb, .57 oz.)
	Recommended PC Specifications
GPU	NVIDIA GeForce GTX 970 equiv or better AMD Radeon R9 290 equiv or better
CPU	Intel i5-4590 equiv or greater
RAM	8 GB or more
Video Output	HDMI 1.3
USB Port	(3) USB 3.0 ports (1) USB 2.0 port
Operating System	Windows 7 SP1 64 bit or newer

(Shanklin, 2016; Digital Trends, 2016)

HTC Vive

Roughly concurrent to the early development efforts surrounding the Oculus Rift, entertainment software developer Valve Corporation of Bellevue, Washington, and HTC, the multinational manufacturer of smartphones and tablets headquartered in New Taipei City, Taiwan, also began a collaboration to develop their own high-end, PC-driven virtual reality display. Initially unveiled to the public in early 2015 and formally referred to as the HTC Vive, the system is now also shipping to customers and is itself an exceptional display.

As shown in Figure 6.3, the HTC Vive is a lightweight stereoscopic wide field of view head-mounted display based on two low-latency AMOLED flat panels with a 1080 × 1200 resolution per eye. Using its own set of proprietary optical elements with a Fresnel diffraction grating, the Vive provides the user with a solid 110° horizontal FOV with minimal distortion or artifacts.

Figure 6.3 The HTC Vive is a first-of-its-kind virtual reality system designed from the ground up for room-scale immersive experiences.
Credit: Images courtesy of HTC

At this point, the Vive and Oculus part ways as other key system functions are handled using very different methods. From the beginning of design efforts, the HTC Vive has been developed with "room scale" tracking technologies in mind in an effort to allow users to navigate naturally by walking around, as well as to use motion-tracked hand controllers to intuitively manipulate objects and interact with the simulation.

As opposed to using a camera to track an array of IR LEDs mounted on the display, the Vive system uses a reverse approach. First, two IR laser base stations are positioned at opposite ends of a room and emit precisely timed IR pulses and X/Y axis IR laser sweeps. An array of IR sensors embedded in the display housing detects these IR pulses and laser sweeps in various combinations. From this information, the system is able to calculate the position and orientation of the display with considerable speed and precision. This system is covered in greater detail in Chapter 11, "Sensors for Tracking Position, Orientation, and Motion."

Another impressive capability of the Vive system that takes user safety into consideration is the "Chaperone" feature, which uses the front-facing camera in the headset to capture and display a representation of the user's physical environment, including walls and obstacles, if the user gets too close.

More detailed specifications for the Vive display hardware can be found in Table 6.2.

Table 6.2   HTC Vive Display Specifications

Feature	Specification
Ocularity	Binocular
Image Source	AMOLED—low persistence/global illumination
Resolution	1080 × 1200 per eye (2160 × 1200 combined)
Refresh Rate	90 Hz
Display Optics	Fresnel
Field of View	110°
Eye Relief	Adjustable to accommodate eye glasses
Interpupillary Dist.	60.2–74.5 mm (adjustable)
Head Tracking	IMU (compass/ accel/ gyro) (2) IR laser base stations w/32IR photodiodes on HMD
Tracking Area	15 × 15 feet
Built-In Camera	(1) Video camera—front facing
Microphone	Integrated microphone
Audio	Ear buds (supplied) w/ 3.5 mm jack
Connections	(1) 3.5 mm audio jack (1) DC barrel jack (1) HDMI port (2) USB 3.0 ports
Phone Integration	Capable of Bluetooth pairing with mobile device
Weight	555 g (1 lb, 3.5 oz.)
Recommended PC Specifications	
GPU	NVIDIA GeForce GTX 970 equiv or better AMD Radeon R9 290 equiv or better
CPU	Intel i5-4590 or greater AMD FX 8350 or greater
RAM	4 GB or more
Video Output	HDMI 1.4 DisplayPort 1.2 or newer

USB Port	(1) USB 2.0 or better port
Operating System	Windows 7 SP1, Windows 8.1, or Windows 10

(Shanklin, 2016; Digital Trends, 2016)

Sony PlayStation VR

Years in the making and intended for console gaming, Sony Computer Entertainment Inc. has introduced PlayStation® VR (PS VR), a virtual reality system that uses the PlayStation® 4 (PS4) gaming console to deliver highly compelling immersive simulations. Originally referred to as Project Morpheus when initially teased in 2014, the new high-performance peripheral has generated significant excitement because it does not require a high-end gaming PC to operate, such as in the case of systems like the HTC Vive and Oculus Rift CV1 mentioned earlier in this chapter.

The PS VR package consists of two major components: a visor style, stereoscopic wide FOV head-mounted display and what is referred to as a breakout box. The display (shown in Figure 6.4) is based on a single shared 1920 × 1080 AMOLED panel providing 960 × 1080 per eye along with proprietary optics providing an approximate 100-degree FOV. The system uses built-in inertial sensors and the PlayStation Camera to accurately track the position and orientation of the display (that is, the user's head) as well as a PlayStation Move (PS Move) Motion Controllers in three-dimensional space.

Figure 6.4 Unlike PC-based virtual reality hardware, Sony's PlayStation VR headset is immediately compatible with more than 30 million PS4 game consoles already in use.
Credit: Image courtesy of Dronepicr via Wikimedia under a CC 2.0 license

The breakout box serves as an interface between the display and the PS4 console. Although the console itself easily handles all graphics-generation tasks, the breakout box handles object-based 3D audio processing, the reverse warping of imagery from one eye, and its output via HDMI to a television for what Sony refers to as *social screen* so others present can share in the gaming experience.

The PS VR system also provides what is referred to as *cinematic mode*, which allows users to enjoy a variety of nonstereoscopic content on a large virtual screen seen while wearing the headset. This content includes standard PS4 games, 360° photos, and videos captured by devices such as omnidirectional cameras via PS4 Media Player (Stein, 2016; Crossley, 2016). More detailed specifications for the PS VR display hardware can be found in Table 6.3.

Table 6.3 Sony PlayStation VR Display Specifications

Feature	Specification
Ocularity	Binocular
Image Source	AMOLED
Resolution	960 × 1080 per eye (single shared 1920 × 1080 panel)
Refresh Rate	90 Hz, 120 Hz
Display Optics	Undisclosed
Field of View	~100°
Eye Relief	Adjustable to accommodate eyeglasses
Interpupillary Dist.	58–72 mm (adjustable)
Head Tracking	6 DoF IMU (gyroscope, accelerometer) Optical tracking of 9 LEDs on headset
Tracking Area	10 × 10 feet
Built-In Camera	No
Microphone	Microphone input
Audio	3D sound, headphone mini-jack
Connections	HDMI, USB
Output	Simultaneous output to headset and TV
Phone Integration	No
Weight	610 g (1 lb, 5.51 oz.)
Console Hardware	Sony PlayStation 4

(Sony, 2016)

OSVR–Open-Source VR Development Kit

One of the surefire ways for the newly emerging virtual and augmented reality industry to slow its own growth is by limiting interoperability between applications and peripheral devices. If gaming or professional software applications, or peripherals, are limited to only one platform or system, things become highly problematic and inconvenient for end users and adoption slows.

By inspiring developers to adopt basic standards early on, greater interoperability is achieved, resulting in faster growth of the industry. It is this particular strategy that has led to the development of OSVR (Open Source Virtual Reality), an open source hardware and software ecosystem for virtual reality development efforts.

The hardware system, known as the Hacker Development Kit and shown in Figure 6.5, consists of a high-quality stereoscopic, wide FOV head-mounted display and the associated cabling. The core of the display is based on a single low-persistence 1080p AMOLED panel (divided in half for separate left- and right-eye views) and crisp, custom design dual-element aspheric optics (lenses whose surface profiles are not portions of a sphere or cylinder). A powerful addition to this display is the diopter (focus) adjustment, a feature lacking in most other head-mounted displays covered in this chapter. Tracking the position and orientation of the display is enabled using an internal nine degree-of-freedom IMU along with a camera that tracks a faceplate embedded with IR LEDs.

Other innovative features for this display include the ability to convert a regular desktop video signal into side-by-side mode so that it can be viewed in the goggle, as well as the ability to accept both 1080×1920 and 1920×1080 video signals. This lets you use the display with a wireless video link.

Figure 6.5 Developed by Razer and Sensics, the OSVR development kit is an open licensed ecosystem intended for use in creating VR experiences across any operating system, including Windows, Android, and Linux.

Credit: Images by Maurizio Pesce via Flickr under a CC 2.0 license

The intent behind the release of this display hardware is to provide developers a wide open, nonproprietary platform for their own system development and testing. All aspects of the display have been designed to be hackable, including the actual designs themselves, which are freely available for download. More detailed specifications for the hardware components can be found in Table 6.4.

Table 6.4 Razer/Sensics OSVR HDK HMD Specifications

Feature	Specification
Ocularity	Binocular
Image Source	Single Panel AMOLED
Resolution	Full Panel: 1920 × 1080p Each Eye: 960 × 1080p
Refresh Rate	60 fps
Display Optics	Dual-element design for < 13% distortion
Field of View	100°
Eye Relief	13 mm
Interpupillary Dist.	Nonadjustable (large eye box accommodates 57–71 mm)
Head Tracking	9 DoF IMU + IR-LED Faceplate and Camera
Tracking Area–	—
Built-In Camera	No
Microphone	No
Connectivity	(3) USB 3.0 Ports—(1) internal, (2) External

(XinReality, 2016)

OSVR is also a software framework. The OSVR API is a platform-agnostic, standardized interface for virtual reality display devices and peripherals. Intended to serve the role of middleware, the OSVR application programming interface (API) is a set of high-performance rendering and device abstraction services enabling augmented reality/virtual reality (AR/VR) applications to provide near-universal support between head-mounted displays, peripherals such as input devices and trackers, and operating systems.

Smartphone-Based Displays

It is without question that one of the key fields enabling a resurgence of virtual reality is mobile telephony. From the ever-increasing performance of mobile processors, to display manufacturers continually packing more pixels into a given screen area, to the introduction of entirely new classes of sensors, these developments have broken through some of the long-standing barriers haunting this field, and in the process, unleashed a wellspring of creativity. One of the highest impact results is the development of simple tools that enable the use of smartphones themselves as the primary platform upon which to drive immersive simulations.

In this section we explore two of these smartphone-based display systems. Although there are dozens of manufacturers for these devices, each with its own take on the overall design, optics, materials, and added capabilities, most have been introduced as a result of the profound success of those appearing in this section.

Google Cardboard

Disruptive innovation is a term originally coined by Harvard Professor Clayton Christensen. It describes a process by which a product or service takes root initially in simple applications at the bottom of a market and then relentlessly moves up market, eventually displacing established competitors.

In the case of Google and its mid-2014 introduction of a smartphone-based virtual reality headset made of cardboard, cheap biconvex plastic lenses, a magnet, washer, and a few tabs of Velcro (see Figure 6.6), shockwaves were sent through high-tech centers around the globe, and in particular, through the meeting rooms of companies still trying to get their higher-end, PC-driven virtual reality displays into consumer hands. Now anyone with $15 and a smartphone could experience virtual reality (albeit in relatively crude form) and even get started developing their own applications with the basic software development kit (SDK) released at the same time.

After the initial shock passed, most industry participants realized that Google's action, while possibly a joking prod at Facebook for its $2 billion dollar purchase of Oculus not three months earlier, was also one of the most intelligent and high-impact moves this field could experience. Suddenly, there was a means available to allow the masses to experience at least a taste of what high-performance immersive virtual reality systems were capable of delivering once they entered the marketplace. The net effect was a massive jump in public awareness and enthusiasm, not to mention the rapid formation of several dozen new companies looking to get involved at some level, be it through producing their own kits with more durable display housings for sale or new content and app providers. As will be covered in Chapter 18, "Education," Google itself has launched a program known as Google Expeditions within which educators in the K-12 sector now make use of the cardboard viewers to engage their classes in virtual field trips. As of November 2015, more than 100,000 students in schools around the world have used Expedition cardboard viewers in their courses.

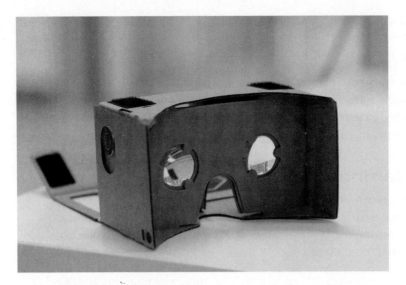

Figure 6.6 A Google Cardboard headset is a cheap and easily accessible standard for experimenting with virtual reality.
Credit: Images by othree via Flickr under a CC 2.0 license

Samsung GearVR

Whereas Google Cardboard and similar devices represent the low end of the smartphone-based display market, the Samsung GearVR device clearly dominates the higher end market. Developed in collaboration with Oculus VR, the headset was first unveiled in late 2014 and released for sale in 2015.

As shown in Figure 6.7, the GearVR headset serves as a viewing device and controller into which any of Samsung's flagship mobile devices can be securely mounted. The system optics expand the display to encompass a 96° horizontal FOV with adjustable focus. Movement of the user's head is tracked across three axes (roll, pitch, and yaw) using an internal IMU with a higher precision than that provided by the IMU within the mobile device. The power for this sensor as well as the side-mounted controls including a touchpad and back button is supplied by the mobile device via a microUSB connection.

More detailed specifications for the Samsung GearVR headset can be found in Table 6.5.

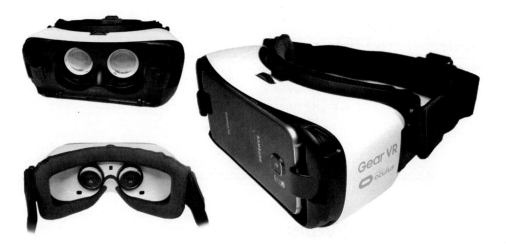

Figure 6.7 Samsung Gear VR is a mobile virtual reality headset developed by Samsung Electronics in collaboration with Oculus VR. The device serves as a housing and controller for any of a variety of Samsung smartphones that acts as the headset's display and processor.
Credit: Images by S. Aukstakalnis

Table 6.5 Samsung GearVR Display Specifications

Feature	Specification
Ocularity	Binocular
Image Source	AMOLED (using recommend mobile devices)
Resolution	Varies based on compatable mobile device.
Refresh Rate	60 Hz (content dependent)
Display Optics	Single biconvex (each eye)
Field of View	96°
Eye Relief / Focus	Eye relief fixed, focus adjustable
Interpupillary Dist.	Accommodates 55–71 mm (nonadjustable)
Head Tracking	3 DoF IMU (gyroscope, accelerometer)
Controls	Touchpad, back key, volume key + Bluetooth (via mobile device)
Audio	Via audio jack on mobile device
Connections	microUSB
Add'l Sensors	Proximity (Mount/Unmount Detection)

(Continued)

Table 6.5   (Continued)

Feature	Specification
Weight	318 g (.70 lbs.)
Compatible Devices	Galaxy S7
	Galaxy S7 Edge
	Galaxy Note5
	Galaxy S6
	Galaxy S6 Edge
	Galaxy S6 Edge+

(Samsung, 2016)

CAVES and Walls

A variety of large-scale, fixed location immersive displays exist for use within the scientific and professional communities. These systems come in a variety of geometries and sizes, including multisided (or multiwalled), rear-projection, or flat panel-based displays, single and multiprojector hemispherical surfaces, and more, each typically displaying field sequential stereo imagery at high resolutions. Most are designed to accommodate multiple users, each of whom wear LCD shutter glasses controlled by a timing signal that alternately blocks left- and right-eye views in synchronization with the display's refresh rate. Most systems incorporate some method of tracking the position and orientation of a lead user's head to account for movement and to adjust the viewpoints accordingly. In such multiuser scenarios, all other participants experience the simulations in 3D, but passively. An example of one such display is shown in Figure 6.8.

Figure 6.8 In this image a research scientist with Idaho National Laboratory views a subsurface geothermal energy model within a computer-assisted virtual environment (CAVE) display.
Credit: Image courtesy of Idaho National Laboratory

Located at the Center for Advanced Energy Studies in Idaho Falls, Idaho, the FLEX CAVE (computer-assisted virtual environment) is a four-walled, reconfigurable, projector-driven 3D display system that allows scientists to, quite literally, walk into and examine their graphical data. Within minutes, the system can be reconfigured into a flat wall display, an angled theater for team collaboration, an L-shape to serve as both an immersive 3D display alongside of a section for 2D data, or a closed room for exploring spatial structures and training applications.

A powerful variation on this reconfigurable room-sized display theme is shown in Figures 6.9 and 6.10. Known as the EmergiFLEX and manufactured by Mechdyne Corporation of Marshalltown, Iowa, the display is composed of a large articulating wall of 24 high-definition panels that can be moved into a variety of configurations, including that of a corner with one extended wall or an open-sided room-like display with an overhead, downward-facing projector.

Figure 6.9 The Mechdyne EmergiFLEX CAVE accommodates multiple users for collaborative design, engineering, and visualization applications.
Credit: Image courtesy of Mechdyne and UALR

As shown in Figure 6.10, each of the three vertical wall sections consists of 8 Barco LED DLP projection cubes. Each cube operates at a 1920 × 1080 resolution. When the 24 cubes are configured as a single wall, the overall display surface measures approximately 10 feet high by 34 feet wide. Two high-resolution overhead projectors are used to create a blended floor image. The floor itself is made from a washable rigid material that has been optimized for front projection (in this configuration it is actually a downward projection) and for color matching with the side walls.

The system incorporates a 24-camera, six-degree-of-freedom optical motion tracking system (see Chapter 11) and is capable of both head and hand tracking regardless of the display system configuration. Here again, users wear polarized glasses to see the 3D graphics presented on the screens.

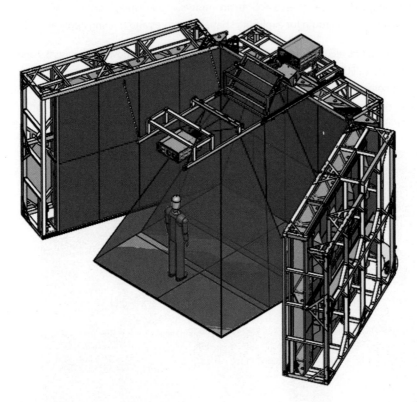

Figure 6.10 The EmergiFLEX CAVE display is composed of an articulating wall of 24 high-definition Barco LED DLP projection cubes as well as overhead projectors to create floor imagery.
Credit: Image courtesy of Mechdyne and UALR

Initially developed by researchers at the University of Illinois at Chicago in the early 1990s under the name Cave *Automatic* Virtual Environment, a large number of variations for the overall room-sized immersive display model have been implemented by a handful of companies. Along with the varied number of implementations have come a seemingly equal number of names and acronyms, including computer-*assisted* virtual environment (shown above), computer-a*ided* virtual environment, COVE, iCube, and still others.

A variety of these displays are detailed in different application case studies found later in this book. Examples of such uses covered include architectural walk-throughs, engineering design reviews, and additional examples of visualization of complex scientific datasets. A list of suppliers for these systems is provided in Appendix B, "Resources."

Hemispheres and Domes

Large format displays are in no way limited to rectilinar geometries. Hemispheres and dome displays are a popular option in many industries, and in particular, those requiring considerable precision in visual representation, room for multiple users, as well as the need to be untethered. As an example, Figure 6.11 shows the advanced joint terminal attack controller training system (AJTS) used by the U.S. Army for skills development and training of joint terminal attack controllers (JTACs). The system simulates virtually any environment and most aircraft and weapons systems utilized by the JTACs.

Figure 6.11 The advanced joint terminal attack controller training system (AJTS) simulator is a domed visual display system used by the U.S. Army to train joint terminal attack controllers (JTACs) and combat controllers.
Credit: Image courtesy of DoD

Developed for the Army by QuantaDyn Corporation of Herndon, Virginia, the core AJTS configuration consists of a domed visual display system with high-resolution projectors, as well as a powerful and intuitive Computer Generated Force (CGF)/Semi-Autonomous Force (SAF) application. A high-fidelity image generator renders scenes in multiple spectrums. A dynamic aural cueing system adds highly realistic audio to supplement the visual display. The simulator is also capable of networking with other offsite simulators, enabling JTACs to communicate and train with real-life pilots in their own simulators at distant locations (QuantaDyn, 2013; Bruce, 2014).

It is important to note that within such large-format displays, it is not always necessary or even desirable to use stereoscopic imagery. As depicted in Figure 6.11, within many simulations there are often no near-field scene features necessitating an enhanced 3D view. Even with this feature's absence, the wide FOV nature of the display still provides users with a highly compelling visual sensation of presence and immersion within the simulation.

Conclusion

Within this chapter we have explored a diverse number of fully immersive displays ranging from handheld and head-mounted stereoscopic viewers to large-scale, fixed placement multiuser systems. In each instance, the majority of the user's FOV is filled with computer-generated or video imagery. Although most head-mounted devices provide a 360-degree viewing experience without interruption of the displayed scene, most of the large-format systems described in this chapter do not because CAVEs and domes have entrances or because the specific applications for which the system is intended do not require this feature.

As will be seen in the application case studies provided later this book, these displays are actively being used in a variety of entertainment, engineering, scientific, and training endeavors with outstanding results.

Most of the flat panel-based head-mounted displays currently available on the market will likely be considered "old technology" within just a few short years. Each of these devices has been engineered around displays originally intended for other purposes. As such, features such as the associated electronics, large, heavy optical elements, and oversized housings are required to bring about functional systems. Although impressive engineering feats and adequate for this stage of the developing industry, this category of displays will be rapidly displaced by new systems designed from the ground up with this application in mind. These trends are discussed in greater detail in Chapter 23, "The Future."

CHAPTER 7

THE MECHANICS OF HEARING

Hearing is arguably one of the human body's most important primary senses. Hearing allows us to communicate with others, is often the first source of information about threats to safety, and reveals extraordinary levels of detail about our surroundings. The addition of an audio component to virtual and augmented reality systems can also enhance usability and the overall sense of "presence" within an artificial space. In this chapter we explore the mechanics of hearing, how our brain localizes and separates sound sources, and how sound cues contribute to overall scene analysis.

Defining Sound

In physics, sounds are defined as variations in pressure. Sounds are produced when an object vibrates, causing a disturbance in the molecules of the medium within which the object is located. For the purposes of this section, that medium is air, although the concept also holds true for liquids. This disturbance moves through the air as oscillating and propagating pressure waves. Figure 7.1 illustrates such a waveform.

There are two main properties of a vibration—*frequency* and *amplitude*—that determine the way air molecules move and, in turn, the way they sound.

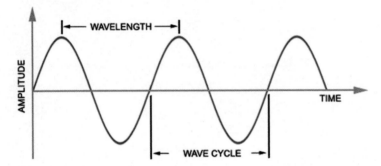

Figure 7.1 This illustration depicts the basic elements of a waveform.
Credit: Illustration by S. Aukstakalnis

Frequency is the rate of movement of molecules set into motion as a result of the vibration of an object and is measured in hertz (symbol Hz) or *cycles per second*. Frequency determines the pitch of a sound. The higher the frequency, or the higher the number of wave cycles passing a specific point in space, the higher the pitch.

Amplitude is the measurement of the maximum displacement of air molecules in a sound wave. Sounds with greater amplitude produce greater changes in atmospheric pressure and result in sounds with higher intensity. The most widely used acoustic measurement for intensity is the decibel (dB).

In the case of pure tones, such as those from a tuning fork, the sounds are made of evenly spaced waves of air molecules experiencing compression, and then rarefaction when molecules are given extra space and allowed to expand (Figure 7.2).

Regardless of the frequency or amplitude, all sound waves generally travel through air at the same speed. At sea level, in dry air at 20°C (68°F), the speed of sound is approximately 761 mph (1225 kph). Thus, sounds with a longer wavelength (lower tones) will arrive at your ear with less frequently, but at the same speed, than sounds with shorter wavelengths (higher tones). Figure 7.3 represents this graphically.

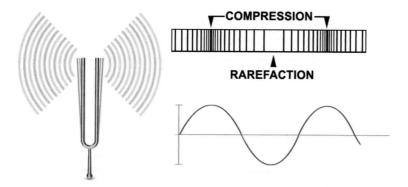

Figure 7.2 This illustration depicts the functional properties of compression and rarefaction in sound waves.

Credit: Illustration by S. Aukstakalnis

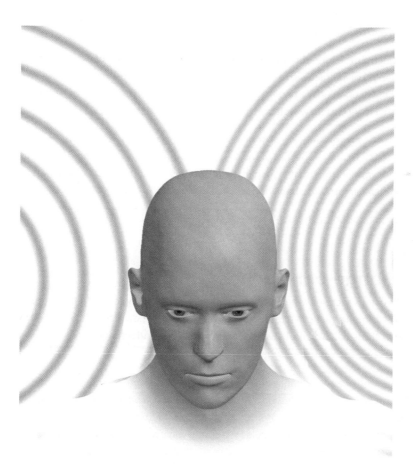

Figure 7.3 Sound wavefronts with longer wavelengths arrive less frequently but at the same speed as those with shorter wavelengths.

Credit: Illustration by S. Aukstakalnis

Echoes and Reverberation

As sound waves propagate through the air and strike a wall or other obstruction, they experience a number of different effects, including reflection, refraction, and diffraction. Most of us have had the experience of shouting down a valley or inside an empty school gymnasium and had those shouts bounced back, albeit at a reduced volume. This is a **reflection** of sound called an **echo**.

If the wall or obstruction is more than 17 meters away, the reflected sound will take 0.1 second or longer to return to your ears due to the speed of sound. If the reflecting surface is closer than 17 meters, the sound will take less than 0.1 seconds to be reflected back to your ears. These reflected waves combine with the original sound waves to form what is perceived to be a single, elongated sound. Different from an echo, this phenomenon is known as a **reverberation** and is perfectly demonstrated by singing in a shower stall. That great-sounding voice you hear is the result of the blending of the original and reflected sound waves.

For clarity, total reverberation time can in fact be much longer than 0.1 seconds as a result of multiple reflections and different time delays. Typically an echo has a single time delay.

Different from a reflection, the term **diffraction** refers to a change in direction of waves as they pass through an opening or interact with a barrier in their path. Similar to the manner in which water waves interact with openings or barriers, the amount of diffraction (or degree of bending) increases proportional to increasing wavelength and decreases with decreasing wavelength.

The third effect, known as **refraction**, is a change in the direction of waves as they pass between mediums (or changing properties of the same medium) and is accompanied by a change in speed and wavelength. As an example, the properties of a sound wave will change when passing from clear air into a fog bank.

As will be seen later in this book, echoes, reverberation, and other dynamic characteristics of sound can be accurately added to virtual environment simulations.

Dynamic Range of Hearing

As covered in the previous sections, when an object vibrates, it sets air molecules into motion in the form of waves. High-frequency vibrations produce high-frequency, high-pitched sound waves such as those of a whistle. Low-frequency vibrations produce low-frequency, low-pitched sound waves such as those from a fog horn.

Overall, the dynamic range of performance of the human auditory system is remarkable. At the lower end of this range, known as the *threshold of hearing*, the ear of a healthy individual is able to detect variations of less than 1 billionth (1×10^{-9}) of the current atmospheric pressure. This corresponds to the displacement of air molecules in a sound wave of less than the diameter of a single atom (Nave, 2012).

The high end of this dynamic range, known as the *threshold of pain*, is in is excess of 120 dB. This represents a range of sensitivity spanning 12 orders of magnitude in sound intensity, across a frequency spread of 20 Hz to 20,000 Hz (Katz, 2002). Table 7.1 summarizes this range and supplies some examples of noises and intensity levels.

Table 7.1   Common Environmental Noise Levels

Intensity (dB)	Source of Noise
0	Healthy Hearing Threshold
10	Normal Breathing
20	Whispering at 5 Feet
30	Soft Whisper
50	Rainfall
60	Normal Conversation
110	Shouting in Ear
120	Rock Concert
150	Jet Engine at Takeoff
170	Shotgun

As will be discussed in the next section, this incredible sensitivity and the ability to perceive such delicate pressure variations at the low end is made possible through amplification of the sound by structures within the outer and middle ear. At the higher end, still other structures help protect our hearing by reducing, or *attenuating*, the forces being transmitted to the middle ear, although this response occurs relatively slowly compared to the speed of sound. The net result is that the ear can still be damaged by sudden loud sounds like a gunshot or explosion.

The Auditory Pathway

Our ears are paired sensory organs enabling us to communicate and experience a broad spectrum of stimuli generated by our surroundings. This process of transforming variations in air pressure into a stream of electrical impulses to be analyzed and interpreted by the brain is one of the most fascinating sensory processes in the entire human body and actually begins outside of the head. In this section we will examine the mechanics of our sense of hearing by progressing through the auditory pathway, from the point where sounds first reach our outer ear to where electrical impulses are sent onto the audio centers of the brain.

The Outer Ear

Our sense of hearing is enabled through a process known as auditory transduction, within which one source of stimuli (sound waves) is converted into another (electrical impulses destined for the brain). As shown in Figure 7.4, key aspects of this process begin when sound waves first reach the external portion of our ear known as the auricle or **pinna** (Latin for *wing*—plural form: *pinnea*).

For the most part immobile, the pinna is composed of cartilage and skin. The hollows, furrows, and ridges are not random structures, but in fact form a complex, highly accurate funnel that channels sound waves arriving from different angles into the auditory canal.

Anatomy of the Ear

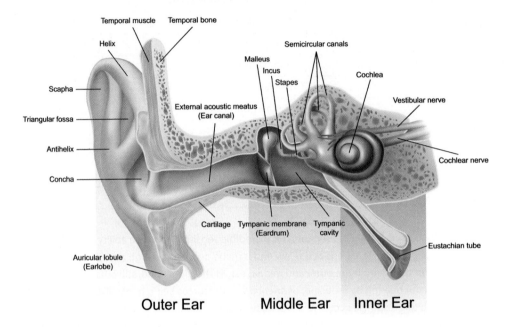

Figure 7.4 Major features of the human auditory pathway.
Credit: Illustration by Peterjunaidy © 123RF.com

Each individual's pinnea are unique, both in overall shape and in the configuration of the irregular surface. In addition to helping channel sound into the auditory canal, sound waves reflect off these surfaces and reverberate slightly. This amplifies certain frequencies and attenuates others, in effect changing the shape of the frequency spectrum (Middlebrooks and Green, 1991). As will be seen later in the chapter, this "coloring" of the sound, often called a *spectral shape cue*, plays a critical role in our ability to localize the apparent source of a sound (Yantis, 2013). The pinnea also serve to enhance the sounds that are important to human behavior and speech communication (Rash et al., 2009).

Once funneled through the pinna, sound waves then enter the auditory canal (*external auditory meatus*). Measuring approximately 2.5 cm (1 in) in length and 0.7 cm (0.3 in) in diameter (Faddis, 2008), the shallow S-shaped canal becomes narrower along its length (Shaw, 1974), provides protection for middle ear structures, and acts as a resonator, further amplifying sounds in the 2,000 to 4,000 Hz range by 10 to 15 db (OSHA, 2013). The outer third of the auditory canal is composed of cartilage covered with skin lined with hairs cells and the glands responsible for the production of ear wax. The inner two-thirds consist of a boney wall covered with a thin layer of skin.

The Middle Ear

The auditory canal terminates at a thin, semi-transparent, oval-shaped membrane approximately 10 mm in diameter called the **eardrum** (*tympanic membrane*). Mounted on an angle between 45° and 60° in relation to the base of the auditory canal, the eardrum is stretched by means of a series of small muscles around its perimeter (Gray, 1918; Stinson and Lawton, 1989). The eardrum is the first of a series of structures in the middle ear that convert sound waves entering the auditory canal into vibrations in the fluid-filled cochlea.

In a process known as *transduction*, when sound waves cause the eardrum to vibrate, a series of three small bones—the **malleus, incus,** and **stapes** (also known as the hammer, anvil, and stirrup and collectively referred to as "ossicles")—transfer these vibrations across the inner ear. The first of these small bones, the malleus (or hammer), is securely attached to the back side of the eardrum, as shown in Figure 7.5. When the eardrum vibrates, the malleus moves in sync. These vibrations are then passed to the incus and to the stapes. The footplate of the stapes bone is itself connected to a membrane covering an opening leading into the inner ear known as the oval window.

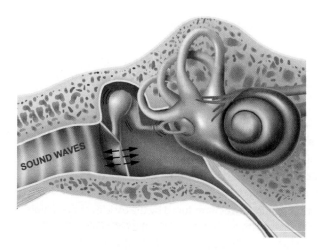

Figure 7.5 This figure illustrates the transduction, or conversion, of sound waves traveling through the ear canal into mechanical vibrations.
Credit: Illustration by Peterjunaidy © 123RF.com

In addition to serving as a transducer of sound waves into mechanical vibrations, these three small bones (the smallest in the human body) also serve as a compound lever to greatly amplify vibrations from the eardrum as they are transferred to the oval window. This lever system, along with the difference in size between the eardrum (approximately 80 square millimeters) and the oval window (approximately 3 square millimeters) increases the molecule-sized sound waves that vibrate the eardrum by a factor of 30 (Aukstakalnis and Blatner, 1992). Without the amplification of the outer ear and middle ear ossicles, only about 0.1 percent of sound energy would make it into the inner ear (Vetter, 2008).

> **note**
>
> The three bones of the middle ear (the malleus, incus, and stapes) are the smallest bones in the human body. They are full size at birth and do not change in size during one's lifetime. All three together can fit on the face of a dime with space left over.

The Inner Ear

Up to this point we have reviewed key properties of sound waves and their mode of transmission, the anatomy of the outer and middle ear, and the process of transforming sound waves back into mechanical vibrations. In this section we explore the mechanisms of the inner ear and the means through which vibrations arriving from the middle ear are transformed into neural impulses sent to the brain that we ultimately perceive as sounds.

The inner ear consists of three primary structures that control hearing and equilibrium. Two of these structures—the semicircular canals and vestibule—are associated with sensing head movement in three spatial planes as well as enabling our sense of balance; they are dealt with at the end of this chapter. However, the **cochlea** is the most important structure in the auditory pathway and critical to our sense of hearing.

The cochlea (Latin for *snail*) is a spiral-shaped cavity in the temporal bone making 2.75 turns around its axis. If uncoiled, this cavity would resemble a tube measuring approximately 35 mm in length, 10 mm in diameter and, as shown in Figure 7.6, is divided into three fluid-filled chambers: the **vestibular canal**, the **tympanic canal,** and the **cochlear duct** (Purves et al., 2001). The three chambers are separated by thin membranes. The vestibular and tympanic ducts, which are responsible for the transmission of pressure waves introduced by the ossicles of the middle ear, connect via a small opening in the apex of the cochlea known as the *helicotrema*. The third chamber, the cochlear duct, contains the highly sensitive Organ of Corti, the central organ for hearing that which ultimately sends electrical impulses to the brain along the auditory nerve.

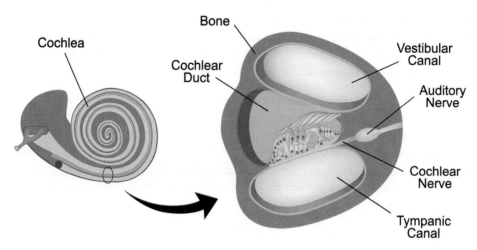

Figure 7.6 This image shows multiple cross-sections of features of the human cochlea.
Credit: Illustration by Alila © 123RF.com

The Oval and Round Windows

As noted in the previous section, vibrations of the eardrum and bones of the middle ear result in a piston-like pumping action of the stapes bone on a membrane covering the oval window, located at the base of the vestibular duct of the cochlea. But unlike air, fluids do not compress. As such, pressure waves created by movement of the stapes bone are accommodated by a second opening, the round window, located at the base of the tympanic duct. As shown in Figure 7.7, when the stapes vibrates and pushes into the oval window, the membrane covering the round window vibrates with opposite phase, bulging out into the air-filled space of the middle ear.

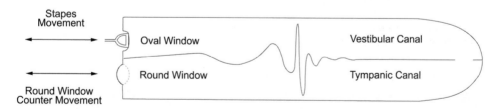

Figure 7.7 This figure illustrates the basic counter movements of the oval and round windows.
Credit: Illustration by Kern A, Heid C, Steeb W-H, Stoop N, Stoop R via Wikimedia under a CC BY 2.5 license—Derivative work—S. Aukstakalnis

These back-and-forth motions of fluid within the vestibular and tympanic ducts caused by pressure waves, in turn, result in the up-and-down movement of the basilar membrane, the first step in converting vibrations of the cochlear fluid into a neural signal that is ultimately routed to the brain and perceived as sound.

An important feature of the basilar membrane is that several of its mechanical properties, such as physical width and stiffness, vary continuously along its entire length. For example, at its widest point the basilar membrane is estimated to be 100 times less stiff than at its narrowest point at the base. The basilar membrane is also *tonotopically* organized, meaning that different frequencies of vibration within the cochlear fluid directly translate into unique moving waveforms along the membrane whose point of maximum displacement takes place at specific locations (Figure 7.8).

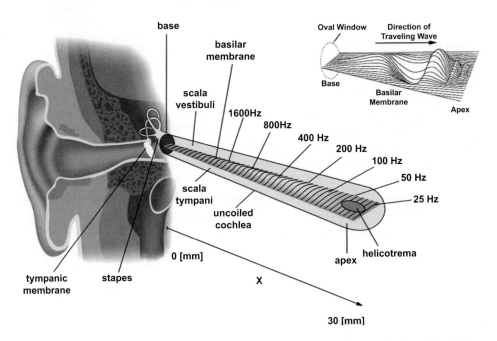

Figure 7.8 This illustration depicts an uncoiled cochlea. Note the tonotopic organization of the basilar membrane.
Credit: Illustration by Kern A, Heid C, Steeb W-H, Stoop N, Stoop R via Wikimedia under a CC BY 2.5 license—Derivative work—S. Aukstakalnis

Organ of Corti

Described as "a masterpiece of cellular micro-architecture" (Fritzsch et al., 2011), the Organ of Corti shown in Figure 7.9 is one of the most amazing sensory mechanisms in the entire human body and arguably the most critical structure in the entire auditory system. Situated on top of the basilar membrane and extending the full length of the cochlear duct, the Organ of Corti is composed of four rows of hair cells (three rows of inner hair cells, one row of outer hair cells) that protrude from its surface. Projecting from the top of each of the cells are tiny hairs known as stereocilia. Overhanging the rows of hair cells is the **tectorial** (roof) **membrane**.

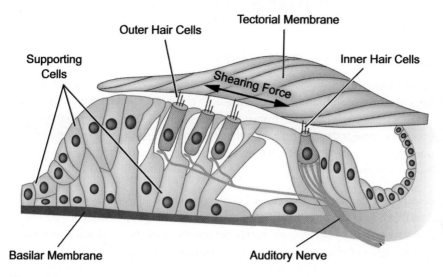

Figure 7.9 This illustration shows a cross-section of the Organ of Corti.
Credit: Illustration by hfsimaging © 123RF.com

As pressure waves pass through the fluid contained within the tympanic canal, waveforms created in the basilar membrane press against the hair cells causing the stereocilia to brush against the overhanging tectorial membrane in a shearing motion (Richardson et al., 2008). This shearing motion bends the stereocilia and triggers a complex electro-chemical process that changes voltages across the hair cell membrane, essentially transforming energy in the form of vibrations into an electrical signal. These electrical signals are sent along the auditory nerve to the audio centers of the brain.

The scale at which the hair cell operates is truly amazing: At the limits of human hearing, hair cells within the Organ of Cori can faithfully detect movements at atomic dimensions and respond in the tens of microseconds (Purves et al., 2001).

> note
>
> Despite its amazing capabilities, the entire cochlea of the inner ear is only about the size of a pencil eraser.

The Auditory Nerve

The *auditory nerve*, also known as the *cochlear nerve*, is responsible for transferring electrical signals from hair cells in the Organ of Corti to the auditory centers of the brain for processing.

In humans, the number of nerve fibers within the auditory nerve averages around 30,000. These nerve fibers exit the cochlea at its base, come together and form a nerve trunk measuring approximately one-inch long, and terminate in the cochlear nucleus located in the medulla of the brainstem (Spoendlin and Schrott, 1989).

From Monaural to Binaural

Thus far we have addressed the human auditory pathway from the perspective of a *monaural* (of, relating to, or involving one ear) system because both of our ears function in precisely the same manner. Once electrical signals from the Organ of Corti of each ear traverse their respective auditory nerve and come together within the *cochlear nucleus complex* located in the brainstem, the processing of auditory information becomes a **binaural** (of, relating to, or involving two ears) process.

In the next section we explore the relationship between the physics of sound energy arriving at our ears and the geometry of our head. The interaction between the two leads to different acoustic phenomena used by our brain to identify not only the location of a sound source, but different characteristics of its nature, including movement and distance.

Sound Cues and 3D Localization

The human brain has the capability to identify the location of sound sources in the environment with considerable precision. Neuroscientists refer to this capability as *localization*. At the heart of this capacity is the fact that we have two spatially separated ears, elegant inner ear transducers and sensors, as well as powerful cognitive centers in our brain for analysis of the incoming acoustic signals. Most animals capable of hearing also have this ability, although acuity varies widely. For example, owls have exceptional sound localization abilities, as do elephants, cats, and mice. Conversely, horses, cows, and goats are notable for poor capabilities in this area (Heffner and Heffner, 1992).

For humans, accurate sound localization adds an amazing level of spatial awareness, richness, and safety to our existence. From the collective (although separate) sounds of a rainforest, to a parent's ability to monitor the location of children at play, to a soldier's ability to hear the approach of the enemy in the dark of night, this aspect of our sense of hearing reveals extraordinary levels of detail about our surroundings.

Sound Cues

There are three primary "cues" identified by researchers that are used by the human brain to identify the spatial position of sound sources in our environment: *interaural time differences* (ITD), *interaural intensity differences* (IID), and *spectral cues*. In describing these phenomena, we will use a common spherical coordinate system based on three elements: *azimuth* (left or right of straight ahead on the horizontal plane, with 0 degrees (0°) azimuth being directly in front, 90° to the right, and 180° being directly behind), *elevation* (the angle above or below the horizontal plane), and distance. This coordinate system is illustrated in Figure 7.10.

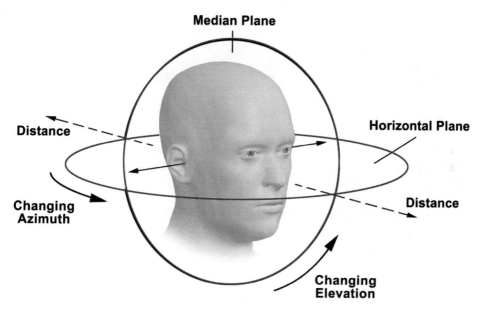

Figure 7.10 This image illustrates the coordinate system commonly used for sound direction and localization.
Credit: Illustration by S. Aukstakalnis

Azimuth Cues

Two of these primary sound cues are most effective in determining the location of sounds in the horizontal plane.

Interaural time difference (ITD) is the difference in the arrival time of a sound between the two ears, the concept for which is illustrated in Figure 7.11. As discussed earlier in this chapter, all sounds travel at the same speed in a common medium regardless of frequency. When sound arrives at our head from either side of the median plane such as depicted in Figure 7.10, there is a difference in length of the path a sound travels to each ear. In other words, the sound will arrive at one ear before the other. The greatest ITD is experienced when a sound source is directly to the left or right side of a listener's head.

If the speed of sound at sea level is ~340 m/s (761 mph), it takes approximately 0.6 ms for sound to travel the width of the average adult human head.

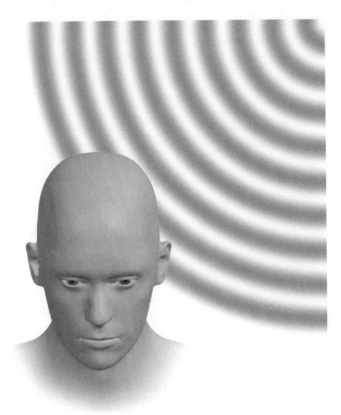

Figure 7.11 This image illustrates the concept of interaural time difference, within which sounds originating from anywhere except along the median plane will arrive at the ears at different times. *Credit: Illustration by S. Aukstakalnis*

It is important to note that when a sound source is directly in front, back, above, or beneath you (that is, from anywhere on the median plane), the interaural time difference is zero, meaning there is no directional information derived.

Interaural intensity difference (IID) is the difference in the intensity of a sound between the two ears and is illustrated in Figure 7.12. If a sound originates from directly in front of or behind a listener, the intensity will be the same in both ears. On the other hand, if a sound originates from a position off to the side, the intensity will be slightly different in each ear. This is due to several factors. First, the distance the sound must travel is different for each, and sound intensity decreases with distance. Second, the head interferes with the sound wave and forms what is referred to as an *acoustic shadow* near the distant ear.

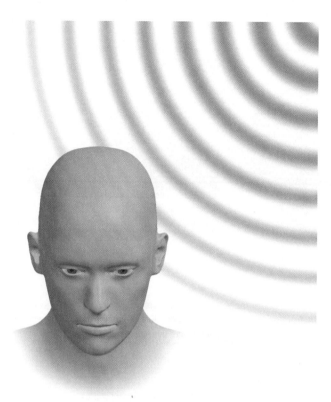

Figure 7.12 This image illustrates the concept of interaural intensity difference, within which sounds originating from anywhere except along the median plane will arrive at the ears at different intensities. *Credit: Illustration by S. Aukstakalnis*

This phenomenon is most common with higher frequency sounds because the sound waves are of short enough wavelengths that they are effectively blocked by the head (Heeger, 2006), (Van Wanrooij et al., 2004). Low-frequency sounds (<1500 Hz) have wavelengths longer than an average adult head is wide. These waves effectively bend around the head (refraction) and do not produce shadows (Harding, 2006).

For some perspective, consider that a 100 Hz wave moving through air is more than 10 feet long. A 1500 Hz wave moving through air is approximately .75 feet long.

The Cone of Confusion

Even with the capability of the brain to rapid identify the variations in the arrival time and intensity of sounds, there are still situations in which it can be difficult to identify whether a sound is coming from in front of or behind you. This is because there are positions to the left and right of your head where sound sources will produce identical ITD and IIDs. This is known as the **cone of confusion** and is illustrated in Figure 7.13.

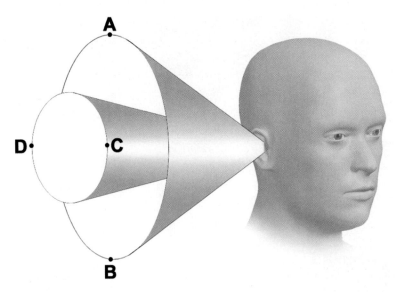

Figure 7.13 The cone of confusion is a cone-shaped set of points, radiating outward from a location midway between a listener's ears, from which a sound source produces identical interaural time and intensity differences. Points **A** and **B** produce identical time and intensity, as do **C** and **D**.
Credit: Illustration by S. Aukstakalnis

Elevation Cues

Judging the elevation of a sound source anywhere along the midline of your head requires more sophisticated processing because there are no variations in arrival time or intensity. This brings us to the third primary sound cue.

Pinna spectral cues, known to sound engineers as *head-related transfer functions*, are changes in the frequency profile of sounds resulting from the size and shape of your head and shoulders, as well as the curves and ducts of your outer ear—the pinna. This concept is illustrated in Figure 7.14. As discussed earlier in this chapter, the physical geometry of the pinnea amplifies certain frequencies and attenuates others, in effect changing the shape of the frequency spectrum. This reliance on the unique shape of the outer ear, as opposed to differences in the sound arriving at different points along the binaural axis, makes this a monaural cue. Neuroscientists have discovered neurons in the audio centers of the brain that appear to be tuned to these spectral changes (Letowski and Letowski, 2012).

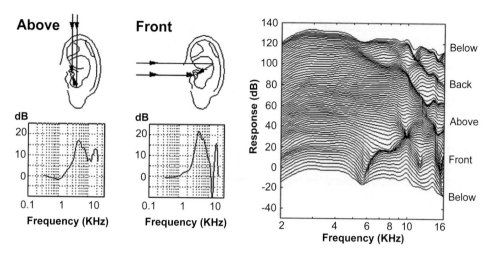

Figure 7.14 This illustration shows how features of the pinna affect the measured frequency response of sounds from two different directions of arrival. The plot on the right shows the frequency response of a sound source moving around an individual along the median plane.

Credit: Images courtesy of Richard O. Duda, "3-D Audio for HCI", http://interface.cipic.ucdavis.edu/sound/tutorial/index.html

Other Cues

In addition to the primary sound cues discussed in the previous section, there are several other phenomena identified by scientists as also contributing to our overall sound localization abilities.

Attenuation, or the reduction in the strength of a sound, can also aid in sound localization because high frequencies in air are dampened faster than low frequencies. Thus, muffled sounds can indicate a distant source. Conversely, high-frequency content of familiar sounds can indicate a source that is closer. **Reverberation** levels can also aid in localization as reverberant energy builds over time, allowing source location to be represented relatively faithfully during the early portion of a sound, although this representation becomes increasingly degraded later in the stimulus (Devore et al., 2009).

Doppler shift is particularly important for sound sources that are moving toward or away from a listener (Schasse et al., 2012). This movement of the sound source results in spectrum shifts between higher and lower pitch (or lower to higher) and provides the listener additional information on where the sound source will be in succeeding moments.

Head movement has been shown to improve the accuracy of sound localization (McAnally and Martin, 2014), particularly in those situations described earlier where sound sources are located along the medial plane or within the cone of confusion.

The Vestibular System

Although not contributing to our sense of hearing, the purpose of the vestibular system is to sense linear and angular acceleration as well as static position of the head. As shown in Figure 7.15, the three **semicircular canals** are positioned perpendicular with respect to each other to sense movement in each of the three spatial planes.

Each canal is set up as an **endolymph**-filled hoop, with the base of each referred to as an ampula. Within the ampula is a single tuft of hair cells extremely sensitive to movement. As the head moves in three dimensions, the endolymph fluid within the canals stimulates the hair cells which, in turn, produce electrical impulses via a neurochemical process. These impulses are sent along the vestibulocochlear nerve to synapse in the brain stem, cerebellum, and spinal cord.

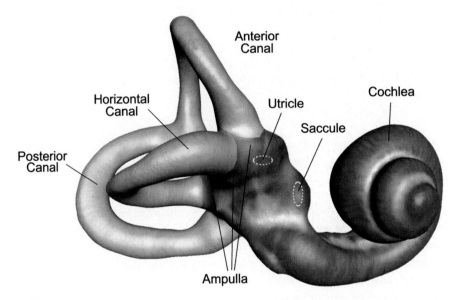

Figure 7.15 This illustration shows the general structure and key features of the human vestibular system.
Credit: Illustration by Ortisa via Wikimedia under a CC 3.0 license.—Derivative work—S. Aukstakalnis

A second set of sensors, the **utricle** and **saccule**, are small patches of hair cells topped by calcium carbonate crystals known as otoconia. These patches are positioned at right angles with respect to each other and detect linear acceleration. In any position of the head, gravity bends the cilia of one of the two patches due to the weight of the otoconia. Here again, this bending triggers a neurochemical process resulting in the generation of nerve impulses sent to the brain stem.

The saccule and utricle serve a primary function of keeping an individual vertically oriented with respect to gravity. If your head and body begin to tilt, signals from these sensors automatically trigger postural adjustments.

When considering the function of these sensors, it is important to remember that they operate in a tightly coupled manner, paired with those of the other ear. When their sensory information is in conflict, such as during a severe infection of the endolymph or following inner ear damage, the result is often severe vertigo and nausea.

Similarly, the vestibular system functions in a manner tightly coupled to the eyes. In fact, a major function of the vestibular system is keeping the eyeballs stable as the head moves. This allows you to remain fixated on an object or point in space as your head swivels and moves up and down, such as when you are walking or running.

Finally, as explained in greater detail in Chapter 21, "Human Factors Considerations," sensory information from the vestibular system is also tightly linked to visual signals from the eyes. When these visual signals are in conflict with those of the vestibular system, such as in some virtual environment simulations where there is a compelling visual sensation of motion without the corresponding inner ear cues, the result is a condition referred to as VIMS, or visually induced motion sickness.

Conclusion

In this chapter we have reviewed some of the basic properties of sound, the process through which acoustic energy is converted by our ears into a neural event, as well as the primary cues derived from these signals by our brain to determine the location of a sound source in our environment. In the next chapter we explore how these key strengths of this powerful perceptual mechanism are being leveraged by scientists to make the use of complex machinery and information systems a much more intuitive experience.

CHAPTER 8

AUDIO DISPLAYS

Although the visual display components of virtual and augmented reality systems play the dominant role in communicating information to the user, they are limited to providing stimuli corresponding to features and events occurring in the direction users are facing within the simulation. The addition of discreet audio cues or even a rich 3D acoustic soundscape can provide significant additional data about the 360-degree virtual environment surrounding the user. In this chapter we explore the various types of audio displays used in virtual and augmented reality systems, examining their functional differences and the types of application settings within which each is most beneficial.

Conventional Audio

It has been said that the ears point the eyes (Blattner et al., 1991; Broze, 2013). Just as with the real world, the use of audio in virtual and augmented reality applications can increase situational awareness (Fisher et al., 1987), improve navigation and way-finding (Ardito et al., 2007), enhance the perception of size, space, and depth (Larsson et al., 2001), and add to the overall sensation of "presence" within a virtual environment (Avanzini and Crosato, 2006).

Conversely, it is also important to understand that not all virtual and augmented reality applications benefit from the addition of sound. In fact, many targeted applications in science and engineering do not use sound at all because it is simply of no benefit. For example, applications such as those focused on the visual exploration and examination of complex geometric models and designs, or analysis of medical imaging or geophysical data, in and of themselves benefit very little from the addition of an audio component.

In the following sections we explore a variety of existing and emerging audio display solutions available for virtual and augmented reality systems, detailing their inherent strengths and weaknesses, and where possible, providing insights into what works best for different applications.

Monaural Sound

Monaural sound (also known as monophonic or simply mono) is a term used to describe a basic sound reproduction format within which all audio signals are combined into a single channel and fed to a single speaker. As illustrated in Figure 8.1, audio output is *perceived* as coming from one position. Monaural sound systems can also use multiple speakers (both clustered as well as separated, such as with aviation headphones), with each receiving identical output signals. An essential identifying characteristic is that monaural audio signals do not inherently contain intensity or arrival time information that can be used by both ears together to simulate directional and depth cues, although Doppler and distance processing (for example, attenuation, filtering, and reverb) can still provide distance cues in mono (interaural time and intensity differences; see Chapter 7, "The Mechanics of Hearing").

Although it is easy to dismiss monaural audio as a basic, limited sound format, there are a variety of application areas within virtual and augmented reality systems where single-channel output is an optimum solution, such as those instances in which a directional property is not required. The simplest of examples could include a warning buzzer or notification tone. In terms of computational load, monaural sound generation requires the least system resources.

Figure 8.1 Illustration depicting a basic monaural sound configuration within which audio signals are intended to be heard as if they were a single channel of sound perceived as coming from one position. *Credit: Illustration by S. Aukstakalnis*

Stereo Sound

Stereo (short for stereophonic, from the Greek words *stereos*, meaning "firm or solid" and *phone* meaning "sound" or "tone") refers to an audio recording or reproduction format within which multiple audio signals are combined into two independent audio channels. As illustrated in Figure 8.2, compared to monophonic systems, stereophonic audio signals do contain intensity or arrival time information that can be used by both ears together to simulate, or reproduce, directional and depth cues. Stereo systems require two or more speakers or a pair of headphones to produce this effect.

Stereophonic systems can be divided into two categories:

■ **Artificial stereo** (also known as "pan-potted" mono) refers to systems within which a single channel audio signal (mono) is reproduced across multiple speakers. Spatialization is simulated through signal processing techniques such as panning (varying the amplitude of the source signal sent to each speaker) to achieve the sensation of left and right source placement or movement, low-pass filters (attenuating a signal above a cutoff frequency allowing lower frequencies to pass through the filter) for front-back movement with distance, and mixed reverb for ambiance effects.

■ **True stereo** (also known as "natural stereo") refers to audio systems with two independent audio channels. Sound signals reproduced in true stereo have a distinct intensity and arrival time relationship between the two channels resulting in a compelling reproduction of the original sound field.

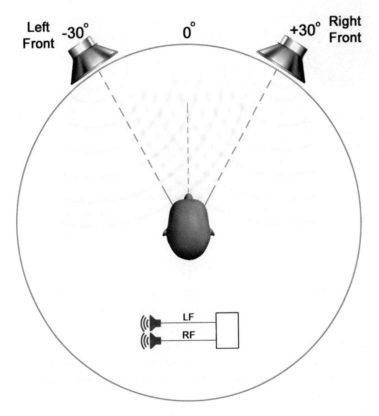

Figure 8.2 This illustration depicts a proper basic stereo speaker configuration within which separate left and right channels are used to project sounds containing distinct intensity and arrival time relationships.
Credit: Illustration by S. Aukstakalnis

Although conventional, fixed speaker stereo systems can produce a compelling spatial sound field, the area within which the effect can be experienced is limited, regardless of whether the audio being delivered is a live recording, the result of extensive mixing in a studio, or generated in real time to supplement a visual simulation application.

As illustrated in Figure 8.3, the best illusion of sound placement and depth is achieved if the listener is positioned on the mid-line between the loudspeakers and back far enough so as to form an equilateral triangle. From this listener position (known as the "sweet spot"), interaural time and intensity differences are minimized and a soundscape can be experienced within the area in front of, but between, the two fixed speakers and spread across a common horizontal plane. If the listeners move out of the sweet spot, the illusion of sound placement and depth falls off dramatically. You will obviously continue to hear the sound, but the rich spaciousness of the sound image will be lost.

Under ideal listening conditions, it is possible to use frequency contouring and crosstalk elimination to move some sound images above and beyond the horizontal plane, although the effect would be perceptible by some and not others because of the differences in the manner in which our individual pinna color the sound before reaching our eardrums (Griesinger, 1990).

In the case of headphones, the spatial effect is quite apparent, although the totality of the sound image is perceived to emanate from the space between your ears.

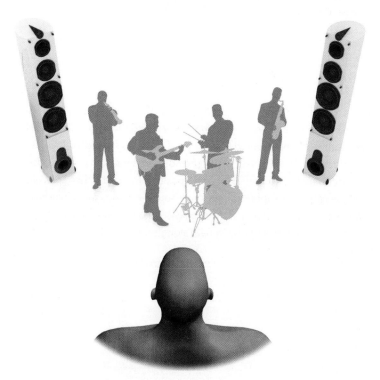

Figure 8.3 Stereo speakers should be arranged to form an equilateral triangle with your listening position. The phantom sound image will appear in front of and between the two speakers.
Credit: Image by iconspro, pisotskii © 123RF.com

note

The use of normal stereo sound within virtual and augmented reality applications requires careful consideration and experimentation given the limited area within which a sound field can be created. As a general rule, you can deliver sounds from the front. Signal processing allows for some flexibility, but the time and effort put forth may warrant simply moving to an alternate solution. The systems in which stereo audio alone could be successfully used are those employing a fixed display where the user is facing in a single direction. Examples might include wide field of view (FOV), theater-like projection systems, hemispherical displays such as those discussed in Chapter 6, "Fully Immersive Displays," within an automobile to complement an on-windscreen display or even in a standalone mode to enhance onboard navigation. In this situation, although the automobile is moving, the operator's position in the driver's seat, and thus, in relation to the speakers, remains relatively constant.

One such application, under development by French automobile manufacturer PSA Peugeot Citroën, optimizes navigation-system voice directions. The virtual placement of sound can create the impression that an instruction to "turn right" is coming from the windscreen area on the right side of the driver (PSA Peugeot Citroën, 2015).

Surround Sound

The phrase *surround sound* refers to an enhanced audio system within which a semi-immersive soundscape is created using a combination of digital signal processing techniques as well as four or more independent audio channels routed to an array of speakers strategically situated around a central listening position. Unlike stereo, which provides the sensation of a soundscape positioned within an arc extending from a central listener's position forward to two speakers (or inside of one's head in the case of headphones), surround sound expands the perceived soundscape to a 360° radius around the listener. If the speakers are correctly positioned, all elements in the soundscape will be perceived to originate along a common horizontal plane, such as is illustrated in Figure 8.4.

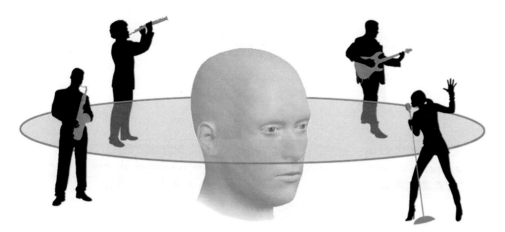

Figure 8.4 Surround sound provides the listener the sensation of sounds originating across a 360° radius in the horizontal plane.
Credit: Image by iconspro © 123RF.com, bogalo/Depositphotos

Surround Sound Formats

There are numerous surround sound formats and speaker configurations available, each of which is described using a unique nomenclature. The most basic surround sound format is known as 5.1 (pronounced 5-*point*-1 or 5-*dot*-1). As shown in Figure 8.5, this format utilizes six separate channels: five normal full-range audio channels (Left Front, Center Front, Right Front, Left Surround, Right Surround) and one low-frequency effects channel (a subwoofer) for extended bass. With such systems there is considerable flexibility in the placement of the subwoofer due to the lack of directionality of these frequencies. (As we learned in Chapter 7, "The Mechanics of Hearing," low-frequency sounds have long wave forms that bend around objects.) Additionally, most professionally mixed audio intended for surround sound systems, such as in the case of movies or soundtracks, typically take advantage of the fact that the audience/listener will likely be facing in one direction and thus, use the front center channel for delivery of character dialogue.

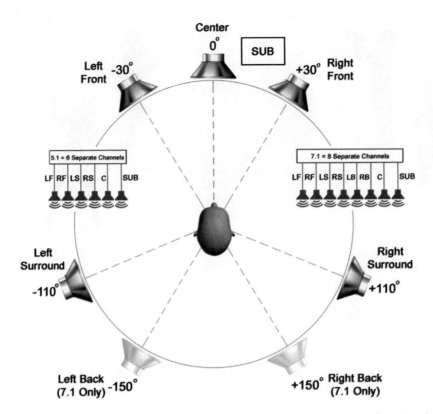

Figure 8.5 Illustration showing basic 5.1 and 7.1 surround sound speaker configurations (max angles).
Credit: Illustration by S. Aukstakalnis

Building on this basic setup, surround sound formats and speaker configurations grow in complexity. For instance, a 6.1-channel system adds an additional channel targeting a single speaker (or array) behind the listener. A 7.1 system adds two additional rear channels for a total of eight full channels. Recent advances in cinematic audio have also resulted in the development of a 7.1.2-channel system, which adds an additional two channels for speakers above the listener.

> ### note
>
> Surround sound is often employed within immersive visualization systems based on large-scale fixed displays such as computer-assisted virtual environments (CAVEs), hemispherical/domes displays, and other wide field of view (FOV) curved-screen systems (each of which is covered in Chapter 6, "Fully Immersive Displays"), as well as various full motion flight simulators. In general, those applications within which an individual or audience remain in a relatively stable position facing in one direction, although sound effects are intended to surround the participants, tend to benefit the most from surround sound solutions.

Object-Based Surround Sound

To this point, each of the fixed-speaker surround sound solutions mentioned in this section are constrained by the need to mix audio to address specific channels (or speakers) and produce the illusion of presence within a sound field. While effective, this method is limiting, particularly if you want sounds to appear well above or below the horizontal plane. An innovative new approach known as **object-based surround sound** now emerging from several manufacturers (Dolby Atmos, DTS:X, Auro-3D) enables audio engineers and designers to treat sound events as individual entities and precisely define their location and movement in 3D space (Dolby, 2015). Although specific methods and approaches vary, each manufacture's system enables sound designers to select a specific position or vector for an individual sound element, and the mixing software determines the correct speakers to target to produce the desired effect. This new approach enables a much larger number of fixed speakers to be employed to produce stunning 3D aural experiences for cinemas and home theaters. But it does not end here.

In an object-based system, the different sound elements are encoded with metadata such as position and vector information during mixing. Each manufacturer has developed proprietary methods to use this metadata in combination with HRTF filters mentioned in Chapter 7 (and discussed in more detail in this chapter) to deliver the same immersive surround sound effects over standard stereo headphones, opening the door for a variety of direct uses in virtual and augmented reality applications.

One such demonstration application, detailed in Chapter 13, "Gaming and Entertainment," involves combining object-based surround sound and 360-degree stereo video (also referred to as spherical video) of a live concert by the musician Paul McCartney, with the end product experienced using a stereoscopic head-mounted display and headphones. Using accelerometers within the display to monitor head orientation and appropriately adjust the visual and audio scene, the user is able to turn to the left or right, look up and down, as if physically standing on the stage.

Binaural audio, also referred to as *3Dsound*, *spatial*(ized) *audio*, or *space-related stereophony*, refers to methods of recording or synthesizing sound to simulate the way our two ears naturally perceive our acoustic surroundings. Considerably different from any of the previously discussed methods of sound reproduction, binaural audio incorporates the localization cues previously discussed in Chapter 7, including the effects resulting from our natural ear spacing (interaural time and intensity differences), as well as the shape of our upper torso, head, and pinna geometry in coloring the frequency spectrum of sound waves before entering our ear canals. The net result is that sound sources can appear anywhere in a 360-degree sphere surrounding the user (Fisher, 1991; Ferrington, 1993; Schauer, 2001; Sontacchi et al., 2002).

Noted sound engineer William B. Snow (San Francisco, May 16, 1903–Oct. 5, 1968), formerly of Bell Labs and assistant director of the U.S. Navy's Underwater Sound Laboratory, offered one of the more eloquent explanations on the difference between stereo and binaural sound: "It has been said aptly the binaural system transports the listener to the original scene, whereas the stereophonic system transports the sound source to the listener's room (Snow, 1953).

The use of binaural sound within virtual and augmented reality systems and applications is enabled through two primary methods: recording and real-time synthesis.

Binaural Recording

Binaural recording is a method of capturing a soundscape—be it in a studio, a concert hall, or in a natural outdoor setting—in a manner similar to the way in which a healthy individual actually hears one's real-world surroundings. In practical terms, this involves positioning two omnidirectional microphones facing away from each other and separated by about 7 inches (17.78 cm), thus approximating the distance between an adult's ears. As discussed in Chapter 7, this separation allows the microphones to capture the interaural time and intensity differences that are used by the audio centers of our brain to localize the direction from which a sound originates along the horizontal plane (the azimuth).

Modern binaural recording systems typically consist of two microphone capsules embedded within a specialized mannequin head that includes external, contralateral (inversely symmetrical) ear forms (pinnea) to also capture the natural reflections and coloration of high-frequency (short wavelength) sound waves that our brain uses to determine the elevation of a sound source. These systems record ambient sounds on two separate and discreet audio channels to preserve these critical interaural differences and pinna spectral cues. This concept is illustrated in Figure 8.6.

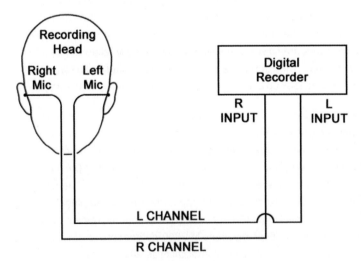

Figure 8.6 Illustration depicting a basic binaural recording setup where left and right channels are kept distinctly separate to preserve binaural sound cues.
Credit: Illustration by S. Aukstakalnis

In general, mannequin head microphone systems provide the most aurally accurate binaural recordings. Upon playback, the listener is able to experience a virtual acoustic image as if one were physically present and positioned at the exact point where the original recording was made (Geil, 1979; Genuit and Bray, 1989). Just as binaural recordings capture the subtle, unique positional cues for each ear separately, the playback of binaural audio recordings over stereo headphones is the most spatially accurate method known for faithfully reproducing the original sound field (Bartlett, 2014; Lombardi, 1997).

MANNEQUIN HEAD RECORDINGS MUST BE EQUALIZED

Binaural recordings produced using mannequin heads are considerably different from any other recording method. As discussed in Chapter 7, just as with a human head, mannequin heads act as an obstacle in a sound field and result in the complex diffraction of acoustic waves and coloration of the frequency spectrum before arriving at the microphones. This diffraction and coloration of the sounds, along with the interaural differences, allows our brain to select and identify the apparent location of sound sources in 3D space.

Now consider what happens when the recorded audio is played back over headphones. Without the proper equalization of the recorded material, a second round of distortions and coloration of the sound spectrum occurs as the sound waves exit the headphone speakers and bounce around the aurical cavity (cavum conchae) and ear canal before actually reaching the eardrum.

In the case of playback over loudspeakers, similar problems arise as a result of the sound spectrum being colored a second time when it strikes the listener's physical body and ears, adding even more distortion.

As a result of these phenomena, each mannequin recording head manufacturer provides either a hardware or a software equalization solution through which the audio signals are to be processed before playback to filter out, or otherwise account for, unwanted distortion.

Hardware Solution Overviews

There are a number of commercial mannequin head recording systems available. Depending on the manufacturer, some models include facial features (which typically have little impact on the overall sound spectrum arriving at the embedded microphones), whereas others dispense with the facial attributes but include neck and torso assemblies to enable the capture of the subtle sound reflections from these features. Still others forgo head and torso assemblies altogether. In general, the single common feature found in most modern binaural recording solutions is contralateral pinna pairs to capture pinna spectral cues as well as to ensure uniform left-right recordings.

The following three hardware solution overviews are presented beginning with a high-end, precision-grade system followed by a consumer-grade unit and then a DIY option. Employed correctly, each provides a compelling binaural audio experience, though accuracy in the capture of the full sound spectrum, and thus, the depth and richness of the end product is considerably different between the high and the low end. Researchers and developers considering the use of binaural recordings in their virtual and augmented reality applications should give careful consideration to the desired quality and end user needs when deciding which hardware to employ. This chapter provides specific details for three binaural recording solutions, but there are many other commercially available systems on the market. A list of these suppliers is provided within Appendix B, "Resources."

The current state of the art in full head binaural recording systems is exemplified by HEAD Acoustics GmbH of Herzogenrath, Germany.

HEAD Acoustics HMS IV Aachen HEAD

The Head Acoustics HMS IV.1 (HEAD Measurement System IV.1) shown in Figure 8.7 is a standalone, high-precision binaural recording and measurement system that includes a mathematically definable upper torso and head. Of particular note is their use of what are referred to as *simplified pinna*. As opposed to other recording heads that incorporate life-like pinna forms with all the curves, ridges, and undulations, Head Acoustics takes a different approach. Based on years of research by company founder Dr. Klaus Genuit identifying the specific structures of the average human auricle demonstrated to be *acoustically essential,* pinna were designed to incorporate only the features and dimensions "important for the directional pattern of the external ear transfer function" (Genuit, 2005; CCITT, 1992). Among the dominant features of the simplified pinna are the cavum-conchae and the asymmetric ear canal entrance, which itself is important for localization cues (Vorländer, 2007).

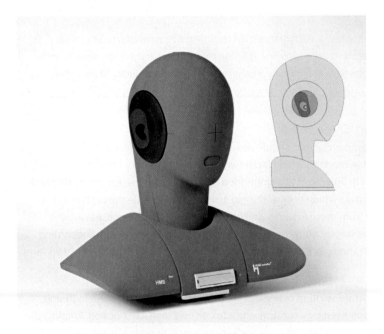

Figure 8.7 HEAD Acoustics HMS IV.1 Artificial Head System and side detail.
Credit: Image courtesy of Prof. Dr.-Ing. Klaus Genuit, HEAD accoustics GmbH

The HMS IV.1 microphone capsules are positioned only slightly recessed into the side of the recording head (5 mm). In this position, sounds waves do not undergo additional coloring and changes that would normally be present if the capsule were positioned deeper into the head in a simulated ear canal. Another interesting result of not embedding the microphone capsules within artificial ear canals is that captured audio is reproduced extremely well over fixed speakers (Wolfrum, 2015), although sweet spot restrictions and limitations of sound placement in 3D space still apply.

The HMS IV.1 is capable of operating in standalone mode, without tethering to external power sources, computers, or recording equipment. Used in this manner, audio is recorded to a CompactFlash card, the reader for which is built into the torso portion of the unit.

The HMS IV.1 system enables any of five different equalization types to be selected: linear (LIN—no equalization), independent-of-direction equalization (ID), free field equalization (FF), diffuse field equalization (DF), and user-defined equalization settings for customized needs.

The HMV IV.1 is renowned for a high dynamic range comparable to that of the human ear, as well as a near-zero frequency response at points along the median plane (Wolfrum, 2015).

It is important to note that the HMS IV.1 is principally intended to serve as a high-end measurement device for such applications as the examination and optimization of the sound quality of technical products, motor vehicles interiors, aircraft cabins, and telephony devices where even the most subtle of acoustic nuances must be measured or captured for study. Thus, this high level of performance can be of significant benefit to virtual and augmented reality applications developers targeting the same level of quality and fidelity.

3DioSound Free Space Pro

Another manufacturer of binaural microphones of note is 3Dio, Inc of Vancouver, Washington. As opposed to microphone capsules being built into a dummy head, the Free Space line of microphones shown in Figure 8.8 simply does away with the head form completely but retains lifelike contralateral pinna mounted on disks separated by about 7 inches approximating the distance between an adult's ears. According to the manufacturer, the discs upon which the ear forms are mounted are specifically designed to provide all the necessary head-shadowing for a perfectly realistic HRTF and binaural experience (Anderson, 2015a).

Figure 8.8 The Free Space Pro II Binaural Microphone from 3Dio, Inc.
Credit: Image courtesy of 3Dio, LLC

Two highly useful features about this microphone include the compact size, allowing for ease of recording in nearly any environment, as well as a hot shoe adapter for mounting with cameras, grip handle, or tripods. The system utilizes XLR outputs that support phantom power, as well as an 1/8-inch stereo output jack enabling audio capture with portable handheld recorders.

The silicone rubber pinna used for these microphones began as a 3D scan of a single ear created using a medical CT scanner (X-ray computed tomography), the resulting model from which was then adjusted for aesthetic appearance and optimization of lower frequency wavelengths[1] (Anderson, 2015b). The company also sells the ear forms independent from the electronics for use in DIY binaural recording projects.

In-Ear Binaural Recording Mics

If you want to completely bypass using artificial head or pinna forms for binaural recording, one of the easiest, most accurate, and least expensive routes to consider is to simply use your own head and ears. There are dozens of commercially available, consumer-level in-ear binaural microphone systems available, each with varying levels of performance and sensitivity (feedback, balance, low noise floor, and so on). One high-quality and reasonably priced option is the Roland CS-10EM shown in Figure 8.9.

---

1   Tests were performed in August of 2015 by the author and two professional audio engineers comparing the recording performance of the Free Space Pro II and HEAD Acoustics HMS IV.1 Artificial Head System. Although the Free Space Pro II proved to be an outstanding microphone in terms of overall performance and low noise floor, the lack of a head form clearly resulted in a weak response to lower frequencies.

This product is unique in that the binaural microphones are built into the same ear buds used for listening, enabling the user to monitor while simultaneously recording. Remember that you will need, at a minimum, a two-channel handheld field recorder such as the Roland R-05 to accommodate the twin microphone inputs. As mentioned earlier, recording on dedicated left and right channels is essential to preserve the embedded localization cues.

Figure 8.9 Roland CS-10EM in-ear binaural recording microphones and R-05 two-channel field recorder.
Credit: Image courtesy of Roland Corporation U.S.

Binaural Recording File Formats

From an engineering standpoint, a binaural recording is generally the same as a stereo audio file. It contains two tracks, and the final edit can be converted into any format. However, encoding into commonly used compressed file formats such as MP3 can significantly degrade the quality of the audio and the spatial feel of the end product. This is due, in large part, to the fact that MP3 (MPEG-1 Audio Layer-3) compression employs psychoacoustics-based algorithms that permit the codec to discard or reduce the precision of audio frequencies that are less audible to human hearing, thus contributing to overall files size reduction (Arms and Fleischhauer, 2005). For general audio applications such as the music playlist on your smartphone, the MP3 format is ideal. For binaural recordings, this compression technique can have a dramatic impact on the directional cues for sound events specifically sought when making binaural recordings.

Researchers and developers producing binaural recordings for virtual and augmented reality applications should always record and manipulate in an uncompressed file format such as WAV (Waveform Audio File Format) or AIFF (Audio Interchange File Format) to capture and preserve the entire frequency spectrum. The finished product can then be mixed down and compressed in postproduction to the desired format, although at the highest bit rate possible to maintain acoustic detail (Anderson, 2013).

HOW IS RECORDED BINAURAL AUDIO USED IN VR AND AR?

Within the context of virtual and augmented reality applications, there are two primary methods in which binaural audio recordings can be utilized.

Environmental Effects

Binaural recordings can be used as a supplement to a computer-generated 3D visual model, and more precisely, for nonspecific environmental effects, as opposed to sound effects for specific events. A simple example to consider could be a 3D visual model of a forest combined with a binaural recording of the same environment. This specific technique is used in some virtual reality gaming applications, but again, only within the context of providing non-event-specific environmental sounds.

Cinematic VR

The second method is to combine binaural audio with 360-degree stereo video (or simple stereo video). Examples of this type of application include music videos, such as *Sound and Vision* by the musician Beck, and *Stone Milker* by the musician Björk. The end products are experienced using a stereoscopic head mounted along with stereo headphones. The detail of a high-end example of this application can be found in Chapter 13, "Gaming and Entertainment."

Real-Time Synthesis of Binaural Sound

The second (and currently more common) method for applying binaural sound to virtual and augmented reality applications takes a completely different approach. As opposed to presenting prerecorded binaural audio to the listener (via distinct left and right channels), existing mono audio samples are instead passed through digital signal processors containing pairs of filters based on measured head-related transfer functions (HRTFs) briefly mentioned in Chapter 7. The net result is that the frequency profile of these audio samples is slightly colored to include the effects that a human torso, head, pinna, and even the acoustic characteristics of the space would have on the sounds. This modification of the audio signal, quite literally, encodes the specific cues used by the brain to help you identify, with comparable precision to real life, the azimuth and elevation from which a virtual sound originates.

Another (albeit loose) way to think of this is that standard sounds passing through these digital filters are colored by interaction with a mathematical representation of a human torso, head, and external ears. Thus, instead of recording and playing back sound that has already been colored by interaction with your physical body (or that of a mannequin head), simple monaural sounds are passed through digital filters that encode the same effects.

In addition to the methods just referenced, there are still other techniques available besides HRTFs and binaural sound used in real-time synthesis of audio. For instance, room and environmental convolution models can actually be obtained offline or can be derived from acoustical physical modeling approaches (Chandak et al., 2012; Taylor et al., 2012).

How HRTFs Filters Are Created

As discussed in Chapter 7, humans perceive the location of a sound source through the use of binaural cues (interaural time and intensity differences) for determining azimuth and monaural cues (changes in the frequency profile of sounds by the pinna) for determining elevation. These specific effects on a sound are known as a head-related transfer function (HRTF) and can be quantified by empirically measuring sounds arriving at the entrance to the ears from hundreds of locations around an actual person or binaural recording head. These individual sound measurements are referred to as a head-related impulse response (HRIR).

In precise mathematical terms, an HRTF is simply a Fourier transform, or *convolution*, of an HRIR.

Measuring Impulse Responses

An HRIR is not only different for each of our ears, but unique for every direction from which a sound might originate. For instance, sounds arriving from a point above a listener along the vertical plane are modified differently (by each ear) than those arriving from a position to the front of the listener.

Thus, it is necessary to measure the HRIR to control tones from hundreds of precisely defined positions around an individual's head (or one of the dummy heads mentioned earlier). The more positions measured, the more precise virtual sounds can be placed, although a multitude of techniques exist to interpolate between data points (Freeland et al., 2002; Ajdler et al., 2005; Keyrouz and Diepold, 2008; de Sousa and Queiroz, 2009).

Numerous methods have been developed for precision measurement of HRIR data. Typically each involves a structure arrayed with equally spaced loudspeakers surrounding a central listening position. One of the most accurate systems currently in operation is found at the Auditory Localization Facility (ALF), located at the Air Force Research Laboratory, Wright Patterson AFB, Ohio. As shown in Figure 8.10, the ALF is a large anechoic chamber that houses a 14-foot-diameter geodesic sphere arrayed with loudspeakers positioned at each of its 277 vertices (Romigh and Simpson, 2014).

Figure 8.10 Measuring head-related impulse responses at the Auditory Localization Facility at the Air Force Research Laboratory, Wright Patterson AFB, Ohio.
Credit: Image courtesy of the U.S. Air Force

Now imagine swapping your physical pinna with those of a friend. The chances are good your ability to accurately localize sounds in the environment around you would be seriously diminished. This should not be surprising given the differences in the geometry of the ear. It is well known that HRIRs, and thus, HTRFs, vary widely from person to person (Kistler and Wightman, 1992). As such, serious localization errors can occur if you listen to sounds filtered through nonindividualized HRTFs. These errors are most pronounced in front-back and up-down judgments (Wenzel et al., 1993; Middlebrooks, 1999; Brungart and Romigh, 2009).

Public Domain HRTF Databases

Although it is currently impractical to produce custom HRTFs for each individual, researchers have developed averaging methods to arrive at generic reference filters that can process sounds with spatial cues perceptible by large segments of the target population. These reference filters are often composed of HRTFs drawn from several high-spatial-resolution collections compiled and placed into the public domain by such institutions as Massachusetts Institute of Technology and University of California at Davis. Details for accessing each of these collections can be found in Appendix B, "Resources."

Position Stabilized Binaural Sound

To this point we have explored the various enabling technology pathways through which binaural sound can be applied to virtual and augmented reality applications, although for the sake of simplicity, these explanations assumed the user would be a passive listener. In reality, most applications will have users swiveling their heads looking around as well as changing their physical position.

The Need for Head Tracking

As we learned earlier in this chapter, listening to stereo audio over headphones provides the aural sensation of a soundscape being positioned between the two speakers within your head. Conversely, binaural audio delivered over headphones provides the aural sensation of your being positioned, or *immersed*, within the soundscape. In other words, the sound field is located outside of your head, just like the real world. For standard audio playback and listening, this is great. But when binaural audio is used in a virtual or augmented reality application, a problem emerges. That problem is head movement.

As you move your head or body, there is no change to the 3D soundscape. It moves with you. The aural sensation of a car horn to your right will always be to your right, even if you physically turn to face the apparent source of the sound.

Thus, just as with the visual component of a virtual and augmented reality application and illustrated in Figure 8.11, it is necessary to track, at a minimum, the orientation (roll, pitch, and yaw) of the user's head and to feed that information to the system delivering the audio. When implemented, the perceived effect is that the 3D soundscape remains fixed as you move within it. This is particularly important because head movements contribute significantly to overall sound localization. Have you ever turned your head to hear something better?

A more in-depth exploration of the various technologies used to track the position and orientation of objects (in this case the human head) is found in Chapter 11, "Sensors for Tracking Position, Orientation, and Motion." Typically the information from one tracking unit is shared by both the visual and the audio components of the virtual or augmented reality system.

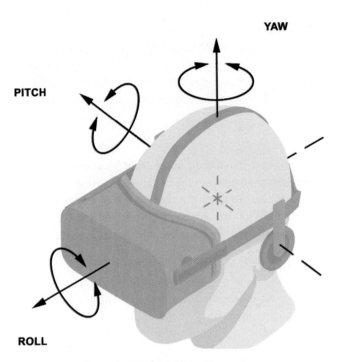

YAW

PITCH

ROLL

Figure 8.11 Binaural audio delivered over headphones requires, at a minimum, tracking the orientation (roll, pitch, and yaw) of the listener's head to present the sensation of a stabilized sound field within which the listener moves.
Credit: Image by andrewrybalko © 123RF.com

What About Binaural Sound over Speakers?

While binaural audio recordings can be played back over conventional stereo speakers, a noticeable loss of spatial quality and directionality of features in the sound is experienced due to crosstalk. In other words, each ear receives the sum of two signals: the signal intended for a specific ear as well as that intended for the other—that is, the crosstalk signal (Khosrow-Pour, 2014). Although crosstalk cancellation solutions have existed for many years for general audio applications, many challenges still exist, such as the need for a listener's physical position to remain relatively stable (that "sweet spot" limitation again).

In the case of real-time binaural *synthesis*, such as that found in gaming applications, the challenges of delivering binaural audio over fixed speakers are significantly greater. Not only is there a need to track the user's head position and orientation to adaptively control the crosstalk canceller, but there is the need to process audio signals through HRTF filters to impart the directional properties to the sounds in the first place. Although significant research and development work is underway to solve these issues, the delivery of a compelling binaural audio scene over fixed conventional speaker systems remains impractical for most virtual and augmented reality applications.

Conclusion

Applied correctly, the addition of a rich, 3D acoustic soundscape to virtual and augmented reality applications can have a powerful impact on the sense of immersion, usability, and overall experience. Within this chapter we have explored a variety of the most common, and still emerging, audio display solutions and methodologies used to achieve this goal. Appendixes A and B should be leveraged for an even greater understanding of this subject matter.

CHAPTER 9

THE MECHANICS OF FEELING

From textures to temperature and vibrations to slippage, our sense of touch serves as the mechanical interface between our bodies and the physical world. This same capability can also be harnessed to provide an added sense of realism to computer-based simulations. To understand the application of tactile sensorial feedback capabilities within virtual and augmented reality simulations, it is important to first understand how we actually feel the real world. In this chapter we explore the mechanics of our sense of touch, its extraordinary range of capabilities, and how tactile and proprioceptive cues supplement sight and hearing.

The Science of Feeling

Consider the touch of a friend, the texture of the different fabrics in your clothing, or the forces you feel as you swing a golf club or baseball bat.

These and other sensations are possible because humans are equipped with a marvelously complex system of sensors, neural pathways, and areas of the brain that together detect, relay, and process thousands of pieces of information each second about the physical environment we are within, the external forces acting on us, as well as the position, orientation, and movement of our body. Collectively referred to as the **somatic sensory system**, there are two subsystems that hold particular relevance to the overall subject matter of this book. The first is responsible for our ability to detect and perceive mechanical stimuli, including those representing external pressure, vibration, flutter, textures, skin stretching, and so on. This is referred to as our *tactile sense*. The second, known as our *kinesthetic sense*, enables us to detect and perceive joint angles, as well as tension and other forces exerted in our muscles and tendons. The combination of the two senses generally falls under the term *haptics*.

> ## note
>
> Use of the word *haptics* has been the source of tremendous confusion and more than a few epic arguments within and between the virtual reality, robotics, and medical communities. Due in part to the "us too" phenomenon, significant disagreement has evolved on proper use of the term. Does haptics refer to our collective tactile and kinesthetic senses, or does it refer to a class of man-machine interfaces providing mechanical stimuli to address these senses, edging out tried and true phrases such as *tactile/force feedback devices*? For clarity, this book will use the term sparingly and in most instances in relation to matters concerning physiology.

In this chapter we will explore both systems. They are crucial to understanding the challenges of implementing tactile and force feedback technologies within virtual and augmented reality systems.

We begin this exploration with the part of our physical body where most of these sensations originate: our skin.

Anatomy and Composition of the Skin

Our skin is the sensory organ responsible for our sense of touch, the first of the five primary senses to develop and respond to stimulation during gestation (Huss, 1977). In fact, a human fetus will actually begin to respond to touch at about the eighth week of development (Rantala, 2013).

A medium-sized organ, our skin spans an area covering approximately 1.6 to 1.9 sq. meters (Rinzler, 2009) and accounts for approximately 15% of our overall body weight (Kanitakis, 2001).

We have two general types of skin—*hairy* and *glabrous* (naturally hairless)—both of which are capable of a remarkably complex set of functions falling into three main categories: protection, regulation, and sensation.

Protection—Located at the interface between the external environment and our internal physiology, skin serves as a protective barrier against a variety of threats, including mechanical impact and pressure (Sembulingam and Sembulingam, 2012), dangerous ultraviolet (UV) radiation (Brenner and Hearing, 2008), and biological pathogens (Nestle et al., 2009).

Regulation—Our skin serves the vital role of regulating and stabilizing body temperature through constriction and dilation of blood vessels (Charkoudian, 2003) and secretion and evaporation of water.

Sensation—Also serving as the primary interface with our physical surroundings, our skin contains an extensive network of nerve cells specifically designed to detect changes in the environment as well as generate sensations we feel related to the properties of our physical world with which we have contact. It is with these nerve cells that we are able to detect the tactile and force feedback cues provided by such devices as a vibrating controller used for navigating in, and manipulation of, augmented and virtual reality simulations.

Skin Layers

As detailed in Figure 9.1, human skin is composed of two primary layers, each of which varies in thickness and function. The top, outermost layer is referred to as the *epidermis* (from the Greek word *epi*, meaning "on top," and *derma*, meaning "the skin") (Oxford, 2015). This layer serves as a physical and chemical barrier separating interior physiology and the external environment (Madison, 2003; Denda, 2000). A dynamic structure, the epidermis is made of tightly packed, scale-like cells that regenerate approximately every 45 days. The epidermis is thinnest on the eyelids (.05 mm) and thickest on the palms and the soles of the feet (1.5 mm) (NIH, 2006).

The second layer, known as the *dermis*, provides support for the epidermis and accounts for approximately 80 percent of the thickness of the skin. The dermis is principally composed of connective tissue (collagen) containing hair follicles, glands, blood vessels, nerves, and sensory receptors. It gives the skin its elasticity and serves the structural purpose of cushioning the body (Boundless, 2015). Also varying in thickness depending on location (1.5 to 4 mm), the dermis layer is highly vascular and contains more than 11 miles of blood vessels (Jablonski, 2013). This venous network keeps the skin oxygenated and supplied with nutrients and plays a vital role in the skin's healing and heat regulation processes.

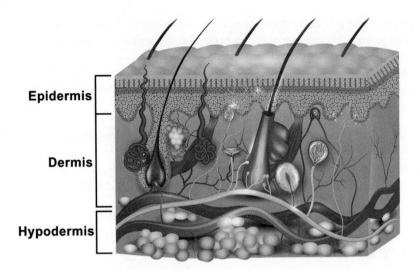

Figure 9.1 Cross-section of human skin detailing the two primary layers and underlying supportive structure of cells specialized in accumulating and storing fats that acts as an energy reserve. *Credit: Image by guniita © 123RF.com*

A third, innermost layer (although technically not considered part of the skin) is known as the *hypodermis* or *subcutis*. This layer is predominantly composed of cells specialized in accumulating and storing fats. The hypodermis also serves to attach the dermis to the muscles and bones and supplies nerves and blood vessels to the dermis. Several sensory receptors are also located in this layer.

Tactile Perception

Tactile sensing is based on sensory information produced by specialized *cutaneous receptors* (those located in the skin) that are triggered through physical contact with the stimuli such as is experienced through active touching (Gibson, 1962) or through an external force acting on our body, such as the touch of a friend, a thumping low-frequency tone from a bass kicker used in flight simulators, or heat from an open flame.

Similar to receptors found in our eyes and ears, cutaneous receptors can also be considered *transducers* because they effectively convert energy, such as mechanical stimulus or thermal energy, into electrical signals (nerve impulses). The receptor types involved in our sense of touch are primarily divided into three categories: ***nociceptors*** (for detection of stimuli producing pain), ***thermoreceptors*** (for detection of stimuli related to temperature), and those with the most relevance to the subject matter of this book, ***mechanoreceptors*** (for detection of mechanical stimuli and physical interaction).

Mechanoreceptors

As detailed in Figure 9.2, human skin contains four major types of receptors that respond specifically to different types of mechanical stimulation resulting from physical interaction with our surroundings: *Meissner corpuscles*, *Merkel disks*, *Pacinian corpuscles*, and *Ruffini endings*. Known as *mechanoreceptors*, these sensors send information to our central nervous system regarding touch, pressure, vibrations, and cutaneous tension (Purves et al., 2001). All four are also categorized as *low-threshold* (or highly sensitive) receptors because each responds to weak mechanical stimulation.

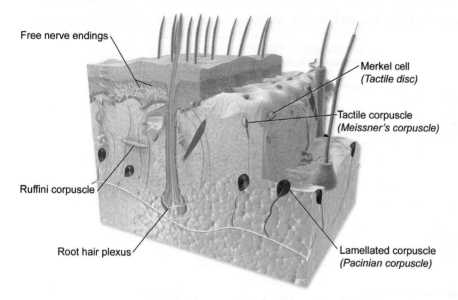

Free nerve endings

Merkel cell
(Tactile disc)

Tactile corpuscle
(Meissner's corpuscle)

Ruffini corpuscle

Root hair plexus

Lamellated corpuscle
(Pacinian corpuscle)

Figure 9.2 Cross-section of human skin detailing cutaneous structures and sensory mechanisms.
Credit: Illustration by BruceBlaus via Wikimedia under a CC 3.0 license

All mechanoreceptors function in the same basic manner:

1. An external stimulus or force acts on the surface of the skin.
2. The force is transferred deeper into the skin where it stimulates a mechanoreceptor.
3. The mechanoreceptor generates an *action potential* (electrical impulse).
4. The action potential is sent along *afferent nerves* to the central nervous system resulting in a conscious perception, behavioral response, or both (Geffeney and Goodman, 2012).

Mechanoreceptor Classification

The four types of mechanoreceptors we will be exploring in this section are classified in two different ways: by their *rate of adaptation* and by the size of their *receptive fields*.

Rate of Adaptation

Mechanoreceptors, like other sensory receptors in the human body, have an interesting performance characteristic known as *adaptation*. When a stimulus acts on our skin, the appropriate mechanoreceptors respond by firing off an initial series of impulses along afferent nerves (nerves carrying impulses from receptors or sense organs toward the central nervous system) signaling the presence of an external stimuli or change in the environment. The stronger the stimulus or displacement of tissue, the greater the frequency of the neural response (Knibestöl, 1973). This response has been shown to logarithmically increase with pressure (Muniak et al., 2007). How quickly the receptors *adapt,* or return to a passive state, depends on the type. The basic concept behind slow and rapidly adapting mechanoreceptors is illustrated within Figure 9.3.

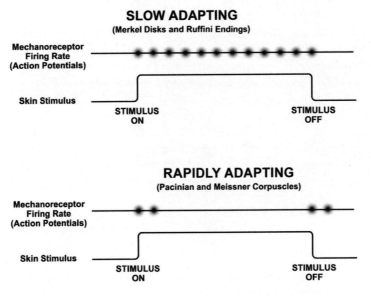

Figure 9.3 This figure illustrates the basic concept of sensory adaptation and the change over time in the responsiveness of a mechanoreceptor to continual stimulation. Slow-adapting receptors continue firing as long as the stimulus is present. Rapidly adapting receptors respond quickly at the initial onset but stop firing if the stimulus remains constant, firing again to signal the removal of the stimuli.[1]
Credit: Illustration by S. Aukstakalnis

Slow-adapting receptors (Merkel disks, Ruffini endings), designated using the initials (SA), optimally respond to contact forces including initial and continuous pressure, edges and intensity, as well as cutaneous tension (skin stretch) (Purves et al., 2001). Your ability to hold this book at your side without dropping it is a direct result of the response from slow-adapting receptors. You are, quite literally, constantly aware of the mass, weight, shape, and edges of the book while it is in your hands. This awareness comes from slow-adapting mechanoreceptors

---

1   There are a number of variations to the slow and rapidly adapting firing patters of different mechanoreceptors based on stimulus, the detailing of which goes far beyond the general scope and intent of this chapter. For more information on this topic, see Johansson and Vallbo (1979, 1983, 2014); Vallbo and Johansson (1984); Burgess (2012); Martini et al. (2013); and Hao et al. (2015).

sending a constant stream of sensory information to the central nervous system. ***Rapidly adapting*** receptors (Meissner corpuscles, Pacinian corpuscles), designated using the initials (RA), optimally respond to rapidly changing stimuli such as vibrations and changes in textures. Rapidly adapting receptors also respond to initial contact and motion, but not to steady pressure (Talbot et al., 1968). Your ability to discern between the feeling of a fuzzy peach and the surface of concrete is a direct result of rapidly adapting receptors. Vibrotactile displays found in gaming controllers and smartphones also rely upon their capability.

Receptive Fields and Mechanoreceptor Distribution

As depicted in Figure 9.4, a mechanoreceptor's receptive field is the region or surface area of skin on the hand and elsewhere that, adequately stimulated, will trigger a response from an individual receptor. Receptor field sizes range from 1 to 2 mm² all the way up to larger areas, including entire fingers and sizeable portions of the palm, depending on receptor type and location on the body (Kortum, 2008; Johansson and Vallbo, 1979). Those receptors with the smallest receptive fields (Merkel disks and Meissner corpuscles) are found in the highest densities and are located in the epidermis layer closest to the surface of the skin. In contrast, those receptors with the largest receptive fields (Ruffini endings and Pacinian corpuscles) are fewer in number and located deeper in the skin within the dermis and subcutaneous layers.

This layering, or overlap, of receptive fields plays a crucial role in our ability to carry out all forms of manual tasks, ranging from grasping and lifting a bulky cantaloupe off the counter in your kitchen to the delicate task of threading a sewing needle or placing a contact lens in your eye.

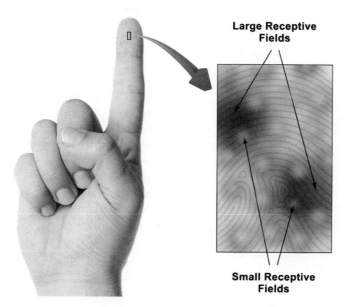

Figure 9.4 Cutaneous receptors form overlapping receptive fields that, when appropriately stimulated, produce action potentials in afferent nerves that carry the signals to the central nervous system. *Credit: Hand image by julenochek © 123RF.com*

Receptor Distribution and Spatial Resolution

It is estimated that there are approximately 17,000 individual mechanoreceptors in the glabrous skin of each hand (Vallbo and Johansson, 1984). Interestingly, tactile perception improves with decreasing finger size, which explains why women have a more finely tuned and delicate sense of touch (Peters et al,. 2009). High-density receptors with the smallest receptive fields (Merkel disks and Meissner corpuscles) have the highest spatial resolutions, enabling us to identify with considerable accuracy where external stimuli are acting on the skin, such as when a mosquito has decided to stop by for a meal. In contrast, low-density receptors with the larger receptive fields (Ruffini endings and Pacinian corpuscles) have a significantly lower spatial resolution. Although they are far less precise in signaling "where" a force is acting on the skin, these receptors are far more sensitive to light touch.

TEST YOUR SKIN'S SPATIAL RESOLUTION

Variations in the spatial resolution, size of the receptive fields, and density of mechanoreceptors can easily be demonstrated by performing a standard two-point discrimination evaluation.

As shown in Figure 9.5, use a draftsman's compass, calipers, or even an unwound paper clip bent into a "U" shape and set the distance between the tips about 2 cm apart. **While you look away,** have a friend lightly touch both tips to the pad of your index finger. Do you feel one point or two? If one, separate the tips a little and try again. Note the distance at which you just begin to clearly discern two points. For accuracy, rotate the placement of the points by 90 degrees. (That is, instead of touching horizontally across the pad of the finger, measure vertically along the pad.) Repeat this process for different places on your body.

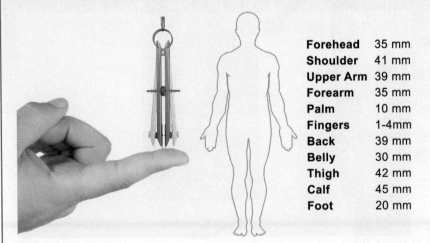

Forehead	35 mm
Shoulder	41 mm
Upper Arm	39 mm
Forearm	35 mm
Palm	10 mm
Fingers	1-4mm
Back	39 mm
Belly	30 mm
Thigh	42 mm
Calf	45 mm
Foot	20 mm

Figure 9.5 Spatial resolution and receptive field size vary by location on the body. Pads on the fingers have a high resolution, whereas the back, thighs, and calf have a low resolution. Numeric list adapted from (Weinstein, 1968).

Credit: Image by vadimmmus, madmaxer, supergranto © 123RF.com

Mechanoreceptor Details

All four main mechanoreceptors differ in physical size, geometry, range of sensitivity to static and dynamic stimuli, location in the skin, population density, specific manner of function, and more. With all of these features, it is important to remember that despite the specificity of the descriptions, there is considerable overlap in the response of different mechanoreceptors to a single stimulus event. As an example, the controller buzzing in your hand as you manipulated an object within a virtual environment or the thump felt on your chest coming from a gaming vest will elicit a response from several different receptors, including those detecting deep pressure, cutaneous stretching, and vibration (which translates into perception of texture).

Merkel Disks

A Merkel disk is a specialized sensory nerve ending characterized by a disk-shaped epithelial cell attached to an afferent nerve fiber. Typically this nerve fiber is a branch of medium-to-large diameter nerves serving a cluster of disks (Netter, 2013). As shown in Figure 9.6, Merkel disks are generally located in skin layers at the boundary between the epidermis and the dermis and are found in the greatest numbers within glabrous skin in such locations as beneath the ridges forming our fingerprints (Bear et al., 2007, p 389). When the appropriate stimulus is present, deformation of the disk wall opens ion channels in the nerve fiber. The influx of sodium (Na+) ions results in action potential firing (Maksimovic et al., 2014).

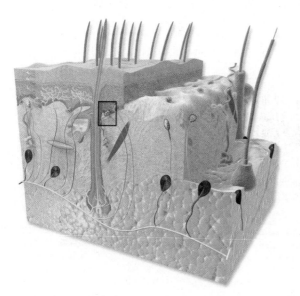

Figure 9.6 Merkel disks are slow adapting, sensitive to light touch and vibration, and respond maximally to low frequencies in the 5–15 Hz range.
Credit: Illustration by BruceBlaus via Wikimedia under a CC 3.0 license

Response Characteristics

Merkel disks are slow-adapting (SA) receptors that are highly sensitive to detailed surface patterns and sustained light mechanical stimulus, and they play a key role in such tasks as reading Braille due to their small receptive field (Noback et al., 2005; Gentaz, 2003). Merkel disk receptors respond maximally to low frequencies (5–15 Hz) (Gilman, 2002).

Meissner Corpuscles

A Meissner corpuscle (also referred to as a tactile corpuscle) is characterized by an elongated, capsule-like geometry. It contains flattened, horizontally stacked laminar cells within which are coiled, meandering, and afferent nerve fibers (Cauna and Ross, 1960). When pressure deforms the corpuscle, the nerve fibers are stimulated and action potentials are produced in the nerve (Dahiya et al., 2010). When the stimulus is removed, the corpuscle regains its shape, producing another series of action potentials (Johnson, 2001).

As shown in Figure 9.7, the boundary between the dermis and epidermis is not uniform, but contains small undulations and protuberances known as dermal papillae extending from the dermis layer up into the overlying epidermis. Meissner's corpuscles are located within about every fourth papilla near the surface of the skin (Freinkel and Woodley, 2001). The highest densities of Meissner's corpuscles are found in glabrous skin most sensitive to touch—notably that of the fingers, palms, and soles of our feet (Johansson and Vallbo, 1979; McCarthy et al., 1995; Dillon et al., 2001; Kelly et al., 2005).

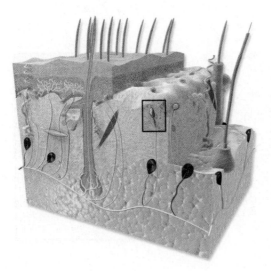 

Figure 9.7 Meissner corpuscles are rapidly adapting receptors found close to the surface of the skin, are sensitive to fine textures and slippage, and respond maximally to mid-range frequencies (20–50 Hz). *Credit: Illustration by BruceBlaus via Wikimedia under a CC 3.0 license*

Response Characteristics

Meissner corpuscles are rapidly adapting (RA) and respond to the onset and removal of the mechanical stimulus. They are particularly efficient in transducing information when textured objects are moved across the skin (Purves et al., 2001; Burgess, 2012), the slippage of objects (Barker and Cicchetti, 2012), as well as shape changes in exploratory and discriminatory touch (Mancall and Brock, 2011). Meissner corpuscles respond maximally to mid-range frequencies (20–50 Hz) (Gilman, 2002) such as might be produced from a smooth cotton shirt (Klein and Thorne, 2006).

Pacinian Corpuscles

A Pacinian corpuscle (alternatively known as a Lamellar corpuscle) is characterized by an oval-shaped geometry and is composed of several dozen concentric lamellae (thin layers) made of fibrous connective tissue separated by layers of fluid. The entire corpuscle is encased on the outside by collagen. At the center of the corpuscle is a cavity containing one or more afferent nerve fibers (Purves et al., 2001).

When physical pressure from an external force acts on the corpuscle and causes a deformation of the structure, the nerve fiber at the center is also bent or stretched, opening ion channels (chemical gates) into the outer membrane and allowing the influx of sodium ions. The greater the external force, the greater the deformation of the corpuscle and the larger the influx of sodium ions, resulting in the generation of an action potential within the afferent nerve fiber that is forwarded to the central nervous system.

The largest of the four major types of mechanoreceptors, Pacinian corpuscles are also the fewest in number (Kandel, 2000). As shown in Figure 9.8, Pacinian corpuscles are located deep in the dermis layer of the skin and even within the subcutaneous fat.

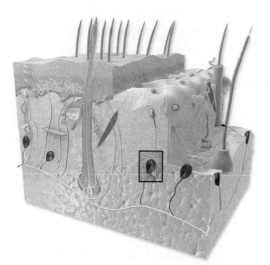 

Figure 9.8 Pacinian corpuscles are rapidly adapting and found deep within the skin; they are sensitive to deep, unsustained pressure and high-frequency vibrations (200–300 Hz range).
Credit: Illustration by BruceBlaus via Wikimedia under a CC 3.0 license

Response Characteristics

Pacinian corpuscles, like Meissner corpuscles, are rapidly adapting (RA) and respond to the onset and removal of the mechanical stimulus. They are most sensitive to deep pressure—such as from a poke—but not sustained pressure. They also respond well to high-frequency vibrations applied to the skin in the 200–300 Hz range (Bear et al., 2007, p 391; Gilman, 2002), although the source is poorly localized due to the size of the receptive field (Noback et al., 2005). Pacinian corpuscles are so sensitive that they have been shown to actually be able to detect sound waves when water is the coupling agent (Ide et al., 1987).

Ruffini Ending

A Ruffini ending (alternatively known as a Ruffini corpuscle) is characterized by a spindle-shaped geometry with complex, tree-like ends (dendritic, from the Greek *déndron*). The structure contains a dense entanglement of nerve endings encapsulated in collagen connective tissue.

As shown in Figure 9.9, Ruffini endings are located deep in the dermis layer of the skin. Found at their highest densities in the folds of the palm, over the joints, and along the edges of fingernails, when the skin is stretched, collagen fibers enclosed in the spindle-shaped capsule compress the nerve endings, resulting in the release of action potentials (Gardner, 2010).

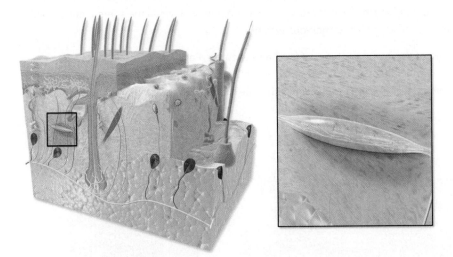

Figure 9.9 Ruffini endings are very slow adapting and sensitive to sustained pressure, skin stretch, and slippage, and they respond to high frequencies (300–400 Hz).
Credit: Illustration by BruceBlaus via Wikimedia under a CC 3.0 license

Response Characteristics

Ruffini ending are slow adapting (SA), sensitive to sustained pressure, skin stretch, and slippage, and contribute to the control of finger position and movement (Barrett and Ganong, 2012; Mountcastle, 2005). Ruffini endings respond maximally to high frequencies (300–400 Hz) and show very little adaptation (Guyton and Hall, 2001).

Mechanoreceptor Performance Summary

Based upon the descriptions provided, Table 9.1 and Figure 9.10 summarize the performance characteristics of the four major mechanoreceptors.

Table 9.1   Summary of Primary Mechanoreceptor Characteristics

Receptor Name	Receptor Field Size	Adaptation Speed	Response Stimuli	Sensitivity Range
Merkel	Small (2–3 mm)	SA	Touch, Vibration	Low (5–15 Hz)
Meissner	Small (3–4 mm)	RA	Touch, Pressure, Slippage	Low (30–50 Hz)
Ruffini	Large (10–15 mm)	SA	Pressure, Stretch, Slippage	High (3–400 Hz)
Pacinian	Large (>20 mm)	RA	Pressure, Vibration	High (2–300 Hz)

Rapidly Adapting

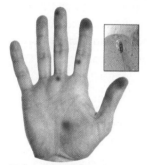

Meissner's Corpuscles

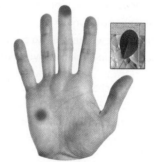

Pancinian Corpuscles

Slow Adapting

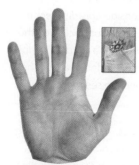

Merkel Disks

Ruffini Endings

Figure 9.10 Based on type, mechanoreceptors in the skin of the palm and fingers vary by distribution and receptive field size.

Credit: Receptor illustrations by BruceBlaus via Wikimedia under a CC 3.0 license., Hand image by ratru © 123RF. com, Derivative work—S. Aukstakalnis

Thus far we have explored the physiology and basic function of the sensors responsible for generating cutaneous tactile sensations. As our fingers explore an object, this information helps our brain understand subtle details about the physical features in our surroundings.

In this next section we will briefly explore the physiology and basic function of an equally important set of sensors responsible for our *kinesthetic* sense, which helps us perceive joint angles, as well as tension and other forces experienced in our muscles and tendons. An example of the relevance to the subject matter of this book can be found in the resistance and rumbling (known as *force feedback*) experienced using a quality gaming steering wheel.

Kinesthetic Sensing

Kinesthesia is the sense that permits us to detect bodily position, weight, and movement in our muscles, tendons, and joints. In short, it is the sense of body awareness. A part of the somatic sensory system described at the beginning of this chapter, *kinesthesia* is a sense we use nonstop without conscious thought. It helps us decide if we will turn sideways (and by how much) when passing someone in a doorway and whether we will fit in the middle seat on a plane flight. It will cue our brain if we are walking off the edge of a step (due to angles in our ankle, knee, and hip) and even help to plant a layup during a game of basketball.

An understanding of this sensory channel is useful because, in addition to the increasing research and development efforts in the area of tactile and force feedback devices discussed in Chapter 10, "Tactile and Force Feedback Devices" (primarily *output* devices), there is experimentation with systems that measure a user's physical *exertion* as a form of input (Ponto et al., 2012).

Proprioceptors

A key aspect of our kinesthetic sense (the adjective form of kinesthesia) is what is known as *proprioception*, which is the unconscious sense of movement, the related strength of effort, and relative positions of neighboring parts of the body (Mosby's, 1994). Considerably different from mechanoreception, where external stimuli trigger a neural response, with proprioception the body itself is acting as a stimulus to its own receptors (Sherrington, 1906). As a simple example, even with your eyes closed, you know if your arms are at your sides or extended over your head, if your fingers are spread apart, or if you knees are bent. There is no need to see them or think about them. You just "know."

When you move your body, be it shifting in your chair, crossing your legs, walking, or reaching for an object, everything begins with nerve impulses from the central nervous system triggering the process. During these movements, tissues in the joints change shape, including skin, muscles, tendons, and ligaments (Adrian, 1929; Grigg, 1994). In turn, various nerves and receptors within these tissues begin firing.

Research suggests that the signals provided by two unique sensory nerves—muscle spindles and Golgi tendon organs—are key to our proprioceptive sense (Proske and Gandevia, 2009, 2012).

Muscle Spindles

Muscle spindles are small, elongated sensory organs enclosed within a capsule and are found in nearly all skeletal muscles of the human body (Purves et al., 2001). As is obvious from Figure 9.11, a muscle spindle derives its name from actual geometry and structure. The concentration of spindles varies depending on specific muscle function, with higher counts found in muscles involved with delicate movements (Taylor, 2006).

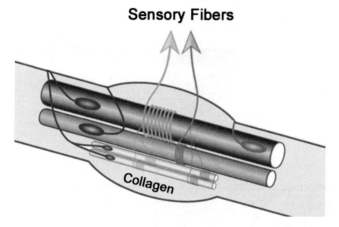

Figure 9.11 A muscle spindle is a proprioceptor located deep within and oriented parallel to extrafusal muscle fibers.
Credit: Image courtesy of N. Stifani, distributed under a CC 4.0 license, Derivative work—S. Aukstakalnis

Similar to Meissner and Pacinian corpuscles, the main body of a muscle spindle is composed of a capsule of collagen. Within this capsule and oriented parallel to the regular muscle fibers are specialized *intrafusal* muscle fibers, around which is wound an afferent nerve ending (dendrite) known as an *annulospiral ending*.

When regular muscle fibers stretch, tension in the intrafusal fibers increases, opening ion gates and stimulating the annulospiral nerve ending. This results in the generation of an action potential. The greater the tension, the greater the frequency of impulses fired off. These impulses quickly reach the central nervous system, and a return signal is sent to control the extent to which the muscle is allowed to stretch and, in doing so, prevent damage (Prochazka, 1980; Sherwood, 2015).

Golgi Tendon Organs

Unlike muscle spindles, which measure stretch, another sensory receptor, the Golgi tendon organ, measures tension in tendons (the tough, fibrous material connecting muscles to bone). When you lift an object, be it a baseball or heavy weight, or a limb is acted on by an external force, Golgi tendon organs tell you how much tension is being exerted by the muscle. From the viewpoint of a force feedback device such as those discussed in Chapter 10, Golgi tendon organs are the sensors that tell you how much force is being imparted to your hand or other limbs.

Muscle spindles are located within actual muscle fibers, as shown in Figure 9.12, but Golgi receptors are located in the tendons that attach a muscle to a bone. The core of a Golgi receptor consists of collagen fibers running parallel to the direction of normal muscle fibers. Interwoven into the collagen fibers are afferent nerve fibers. When a muscle stretches, tension is produced within the tendon. In turn, this tension results in the collagen fibers being pulled tight, stimulating the afferent nerve. Variation in the tension of the collagen fibers results in a variable firing rate of the nerve. These signals, in turn, enable physical output to be modulated (Grey et al., 2007; Mileusnic and Loeb, 2006).

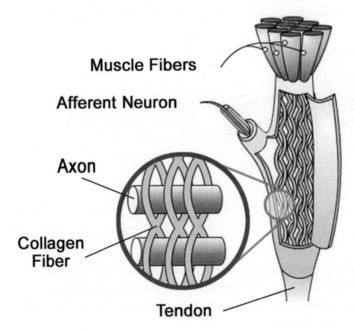

Figure 9.12 Golgi tendon organs consist of sensory nerve endings interwoven among collagen fibers. When tension in the tendon increases due to muscle stretching, the collagen fibers stimulate the nerves. *Credit: Derivative work based on public domain image courtesy of Neuromechanics via Wikimedia*

Conclusion

In this chapter we have explored the primary mechanisms enabling our sense of touch, from the sensors responsible for generating cutaneous tactile sensations that help our brain understand subtle details about the physical features of objects and our surroundings, to those enabling us to perceive stronger mechanical forces acting on our body. In Chapter 10 we will explore a range of technologies and devices leveraging these processes and mechanisms enabling more intuitive man-machine interfaces.

CHAPTER 10

TACTILE AND FORCE FEEDBACK DEVICES

Although visual and audio displays garner the most attention in virtual and augmented reality applications, the number of interfaces harnessing the strengths of our tactile and kinesthetic senses has grown steadily in the past several years. Significant technological challenges remain, however. In this chapter we will explore a number of these devices, highlighting the underlying technologies used, their range of performance in simulating actual tactile and kinesthetic cues, and the obstacles facing developers attempting to leverage the power of this incredible sense.

Haptic Illusions

Of the three primary senses typically addressed with the advanced human-computer interface technologies covered in this book, two of these channels, sight and hearing, have received the greatest amount of development emphasis. This is due, in part, to the sheer information bandwidth and broad reliance on the two channels in real life, the fact that technological barriers such as the need for higher resolution displays and low-latency sensors are principally being addressed in other more advanced markets, as well as overall need. In comparison, significantly less commercial development has taken place with technologies leveraging our sense of touch.

As we learned in Chapter 9, "The Mechanics of Feeling," our somatic sensory system has two major subsystems contributing to our overall sense of touch. The first, our *tactile* sense, is responsible for our ability to detect and perceive mechanical stimuli such as external pressure, vibration, flutter, textures, and skin stretching. The second, our *kinesthetic* sense, enables us to detect tension and other forces exerted in our muscles and tendons. Just as each is highly specialized in the various types of mechanical stimulation it is able to detect, each also requires highly specialized technologies to artificially produce the range of mechanical stimuli necessary to harness our sense of touch in a manner useful to within virtual reality/augmented reality (VR/AR) applications.

To this end, the enabling technology examples shown in this chapter are divided into two broad categories: those providing predominantly tactile feedback and those providing force (kinesthetic) feedback. As with other chapters covering enabling technologies within this book, it is important to stress that the solutions presented here are by no means a comprehensive list and represent only a fraction of the dozens of development projects underway in government, university, and corporate research labs spread out around the world.

Tactile Feedback Devices

It is reasonable to assume that all individuals reading this book have experienced the sensation of a mobile device buzzing in their hand or the grinding vibrations of any of dozens of different video game controllers and input devices. These sensations are most often produced by a class of mechanical actuators referred to as *eccentric rotating mass* (ERM) vibration motors. As shown in Figure 10.1, an ERM is a miniature DC motor with an off-center, or eccentric, mass attached to the shaft. When the shaft rotates (typically at very high speeds), the eccentric mass creates a *centripetal* force perpendicular to the axis of rotation of the drive shaft. This force is transferred to the object or component to which the motor is attached, resulting in vibrations.

Simple in design and highly effective, the speed, and thus centripetal force and frequency of the vibration, can be easily controlled by varying the voltage applied to the motor. Eccentric rotating mass motors are available in a variety of sizes and vibrational force levels to support the creation of a range of tactile sensations.

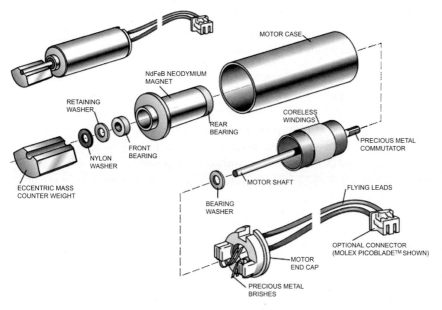

Figure 10.1 This is an exploded view of an eccentric rotating mass vibration motor.

Credit: Image courtesy of Precision Microdrives Haptic Motors: www.PrecisionMicrodrives.com

The continual push to pack more components and capability into mobile computing platforms and input devices has contributed to the development of a related type of ERM motor referred to as a *pancake vibrator motor*. As shown in Figure 10.2, pancake motors function under the same general principle as other ERMs; an eccentric mass disk is rotated inside of a thin, enclosed housing, creating a centripetal force that is transferred to the object or component to which the motor is attached, resulting in vibrations (Precision, 2015).

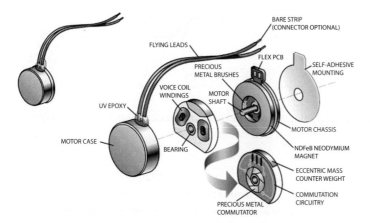

Figure 10.2 This is an exploded view of a Pancake Vibrator Motor, a variant of an Eccentric Rotating Mass vibration motor.

Credit: Image courtesy of Precision Microdrives Haptic Motors: www.PrecisionMicrodrives.com

Depending on the application, pancake vibrator motors have several advantages, the most obvious of which are the compact size as well as no external moving parts, thus enabling more efficient use of space within tightly packed component designs.

Another class of actuator used in the generation of vibrotactile cues is known as a linear resonant actuator (LRA) vibration motor. As shown in Figure 10.3, a magnetic mass is situated between a spring and a voice coil. When current is applied to the coil, the magnetic mass is forced back against the spring along a single axis. Changing the current direction through the coil results in movement in the opposite direction (obviously making this an AC device, as opposed to ERMs, which are DC). Similar to the pancake vibrator motors, LRAs are compact in size and have no external moving parts, making their application ideal within devices of a small form factor intended to generate tactile cues.

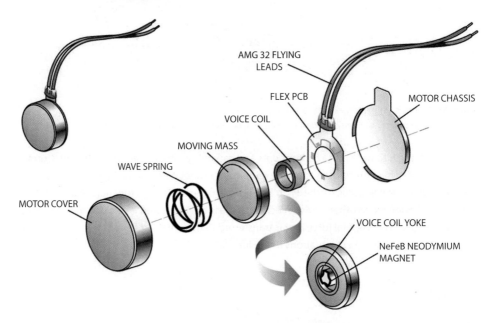

Figure 10.3 This is an exploded view of a linear resonant actuator vibration motor.
Credit: Image courtesy of Precision Microdrives Haptic Motors: www.PrecisionMicrodrives.com

Varying combinations of eccentric rotating mass and linear resonant actuator vibration motors can be found in the next two devices described in this section.

Gloveone

One of the most promising mass market tactile feedback-enabled input devices developed to date is the **Gloveone** interface by NeuroDigital Technologies of Almería, Spain. Several years in development, the lightweight glove is laden with sensors and vibrotactile actuators to provide detailed tactile sensations resulting from interaction with virtual objects seen on a computer screen or within a head-mounted display. As shown in Figure 10.4, Gloveone's components can be separated into the following subsystems:

- **Actuators**—Gloveone contains 10 miniature LRAs, one in each fingertip and five arrayed across the palm.

- **IMU Sensors**—(6)3-axis IMUs track flexion, extension, and sideways movement of the fingers. Whole-hand orientation is tracked with (1) 9-axis IMU located within the controller.

- **Conductive Fabric**—A conductive knit fabric is used in the tips of the thumb, index, and middle fingers, as well as in the palm near the crotch of the thumb, to enable gestural triggering of commands (pinch, fist, and so on).

- **Controller**—Mounted on the back of the hand, the master controller contains the device's motherboard, Bluetooth 4.0 sensor, IMU, USB port, power button, and Li-Po battery.

Figure 10.4 The GloveOne interface by NeuroDigital Technologies uses 10 individual actuators arrayed across the fingertips and palm to create compelling tactile sensations.
Credit: Image courtesy of Neurodigital Technologies

Each of the 10 vibrotactile actuators is capable of 1024 different intensities and frequencies, providing a broad capacity (10 × 1024 individual settings or combinations) for the creation of tactile sensations. As of the time of this writing, although IMUs are used to track finger movements and rotation of the hand, tracking the position (X, Y, and Z) of the device, and thus, the user's hand, is accomplished using a third-party device such as a Leap Motion Controller, Intel RealSense, and Microsoft Kinect. According to the manufacturer, this is due, in part, to a desire to limit onboard sensor latency currently in the 10–15 millisecond range.

The GloveOne Manager software utility provides overall control of the device and allows for extensive development and testing. Screenshots from this utility are shown in Figure 10.5.

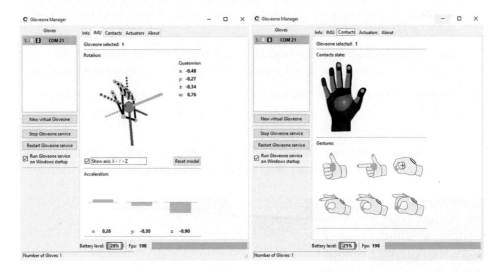

Figure 10.5 These screenshots from the GloveOne Manager software utility show the device in actuator setup and testing mode.
Credit: Image courtesy of Neurodigital Technologies

This device was initially targeted toward the gaming and entertainment markets, but other applications are already underway. For instance, in late 2015 it was announced that NeuroDigital Technologies had partnered with King's College London to jointly develop a Laparoscopy Virtual Trainer that would make use of the GloveOne device within the simulation procedure (Cuthbertson, 2015).

TeslaSuit

The use of electrical impulses on bodily surfaces to transmit tactile information is generally referred to as *electrotactile* or *electrocutaneous* stimulation (Bobich et al., 2007; Kajimoto et al., 2004; Kaczmarek and Haase, 2003; Kaczmarek et al., 2000; Menia and Van Doren, 1994; Higashiyama and Rollman, 1991; Tashiro and Higashiyama, 1981). Although these techniques have been investigated for decades, most efforts have focused on applications related to sensory substitution (using the function or output of one sense as the stimuli for another sense), advancing the functionality and usability of prosthetics, as well as telerobotics (Danilov et al., 2008; Tang and Beebe, 2006; Monkman et al., 2003).

Electrotactile stimulation is closely related to *neuromuscular* stimulation, a therapeutic treatment widely used in medicine and professional sports within which electrical impulses are used to stimulate select muscle groups (Doucet et al., 2012; Sheffler and Chae, 2007; Lake, 1992). The technology has been employed in a variety of other application areas as well, including orientation, navigation, intra-cockpit communications, and vestibular substitution (Van Erp and Self, 2008; Danilov, 2008; Zlotnik, 1988).

To date, few electrotactile or neuromuscular capabilities have been effectively employed within the entertainment industry, and fewer still as an enabling technology within virtual and augmented reality systems. This is due, in part, to the technological challenges of miniaturization, prohibitive costs, and a limited understanding of several relevant physiological factors, such as the differences between the size and functionality of the electrotactile versus mechanoreceptive fields, along with their respective variations across different parts of the body. But one by one, these and other barriers are being addressed and, in turn, allowing promising headway to be made in advancing the state of the art in tactile interface design.

One example of a system employing such advances is the **TeslaSuit DK1** shown in Figure 10.6, developed by Tesla Studios of Saint Andrews, Scotland.

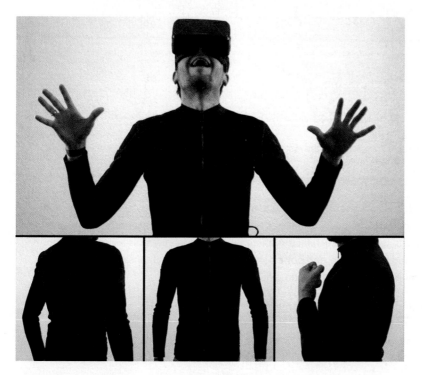

Figure 10.6 The full body TeslaSuit DK1 is modular and includes a vest, trousers, belt (with a central control unit), and gloves. The full system currently incorporates 60 electrotactile stimulation points.
Credit: Image courtesy of Tesla Studios

As discussed within Chapter 9, the human skin is heavily populated with a complex network of specialized cutaneous tactile receptors. When mechanically excited, these receptors send small electrical impulses along afferent nerve fibers to the central nervous system. As shown in Figure 10.7, the TeslaSuit DK1 stimulates these same afferent nerve fibers using miniature electrodes embedded into the fabric of the garment that provide minute, controlled, painless electrical impulses to a user's skin across dozens of strategically selected points.

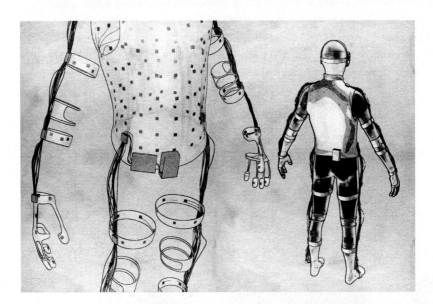

Figure 10.7 This illustration shows the distribution of electrotactile stimulation points within the TeslaSuit DK1.
Credit: Image courtesy of Tesla Studios

A software suite the manufacturer refers to as a *tactile editor* is used to control the encoding of the impulse patterns, enabling users to customize their own tactile sensations for various application needs. By varying such factors as stimulation frequency, pulse width/duration, intensity/amplitude, ramp time, and pulse pattern, a wide variety of sensations can be produced simulating actual physical stimulation.

The full-body TeslaSuit is composed of multiple components, including a jacket, trousers, belt, and gloves. At present, the full suit incorporates 60 individual stimulation points. A high-performance micro-controller located in the belt communicates with other suit components via a Bluetooth 4LE (low-energy) connection.

The Tesla Suit DK1 also incorporates multiple 9-axis IMU sensors (see Chapter 11, "Sensors for Tracking Position, Orientation, and Motion") to accommodate motion capture needs.

Haptic Audio and Tactile Sound Transducers

The tactile and kinesthetic receptors discussed in Chapter 9 can also be stimulated with sound. For instance, most would agree that a cinematic movie experience is a much more engaging and immersive experience when sound effects generate tactile sensations, such as the low rumble of a plane, the thumping of an approaching helicopter, or an explosion, seemingly causing the floor and seats to vibrate. In fact, there is a whole class of highly specialized electromechanical devices that are specifically designed to take what normal speakers would produce as low-frequency sounds and instead produce vibrations. Designed to drive large surfaces as opposed to speaker skins, these devices, known as tactile sound transducers or bass shakers, are used extensively in military simulation applications, in the floors of nightclubs, as well as in amusement parks such as Disney and Universal Studios.

Given the dramatic resurgence of interest in virtual and augmented reality over the past several years, a number of these devices have found a new application niche within the gaming and entertainment sector.

The SubPac

Originally designed for use by sound engineers and DJs who need to physically experience the full range of their audio productions, such as the deep thumping bass lines of a new music track or the special sound effects being added to a movie, the **SubPac S2** (studio) shown in Figure 10.8 is a tactile sound transducer you strap to your chair. With a frequency response range between 5 and 130 Hz (remember from Chapter 7, "The Mechanics of Hearing," that the low end of human hearing is in the 20 Hz range), the SubPac contains a set of transducers that transfer the low-frequency vibrations to your body, allowing the user to, quite literally, "feel" the sound.

For the dedicated gamer or VR enthusiast, the SubPac continually receives impressive reviews for its ability to add highly compelling tactile sensations and depth to low-frequency sound effects. Unlike standard sub-woofers that would shake your walls, the SubPac itself is relatively quiet. Again, you don't actually hear the sound through this device. You feel it.

SUBPAC M2
(Wearable)

SUBPAC S2
(Seatback)

Figure 10.8 SubPac S2 is one of the most powerful and accurate seated tactile bass solutions available. The SubPac M2 incorporates the same proprietary tactile transducers in a wearable version. *Credit: Image courtesy of Marwan Balaïd/http://mar-one.tumblr.com/*

The SubPac's soft, neoprene exterior and well-designed ergonomic shape provide maximum contact with the user's back. The SubPac is secured to a chair with a three-point strapping system. A small control unit can accept audio input via a standard 3.5 mm stereo jack or via Bluetooth 4.0 with A2DP Streaming. An output jack is also provided for headphones.

For those applications requiring a mobile solution, SubPac produces a wearable version known as the M2 (mobile) offering the same range of performance and features.

The Woojer

Another tactile sound transducer gaining considerable popularity within the gaming side of the virtual and augmented reality community is the **Woojer**, a wearable mobile accessory produced by Tel Aviv, Israel-based Woojer, Ltd. As shown in Figure 10.9, the Woojer is a silent, wearable polyphonic (producing many sounds simultaneously) transducer just slightly larger than a matchbox that is placed in direct contact with the user's chest using an elastic strap, attached to a shirt with a magnet, or clipped to a belt.

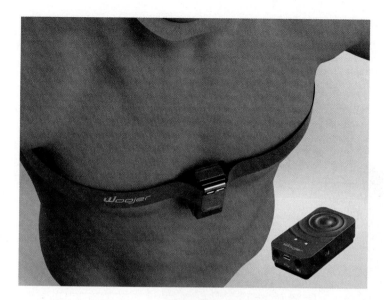

Figure 10.9 The Woojer is a wearable tactile device that uses a patented polyphonic transducer to transfer rich, emotional infrasonic bass tones into the body, enabling the user to feel the sensation of sound.
Credit: Image courtesy of Woojer—Born to FEEL

According to the manufacturer, the Woojer relies upon *perceptual inference*, which refers to the ability of the human brain to infer sensory stimuli from predictions that result from internal neural representations built through prior experience (Woojer, 2013; Aggelopoulos, 2015).

A highly unique feature of the product is the fact that there is no software or algorithm use in the generation of the polyphonic vibrations. This means there is minimal latency (~1 ms) between when the signal from the audio input is received and when corresponding vibrations are produced, eliminating the decoupling of what the ears hear and what the body feels.

Specifications for Woojer 1.0 include a frequency response range between 0 and 500 Hz, a 3-position vibration-level control switch, a rechargeable lithium-ion battery, a Micro USB charger port, a green/red LED to indicate on/off and overdrive, a blue LED that flashes in sync with vibrations, as well as twin 3.5 mm analog audio ports (one for player, one for headphones). Woojer 2.0 is slightly smaller and is Bluetooth 4.0 enabled to eliminate cabling.

Clark Synthesis Full Contact Audio Tactile Sound Transducers

Another class of tactile transducers exist that are meant to be firmly attached to an object or surface such as a seat, couch, or floor. In most, the transducer houses a small weight driven by a coil or magnet to provide high-fidelity sound-motion augmentation. In the world of high-performance simulation and training, this type of tactile and kinesthetic cueing helps develop accurate psychomotor reflexes and adds richness to the training experience.

One of the leading companies producing high-performance transducers for this market is Clark Synthesis of Littleton, Colorado. As shown in Figure 10.10, the TST329 Gold Transducer, one of several models offered, is used worldwide in professional audio/video applications ranging from theaters to commercial/military vehicle simulators.

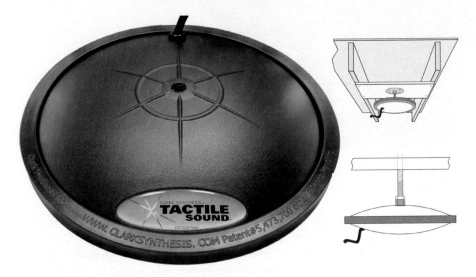

Figure 10.10 The Clark Synthesis TST329 Gold Transducer is a high-fidelity sound-motion augmentation device used in professional simulation and training applications around the world.
Credit: Image and illustrations courtesy of Clark Synthesis

This class of tactile sound transducer typically requires an amplifier for proper operation. In the case of the Clark TST329 Gold, 125–150 watts with an impedance of 4 ohms achieves the full range of performance. Measuring 8 in. in diam. by 2.25 in. in height, the frequency response of the device ranges from 10 Hz to 17 kHz.

Force Feedback Devices

Force feedback devices engage the sense of touch by applying contact forces, vibrations, or motions to the user (Robles-De-La-Torre, 2010). To provide a compelling experience and match human performance, the maximum force exerted by the device should meet or exceed the maximum force humans can produce (Raisamo and Raisamo, 2007). In this section we explore a variety of innovative force feedback solutions being integrated into augmented and virtual reality systems.

CyberGlove Systems CyberGrasp

There are myriad highly specialized industrial and defense applications requiring the ability for human operators to be able to manually interact with, and actually feel, computer-generated models or to accurately control the dexterous end effectors of robots. Such applications range from complex simulation and training scenarios in various areas of manned space flight to telerobotics applications within which the handling of hazardous materials need to be carried out at a safe distance. In such critical tasks, one of the leading devices employed worldwide is a force-reflecting exoskeleton known as the **CyberGrasp**, manufactured by CyberGlove Systems of San Jose, California.

As shown in Figure 10.11, the CyberGrasp device is a lightweight, force-reflecting exoskeleton that provides resistive force feedback to each finger via a network of tendons (cables) routed from five actuators in a desktop unit to the fingertips of the device. The maximum force the CyberGrasp is able to exert on each finger is 12 Newtons (equal to approximately 2.7 pound-force (lb_F)). In use, the CyberGrasp device imparts forces (or restrains the fingers) in a direction roughly perpendicular to the fingertips throughout their entire range of motion. The entire device is highly configurable, with each finger individually programmable.

Most uses of the CyberGrasp also require precise measurement of flexion and extension of the fingers to control a virtual character or teleoperated system. In such instances, the manufacturer is also the leading global supplier of data glove input devices, such as the CyberGlove shown in Figure 10.11. An advanced version of CyberGlove is detailed within Chapter 12, "Devices to Enable Navigation and Interaction."

Use of the CyberGrasp system is not limited to a fixed laboratory or worksite. For those applications requiring mobility of the human operator, the desktop actuator and controller can be worn in a specialized backpack designed for this specific purpose.

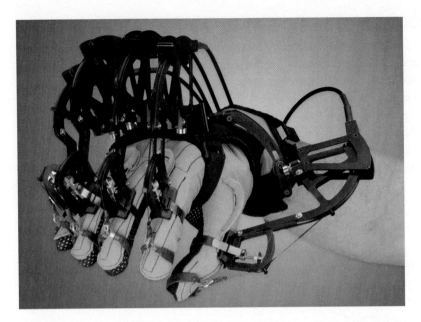

Figure 10.11 The CyberGrasp is a lightweight, force-reflecting exoskeleton that fits over a CyberGlove data glove to provide resistive force feedback to the user's fingers.
Credit: Image courtesy of CyberGlove Systems/CyberGrasp®

Geomagic Touch X Haptic Device

From model makers to surgeons, and chemists to engineers, there exist a host of application areas where individuals need to create, manipulate, sculpt, shape, or otherwise manually interact with complex 3D structures. For a surgeon, this may be practicing the cutting and shaping of a bone before carrying out the actual procedure in an operating room, a chemist attempting to dock drug molecules into a receptor site, or a mechanical engineer working with complex virtual assemblies.

For such applications, an extensive class of bidirectional, highly intuitive force feedback devices that can produce high forces at high resolutions is available to enable close manual interaction with digital models. On the smaller end, one of the most widely used is the **Touch X** desktop haptic device from Geomagic, Inc of Morrisville, North Carolina.

As shown in Figure 10.12, the Touch X is a force-reflecting robotic haptic device with a pen-like stylus. In operation, the user freely moves the stylus, where it is accurately tracked across 6 DOF resulting in precise, corresponding movement of onscreen tools. The interaction of the onscreen tool with geometric objects results in the real-time generation of lifelike, high-fidelity, low-friction force-feedback output to the stylus along each axis (x, y, and z).

Figure 10.12 The Geomagic Touch X is a desktop haptic device that applies force feedback to the user's hand, allowing one to feel virtual objects and true-to-life tactile sensations as onscreen objects are manipulated.
Credit: Image courtesy of 3D Systems

As shown in the patent illustration (#6985133) within Figure 10.13, forces are produced using actuators and cable drives to power each rotary axis. In normal operating mode, the device is capable of positional resolutions greater than 1100 dpi (.023 mm). The maximum exertable force on the stylus is 7.9 Newtons (equal to approximately 1.8 pound-force (lb_F).

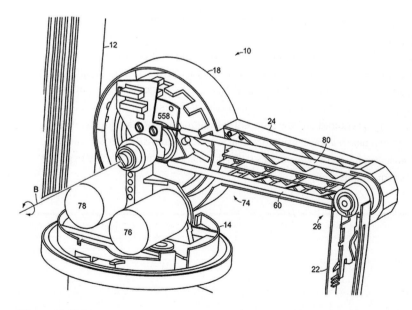

Figure 10.13 This patent illustration shows the inner workings of the Geomagic Touch X desktop haptic device.

Conclusion

As can be seen in this chapter, the implementation of tactile and force feedback capabilities within user interfaces employed in virtual and augmented reality systems, while making great strides, faces significant challenges given the very nature and complexity of this physiological information pathway and the broad range of stimuli it is able to detect. Being able to accurately and cost effectively produce stimuli such as variable pressure, flutter, textures, shearing forces, edges, and more—all in a reasonably sized device that can be held in one's hand, placed on a desktop, or worn on one's body—is an engineering and development task facing tremendous technological obstacles.

Another challenge faced in the development and production of consumer market tactile and force feedback devices, for large and small companies alike, can be found in the area of intellectual property barriers. Beginning in 2001, a number of strong, far-reaching patents were issued that locked up many of the technology avenues for imparting tactile and force feedback effects to a variety of controllers and mobile devices, essentially shelving many promising products for those companies unwilling or unable to pay licensing fees. These patents include 6,424,333; 6,275,213; 6,429,846 (including updates 7,592,999; 7,982,720; 8,031,181; 8,059,105); and 7,969,288. In fact, massive infringement lawsuits have been visited upon such companies as Microsoft, HTC, Sony, Motorola (settled by Google after acquisition), and others. But business is business, and the intellectual property holder, Immersion Corporation of San Jose, California, is entitled to licensing fees.

It is for these and other reasons that this author firmly believes the breakout enabling technology pathway to accurately harnessing the human sense of touch will be some form of neurotactile stimulation, such as that written about earlier in the overview of the TeslaSuit by Tesla Studios of Saint Andrews, Scotland. As we learned in Chapter 9, most tactile sensations are nothing more than a series of highly structured electrical impulse patterns generated by specialized receptors that are sent to processing centers of the brain. Once a greater understanding is acquired on how different sensations are encoded (does feeling the surface texture of a peach always result in similar impulse patterns?), methods can be developed to measure, catalog, and reproduce them in a manner that completely bypasses the mechanoreceptors themselves.

SENSORS FOR TRACKING POSITION, ORIENTATION, AND MOTION

From tracking the position and orientation of a display or input device to monitoring the direction and magnitude of your physical input and the commands or actions you want to trigger, virtual and augmented reality systems make extensive use of sensors. In this chapter we explore a variety of key sensor technologies, highlighting their mode of operation, and the strengths and weaknesses in each.

Introduction to Sensor Technologies

Sensors are a key enabling technology in all virtual and augmented reality systems. They are used to track a participant's location and the position and orientation of a user's head (and thus, that of a head-mounted viewing device) and hands (or any manual interface) in 3D space. Sensors tell the computing system where you are looking so it knows what scenes to draw, as well as what events to trigger as a result of interaction with a virtual environment and the objects contained therein. Sensors are absolutely critical to conveying a feeling of presence within, or interactions with, virtual spaces and their content.

In this chapter we explore a variety of sensor technologies used to track the position (X, Y, and Z) and orientation (roll, pitch, and yaw) of a user, as well as input and output devices most common to current virtual and augmented reality systems. These solutions are subdivided into categories based on optical, electromagnetic, inertial, and acoustic methods, each of which carries its own set of strengths and limitations. For instance, although some require direct tethering or mechanical connections, others require an unobstructed line of sight between a transmitter and receiver, and still others are influenced by environmental factors such as ambient noise, natural lighting, or the presence of conductive materials within the operating area. Each of the solutions also varies widely in terms of accuracy and system latency (the time interval between movement and response).

As with other chapters in this book dealing with enabling technologies, it is simply impossible to provide coverage of each commercially available solution. As such, the specific products and functional methodologies covered are intended only as representative of a particular sensor or technology category. A detailed list of suppliers for each is provided in Appendix B, "Resources" at the end of this book.

Optical Trackers

Optical tracking generally refers to a variety of techniques within which cameras are used to monitor the movement of objects. These techniques range from single and multiple camera systems that track active and passive infrared markers as a person or object moves, to single camera systems that measure the time required for a light impulse to be sent from a transmitter, bounce off an object, and arrive at a receiver, to systems that project infrared light in a known pattern and then calculate movements based on distortion of that pattern. For convenience, we will begin with multicamera systems, the most common optical solution currently employed within the virtual and augmented reality arenas.

Multicamera Optical Tracking

Multicamera optical trackers operate on the basic principle of measuring movements of a person or object arrayed with either infrared retro-reflectors (passive markers) or infrared

LEDs (active markers). Changes in position and orientation are derived using triangulation calculations. Figure 11.1 illustrates a basic multicamera implementation. Each camera is outfitted with a ring of near-infrared LEDs surrounding the lens. These LEDs illuminate the measurement area, with passive markers on the objects being tracked reflecting the light back to the cameras. The cameras typically use optical band-pass filters to eliminate the interference of ambient light of other wavelengths, making the identification of the markers a reliable process.

Figure 11.1 Objects to be tracked are equipped with retro-reflective markers that reflect the incoming IR light back to the cameras.
Credit: Images courtesy of OptiTrack

Applications that call for the tracking of an object arrayed with LEDs as opposed to reflectors operate in essentially the same manner, although it is unnecessary to provide illumination from a remote source. It is important to note that infrared trackers require a minimum of three noncollinear reflectors or LEDs to track movement across six degrees of freedom (6 DOF). This allows the processing unit to use simple triangulation techniques based on the known geometric configuration of the markers along with the fixed distance between camera units.

More immersive applications, such as those experienced in computer-assisted virtual environments (CAVEs), hemispherical, or large-format panoramic displays, require the use of additional cameras to ensure the object or person being tracked is always within view of multiple units. Figure 11.2 illustrates this concept.

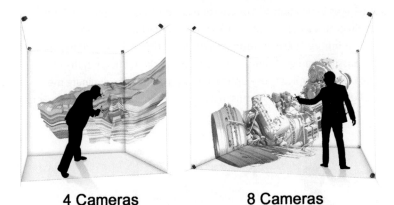

4 Cameras   **8 Cameras**

Figure 11.2 Optical tracking systems often include extra cameras to ensure that regardless of the user's physical position, multiple cameras are able to illuminate and image retro-reflective markers. *Credit: Images courtesy of OptiTrack*

Some important points to consider regarding use of this type of optical tracking solutions:

- Systems capable of tracking passive reflectors have the benefit of fewer tethers but are more expensive given the added complexity of the cameras and controllers. In many cases they also require the geometry of the markers to be fixed.

- Systems designed to track objects arrayed with infrared LEDs may be less expensive, but the LEDs must be powered. This means they are either tethered or require onboard batteries.

In general, the use of fixed cameras to track either IR LEDs or reflective markers is referred to as an **outside-in** tracking method.

The inverse, known as an **inside-out** tracking method, involves placement of infrared emitters in fixed positions around the user (such as on a computer monitor, walls, or ceiling) and then using a camera mounted on a head-mounted display to track position and orientation relative to those emitters. An innovative example of such an implementation is the Valve lighthouse tracking system described later in this chapter.

Still others forego the use of infrared illumination or LEDs altogether and instead use stick-on visible markers with a design easily recognized by the processing unit.

Finally, there is the brute force method of on-the-fly comparison of sequential images looking for changes.

Optical Sensors

Science fiction movies such as *Minority Report* and *Iron Man* have dazzled audiences with depictions of amazing computer interfaces allowing users to reach into the air and interact with holographic data, moving graphical elements around, adjusting CAD models, and so on. At the core of each was the assumption of a technology that, without gloves or worn sensors of any type, tracked the position and orientation of a user's hands in 3D space. Such technologies have now begun to emerge, and they hold significant promise within the field of virtual and augmented reality.

Leap Motion Controller

One such example is the Leap Motion Controller, a consumer-grade optical sensor developed by Leap Motion of San Francisco, California. The device is intended to enable touch-free 3D hand gesture control of computer systems with declared 1/100th millimeter accuracy and no visible latency (Leap, 2013). As shown in Figure 11.3, the Leap device consists of two cameras with wide angle lenses and three infrared LEDs. The cameras are tuned to capture infrared light at a wavelength of 850 nanometers, which is outside the visible portion of the light spectrum.

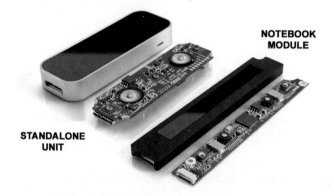

NOTEBOOK MODULE

STANDALONE UNIT

Figure 11.3 This image shows the circuit board of the standalone Leap Motion Device alongside the reduced size sensor module designed for use in the HP ENVY 17 Leap Motion SE Notebook and HP Leap Motion keyboard.
Credit: Images courtesy of Leap Motion

As shown in Figure 11.4, when placed on a desk, the interaction space above the device covers an area measuring eight cubic feet in size—approximately 2 feet above the controller, 2 feet to either side (equal to approximately a 150° angle), and 2 feet in depth (equal to approximately a 120° angle).

The limits to this operational area are determined, in part, by a basic physics principle known as the *inverse-square law*. This law states that intensity of illumination is proportional to the inverse square of the distance from the light source. In simple terms, as light travels away from the source, it spreads both horizontally and vertically. As it does, the intensity decreases. Although the total power of the infrared light waves remains the same, it is spread over an increasing area as the light moves away from the source. Beyond the ranges listed earlier, the intensity of the infrared light drops off to such a level that the cameras can no longer gather enough reflected light to reliably measure the user's hand positions.

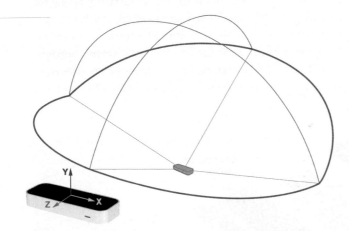

Figure 11.4 The lines in this illustration represent the effective interaction area above the Leap Motion Controller. This area measures 2 feet above the device by 2 feet on each side.
Credit: Images courtesy of Leap Motion

The operating principle behind the Leap Motion device is considerably different from that of other optical sensors described in this section. As the user's hands move through the interaction space above the device, the stereo cameras collect scene information that is streamed to the host computer. Control software then reconstructs and interprets a 3D representation of what the cameras see, including the generation of tracking data from which gestures can be recognized and used to control virtual objects.

Although initially intended as a desktop interface, soon after the initial release, developers began experimenting with the software pathways necessary to enable the use of the Leap Motion sensor data as a natural input mechanism for immersive virtual reality applications.

As shown in Figure 11.5, mounted on the front of a head-mounted display such as those available from Oculus, HTC, and OSVR, the scene taken in by the stereo cameras easily encompasses the user's lower arms and hands.

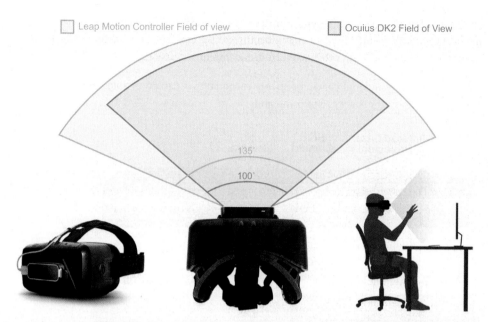

Figure 11.5 The center image shows a field of view (FOV) comparison between the Leap Motion Controller and the Oculus Rift. Because the Leap's FOV is wider than the Rift's, hand movements can be tracked even if outside of the user's visual field.
Credit: Images courtesy of Leap Motion

To predict the positions of fingers and hands not clearly in the view of the system cameras, the Leap Motion application programming interface (API) provides extensive utilities that enable accurate hand and finger tracking. The API allows developers to extract position and measurement data of the bones in the hand, including joint positions and bone lengths. This capability is at the core of enabling virtual hands to interact with virtual objects.

Microsoft Kinect

Another powerful series of optical tracking technologies serve at the heart of the Kinect line of motion sensing input devices by Microsoft. Initially intended for gesture recognition and motion tracking with Xbox video game consoles, additional versions of the hardware have been released for use with Windows PCs as well as custom systems.

Early versions of the Kinect sensor used a multistage process to infer body position. As shown in Figure 11.6, the system consists of an infrared laser projector as well as RGB and infrared Complementary Metal-Oxide Semiconductor (CMOS) cameras. Using a technique known as *structured light*, a depth map is constructed by analyzing a spatially encoded speckle pattern of infrared light projected onto the scene. In front of the infrared projector is a specialized *astigmatic* lens that provides a different focal length on two different perpendicular planes, resulting in the vertical and horizontal components of the projected image to be in focus at different distances. Thus, circular dots of light would be projected and focused as ellipses, the orientation of which would depend on the depth from the lens. The scene gathered by the IR camera is then analyzed, a depth map created, and motion monitored.

A microphone array and multilanguage speech recognition capability enables control of the main computing system using voice commands.

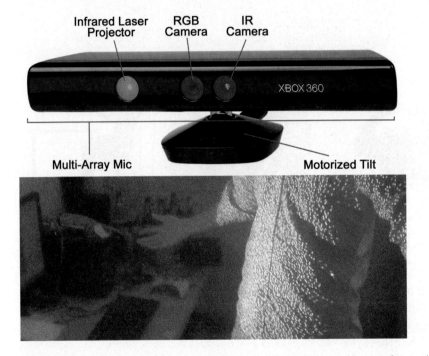

Figure 11.6 This image shows the early version of the Kinect device and its use of a speckle structured light pattern to create a depth map and monitor motion.
Credit: Kinect device image by James Pfaff, dot pattern image by Jeff Warren, both via Flickr under CC 2.0 licenses

More recent versions of the device, such as Kinect for Windows, come at the tracking challenge from a completely different angle. As opposed to analyzing dot patterns and their geometry, newer sensors employ what is known as a *time-of-flight* technology. In a simple explanation, this sensor measures the time it takes for photons of light to travel from a laser projector, reflect off a target surface, and then back to an image sensor.

As shown in Figure 11.7, the new technology system uses *active infrared imaging* (direct infrared scene illumination), which results in the generation of depth maps containing significantly greater scene detail, enabling the ability to recognize facial features, hand and finger positions, and even the individual folds, wrinkles, and waves of clothing.

RGB   IR   Infrared
Camera   Camera   Blasters

Multi-Array Mic

Figure 11.7 This image shows a more recent version of the Kinect device and its use of an active infrared imaging and time-of-flight technology to create a depth map with considerably more detail. *Credit: Kinect device image by BagoGames, scan image by Kyle McDonald, both via Flickr under CC 2.0 licenses*

The release of a software developer's toolkit has enabled the integration of the Kinect device into a number of intriguing immersive applications, including AltspaceVR, an online virtual reality social, chat, and gaming community.

> **note**
>
> **PHOTOSENSITIVE SEIZURE WARNING**   It is important to point out that early versions of this product come with a photosensitive seizure warning. According to the Epilepsy Foundation, for about 3 percent of individuals with epilepsy, exposure to flashing lights or certain visual patterns can trigger seizures. The condition is known as photosensitive epilepsy and is more common in children and adolescents, especially those with generalized epilepsy, and a type known as juvenile myoclonic epilepsy (Shafer and Sirven, 2013).

Beacon Trackers

Beacon tracking is a new method for monitoring position and orientation within which infrared emitters are placed at strategic positions around the user. Infrared sensors mounted on an object are then used to track position and orientation relative to the fixed infrared emitters. Developed by Valve Corporation of Bellevue, Washington, this tracking method is used by the HTC Vive virtual reality system.

As shown in Figure 11.8, this implementation consists of two "Lighthouse" base stations mounted at elevated positions in opposing corners of a room. Each base station consists of an infrared beacon that emits a synchronization pulse, as well as two flywheels upon which infrared lasers are reflected to produce vertical and horizontal lines that sequentially sweep the tracking volume. The combination of the synchronization pulse as well as sweeps of the lasers allow sensors on the Vive headset and hand controllers to be used to detect their position and orientation relative to the base stations.

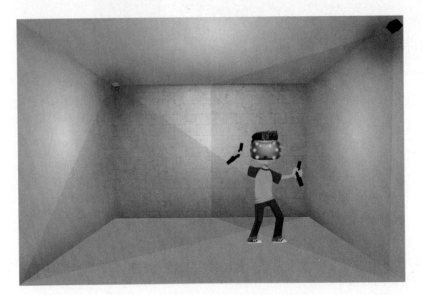

Figure 11.8 The Lighthouse tracking system used with the HTC Vive system employs sensors in the headset and controllers to detect infrared laser sweeps and flashes from wall-mounted emitters.
Credit: Room image and character by stryjekk, subarashii21 © 123RF.com—Derivative work—S. Auksakalnis

Electromagnetic Trackers

Electromagnetic tracking systems have played a key role in virtual reality systems for more than two decades. One of the earliest entrants in the field and still a major workhorse solution for some of the most demanding mission-critical applications is the FASTRAK system developed by Polhemus, Inc of Colchester, Vermont.

The general operating principle behind magnetic tracking systems is rather simple. As shown in Figure 11.9, the transmitter is a small stationary cube that contains three coils of wire mounted at right angles to each other. When electrical current is sequentially pulsed to the three coils, three dipole magnetic fields are produced, each of which is orthogonally oriented with the others.

The sensor itself is of the same general design as the transmitter, although it's considerably smaller in size. As the object upon which the sensor is mounted moves through the three magnetic fields, electrical currents are produced in the three coils that are proportional to the flux of the magnetic field. These signals are sent via a tether or wireless connection to a controller where the receiver's position and orientation relative to the transmitter are calculated.

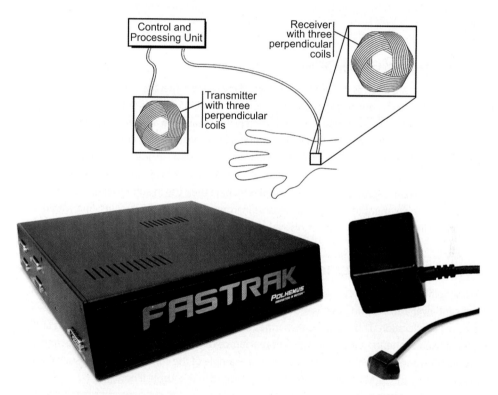

Figure 11.9 This figure illustrates the orthogonal winding of coils within the transmitter and receiver of the Polhemus FASTRAK electromagnetic tracker.
Credit: Image courtesy of www.polhemus.com

The FASTRAK system provides a position update rate of 120 Hz (divided by the number of sensors) with a latency of approximately 4 milliseconds. The standard operational range for the device is 4 to 6 feet, although this can be extended to 10 feet with system add-ons. Measurement accuracy is 0.03 inches RMS for the X, Y, or Z position and 0.15° RMS for receiver orientation.

There are two general varieties of magnetic position sensing devices available on the market: those generating magnetic fields using AC current and those using DC current, although AC solutions tend to dominate the virtual reality arena. AC systems provide precision measurement capabilities at greater operational ranges as well as low signal-to-noise ratio, meaning multiple units can be used in the same general space with minimal crosstalk.

Like all other tracking solutions in this chapter, there are limitations and implementation challenges. Perhaps the most well known is the impact of the conductive materials within the operating range of the device. As the AC current used to generate the magnetic field fluctuates, eddy currents can be created in conductive materials, resulting in distortions to the magnetic fields and the degraded performance of the system. A number of corrective solutions, including adaptive filtering, have been developed to mitigate the effect.

Inertial Sensors

Inertial sensors are devices that measure forces. Many modern inertial sensors, and in particular, those within general consumer goods, are a category of MEMS devices (Micro-Electro-Mechanical System). They combine accelerometers (for measuring acceleration), gyroscopes (for measuring angular velocity) and magnetometers (for measuring orientation relative to the earth's magnetic field—that is, a compass). Manufactured using fabrication techniques and materials common to all micro-electronics, inertial sensors are now found in a wide variety of goods and systems. Some application examples include their use in automobiles (to detect impacts for deployment of airbags), tilt sensors in irons and gaming controllers, and within mobile devices to reorient onscreen displays.

How Inertial Sensors Function

In a simplified explanation, the central element in a MEMS inertial sensor is a *proof mass* such as a cantilever arm or spring that is moved from its neutral position under the influence of external acceleration. This movement changes the capacitance between the proof mass and a set of fixed elements. It is this change in capacitance that is measured and used to quantify acceleration and rotation. Figure 11.10 shows an example of the complexity of one such MIMS inertial sensor, the ST Micro three-axis gyroscope found in the Apple iPhone 4.

Over the past decade, inertial sensors have advanced to such an extent that developers in the virtual and augmented reality arenas have naturally gravitated toward their use due to the multiple benefits they offer, including small size, low cost, high update rates, and low latency. Used standalone, as well as in combination with other sensor technologies (otherwise referred to as *hybrid systems*), inertial sensors are beginning to have a significant impact on the overall performance, size, and applicability of the core enabling technologies of this field.

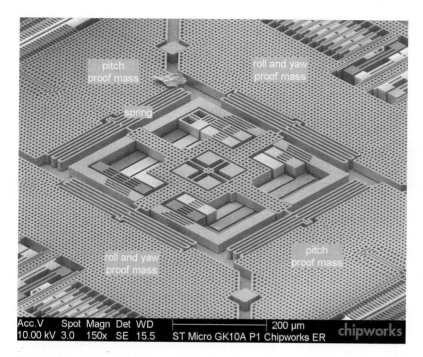

Figure 11.10 This image shows a detailed view of the iPhone 4s 3-axis gyro. The multilevel MEMS structures are clearly visible.

Credit: Photo courtesy of Chipworks, Inc

Integration Example

An ideal example is the use of an inertial sensor within the Google Glass display. (See Chapter 5, "Augmenting Displays.") Hidden deep within the compact electronics design is a small chip known as the InvenSense MPU-9150 shown in Figure 11.11. This inertial sensor is the world's first 9-axis motion-tracking MEMS device and contains a 3-axis gyroscope, 3-axis accelerometer, and 3-axis digital compass. Similar inertial sensors can be found in the R7 Smart Glasses augmenting display manufactured by Osterhut Design Group of San Francisco, California.

A number of other input devices covered within this book incorporate MEMS inertial sensors, and this field is still in its commercial infancy. Readers can expect to see such technologies increasingly at the heart of new products as hardware designers continue the quest to reduce the size of key components such as displays and input devices.

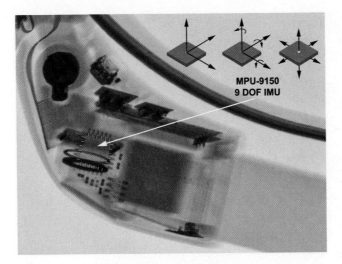

Figure 11.11 This x-ray of a Google Glass display shows the position of the InvenSense MPU-9150 9-axis motion tracking MEMS sensor.
Credit: Image courtesy of Andrew Vanden Heuvel, AGL Initiatives

> ## note
>
> An IMU is what is referred to as a dead-reckoning or ded-reckoning (for deduced reckoning) device. Dead-reckoning is the process of calculating a current position by using a previously determined fix and advancing that position based upon known or estimated speeds over elapsed time and course. Thus, bias-corrupted measurements produce large errors in calculations over time. It is for this reason that IMUs are typically used in conjunction with another sensor, such as chip-based GPS, to correct for drift.

Acoustic Sensors

As of the time of this book's preparation, there were few viable acoustic tracking solutions commercially available and in use within the virtual and augmented reality arena. Regardless, acoustic sensors, or more specifically, ultrasonic trackers, can be a powerful solution under the right circumstances. The dominant player in this sensor category is the high precision IS-900 system manufactured by InterSense Corporation of Billerica, Massachusetts.

In a typical configuration, the IS-900 system uses devices known as SoniStrips, which are lined with transponders to deliver ultrasonic pulses. As shown in Figure 11.12, the SoniStrips are normally mounted above the tracking workspace to maintain an unobstructed line of sight with the sensors embedded in either a handheld controller or sensor bar mounted to a viewing device or other object. Once the SoniStrips are installed, the relationship between each of the SoniStrips and the sensors must be carefully calibrated to enable accurate tracking across all six DOF.

Figure 11.12 This image shows an array of InterSense SoniStrips embedded with ultrasonic transponders in an elevated position within a U.S. Army man portable air-defense (MANPAD) simulator.
Credit: Image courtesy of the U.S. Marines

With the InterSense system, the ultrasonic tracking components are principally used for ranging measurements to determine the location of an object within the tracking workspace using Cartesian coordinates (X, Y, and Z). The orientation (roll, pitch, and yaw) of the object being tracked is measured using a high precision inertial sensor known as an InertiaCube embedded within the handheld controller or sensor bar such as those devices shown in Figure 11.13. The measurements of the movement of these devices are sent to a rack-mounted base unit via tethered or wireless connection.

This use of multiple tracking technologies is referred to as **sensor fusion** and can be found in a variety of combinations throughout the industry.

Figure 11.13 This image shows the wireless hand controller and tethered sensor bar components of the InterSense IS-900 inertial-ultrasonic tracking system.
Credit: Image courtesy of Idaho National Laboratory via Flickr under a CC 2.0 license

In addition to widespread use within the simulation and training community, the IS-900 is also used within a large number of CAVE, Powerwall, and hemispherical display installations as an alternative to optical tracking solutions mentioned earlier in this chapter.

In general, acoustic trackers are finicky systems requiring extensive initial setup and calibration. They are also highly susceptible to errors induced by ambient noise, particularly in those wavelengths close to that of the carrier signals. For those applications in which you have complete control of the operational environment, such as within a flight simulator, this tracking solution is ideal.

Conclusion

Accurate, efficient, and affordable sensors are a basic requirement that permeates virtual environment systems. Just as virtual and augmented reality are having a transformational impact on a variety of industries, many of these key advances come about as a result of sensor advancements, although challenges still remain. This is not an issue with the weakness of the technological solutions but the relative youth of the field.

One of the most challenging issues facing system developers when deciding which sensor technologies to employ is a general disparity on methods for measuring and expressing performance, although this problem will likely sort itself out when enough established companies are participating in the field that strict industry standards begin to emerge.

CHAPTER 12

DEVICES TO ENABLE NAVIGATION AND INTERACTION

One of the most fundamental and essential baseline technology components of any virtual or augmented reality system is the mechanism with which a user navigates within and interacts with the simulation. In addition to dramatically extending the usefulness of these systems, it is considered crucial to the overall sense of immersion. In this chapter we explore a number of the current and emerging solutions being put forth, as well as look at why this single hardware component can determine the future of this industry.

2D Versus 3D Interaction and Navigation

Interactive, immersive virtual reality applications typically require a means of enabling user input, whether it is intended for model/data interaction, navigation, or both. Specialty systems aside, standard 2D input devices such as a mouse, touchpad, or basic game controller are of limited use unless features and utilities within the application are bound to translation along a 2D plane. For instance, within architectural walk-throughs or gaming applications where your viewpoint is generally limited in its range of movement along the Z-axis (up and down), the use of a 2D input device may be an entirely appropriate and ideal solution. Once user movement along the Z-axis is enabled such as within applications involving flight, navigation is likely to become hampered, impossible, or considerably less intuitive.

For clarity, not all 2D interfaces are manual devices. As shown in Figure 12.1, treadmills of various configurations are frequently combined with immersive display solutions and are in wide use within research institutions, large architecture firms, and simulation and training applications. In most cases, the systems facilitate translation of viewpoint position exclusively along the XY plane, although some specialty systems are capable of transitioning to an inclined plane. Invariably, most treadmill-based systems include some provision for tracking a user's head movement across 6 degrees of freedom (DOF) completely independent of the technology used to track movement of the feet. Thus, although a user may be walking on a treadmill in one direction, he is able to swivel the head up, down, and side to side as if maneuvering in a real-world setting.

Figure 12.1 This image shows three examples of treadmill systems used to translate a participant's viewpoint along the XY plane within immersive virtual reality applications. Shown here are a standard treadmill within a computer-assisted virtual environment (CAVE) display at the Beckman Institute Illinois Simulator Lab, University of Illinois at Urbana-Champaign (left), and omnidirectional treadmills by Virtuix (center) and Omnifinity (right).

Credit: Images courtesy of Illinois Simulator Laboratory (University of Illinois), Czar via Wikimedia under a CC 2.0 license, and Johan Schmitz

The Importance of a Manual Interface

As explained in Chapter 1, "Computer-Generated Worlds," there are a variety of immersive visualization scenarios currently carrying the title of *virtual reality*. These can range from situations in which participants are merely "along for the ride" and limited to swiveling their heads as a 3D simulation or 360° video plays, or perhaps a scenario in which several individuals crowd into a CAVE display while one person navigates, to single or multiuser interactive experiences involving the use of head-mounted displays. Each scenario may provide a powerful visual sensation of presence within a computer-generated space or model, but those systems allowing first-person navigation through and direct interaction with the objects in the simulation tend to be the most engaging and compelling and provide the greatest sense of immersion, particularly when some form of tactile and force feedback is also provided (Monroy et al., 2008; Kechavarzi et al., 2012; McGloin et al., 2013).

To this end, it is important to remember that outside of specialty applications or systems incorporating cameras such as the HTC Vive, when wearing a fully occluding head-mounted display, users typically have no visual reference to their real-world surroundings. This includes keyboards, mice, trackballs, gaming controllers, and more. Thus, it is essential that any input device intended for use in this application setting be intuitive and easy to operate. Physicist, author, and former Atari game designer Chris Crawford, in his 1984 book titled *The Art of Computer Game Design*, provides an insightful description of this requirement:

"Given a bat and told that the goal in baseball is to hit the ball, few would have problems deciding that swinging the bat at the ball should be their goal. A computer baseball game is not so easy to decipher, however. Should one hit H for "hit" or S for "swing" or B for "bat"? Should one press the START key or press the joystick trigger? Without directions, the goal remains unclear" (Crawford, 1984).

Although Crawford's analogy was not referring to an immersive virtual reality application, his statement clearly illustrates the complexity of the task faced by the designers of manual interfaces and controllers intended for this field. What is the right size and shape? Where should buttons and triggers be located? What is an appropriate weight? What tactile and force feedback cues should be incorporated? Should buttons and triggers be labeled with icons? Can a device designed for general entertainment applications (where the largest user base for VR will be found) also serve as an effective solution for an architect or engineer?

Throughout the remainder of this chapter, we will explore a variety of input devices specifically intended for this field, as well as a few developed for alternate uses but which are finding added applicability within this general arena.

As with other chapters detailing specific products, it is impractical to provide coverage of each and every commercially available solution. As such, the specific products and functional methodologies mentioned next are intended as representative of a particular device category. A more comprehensive list of suppliers is provided in Appendix B, "Resources," at the end of this book.

Finally, several devices that would logically be included in this chapter have already been described in detail elsewhere in this book in the course of explaining core enabling sensor technologies. These include the Leap Motion device that uses infrared light and stereo cameras to track hand movements, Microsoft's family of Kinect sensors that utilize structured light fields and time-of-flight measurements to enable user tracking and interaction, and others. References to the location of those device descriptions can be found in the appropriate sections of this chapter.

Hand and Gesture Tracking

Beyond actually using fully immersive, head-mounted display-based virtual reality systems for yourself, it is also a fascinating experience to closely observe the reaction of others using them for the first time. In many instances, a common action that will be seen is a new user raising one or both hands, physically reaching out and attempting to grab or otherwise interact with virtual objects they are viewing. This is an instinctive response, just as reaching out and attempting to manually explore and interact with objects in the real world. So important is a manual interface to the overall goal of *suspended disbelief* that it may actually turn out to be a "king maker" of sorts and a key deciding factor on which companies participating in this field ultimately dominate the marketplace, such as with the gaming controllers manufactured by Microsoft and Sony. Fortunately, given the broad number of application areas for virtual and augmented reality, there is ample market share to go around.

We begin this section by exploring those input devices that enable the most natural and intuitive means of interacting with virtual environments and the objects contained therein.

Gloves

From the earliest days of the virtual reality/augmented reality (VR/AR) industry, the primary (and preferred) interfaces used for interaction and navigation in virtual environments have been those based around a basic glove to leverage the strengths, dexterity, range of motion, and accuracy of our hands, our most natural means of interaction with the physical world. Dozens have been produced over the years to one measure of success or another, although one company in particular, CyberGlove Systems LLC, of San Jose, California, has managed to carefully navigate the ups and downs in this industry and continues to produce high-quality precision devices in wide use by Fortune 500/Global 500 corporations, government agencies, and universities worldwide. One such device is shown in Figure 12.2.

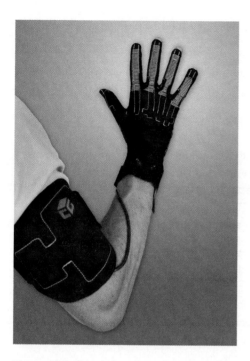

Figure 12.2 The wireless CyberGlove III motion capture data glove uses up to 22 high-accuracy joint-angle sensors to accurately transform hand and finger motions into real-time digital joint-angle data.

Credit: Image courtesy of Cyberglove Systems, LLC

CyberGlove III

The CyberGlove III is a wireless, hand-centric 3D motion capture device that accurately quantifies the movement of a user's fingers and hand, and, in conjunction with control software, maps these movements to a graphical representation of a hand within a virtual environment or on a computer screen. This allows users to "reach in and manipulate" digital objects as if they were physical objects (CGS, 2015).

Depending on the model, the CyberGlove III is capable of high-accuracy joint-angle measurements using proprietary resistive bend-sensing technology across 18–22 different points on the device. These include bend sensors on each finger, abduction sensors, as well as sensors for measuring thumb crossover, palm arch, and more. The base glove itself is constructed of stretchable fabric and a mesh palm for ventilation. The sensor data rate ranges from 100 records/sec (SD card) to 120 records/sec (USB and Wi-Fi). Wireless data transfer is enabled via 802.11g Wi-Fi.

It is important to stress that in its basic form shown in Figure 12.2, this device does not provide tactile or force feedback cueing, although such capability is available via add-on systems.

An example of such an offering is the CyberGrasp force-reflecting exoskeleton detailed in Chapter 10, "Tactile and Force Feedback Devices."

For those applications requiring the tracking of movement of the user's hand in 3D space, the glove needs to be paired with one of the tracking technologies detailed in Chapter 11, "Sensors for Tracking Position, Orientation, and Motion."

Peregrine USB Glove

On the consumer side, the Peregrine USB Glove shown in Figure 12.3 holds significant promise as a cost-effective natural interface for the virtual and augmented reality industry. Developed by Iron Will Innovations of Lloydminster, Alberta, and originally intended as a "wearable keyboard" for task-intensive real-time strategy (RTS) games such as *Minecraft*, the Peregrine is finding a new family of users within the virtual reality gaming community.

Built from a durable, stretchable, and washable spandex and nylon mesh, the glove includes three conductive contact pads: one across the palm of the hand and two located on the thumb. There are also 18 touch points spread across the inside of the fingers (5 each on the index, middle, and ring fingers and 3 on the pinky). Touching any of the 18 finger points to a contact pad sends a unique control signal to the game or other application. Control software allows the user to customize and calibrate more than 30 user-programmable actions based solely on gestures, which result in unique touch combinations.

Figure 12.3 The Peregrine USB Glove uses conductive contact pads and touch points spread across the fingers and palm of the device to translate gestures into general computer and software application commands.
Credit: Image courtesy of Iron Will Innovations Canada Inc

The Peregrine is connected to a computer via a USB cable that itself is attached to a break-away magnetic pod mounted on the back of the glove. If your motions and gesticulations exceed the length of the cable, the break-away pod simply pulls off, preventing potential damage to the glove and sensors.

Here again, this device does not provide any form of tactile or force feedback cueing. For those applications requiring the tracking of movement of the user's hand in 3D space, the glove needs to be paired with one of the tracking technologies detailed in Chapter 11.

Dual Wand/Paired Controllers

Try a simple experiment. Stick one hand in your pants pocket and go on about your day. See how long you last before frustration sets in and you end the experiment. To some extent, the same concept holds true when using a virtual reality system with great frequency or for extended periods of time requiring manual interaction. We have two hands for a reason. Dual wand/paired controllers provide increased bandwidth for information gathering from our environment, greater functionality and dexterity, and the easier completion of tasks. In this section we explore a variety of dual wand and paired controllers designed to facilitate interaction and navigation within immersive virtual environments.

HTC Vive SteamVR Controllers

Designed specifically for use with the HTC Vive virtual reality system, the Vive controllers shown in Figure 12.4 are of a balanced, ergonomic design incorporating a textured circular touchpad, dual stage trigger under each forefinger, two grip buttons, as well as system and menu buttons. In addition to aesthetic appeal, the toroidal shape of the controller head is necessary to separate sensors used for tracking position and orientation of the device. The controllers are powered using integrated rechargeable lithium polymer batteries and charging via micro USB cables. A single charge is reported to provide multiple hours of runtime.

Figure 12.4 The HTC Vive/Steam VR Controllers are state-of-the-art 3D input devices designed with the sole purpose of enabling smooth, versatile interactions with and navigation through virtual reality simulations.
Credit: Images courtesy of HTC

The position and orientation of these controllers are monitored using a combination of internal MEMs sensors as well as the same Lighthouse 3D spatial laser-tracking technology as the HTC Vive head-mounted display detailed in Chapter 11. Data from the interface controls and internal sensors are sent via wireless transmitter to a receiver in the Vive head-mounted display, well displaced from potential interference noise generated by the host computer. Light haptic effects are provided using vibrotacticle cueing.

Oculus Touch

One of the most innovative user interfaces developed to date, Oculus Touch is a pair of handheld wireless controllers initially intended for use with the Oculus Rift virtual reality system. Yet another example of the impact quality industrial designers can have on the outcome of a product, the Touch controllers embody many of the necessary features mentioned earlier in this chapter. The devices sit easily in your hand at a relaxed state, and it takes only seconds for a user to figure out how they function. As shown in Figure 12.5, each unit includes a well-placed trigger for the index finger, a second for the middle finger, a perfectly placed analog thumb stick, as well as two clearly labeled buttons. The overall geometry of the device leaves the user's fingers unencumbered and in such a position that natural gestures like grabbing, pointing, and waving are possible. Capacitive-sensitive surfaces on the triggers and elsewhere on the device help the system recognize these hand poses, thus enabling a range of additional control possibilities.

Figure 12.5 Oculus Touch controllers employ a variety of sensors, including IR LEDs, to aid in tracking position and orientation, as well as capacitive-sensitive control surfaces to track natural hand poses like pointing and waving.
Credit: Image courtesy of eVRydayVR via Flickr

The position and orientation of these controllers are monitored using the Oculus Constellation tracking technology, which is an infrared camera that monitors the position of IR LEDs arrayed around the each device. Data from the interface controls and internal sensors, such as those that detect whether user fingers are touching buttons or are in certain positions, are sent via wireless transmitter to a receiver in the Oculus head-mounted display, well displaced from potential interference noise generated by a PC.

The Oculus Touch controllers provide haptic feedback via vibrotacticle cueing, which is variable in both frequency and amplitude, giving application developers significant latitude and creativity in matching tactile sensations with observed or user-initiated events.

Sony PlayStation Move VR Controllers

The cornerstone of the Sony PlayStation line for several years, the Move VR controllers shown in Figure 12.6, although less artistic and ergonomically driven than others shown in this chapter and built for a rougher user environment, still function exceptionally well in the tasks for which they were designed to perform. Each Move controller features nine input buttons, including four control buttons (O, □, Δ, X), start and select buttons on the side, a standard PS button, a trigger button, and a large Move button. A novel feature found with these controllers is that the illuminate balls at the top of the device (used for position tracking) actually change color while in use.

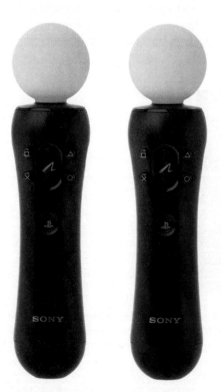

Figure 12.6 The Sony PS Move Controller tracks both fast and subtle movements of a user's hands in 3D space.

Credit: Image courtesy of Evan-Amos

An internal lithium-ion rechargeable battery provides 10 hours of operational time on a full charge. The position of these controllers is monitored using the Sony Playstation Camera (actually contains stereo cameras for depth vision). Orientation of the device is tracked using an internal MEMS gyroscope, accelerometer, and three-axis compass, measuring both fast and subtle movements. Information from these sensors is transferred to the PlayStation base unit via Bluetooth transmitter.

The PlayStation Move VR controllers provide haptic feedback via vibrotacticle cueing, or what system users frequently refer to as *rumbling*.

Whole Body Tracking

There are a host of immersive virtual reality application scenarios requiring the tracking of full body dynamics. A striking example is the use of such technologies by law enforcement and the military in the development of essential tactical skills used in such activities as room clearing operations and dealing with active shooter situations. By tracking the movement of multiple points on a participant's body and well as his weapon during immersive training scenarios, detailed after-actions analysis can be undertaken, problems identified, and skill sets refined. Figure 12.7 shows one such implementation.

Figure 12.7 Soldiers of the 157th Infantry Brigade, First Army Division East, take advantage of the Dismounted Soldier Training System. Although the DSTS does not replace training, the system augments exercises by providing the ability to change or repeat scenarios, analyze individual and team movements, and more.
Credit: Image courtesy of DoD

The methods used to carry out these detailed movement studies fall into a category of technologies referred to as *motion capture* (MOCAP), which come in two distinct types: optical and nonoptical. Several optical tracking technologies are described in Chapter 11. Several examples of the use of optical MOCAP systems in immersive virtual reality applications can be found in Chapter 15, "Science and Engineering."

Perception Neuron

The emergence of new inertial tracking technologies has opened doors for the introduction of significantly less expensive alternatives to optical MOCAP solutions. One such alternative comes in the form of a system of sensors known as Perception Neuron, manufactured by Noitom Ltd of Beijing, China. As shown in Figure 12.8, the Perception Neuron system is based on interchangeable motion sensors called Neurons, each about 1 cm × 1 cm, that connect to a Hub. A Neuron houses an inertial measurement unit (IMU) composed of a gyroscope, accelerometer, and magnetometer. The ingenuity of the system is that every Neuron is interchangeable and can be placed anywhere it's needed in an endless number of combinations, such as on a hand for detailed movement, on specific parts of the body, or even on accessories. A single Hub can connect from 1 to 30 Neurons.

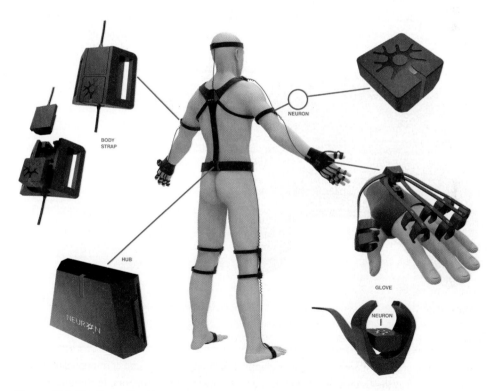

Figure 12.8 The Perception Neuron motion capture system uses up to 32 individual, interchangeable sensors to track movement of a user's body and limbs.
Credit: Image courtesy of Noitom Ltd

The Perception Neuron system can function wirelessly via Wi-Fi or onboard recording or wired via USB, providing extensive application flexibility. Several variations on this system are available for purchase, ranging from 18 to 32 individual Neuron sensors. Also, it has already been widely demonstrated to function relatively seamlessly with VR systems from both Oculus and HTC Vive as well as a host of software solutions including Maya, 3ds Max, Unity, and Unreal.

Gaming and Entertainment Interfaces

There are numerous commercially available gaming controllers already in wide use with smartphone-based head-mounted displays such as Samsung's Gear VR. In this usage scenario, although many Bluetooth-enabled controllers of this type will connect with the Android powered Samsung mobile devices such as the Galaxy S7, S6, S6 Edge, S6 Edge+, and Notes 4 and 5, the control scheme of a particular device may require remapping to function correctly. To this end, a variety of instructions to enable such configurations can be found on the Internet.

At the time of this book's preparation, the initial Oculus Rift commercial headset (detailed in Chapter 6, "Fully Immersive Displays") was bundled with a Microsoft Xbox One controller shown in Figure 12.9, demonstrating the viability of these interfaces in fully immersive applications.

Figure 12.9 The Xbox One gamepad is the initial manual controller bundled with the consumer version of the Oculus Rift head-mounted display.
Credit: Image by BagoGames via Flickr under a CC 2.0 license

Among some of the first immersive gaming applications developed upon commercial release of devices such as the Oculus Developers Kit1 and 2 were driving simulators. To this end, some of the highest fidelity gaming steering wheels available and in use for this particular application scenario are produced by Logitech International of Romanel-sur-Morges, Switzerland. One such system, the G29 Driving Force Racing Wheel and associated shifter, is shown in Figure 12.10. Of particular note is the extensive incorporation of high-resolution tactile and force feedback cueing described in Chapter 9, "The Mechanics of Feeling." The peripheral is compatible with various gaming consoles as well as Windows-based PCs.

Figure 12.10 The Logitech G29 Driving Force Racing Wheel is a simulator-grade, helical geared force feedback input device that has been paired with the Oculus for deeply compelling driving simulation experiences.
Credit: Image courtesy of Logitech

Navigating with Your Mind

The human brain is an extraordinarily fascinating and complex organ. It contains 100,000 miles of blood vessels (Turkington, 1996); an estimated 100 billion neurons, each having between 1,000 and 10,000 synapses (Chudler, 2011); and a memory storage capacity estimated in the range of 2.5 petabytes (a petabyte is 1 million gigabytes, or 1,000 terabytes) (Reber, 2010). IBM's chief scientist for brain-inspired computing, Dharmendra S. Modha, conservatively estimates the human brain has 38 petaflops (a petaflop is 1 thousand trillion operations per second) of processing power (Greenemeier, 2009). And all this capability is contained within a roughly 3-pound mass composed of 75% water with the overall consistency of gelatin (Juan, 2006).

Given this amazing functional capacity that manifests itself every moment of our existence, works of science fiction are replete with examples of direct brain-machine interfaces (BMIs). The complete elimination of the boundaries between man and machine is highly unlikely in the near term, but the line is certainly blurring. Significant advances have been achieved over the past decade using both invasive and noninvasive methods of creating a direct communication pathway between the human brain and complex information systems, with the primary goals of assisting, repairing, or augmenting human cognitive and sensory-motor functions.

Although the driving force behind these efforts has not been focused on interfaces for augmented or virtual reality per se, the field is most certainly taking advantage of these advances and the products resulting from this work.

One such device is the EPOC multichannel EEG (electroencephalogram) acquisition system developed by the bioinformatics company Emotiv, Inc of San Francisco, California. Shown in Figure 12.11, the device features 14 individual sensors (and two reference/positioning sensors) through which electrical signals in the brain are measured. Initially, a user "trains" the system by thinking about movement-based actions while brain activity is recorded and analyzed. Eventually the system is able to differentiate between distinct thoughts. These detections can then be assigned or mapped to any computing platform or application (Le, 2010), although many challenges still exist due to high variability and non-normality of attention and meditation data (Maskeliunas et al., 2016).

Figure 12.11 The EPOC headset is a high-resolution, multichannel, portable EEG system that can enable a user to navigate through immersive virtual environments using only one's thoughts.
Credit: Images courtesy of Bruno Cordioli and Bownose via Flickr under a CC 2.0 license

The breakthrough capability allowing the development of a mass market product came about through the development of algorithms that mathematically flatten the cortical folds of a user's brain, enabling the mapping of signals closer to their true source despite the fact that this folding pattern is as unique to each individual as a fingerprint (Le, 2010).

This device is already in wide use around the world as an interface for a host of immersive virtual reality and robotics applications.

Conclusion

Input devices, controllers, and other means of enabling user input are a key component to most immersive virtual reality systems and applications. From manual interfaces such as sensor-laden gloves, rings, wands, and a myriad of gaming interfaces to motion capture systems, omnidirectional treadmills, and devices for tracking the direction of your gaze or EEG activity, these tools are essential for movement through, and interaction with, computer-generated environments.

The variety of application areas for immersive virtual reality systems necessitates an equally broad and varied selection of input devices. For instance, engineers evaluating the designs for a new space station module will need entirely different tools than gaming enthusiasts or surgeons practicing a delicate laparoscopic technique. It is for this reason that, aside from actual applications and content, devices to enable interaction and navigation will likely be the most dynamic and changing aspect to this industry.

CHAPTER 13

GAMING AND ENTERTAINMENT

Despite the youth of the field, virtual and augmented reality are on the verge of transforming the arts, gaming, and entertainment industries. From entirely new mediums and forms of artistic expression, to immersive games with action surrounding the user, to stereoscopic 360° cinema, these technologies are already beginning to redefine traditional media in these application areas. In this chapter we explore some of the unique applications for immersive systems in arts and entertainment, highlighting strengths and benefits as well as challenges posed in harnessing this new medium.

Virtual Reality and the Arts

For artists, virtual reality represents an extraordinary new medium for expression… a new type of canvass for the externalization and sharing of ideas. But unlike more traditional mediums, virtual reality is not limited by physics or improbabilities. Works can now be created that were unimaginable just a few short years ago. For instance, scale is no longer an issue. Painters are no longer limited to a 2D canvas or surface. Sculptors can create pieces that change shape based on a user's hand gestures or facial expressions, and one's varied creations are not the slightest bit fragile nor subject to the normal laws of entropy. In fact, the only realistic limitations to the manifestation of such creations are one's programming skills or the ability to properly leverage the tools of content creation.

To this end, one of the more impressive software applications to be released thus far in support of the use of virtual reality as a medium for artistic expression is Tilt Brush (originally developed by the software company Skillman and Hackett, which was acquired by Google in 2015). As opposed to being yet another 2D painting utility, Tilt Brush adds a whole new dimension by allowing users to paint in 3D space while using a head-mounted display and paired hand controllers. With an extensive toolset of brushes, patterns, color palettes, and innovative utilities, users are able to create their works of art using techniques that have simply not existed prior to its introduction. You can even paint with smoke, fire, and light.

A stunning example of the power of such tools in the hands of a talented individual can be seen in Figure 13.1. This 3D creature was "painted" in less than 15 minutes by UK artist Alix Briskham while wearing an HTC Vive stereoscopic head-mounted display (see Chapter 6, "Fully Immersive Displays") and the associated paired hand controllers (Opposable VR, 2015).

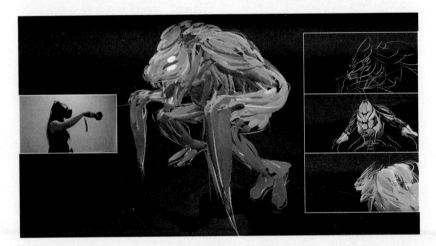

Figure 13.1 This image shows screenshots of a 3D painting created by UK artist Alix Briskham while using an HTC Vive head-mounted display, manual controllers, and the 3D painting program from Google known as Tilt Brush.
Credit: Opposable Group Limited

A similar package known as Medium has been developed for the Oculus Rift system. Although the control schemes for both Tilt Brush and Medium present the user with a virtual palette and brush, Medium is more of a sculpting program intended as a collaborative tool.

Gaming

Given the myriad of potential application areas for virtual and augmented reality, the present market segment holding the greatest potential and number of enthusiasts is gaming. Every company participating in the electronic gaming field, be it software, hardware, or peripherals, has development projects underway to capitalize on what appears to be the next great advancement for this market space. In fact, the size and profitability of the computer gaming market has been a significant driving force behind the speed of advancement in graphics processing unit (GPU) performance and the reemergence of the entire field of virtual reality.

Single-User First-Person Games

Despite the relative youth of this field within the gaming arena, the number and variety of computer games either specifically designed for use with a stereoscopic head-mounted display or ported for such use after the fact is impressive, and growing. Themes range from flight and driving simulations, to navigating labyrinthine dungeons and fighting monsters, to surgery simulators and standard military-style first-person shooting games. A scene from one popular example, *Gunjack*, by CCP Games of Reykjavik, Iceland, is shown in Figure 13.2. Thematically set in space, this visually stunning game has players operating a gun turret on a mining vessel to fight off pirates.

Figure 13.2 This is a screenshot from *Eve: Gunjack*, a first-person action shooting game designed specifically for use with virtual reality systems.
Credit: Image courtesy of Bryan Ward via Flickr under a CC 2.0 license

Built using the Epic Games' Unreal Engine 4 suite of development tools, Gunjack was specifically designed for use with the smartphone-based Samsung Gear VR head-mounted display (CCP, 2015). (See Chapter 6, "Fully Immersive Displays.") User navigation through and interaction with features in the game is accomplished using one of a variety of handheld game controllers. (See Chapter 12, "Devices to Enable Navigation and Interaction.")

There are hundreds of additional single-user, first-person games now available and supported by VR systems such as Oculus, HTV Vive, Sony PS4 VR, OSVR, and others.

Multiplayer First-Person Games

Since the introduction of the first commercial virtual reality systems in the mid-1980s, the concept of multiuser or "shared" virtual environments has been a cornerstone of the general discourse on the topic. Scientists and engineers rave about the ability to have multiple participants collaborating on a common project from remote locations, specialists in education are eagerly exploring ways to create decentralized virtual classrooms, and social networking companies such as Facebook unequivocally state that they see virtual reality as one of the primary tools facilitating social interaction in the future (Metz, 2016). Fans of computer gaming are no different. From joining forces to achieve a common objective to highly competitive games of skill, a major consideration in the development of gaming software for virtual reality systems is the accommodation of multiple users, and for good reason. Standard computer games supporting multiple users, be they seated on the same couch or spread out around the world, are some of the highest grossing, most popular titles in the industry. But unlike standard computer games, multiuser virtual reality applications pose an interesting set of computing and connectivity challenges.

At the most basic level, fully immersive virtual reality systems require a stereoscopic head-mounted display, at least one input device or controller, and sensors to track position and orientation of, at a minimum, a user's head. Because it is already a computationally intensive task to drive all this hardware, it remains impractical to support multiple users off of a single system. This means that multiuser virtual reality games are being designed with some form of networking capability, the specifics depending on the platform and source of the title.

Massively Multiplayer First-Person Games

This connectivity challenge, and potential, extends far beyond three or four friends getting together for an evening of virtual sword fights or an urban bloodbath. Following in the footsteps of existing massively multiplayer first-person games (MMFPG) such as *World of Warcraft* and *EVE Online*, numerous software manufacturers are actively developing the gaming applications and networking infrastructure to support the use of virtual reality systems. One such endeavor is *Wizard Online*, a scene from which is shown in Figure 13.3 (Olivetti, 2016).

Figure 13.3 This is screenshot from *Wizard Online*, a massively multiplayer first-person game designed for use with both virtual reality systems as well as desktop computers.
Credit: Playwizardonline.com. Gameplay was programmed by the founder Mahir Ozer

Location-Based Entertainment

Virtual reality gaming is not limited to a home (or work) setting. Out-of-home entertainment and gaming venues involving immersive virtual reality systems are being established in a number of locations around the world. These operations take on the form of both mixed reality as well as free-roam settings and are detailed next.

Mixed Reality Gaming

A *mixed reality* is a merging of real and virtual worlds where objects in the actual physical surroundings play a direct functional role within the virtual environment simulation. Imagine a setting in which a physical warehouse space is converted into multiple intricate mazes of featureless halls, corners, and rooms with large, similarly featureless cylinders, cubes, and spheres placed about. Now imagine putting on a head-mounted display and being presented with an impeccably designed, detail-rich virtual environment perfectly aligned and correlated to the featureless physical space within which you are standing. This is a mixed reality. It is also the basis of a new location-based game center known as The Void, located in Lindon, Utah.

The Void blends a generally featureless, reconfigurable physical environment known as a "Pod" with beautifully designed graphics seen within the head-mounted display to produce a highly compelling sensation of actual presence within the gaming scenario. Additional sensory cues such as misting, heat, smells, wind machines, and surround sound dramatically increase the realism of the simulation. Similarly, effects such as vibrating walls and floors and 3 degree of freedom (DOF) motion platforms can be used to simulate, say, an elevator ride to a different level or transport to a distant battlefield, giving the perception of a gaming space significantly larger than the actual 60 square foot physical space within which the scenario plays out (The Void, 2015).

Accommodating between six and eight players at a time, actual enabling technologies employed in the simulations include a custom-designed, wide field of view (FOV) stereoscopic head-mounted display. Graphics are generated using a portable lightweight computer worn on the user's back. Position and orientation of the display, hands, and handheld weapons are monitored using a combination of optical and inertial sensors.

Mixed Reality Using Augmenting Displays

Another mixed reality implementation approaches the paradigm from a dramatically different angle. As opposed to having the user interact with his physical surroundings while viewing precisely correlated imagery within a fully immersive display as described earlier, augmented reality displays can be used to place computer-generated objects within the user's real-world surroundings. Recent examples include a tabletop implementation of *Minecraft* viewed using the Microsoft HoloLens display.

Free Roam

Unlike mixed reality settings, free-roam gaming relies exclusively on graphic representations of a virtual environment delivered via a head-mounted display, with users free to move about inside of a defined volume of open space. One such gaming center is Zero Latency PTY LTD of Melbourne, Australia. As shown in Figure 13.4, Zero Latency provides participants with a fully immersive wide FOV head-mounted display driven by a compact Dell Alienware Alpha gaming computer within a small backpack. Position and orientation of the user's head and weapon are monitored using a combination of optical tracking (as denoted by the single-point illuminated spheres) as well as inertial sensors. The actual gaming space within which multiple participants engage in 50-minute missions measures 400 square meters (4,300 square feet) (Simpson, 2015).

Figure 13.4 This split screen shows a free roam gaming implementation used at Zero Latency virtual entertainment center in Melbourne, Australia.
Credit: Images courtesy of Zero Latency Pty PTD, Melbourne, Australia

Given the relative youth of the commercial availability of the enabling technologies (in many cases still in prototype stage), location-based entertainment venues such as those just shown are not without their rough spots, as is always the case with early technology adopters. Still, these firms provide a powerful example of the direction that location-based entertainment is headed.

Immersive Video/Cinematic Virtual Reality

The general concept of immersive video is a fairly straightforward concept. With traditional video or filmmaking, a director or camera operator chooses, or frames, specific scenes to be captured. An editor then pieces these clips together, ultimately controlling what the end user sees. With immersive video, specialized camera systems are used to capture imagery in all directions simultaneously, and it is the end user who determines what direction and features within the video to watch.

Although standard 360° video (simply a flat equirectangular video morphed into a sphere) has been available for a number of years and is fairly common, the major advancement in the field is the introduction of stereoscopic 360° cameras, such as those shown in Figure 13.5. In each of these systems, separate left and right eye 360° views are captured, the output from which is viewed within a stereoscopic head-mounted display.

Figure 13.5 The three camera systems in this image are designed to capture stereoscopic 360-degree video. Shown are the Jaunt ONE (top center), the NextVR Virtual Reality Digital Cinema System (left), and the Vuze consumer-oriented 3D camera (right).
Credit: Images courtesy of NextVR, Inc., Jaunt, Inc. and Humaneyes® Technologies, LTD

This technology has powerful applications, as well as implications, across a variety of entertainment fields, ranging from an outdoorsman capturing the remarkable beauty of a walk through a tropical rain forest, to professional productions where these specialized cameras are strategically positioned in venues to capture and stream immersive 360° stereoscopic video of a sporting event live over the internet.

One of the early, more compelling applications that made both the music and the film industries sit up and take notice occurred in August 2014 when musician Paul McCartney partnered with Jaunt Inc. of Palo Alto, California to capture a 360° stereoscopic recording of a concert he performed at Candlestick Park in San Francisco. Figure 13.6 shows an early version of the Jaunt camera rig in Figure 13.5. Three of the early systems were positioned at different locations on the stage to capture different viewpoints. Ultimately, a free smartphone app for Google Cardboard/Samsung VR type displays was published allowing the viewer to watch McCartney playing "Live and Let Die" in 360° stereoscopic video while listening (via headphones) to the accompanying binaural audio (Ong, 2014).

Figure 13.6 This still shot shows the musician Paul McCartney within a concert venue while being recorded in stereoscopic 360° video using an early version of the Jaunt ONE camera system.
Credit: Image courtesy of Jaunt, Inc

Although the configuration of this camera is changing, at the time of this book's preparation, the Jaunt camera rig incorporated 16 individual cameras on the equator, as well as 4 on both the top and bottom, each of which records at 4K resolution. Output from a recording comes in the form of 24 individual files, which are then uploaded as a set to Jaunt's cloud-rendering pipeline. There, the 24 videos are merged into a single file with left- and right-eye panoramic video, the format for which can be imported and read by most video editing packages (Murie, 2016).

Even major Hollywood studios have begun working with such systems, albeit initially from an exploratory and experimentation standpoint given it is an entirely new medium for entertainment and media. Whole new ways of capturing and delivering narrative through cinematic virtual reality must be developed first.

Conclusion

From the time of the introduction of the first computer games such as *Pong*, developers have been on a nonstop quest to introduce tools and techniques to draw users more fully into the player experience. Since that time, this fast-paced industry has enabled stunning advances in the quality of graphics and displays, tools for interaction, and a shift from standalone arcade-style games into which were fed mountains of quarters to globally networked first-person games connecting thousands of living rooms at a time. Virtual reality is clearly the next step in this evolution and will likely serve as the primary revenue-generating market segment of the virtual reality industry for years to come.

The same holds true with augmented reality gaming applications. Although still very young in terms of development and release into the marketplace, this particular paradigm holds significant potential due to the entirely new class of gaming experiences possible. There are also a number of benefits to be gained over fully immersive implementations, including the reduction of nausea and collision with walls and physical objects, as well as an infinite variety of actual gaming environments.

Cinematic application of these technologies is a different matter entirely. When the first personal computers were introduced in the mid-1970s, many people scratched their heads and wondered just how such technology would ultimately be utilized. Most could never envision the depth of integration that complex information systems would have in modern society. In many respects, the same questions are now being asked about how virtual reality can ultimately come into play in Hollywood productions. Sure, the initial answer is invariably some form of the phrase *interactive cinema*. But burrowing down on this topic, at least for the moment, reveals infinitely more questions than answers. Filmmaking professionals know they have an immensely powerful tool at hand, but how to begin harnessing its capabilities is only now beginning to be explored.

For instance, an entire art and science for filmmaking has evolved over the past 100+ years covering everything from camera position and movement through a scene, effective use of lighting, guiding a viewer's eyes and attention around a frame, and ultimately, controlling every aspect of what an individual sees and hears. These and thousands of other well-defined methods and techniques constitute a visual and audio language through which filmmakers ultimately communicate on a 2D plane with an audience. It is through this complex visual and audio language that producers, directors, and postproduction teams are able to transport a viewer to another place and manipulate emotions, the effects of which occasionally last a lifetime. Changing the very medium, whether it is simply surrounding the viewer with scene action or even allowing some form of interaction, directly impacts the art and science underpinning this language.

Some answers are being found with the increasing use of straight 360° video capture and real-time delivery, or delayed playback, of specific events such as in major league sports, concerts, and more. Slowly, the language of this new medium is being constructed.

CHAPTER 14

ARCHITECTURE AND CONSTRUCTION

From assisting architects in refining design concepts, to enabling general contractors to more effectively manage large projects involving teams from widely varying disciplines, to aiding in the sale of existing real estate, immersive virtual reality systems are having a transformational impact on the architectural, engineering, and construction industries. In this chapter we present case studies involving companies both large and small to illustrate the widely varying ways in which these new display tools are being used to solve design, communication, and project management challenges.

Artificial Spaces

Spatial visualization—the ability to mentally envision and manipulate 2D and 3D figures—is yet another amazing capability of the human mind. In the field of architecture, this ability enables designers to mentally envision the complex 3D geometry of spaces and forms, their differences based on material selections and variable lighting conditions, and interactions of widely varying building systems and processes.

But there are limits to this ability. For instance, the greater the complexity of a structure or space under consideration, the greater the need for these mental images to be externalized to enable more detailed visual inspection and confirmation as well as to communicate these design ideas to clients.

The traditional methods used by an architect to externalize, evaluate, and communicate their design concepts and decisions prior to construction range from 2D representations such as hand illustrations and realistic computer-generated renderings to endoscopic exploration of physical table-top models and real-time walk-throughs on a workstation. These methods do assist in providing some sense of how the architectural space may *appear*, but the architect, and perhaps more importantly an untrained client, still carries the enormous task of trying to form an accurate mental image of the structure at scale in an attempt to gain an understanding of the complex geometry, metrics, and spatial interrelationships of the design.

From the earliest instances that the individual enabling technologies were cobbled together to create functioning, fully immersive virtual reality systems, architecture has been one of the primary application areas explored. Since this time, immersive architectural walk-throughs have become increasingly relied upon by architects and engineers, students in training, real estate agents, and others to effectively externalize and experience complex, habitable 3D structures.

In this chapter we will explore the variety of ways in which immersive and semi-immersive virtual and augmented reality technologies are employed in this field. As with other application areas detailed in this book, these examples are intended to be representative and seeds for additional thought on the variations and creative ways in which virtual interface technologies can be employed.

Architectural Design: Mangan Group Architects

It's one thing for an architect or engineer to view a 3D CAD model of a structure on a conventional 2D display and mentally envision the actual spatial characteristics of the interior of the design. It is another matter entirely to put on a head-mounted display and navigate through the same CAD model, but on a 1-to-1 scale, evaluating the physical and functional characteristics of a space or perhaps searching for plumbing and HVAC clashes, all before a single spade of dirt is turned in the construction process. This is precisely what is taking place in the back offices of an increasing number of architectural firms around the world. Invariably, these same tools are also used to allow clients to review designs and make changes before locking a project and seeking construction bids.

An ideal example of the simple, but powerful application of these technologies is Mangan Group Architects of Tacoma Park, Maryland. A small, full-service architectural firm specializing in remodels, production homes, and small commercial projects, Mangan Group regularly utilizes immersive virtual reality simulations to enable efficient communication and collaboration within the design team, as well as provide clients with the opportunity to tour designs on a 1-to-1 scale, choose between feature options and, where desired, request changes.

One such project was a recent hotel remodeling within which a commercial developer client was able to visualize rooms, the roof deck, and other aspects of the proposed design. During the review process, the client was able to tweak layout and design features, as well as switch between multiple preprogrammed variations of appearance and component functionality (such as sliding versus fixed panels) with the push of a button.

As shown in Figure 14.1, the basic hardware used in that office is an Oculus DK2 stereoscopic head-mounted display (see Chapter 6, "Fully Immersive Displays"), a small infrared sensor (mounted on the desktop monitor) to track position and orientation of an IR-LED array built into the display, as well as a Microsoft Xbox hand controller to facilitate easy navigation and viewpoint changes.

Figure 14.1 This photo shows a Mangan Group client during an immersive architectural walk-through of a proposed design.

Credit: Image courtesy of Mangan Group Architects

As depicted within the stereo pair shown in Figure 14.2, the Oculus DK2 head-mounted display presents the client a moderately bright, medium resolution Active Matrix OLED (AMOLED) image (960 × 1080 per eye) of the design as the user maneuvers his viewpoint through the model using the controller. With <20 ms latency in the position/orientation tracking, images translate smoothly as the user moves his head.

A simple software pathway enables the preparation of industry-standard CAD models for deployment within the Oculus system. In one example, CAD files are imported directly into the Unity 3D gaming engine where visual effects can be applied, including custom material textures, lighting and shading, as well as other treatments needed to reflect the designer's ideas.

Figure 14.2 While a Mangan Group client tours a proposed design using the head-mounted display, the stereo pair of images delivered to the headset is simultaneously shown on a standard desktop monitor, enabling designers and others to view where a client is looking within a model at any given moment.
Credit: Image courtesy of Mangan Group Architects

According to principles of the Mangan Group, the application of these technologies within their workflow is having a demonstrably positive impact on their design projects, and perhaps more importantly, their ability to provide clarity, insight, and design understanding to the client, enabling more informed decisions while still in the design stage.

It is important to highlight that use of these technologies within this particular application area is no longer just the realm of well-funded research institutions or company laboratories. In fact, the Mangan Group points out that it is only a 6-person operation generating just under $1 million in annual gross revenue, clearly demonstrating that these technologies are accessible and applicable even within a small businesses.

Construction Management

The larger a capital construction project, the greater the need for close collaboration between the designers, the engineers, the builders, and the client. One of the latest means of achieving this depth of collaboration is the adoption of **Building Information Modeling** (BIM) practices, which is the term describing a process used by architects, engineers, and contractors to coordinate project data, drawings, designs, and other information from multiple disciplines into a single 3D virtual model. Whereas traditional collaborations were based on 2D designs and data from each discipline that were layered, checked, and manually verified, BIM brings together and integrates the data from multiple disciplines and sources into a single, commonly accessible virtual model.

Another powerful aspect to BIM practices is the ability to add a fourth dimension, or time component, to the model. By assigning time- or schedule-related information to individual 3D CAD elements and assemblies, architects, engineers, contractors, and other stakeholders are able to visualize an accurate sequence of events in the 3D model at different phases of the project, providing increased understanding of construction progress and improving overall project management (McKinney et al., 1996; Jacobi, 2011).

The use of BIM in design and construction projects both large and small is having a wide-ranging impact on the architecture, engineering, and construction industry. It facilitates efficient collaboration, communication, and easy identification of conflicts between systems by enabling all the parties to access and review a single, common model and to immediately propose solutions to uncoordinated or conflicting design features. In the past, many of these conflicts would emerge as problems encountered by the builders after construction had already begun.

As the following case studies show, the combination of BIM with high-performance immersive visualization techniques is further enhancing the impact these technologies are having on large-scale design and construction projects.

Mortenson Construction

Mortenson Construction of Minneapolis, Minnesota, one of America's largest private companies and a top-rated general contractor and construction management firm, is well known for its expertise in virtual design and construction. For more than a decade, the company has been actively working with BIM, along with innovative immersive visualization tools, to the benefit of its clients, subcontractors, and project team members.

One of the many projects of note to which these technologies have been applied is the Pegula Ice Arena shown in Figure 14.3, located in University Park, Pennsylvania, on the campus of Penn State University. This $100 million, 228,000 square foot, 6,000-seat facility contains two NHL regulation-size ice surfaces, a main competition ice arena and practice rink, eight locker rooms, offices, player areas, and a variety of other facilities.

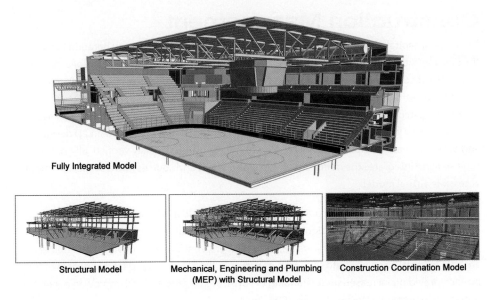

Fully Integrated Model

Structural Model

Mechanical, Engineering and Plumbing (MEP) with Structural Model

Construction Coordination Model

Figure 14.3 This composite image shows the various levels of detail of the Pegula BIM model available to design and construction team members for standard visualization tasks as well as immersive architectural walk-throughs.
Credit: Image courtesy of Mortenson Construction

While still in the design phase of the project, Mortenson, along with Crawford Architects of Kansas City, Missouri, and the clients, was able to tour and evaluate detailed virtual models of the facility at a 1-to-1 scale during various stages of completion. This was accomplished using a computer-assisted virtual environment (CAVE) display system (see Chapter 6) located at the Applied Research Laboratory on the Penn State campus.

As shown in Figure 14.4, the Penn State CAVE system is a four-sided room composed of rear projection screens. Stereoscopic imagery is reflected onto these surfaces using four high-resolution Barco projectors. An overhead, downward-facing projection system is used to accommodate continuation of simulation imagery onto the floor. While inside of the CAVE, users wear polarized glasses to see the 3D graphics generated by nearby servers.

Figure 14.4 Similar to that shown in the image, the Penn State Applied Research Laboratory CAVE is composed of four rear projection screens serving as walls. Stereoscopic imagery from high-resolution projectors is reflected off mirrors and onto the respective display surfaces.
Credit: Image courtesy of Dave Pape via Flickr under a CC 2.0 license

The first of the walk-throughs was conducted 18 months before a single spade of dirt was turned in the construction process and played a key role in the refinement of the design, as well as construction, of what is considered one of the finest collegiate ice arenas in the United States.

During these preconstruction tours, a variety of design flaws were identified in the public areas, training facilities, office spaces, and underground communications infrastructure, many of which would have remained hidden until well into the construction phase. In one example shown in Figure 14.5, a line of interior windows overlooking the practice rink in the facility were found to be of an insufficient length, resulting in an obstructed view of a team bench below. By extending the length so that the window ended at the floor instead of waist height, clear unobstructed views were created. As the participants have explained, this issue would likely have been impossible to identify had the immersive, 1-to-1 scale visualization capabilities of the CAVE not been utilized.

Figure 14.5 The image pair on the left shows the design of a line of viewing windows overlooking the Pegula Ice Arena practice rink before and after a design flaw was identified during virtual tours of the facility. The photograph on the right shows the real-world result of the design change.
Credit: Image courtesy of Mortenson Construction

Other problematic design issues were identified during these walk-throughs, including scope and layout of office space, reconfiguration of the coaches' locker room, and relocation of lighting within a mechanical room. The discovery of these issues while still in the design phase allowed adjustments to be made at absolutely no cost to construction. Mortenson estimates that the use of the CAVE in these design reviews directly averted more than $475,500 in changes during or after construction (Mortenson, 2013). Figure 14.6 is a photograph taken inside of the CAVE display during a walkthrough of the proposed facility design.

Figure 14.6 This image shows Guy Gadowsky, head coach of the Penn State University men's ice hockey team, wearing polarized stereo glasses during a walkthrough of the Pegula Ice Arena model within the CAVE display at the Applied Research Laboratory on the Penn State campus.
Credit: Image courtesy of Penn State Intercollegiate Athletics

It is interesting to note that, in addition to using the CAVE for design evaluation purposes, the Penn State coaching and athletic staff used the system for virtual tours of the ice arena to assist in recruiting and signing key players for their first season of Division 1 play.

Nabholz Construction

Nabholz Construction of Conway, Arkansas, one of the top commercial general contractors and construction management companies in the United States, has also found tremendous benefit in combining BIM with high-performance immersive and interactive visualization technologies. Here again, this application area brings various project participants and stakeholders together for closer collaboration and design reviews, as well as to demonstrate to clients precisely the end structure to be delivered.

Through a partnership with the Emerging Analytics Center (EAC) at the University of Arkansas at Little Rock (UALR), the Nabholz team regularly utilizes the EAC's state-of-the-art CAVE display system custom-designed and built by Mechdyne Corp. of Marshalltown, Iowa, as part of the preconstruction design review process.

One example of the use of this display system by Nabholz was architectural walk-throughs of the Central Arkansas Radiation Therapy Institute (CARTI) Cancer Center during both the design and the construction phases of the project. This $90 million, 170,000 square foot facility in Little Rock, Arkansas, provides medical, surgical, and radiation oncology, as well as diagnostic radiology and hematology services. As reflected in Figure 14.7, the CAVE display was used extensively by architecture, engineering, and construction teams in a variety of configurations for collaborative design reviews, constructability assessments, structure, plumbing, and HVAC clash discovery and resolution, as well as overall project management between disciplines.

Figure 14.7 This image shows Nabholz Construction team members working with Polk Stanley Wilcox Architects within the University of Arkansas Emerging Analytics Center's state-of-the-art CAVE system on the Central Arkansas Radiation Therapy Institute (CARTI) Cancer Center project.
Credit: Image courtesy of Nabholz

The use of these visualization technologies on this project resulted in a number of quantifiable benefits. These included decisive design reviews leading to early detection of flaws, on-the-fly decision-making and design changes while there were still minimal cost implications, as well as net measureable schedule and cost savings.

Real Estate Sales Applications

In addition to assisting in the design and construction process, immersive and semi-immersive virtual reality systems are proving to be a powerful tool through which to facilitate existing real estate sales. In one example, Los Angeles–based Matthew Hood Real Estate Group at Sotheby's International Realty is using various implementations of the technologies to showcase luxury properties in Southern California and New York.

As shown in Figure 14.8, Hood's team uses a motorized, tripod-mounted Matterport camera that spins in place, simultaneously capturing high dynamic range (HDR) imagery and detailed 3D spatial data in the form of a point cloud. Using a tablet application to control the camera, multiple scans are captured along a path winding through the home or condo with the entire process taking just a few short hours. This data is then uploaded to Matterport's cloud servers, which calculate the interrelationships between the points to create a polygonal mesh, as well as seamlessly stitch together the various scans.

Figure 14.8 The Matterport Pro 3D Camera is used to gather high-resolution 3D scans of interior spaces. The room in this image is a single viewpoint shot from an actual scan of a space.
Credit: Image courtesy of MatthewHoodRE.com/Matterport, Inc

The net deliverable is a high-resolution, dimensionally accurate, and visually realistic 3D model of a full property such as is depicted via the "dollhouse" view in Figure 14.9. This model can then be imported into a variety of common design utilities such as Maya, AutoCAD, Revit,

SolidWorks, and the Unity software framework or other graphics engines for viewing through a variety of displays ranging from handheld viewers and mobile devices to head-mounted displays.

Unlike a panoramic photo which depicts a space from one fixed viewpoint, or a spherical video in which the viewer is similarly limited to changes in viewpoint orientation (roll, pitch, and yaw) while "along for the ride," 3D geometric models created using scanners such as Matterport enable the free exploration of the captured 3D geometry.

Figure 14.9 This image shows an example of a 3D dollhouse model created using multiple scans produced with a Matterport Pro 3D Camera. This model is imported into a simulation utility for viewing within a stereoscopic head-mounted display.
Credit: Image courtesy of Matterport, Inc

Potential buyers are currently provided with a Samsung GearVR display (see Chapter 6) and hand controller to enable them to freely navigate through the models. Because the broker is able to see where the user is looking at any given moment simply by glancing at a desktop monitor, detailed tours of a property can be provided and features of interest explained as though visiting the physical site.

The application of these enabling technologies is particularly well suited for the geographic region as well as the high net worth buyers and sellers that Hood serves. The efficiency of providing in-depth tours of multiple properties from a single location to narrow down interests saves considerable time and effort and eliminates unnecessary travel in an area notorious for challenging traffic patterns.

Adoption of these technologies has proven to be a powerful tool for Hood's firm, with efforts underway to expand these capabilities to other offices across the United States. Such a strategy would enable brokers on the other side of the country, or in other regions of the world, to show virtual models of properties to clients who would normally have to undertake time-consuming travel to visit the actual sites.

Architectural Acoustics

Modeling and simulation of architectural spaces is not limited to the visual realm. A growing number of architectural design firms are now employing sophisticated acoustic modeling software utilities as a means of predicting sonic performance of a space or structure to further enable clients to make optimal design decisions. These software packages import basic CAD geometry as well as the acoustical properties of building materials to model reflection, transmission, diffraction paths, and more. Functional at interactive rates, these simulations can be combined with real-time visual walk-throughs to give architects and clients accurate multisensory representations of proposed designs and alternatives.

These capabilities are also increasingly employed within computer games and other immersive entertainment settings to further add to the realism of the simulations. One of the leading software developers in this field is Impulsonic, Inc. of Carrboro, North Carolina.

Conclusion

This chapter has presented several case studies demonstrating a range of applications for immersive virtual reality technologies within the fields of architecture, construction, and real estate sales. While the approach and technology solutions varied, the ultimate objectives were essentially the same: to provide a means of visualizing, on a 1-to-1 scale, the complex geometry of an architectural space to designers, builders, and clients. Similar implementations can be found in hundreds of architectural, construction management, and real-estate offices across North America and around the world. Given the growing commercial availability of enabling hardware and software tools, the continued adoption of these technologies within these applications areas is all but assured.

The application of augmenting visualization solutions within these fields also holds significant potential and promise, although development of the necessary hardware and software solutions is occurring at a much slower pace than that of fully immersive systems. As pointed out in several areas in this book, the single largest source of delay is in the availability of optical see-through displays of sufficient resolution and field of view (FOV). Once this display hurdle is overcome (only a matter of time), the enabling software utilities will appear rather quickly.

CHAPTER 15

SCIENCE AND ENGINEERING

The use of interactive immersive display systems is in widespread use across a host of engineering fields. From the start of the design process through facilitating decision-making between multidisciplinary teams spread out across multiple locations globally, these technologies are having a profound impact on design quality, cost control, and workflow efficiency. In this chapter we explore a number of applications within varied engineering disciplines, highlighting the common challenges faced as well as the quantifiable benefits the systems provide.

Simulate and Innovate

Virtual and augmented reality are becoming vital tools in a number of engineering fields ranging from aerospace and automotive design to naval architecture and civil projects. Far more than a means to present design ideas to clients, these tools are having a demonstrable and quantifiable impact on actual engineering, manufacturing, and maintenance processes resulting in higher quality deliverables, fewer design flaws, and increased savings in terms of costs and man-hours. These benefits are being achieved through the ability to visualize and review large data sets at scale, often resulting in the reduction or elimination of the need for physical prototypes, through early error identification, the facilitation of efficient collaboration and decision-making, and the ability to analyze complex systems from viewpoints impossible to achieve using traditional displays. So important are these tools to the broader field that the National Academy of Engineering has designated the enhancement of virtual reality systems as one of the 14 Grand Challenges for Engineering in the 21st Century (NAE, 2015).

In this chapter we explore a number of key application examples within several engineering fields. Separated by industry, these examples will highlight both the design challenges faced as well as the benefits realized as a result of the use of various virtual and augmented reality systems.

Naval Architecture and Marine Engineering

Naval architects and marine engineers face a variety of design challenges similar to, but often well in excess of, those experienced by traditional architects. Within a self-contained entity of limited volume, engineers must include systems for propulsion and maneuvering, power generation and distribution, heating ventilation and air conditioning (HVAC), water distribution and sewage, cargo handling, and more. Because most ships have a human crew, naval architects must also include birthing spaces and passageways, galleys, heads, and other necessities. Hulls must be designed to move through a fluid medium with minimal resistance and, in some cases, leaving minimal disturbances on the surface. Given the harsh operating environment, ships must be designed with multiple watertight compartments, often with more than one hull, and they must be able to deal with the immense forces being exerted by wave action and the environment. And this is just what is necessary to have a functioning, seaworthy, independently operating vessel. Depending on the intended use or mission, the list of additional shipboard systems can grow significantly. In the case of warships, it includes all of the above, as well as offensive and defensive weapons systems, the ability to store, service, launch, and recover aircraft or smaller vessels, incredible arrays of sensors, and more.

In an effort to convert the functional specifications of massive shipbuilding programs into effective, cost-efficient designs, ship builders have been some of the earliest adopters of immersive 3D visualization techniques, with their use beginning from the start of the engineering process—often years in advance of the first pieces of steel being cut in the building phase. One such company is the British multinational defense, security, and aerospace company BAE Systems, headquartered in London.

British Royal Navy Type 26 Global Combat Ship

In two of the most recent examples, engineers with BAE are employing large-scale immersive 3D display techniques in the design and prototyping of the new Type-26 Global Combat Ship as well as the Offshore Patrol Vessel for Britain's Royal Navy (shown in Figure 15.1). With both expected to enter service between 2017 and 2020 (RINA, 2011), the new multimission warships are being designed for joint and multinational operations across the full spectrum of warfare, including complex combat operations, counter piracy efforts, as well as humanitarian and disaster relief.

Figure 15.1 London-based BAE Systems utilizes a variety of immersive displays to assist in the design of surface combatants for the British Royal Navy.
Credit: Image courtesy of BAE Systems plc

Using the Sener FORAN CAD/CAM ship design system and the Windchill Product Lifecycle Management (PLM) program from PTC, Inc. (formerly Parametric Technology Corporation), engineers across a host of disciplines are able to visualize the ship's models at various stages within the design, fabrication, and assembly phases using large-format 3D display solutions from Virtalis, LTD of Cheshire, UK. At least five visualization suites of varying configurations have been constructed, including three at BAE's Glasgow shipyard, and one each at its Portsmouth and Bristol bases. All the systems are networked, enabling close collaboration by geographically separated groups.

As shown in Figure 15.2, the various systems allow single and multiple engineering personnel, at single and multiple locations, to explore and evaluate every inch of the ship design from angles, scales, and in subsystem combinations impossible to achieve with comparable insight using traditional techniques.

Figure 15.2 BAE Systems engineers use multisided computer-assisted virtual environment (CAVE) displays and large 3D projection walls to freely explore the complex designs of forthcoming warships. *Credit: Image courtesy of BAE Systems plc*

Although the initial launch of the Type 26 shipbuilding effort will not begin until late 2016, extensive use of these simulation and visualization systems is now underway finalizing key design changes from stakeholders. In one example, following a request by the Royal Navy for the addition of a new observation station for an officer to monitor launch and recovery of Merlin helicopters on the vessel's helo-deck, design changes were quickly implemented and field of view (FOV) and line of sight studies performed using the simulation system to ensure proper implementation of the design change.

British Royal Navy Astute Class Nuclear Submarines

These warship projects are not the first instances BAE has applied these visualization technologies in the design and construction of ships for the Royal Navy. An earlier example was the design and construction of the Astute Class of nuclear powered submarines, some of the most complex machines ever developed. A highly unique aspect specified for this project's implementation of immersive display technologies was that the visualization solution had to be easily accessible not only to a multidisciplinary engineering team, but also to the actual welders, pipe fitters, electricians, and other workers within the shipbuilding and assembly complex located at Barrow-in-Furness, England, during the construction process.

To accommodate this requirement, in addition to three "VR suites" located at different design facilities, Virtalis has also supplied BAE with two rear projection–based "VR-cabins" that are positioned on gantries surrounding the submarines under construction, providing a direct replacement for expensive physical mockups. Workers are encouraged to visit the cabins and use the systems to better familiarize themselves with specific aspects of their work compartment or to analyze construction or installation problems with which they are struggling (Virtalis, 2010). BAE reports significant benefits in this particular system's implementation, including a reduction of time, money, and effort spent on physical prototypes, an increase in design/build productivity, as well as early identification of design conflicts. As of 2015, seven boats have been ordered, three of which have already been delivered and are in service, with the remaining four slated for delivery through 2024. With the completion and deployment of each new boat, design changes and updates are then implemented for the next boats in the production line. To date, the virtual reality systems remain an integral part of the design/build process.

Automotive Engineering

Automotive companies face a number of unique design and engineering challenges in the annual development of new makes and models of cars and trucks. Automobiles are sophisticated machines comprising tens of thousands of individual parts and dozens of subassemblies, all of which must come together within specific tolerances and performance standards to ultimately meet high customer expectations for reliability and appearance. Not only do the complete automobiles need to be designed, detailed, and rigorously tested, but the same holds true for the actual assembly processes. Thus, from the major manufacturers all the way down to the small 10-man design shops who support their efforts, engineers are constantly on the prowl for new tools and methods enabling more accurate, efficient, and cost-effective delivery of competitive products. To this end, immersive virtual environment simulation technologies are proving to be powerful solutions with which to meet these goals.

Ford Motor Company

Among the numerous automotive manufacturers to implement the use of these technologies is Ford Motor Company of Dearborn, Michigan. Using a variety of immersive display methodologies, Ford designers and engineers around the world collaborate in real time on tasks ranging from design of mechanical systems, vehicle appearance, and overall customer experience, to overall manufacturing feasibility reviews, process layout, and ergonomic studies for the safety of employees on the production line.

Design Analysis

As shown in Figure 15.3, one visualization system used in such tasks relies on an nVisor ST50 stereoscopic head-mounted display from NVIS, Inc (see Chapter 7, "Augmenting Displays") to present designers and engineers with high-resolution stereoscopic imagery of vehicles under development.

Figure 15.3 Ford Motor Company makes extensive use of immersive visualization tools, including stereoscopic head-mounted displays, in the evaluation of automobile designs.
Credit: Image courtesy of Ford Motor Company

Not only do the visualization tools allow workers to explore full-scale lifelike 3D models of the interior and exterior of a vehicle design down to precise evaluation of margins, gaps, and fit-and-finish, they also enable engineers and designers to freely examine a vehicle's underlying structure to study how mechanical and electrical systems interact within the architecture.

In addition to the main Immersion Lab at Ford's headquarters in the United States, the company has established design collaboration centers with similar capabilities in Australia, Germany, China, India, Brazil, and Mexico. These facilities enable multidisciplinary groups of engineers and designers to collaborate in a common virtual environment long before a physical proto-type is ever constructed. The quality of the simulations is exceptional, providing the design teams highly accurate gradation of colors, contrast, shadows, textures, lighting, and reflections.

In 2013 alone, Ford designers and engineers used these technologies to inspect more than 135,000 details on 193 virtual vehicle prototypes (Ford, 2013).

Production Simulation

In keeping with the multidisciplinary approach to the use of these systems, while automotive designers focus on a vehicle's look and the customer experience, Ford virtual manufacturing experts perform detailed studies on design feasibility and the safety of employees on the production line. Here again, these studies can take place two to three years in advance of a new-vehicle launch.

3D printing is also used within these simulation scenarios. In one example shown in Figure 15.4, a physical mockup of a transmission for the 2015 F-150 pickup was prepared to carry out studies of the assembly line mating process. (Note the reflective markers on the transmission mockup, hand of the operator, and head-mounted display along with the infrared optical tracking system on the scaffolding.)

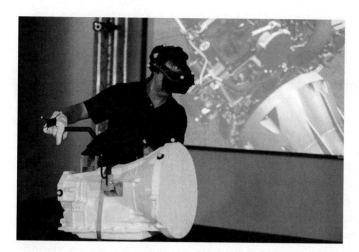

Figure 15.4 This figure shows an example of a Ford engineer using a simple 3D printed transmission mockup along with a virtual reality simulation to validate an assembly line mating procedure for the 2015 F-150 pickup truck. Such tests have proven to be highly reliable when compared to standalone virtual simulations and help to drive better production decisions.
Credit: Image courtesy of Ford Motor Company

According to Ford, these simulation studies, in addition to new ergonomics technologies, lift-assist devices, workstation redesigns, and data-driven process changes, have reduced injury rates by 70 percent for its more than 50,000 "industrial athletes" in the Unites States, and many more around the world (Ford, 2015).

Aerospace Engineering

Aerospace engineering is a field principally focused on the design, development, and testing of airborne and space-borne systems. From aircraft and both manned and unmanned spacecraft, to rockets and missiles, these systems pose highly unique design challenges due to their overall complexity, demanding operating conditions, and mission-critical nature. As the complexity of these systems increases, so too does the need for the best possible multilevel design and development review process to minimize errors and system conflicts, as well as maximize returns on capital-intensive projects.

Lockheed Martin Corporation

An ideal example of the comprehensive application of these visualization technologies within the aerospace arena is the global security and aerospace company Lockheed Martin, based in Bethesda, Maryland. The company operates several virtual simulation facilities, but one of the most comprehensive is the Collaborative Human Immersive Laboratory (CHIL) located in Littleton, Colorado. The following examples offer an overview of how these technologies have been applied to a variety of programs within Lockheed Martin's various business units.

Space Systems

Lockheed Martin is the prime contractor selected by NASA to design, develop, and build the Orion Multi-Purpose Crew Vehicle, NASA's first spacecraft designed for long-duration, manned deep space exploration. Orion is intended to carry astronauts to destinations beyond low Earth orbit including the moon, asteroids, and eventually Mars, and then return them safely to Earth.

As depicted in Figure 15.5, prior to Orion actually being manufactured on Lockheed's production floor in preparation for its initial test flight on December 5, 2014, the entire spacecraft was assembled in virtual space using a variety of visualization tools at the CHIL facility, including a CAVE and stereoscopic head-mounted display. This process enabled critical reviews of the entire system design and assembly effort, all the way down to such minutia as where specific technicians should be positioned, to turn up and resolve any problems ahead of time. The net result was a measurable savings of time and expense in the overall project.

Figure 15.5 Lockheed Martin used state-of-the-art immersive CAVE systems and head-mounted displays to fully evaluate the design and assembly of NASA's Orion Multi-Purpose Crew Vehicle.
Credit: Image courtesy of Lockheed Martin Corporation

The Orion program is just one of many such projects within which these tools have been applied with great success and quantifiable outcomes. In fact, most of Lockheed's major space programs are now carried out using a strategy the company refers to as "virtual pathfinding," which makes use of digital data throughout the entire design and production process to reduce the time and expense required to build products.

Another example is their application in projects associated with developing the next-generation GPS III satellites as well as unmanned systems such as the Mars Atmosphere and Volatile EvolutioN Mission (MAVEN) space probe shown in Figure 15.6. Here again, not only did the actual spacecraft undergo extensive design reviews via simulation, but so too did the final build and testing procedures.

Figure 15.6 This side-by-side image shows a virtual simulation, and the real instance, of the movement of the Mars Atmosphere and Volatile EvolutioN Mission (MAVEN) spacecraft into Lockheed Martin's Thermal Vacuum Chamber (TVAC) in Littleton, Colorado.
Credit: Image courtesy of Lockheed Martin Corporation

Aeronautics

Lockheed programs within which these immersive simulation technologies are being utilized also extend into the aeronautical business unit and include extensive use of motion capture technologies to carry out ergonomic studies. Similar to earlier descriptions of their application in the manufacturing of automobiles, by enabling engineers to conduct virtual assembly and maintenance tasks well before a product is physically produced, obstacles to completion such as improper tool clearances, worker accessibility, and safety can be identified early on and the appropriate design changes or other accommodations made before they are encountered in production or in the field. As is shown in Figure 15.7, these capabilities have already been used in such tasks as developing proper arming and refueling procedures associated with the F-35 Lightning II multirole fighter.

Figure 15.7 Lockheed Martin engineers make extensive use of motion capture technologies for virtual design reviews and development of arming and refueling procedures associated for the F-35 Lightning II multirole fighter.
Credit: Image courtesy of Lockheed Martin Corporation

Lockheed Martin has also adopted the use of augmented reality visualization solutions into a number of its aeronautics programs in an effort to increase the effectiveness and efficiency of inspection and maintenance solutions. Most notable are their application with the F-35 and F-22 fighter programs. Using a unique set of software utilities developed by NGRAIN, Inc of Vancouver, British Columbia, technicians are able to use a mobile tablet device or an optical see-thru head-mounted display to precisely overlay live systems data and 3D graphics on top of a particular task area, including instructions and animated equipment procedures. The net result has been a significant and quantifiable reduction in repair time and the minimization of errors, both of which are critical to these platforms because even the smallest amount of surface damage to a stealth aircraft can dramatically impact radar visibility.

Nuclear Engineering and Manufacturing

Manufacturing represents a sizeable contribution to the economy of the United Kingdom. In an effort to position the UK industrial base with the expertise and capabilities necessary to increasingly draw high-value manufacturing (HVM) projects from abroad, the government has invested hundreds of millions of British Pounds into a series of seven elite centers of excellence, each of which is focused on accelerating the capability for innovation in specific areas and helping to drive future economic growth with globally competitive products and services. Known as Catapult Centers, these facilities bridge the gaps between government industrial policy, academic research, and business and span fields ranging from biologics and composites to low carbon transport systems and satellite applications for the exploitation of space.

A number of the Catapult Centers make extensive use of immersive virtual reality systems in the course of their operations. Of particular relevance to this chapter are those applications found at the Nuclear Advanced Manufacturing Research Center (NAMRC) located in Sheffield, South Yorkshire. Led by the University of Sheffield, the NAMRC works with UK companies to improve capabilities in manufacturing the highly specialized components found in nuclear power facilities and other energy sectors.

The engineering and manufacturing tasks encountered within the nuclear industry are similar, although in many ways uniquely different, than many of the other examples provided in this chapter. One of the most significant differences is in the sheer size and weight of components and systems involved. Most nuclear reactors generating power for civilian use are massive structures, with individual precision components in some cases weighing many tens of tons, such as shown in Figure 15.8 (Virtalis, 2010).

As these individual components are completed and then combined with others, they must be moved, leading to significant safety risks and logistical challenges. Often other work has to stop while these large components and structures are being lifted and moved from station to station through a facility. In fact, just moving parts of this size is estimated to account for a fifth of the total manufacturing lead time (NAMRC, 2012). This lost time translates into lost productivity and significantly higher costs across the span of a construction project.

Figure 15.8 This image shows the immense scale of just one section of a steam turbine used within a nuclear power plant. This single unit weighs 20 metric tons.
Credit: Image by photosoup © 123RF.com

Additional challenges are faced in ensuring absolute design precision ideally before manufacturing, but most importantly, before final assembly. Given the size and weight challenges mentioned earlier, it is essential to identify design conflicts and imperfections as early in the process as possible.

Some of the many ways in which NAMRC is helping companies such as Rolls Royce optimize manufacturing efforts (and thus more successfully compete for business in the global nuclear industry supply chain) is through visualization of factory layout and process planning, collaborative design reviews, virtual prototyping (as shown in Figure 15.9), and human factors assessments.

Figure 15.9 Engineers with the UK Nuclear Advanced Manufacturing Research Center use a variety of state-of-the-art immersive displays to assist companies such as Rolls Royce in optimizing processes for manufacturing and movement of large components for nuclear power plants.
Credit: Image courtesy of Nuclear AMRC

As an example, production processes and movement of these large components have been modeled using discrete event simulation (DES) software and combined with a virtual model of the fabrication facility to evaluate the complete factory cycle over time. The result is identification of where parts are interacting and potentially causing delays, which is particularly useful in nonlinear routed flow factories (NAMRC, 2012).

The tools used in these services span the entire range of immersive display solutions currently available, including a variety of different stereoscopic head-mounted devices, a 3.2 square meter CAVE-like display from UK-based Virtalis known as an ActiveCube, which can accommodate up to four individuals, and an ActiveWall 3D visualization system that can be used by up to 25 participants.

Conclusion

As shown in this chapter, the use of immersive visual display technologies is proving to be a powerful extension to current practices in a variety of engineering fields. These technologies directly support and complement an engineer's application of science, mathematics, and empirical evidence to invent, innovate, build, and improve structures, machines, and processes. The broad availability of software pathways enabling the use of the most common computer-aided design/computer-aided manufacturing (CAD/CAM) and computer-integrated manufacturing (CIM) software from which model geometry originates has dramatically accelerated this widespread adoption.

Among the many benefits that immersive display technologies provide is that these systems enable multidisciplinary teams of professionals to communicate and collaborate using the common language of 3D visualization. Watching a group of engineers from different fields enter a CAVE or otherwise participate in a common simulation is a fascinating process in and of itself. Invariably, the result is new insights, ideas, and solutions, leading to faster design decisions and fewer errors. These and the many other benefits outlined in the case studies in this chapter lead this author to believe that application of immersive displays within the engineering sector will likely be some of the highest impact uses of these technologies.

In comparison, at the time of this book's preparation, the widespread use of augmenting displays within the broader engineering arena is still in its relative infancy, with the primary bottleneck to date being a lack of affordable, commercially available, optical see-through displays, although this is changing fast. While the industry waits for a number of promised solutions to enter the commercial marketplace, interim platforms such as smartphones and tablets are serving as ideal systems for applications development.

CHAPTER 16

HEALTH AND MEDICINE

From education, training, and procedure rehearsal, to enhancing a surgeon's situational awareness, to tools that aid in recovery and rehabilitation, a growing number of applications of virtual and augmented reality–enabling technologies within the physical and mental health fields are showing demonstrable results, as well as significant potential for future development. In this chapter we explore a number of these applications, highlighting the specific problems they solve, their major enabling technology components, and their strengths compared to solutions traditionally employed.

Advancing the Field of Medicine

The application of virtual and augmented reality within the physical and mental health fields is having a transformational impact on a number of areas in the practice of medicine. From powerful, clinically validated procedural simulators to innovative information displays designed to increase a physician's level situational awareness and optimize workflows, great strides are being made to apply these technologies in a manner that ultimately results in better care being rendered, more favorable patient outcomes, and more efficient use of resources.

In this chapter we will explore several innovative applications of immersive, semi-immersive, and augmented display technologies, detailing the specific problem being addressed, the solution employed, as well as quantifiable benefits. These examples represent only a small fraction of the number of solid, deployed applications, development efforts, and clinical trials underway at dozens of universities and hospitals around the world, not to mention the fascinating offerings of many companies formed in the past few years with hardware and software solutions targeting this field. To attempt to do so would far exceed the scope and intent of this chapter, and perhaps even this entire book. As such, the cases highlighted are selected with the specific goal of illustrating the broad range of applications possible with careful thought and planning, as well as their far-reaching, problem-solving impact.

Training Applications

Every human being comes to understand the reality of the old adage "practice makes perfect." In nearly all areas of human endeavor, from the most basic skills like children learning to accurately guide food into their mouth instead of their nose, to mastery of a range of particular talents as adults, there is no question that practice and training improve human performance across most physical and mental activities. And the greater the complexity of a task, the more practice is needed, not only to initially develop a skill but often to maintain performance levels. These truths are no more apparent than in the varied fields of medicine, where the health and well-being of individuals is at stake.

To this end, the past decade has seen a dramatic increase in the number of simulation and training utilities developed for the medical community based on, or incorporating, virtual and augmented reality–enabling technologies, and their adoption is having a transformational effect on the field. From assisting students and practitioners in developing and refining specific skills ranging from delicate microsurgical techniques to complex invasive procedures, the benefit of using these technologies over more traditional methods of skills development has been well documented.

Perhaps one of the greatest benefits to the use of computer-based simulation technologies in the medical field is the creation of an environment where the student or practitioner is able to fail without consequence. Failure is absolutely critical to the learning process, although in medicine, it can have dire consequences. Thus, it is obviously far better to make mistakes in training and procedure rehearsal than in a clinic or operating suite.

HelpMeSee Cataract Surgery Simulator

According to the World Health Organization, the leading cause of blindness worldwide is untreated cataracts, which are a clouding of the eye's natural lens resulting in the reduced transmission of light to the retina. (See Chapter 3, "The Mechanics of Sight"; WHO, 2014a.) According to the latest assessments, more than 20 million people worldwide, or approximately half of all cases of blindness globally, are the result of this condition. In most instances cataracts are a normal result of aging, although children are sometimes born with the condition. By the age of 80, more than half of all Americans will either have a cataract in one or both eyes or have had cataract surgery (WHO, 2014b; NEI, 2009).

Although corrective surgery, normally an outpatient procedure, is easily obtained in developed regions of the world, there are significant barriers to access in less developed nations, including the costs of treatment, few trained practitioners, and lack of awareness (Tabin, 2005).

To combat this growing problem, HelpMeSee, a U.S.-based nonprofit organization and global campaign to eliminate cataract blindness, has joined with a number of partners— including Moog, Inc (New York, New York), InSimo (Strasbourg, France), and SenseGraphics (Kista, Sweden)—in the development of a high-performance surgical simulator used to train in-country specialists in a fast, effective, and high-quality procedure to correct the condition and restore vision.

Known as the Manual Small Incision Cataract Surgery (MSICS) simulator, the system is used to train specialists to perform a low-cost, highly effective, small-incision surgical procedure that enables the removal of a clouded, cataractous lens and replaces it with an artificial intraocular lens implant in as little as 5 minutes for an adult patient and 15 minutes for a child (HelpMeSee, 2014a).

As shown in Figure 16.1, the MSICS simulator is a self-contained, cart-based system incorporating an armature-mounted, high-definition (HD) stereoscopic display taking the place of what would normally be a stereo microscope. As with the real surgical procedure, the human operator would be seated near the head looking into the viewing device. Peering into the viewer, the operator is presented with an exceptionally detailed graphical model of a human eye. The simulator's main user interface consists of bimanual surgical instruments that are identical to those used in the actual surgical procedure.

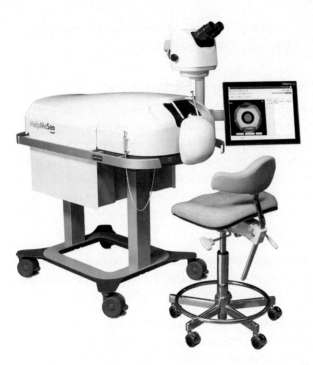

Figure 16.1 The Manual Small Incision Cataract Surgery (MSICS) simulator developed by HelpMeSee, Moog Industrial Group, and several software partners will be used to train thousands of cataract surgical specialists in developing nations.
Credit: Image courtesy of Moog, Inc/HelpMeSee

As the operator moves the instruments and interacts with the virtual eyeball, high-fidelity haptics technologies developed by Moog, combined with physics-based virtual tissue models and a simulation engine from SenseGraphics and InSimo, provide a level of realism, both visually and tactually, that is virtually indistinguishable from that experienced during a live procedure performed by an experienced surgeon (HelpMeSee, 2014a).

The system also includes an instructor workstation and courseware that will ultimately encompass more than 240 training tasks and complications that cataract specialists could encounter during live surgical procedures (Moog, 2015; Singh and Strauss, 2014).

System rollout is intended to begin in 2016 with the establishment of up to seven training centers spread across Asia, Africa, and Latin America, each capable of training up to 1,000 MSICS surgeon candidates annually, with each trainee expected to undergo between 400 and 700 hours of learning with roughly 60% of this time spent working with the simulator (Broyles, 2012). According to HelpMeSee, each surgical specialist trained in this procedure is capable of performing upward of 2,500 procedures per year at the cost of approximately $50 USD per operation (HelpMeSee, 2014b; 2014d).

Simodont Dental Trainer

In dental schools worldwide, students have traditionally developed their clinical skills by using drills and other tools on plastic teeth within "phantom heads." This is an expensive, time-consuming process and, from an instructor's viewpoint, highly subjective in terms of evaluating a student's performance. To help students build a stronger set of essential skills earlier, and at considerably less expense, Moog Industrial Group and the Academic Centre for Dentistry in Amsterdam (ACTA) collaborated in the development of Simodont, a high-quality, high-fidelity, bimanual dexterity simulator that combines 3D visualization, tactile, and force feedback technologies as well as audio to deliver highly realistic training in operative dental procedures (Forsell, 2011; Moog, 2011).

As shown in Figure 16.2, the user is seated in a position similar to that of a dentist in a clinical setting. Wearing polarized stereo glasses, the operator looks into a viewing window and is presented with a sharp, correctly sized 3D model of a patient's mouth directly in the physical workspace of the hand instruments to be used within the specific lesson (handpieces, burs, mirror, and so on). As the user moves the hand instruments, which are the same as the standard tools she would be encountering in a clinical setting, the virtual tools mimic those movements precisely. When the virtual drill interacts with a virtual tooth, the simulation engine and haptics drivers provide a full visual, audio, and haptic experience of drilling a physical tooth, including crisp rendering of drill and contact forces as well as hardness of a tooth's enamel. As with a drill in a dentist's office, a foot peddle controls the speed of the virtual drill.

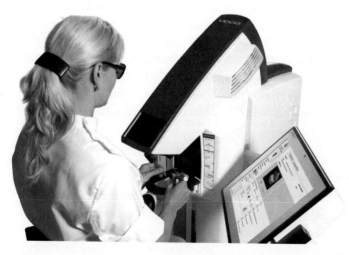

Figure 16.2 The Simodont Dental Trainer developed by Moog Industrial Group and the Academic Centre for Dentistry in Amsterdam (ACTA) is used by dental students around the world to practice and refine many of the manual skills they will need when treating live patients.
Credit: Image courtesy of Moog, Inc

Sophisticated courseware developed by ACTA provides a range of training procedures and scenarios, as well as the ability of an instructor to play back and review a student's movements to provide feedback in a more objective manner. The system also enables scans of real teeth to be imported to infinitely expand the selection of case scenarios.

The Simodont dental trainer has proven so successful at building student skill set that it is now in use at dentistry schools around the world.

As with other medical procedure simulators, the value that such systems bring to a learning environment cannot be overstated. From a student's perspective, simulators provide a powerful tool with which to develop and refine skills essential to treating patients once they progress from a preclinical to a clinical environment. For instructors, simulators such as Simodont enable significantly greater flexibility in development of training scenarios and pedagogical options to ultimately turn out better graduates.

Treatment Applications

"Ain't it funny how a melody can bring back a memory?
Take you to another place in time,
Completely change your state of mind."

—Clint Black, *State of Mind*, 1993

These lyrics from the 1993 country music hit *State of Mind* by Clint Black perfectly illustrate the power of the human brain to store and retrieve memories based on sounds, sights, smells, and a variety of other environmental cues. Clinically classified as *episodic autobiographical memories* (EAMs), they are an involuntary function of the human perceptual and memory systems that add both tremendous benefit, and more than occasional troubles, to our existence. One of the areas where this function is highly problematic is in retention of sensory information and memories from times of extreme mental and physical trauma, such as is experienced on war-time battlefields.

Post-Traumatic Stress Disorder

Since September 11, 2001, America's armed forces have endured more than 14 years of high-intensity ground combat operations and a deployment tempo that has led to significant behavioral health challenges within our active duty and veteran population (Rizzo et al., 2012). As of 2014, some 2.5 million U.S. service members had deployed one or more times in support of Operation Enduring Freedom (OEF) and Operation Iraqi Freedom (OIF) (Ramchand et al., 2014; Hautzinger et al., 2015). Of these numbers, it is estimated that upward of 18% of all returning service members are struggling with psychological injuries, and a majority of those deployed report exposure to multiple life-changing *stressors* (Hoge et al., 2004; APA, 2007).

Collectively, these psychological conditions are classified under the official label of *post-traumatic stress disorder* (PTSD) or *post-traumatic stress injury*, which the American Psychological Association defines as an anxiety disorder that can develop after a person is exposed to one or more traumatic events, such as major stress, warfare, or other threats on a person's life (DeAngelis, 2008)[1]. Research shows this is a disorder that, once manifested, often becomes chronic (Hoge et al., 2004).

To date, published research suggests one of the most widely used and empirically validated psychotherapeutic treatments for the condition is known as **prolonged-exposure therapy,** which consists of two components: *imaginal* and *in vivo* exposure. As the name would suggest, imaginal exposure involves a trained therapist carefully guiding the client to verbally recount, in a gradual, controlled, and repeated manner, the traumatic experiences from memory. *In vivo* exposure involves a simulated exposure to feared objects, activities, or situations, in both a rapid as well as progressive manner. Both components are said to allow the individual to safely engage, evaluate, and emotionally process the stressors, enabling the person to overcome excessive fear and anxiety (Foa et al., 2007; DeAngelis, 2008).

Although published research clearly demonstrates a high rate of effectiveness using prolonged-exposure therapy in the treatment of PTSD, significant challenges still exist with its traditional delivery. One of the most formidable obstacles has been the reliance on the patient to mentally visualize the traumatic experiences. This is a major impediment because avoidance of trauma reminders is one of the key identifying symptoms of PTSD (Rizzo et al., 2006). There is also an obvious hindrance in the ability to put the patient and clinician into a convincing setting that enables controlled re-exposure to widely varying traumatic stimuli. In other words, there is only so much that can be done within a clinician's office to effectively simulate the stressful situations and environment of a combat zone. That is, until recently.

Bravemind (Virtual Iraq and Afghanistan)

Leveraging advances in immersive displays, increased computational performance, as well as scene and character modeling, researchers with the University of Southern California/Institute of Creative Technologies (USC/ICT) have developed the basis for a new clinical tool that facilitates the manner and effectiveness in which prolonged exposure therapy is delivered to soldiers suffering from combat-related PTSD.

A collaborative effort between USC/ICT, Georgia-based Virtually Better Inc., Naval Medical Center-San Diego (NMC-SD), and the Geneva Foundation and known as *Bravemind*, the system enables the controlled, gradual exposure of patients to fully immersive virtual representations of the experiences that underlie his/her traumatic combat-related memories until there is a diminishing, or *habituation*, to the anxiety-producing stimuli (Virtually Better, 2008).

---

1   Although PTSD is discussed within this chapter in direct relation to military personnel, such psychological injuries and conditions are also experienced by many others, including victims of rape, terrorist attacks, first responders, and more.

As shown in Figure 16.3, the key hardware components of a Bravemind system consist of commercial off-the-shelf technologies including a PC, dual monitors, a Sony HMZ T3W stereoscopic head-mounted display, a position/orientation sensor, and a handheld controller neatly built into a medical-grade mobile cart. Not limited to just the sights and sounds of a battlefield environment, the Bravemind system also includes a tactile feedback component in the form of a small floor platform into which is built a sub-woofer to simulate vibrational cues such as engine rumbling, explosions, firefights, and corresponding ambient noises. A scent machine is also provided that can deliver situation-relevant odors (including cordite, burning rubber, diesel fuel, garbage, and gunpowder).

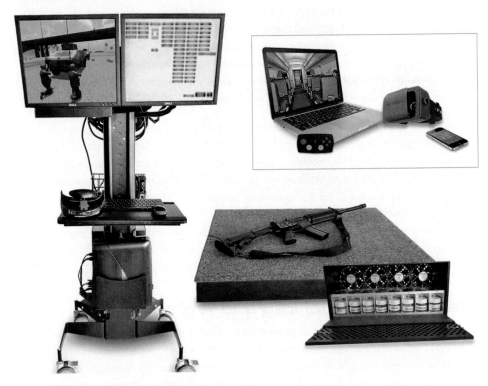

Figure 16.3 The Bravemind simulator developed by the University of Southern California/Institute of Creative Technologies is specifically designed to provide immersive virtual reality exposure therapy to soldiers suffering from post-traumatic stress disorder (PTSD).
Credit: Image courtesy of Virtually Better, Inc. www.VirtuallyBetter.com

At the time of this book's preparation, two main virtual environment simulation software packages were available: Virtual Iraq and Virtual Afghanistan. Both contain baseline models of various battlefield environments resembling Middle Eastern cities as well as desert road environments. Clinicians are provided considerable flexibility and control in engaging users within a variety of different scenarios and intensity levels, including foot patrols, urban warfare, vehicle convoys, bridge crossings, and medical evacuations via helicopters.

Quantifiable Benefits

Across a number of studies (Rizzo et al., 2015; Gerardi et al., 2008; Reger and Gahm, 2008; Rizzo et al., 2007; Difede et al., 2007; Difede and Hoffman, 2002), outcomes resulting from the use of virtual reality exposure therapy in the treatment of post-traumatic stress disorder have been both statistically and clinically significant. This includes patients with no prior PTSD treatment, those who previously underwent more traditional exposure therapy, as well as active duty service members actually treated in the war zone.

So promising are the outcomes of the use of these simulation utilities that the Bravemind system is in active use at more than 50 sites around the United States, including VA hospitals, military medical centers, and university research centers, to study and treat PTSD.

Phobias

Virtual reality exposure therapy (VRET) has also been demonstrated in a number of investigations to produce statistically and clinically significant outcomes when used to treat a variety of phobias, including the fears of flying, heights, and storms.

Fear of Flying/Fear of Heights/Fear of Storms Treatment Suites

Georgia-based Virtually Better Inc. has produced several commercially available PC-based VRET software suites specifically designed to be used in the treatment of common phobias and addictions, as well as others for pain distraction and relaxation. Unlike systems requiring more robust capabilities and peripheral devices such as the Bravemind system mentioned earlier, some of these VRET suites, as illustrated in Figure 16.4, can be run on a notebook PC and utilize a smartphone-based stereoscopic head-mounted display. (See Chapter 6.)

Figure 16.4 Virtually Better Inc. has developed several PC-based virtual reality exposure therapy applications specifically for treatment of phobias such as the fear of flying, fear of heights, and fear of storms.
Credit: Image courtesy of Virtually Better, Inc. www.VirtuallyBetter.com

Accelerometers within the smartphone handle tracking of the user's head orientation (roll, pitch, and yaw), while a small hand controller enables the patient to safely translate, at her own pace, her viewpoint through the simulation models. Here again, clinicians are provided considerable flexibility and control in engaging users within a variety of different scenarios to achieve the desired outcomes for the specific treatment plan.

Quantifiable Benefits

A 2015 meta-analysis (a statistical technique for combining the findings from multiple independent studies) of 14 VRET clinical trials on specific phobias arrived at two powerful findings: patients performed significantly better on post-treatment behavioral assessments than before treatments and, the results of behavioral assessments at post-treatment and during follow-up showed no significant differences with traditional in vivo techniques. The net takeaway from the study is that VRET can produce significant behavioral changes in real-life situations (Morina et al., 2015). Extrapolating beyond these core findings, you can easily see that, applied correctly, the use of VRET can have a significant impact in terms of increasing treatment efficiency as well as lowering costs given the reduced need for the patient and clinician to make offsite visits to engage in *in-vivo* treatment scenarios.

Vascular Imaging

Accessing a vein to draw blood or to provide intravenous (IV) therapy is one of the most challenging clinical tasks faced by health professionals, including lab techs and nurses, EMTs, military field medics, anesthesiologists, and everyone in between. Although it is one of the most routinely performed invasive procedures globally, a variety of circumstances and conditions can make this seemingly simple task exceedingly difficult, including tiny spidery veins, subcutaneous fat, darker complexions, vasoconstriction due to cold temperatures, dehydration, hemodialysis, and more.

Evena Eyes-On Glass

To make this process easier, California-based Evena Medical has developed a head-mounted, stereoscopic, augmented reality display that allows a health worker to peer through the skin and visualize the underlying vascular structures in near real time, enabling the selection of the best veins for the invasive procedure. As shown in Figure 16.5, this device, known as Eyes-On Glass, uses a patented multispectral lighting system built into the brow piece of the display that projects four near-infrared (NIR) wavelengths of light falling between 600 and 1000 μm to illuminate the targeted area of the body. As blood absorbs these wavelengths of light at greater levels than surrounding tissues such as skin and muscle, it appears darker, and thus, an optical contrast is produced. Two custom-designed cameras sensitive to these particular wavelengths (one camera for each eye) collect video imagery, which is transferred to a belt-worn controller.

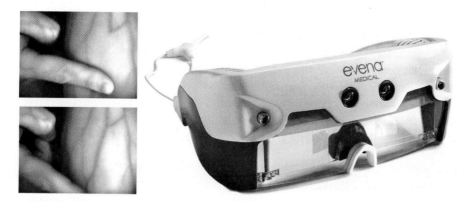

Figure 16.5 Evena's Eyes-On Glass helps clinicians visualize a patient's veins by using a unique lighting and video system to overlay an enhanced view onto the wearer's real-world view.
Credit: Kent Lacin Photography, Evena Medical

The controller interlaces the video imagery from across the four different wavelengths (separately for each eye). The result is then returned to the display portion of the headset, which is itself built around the display subassembly of the Epson Moverio BT-200. (See Chapter 5, "Augmenting Displays.") Projectors in the display then overlay the separate left and right video channels on top of the wearer's real-world scene, resulting in a clinically useful stereoscopic 3D view of the worksite that dramatically enhances the healthcare worker's view of the venous network.

As shown in the inset of Figure 16.5, the effect of this device in revealing what is normally an invisible vascular structure is plainly obvious.

Quantifiable Benefits

The benefits of this type of device in a clinical environment are numerous. In the United States alone, more than 2.5 million venipuncture procedures are performed daily (Walsh, 2008; Ogden-Grable and Gill, 2005). It has been estimated that up to 60% of children and 40% of adults require multiple attempts to access a vein (Frey, 1998; Harris, 2004). With such failure rates, this basic procedure experienced by nearly everyone who enters a hospital for treatment is one of the leading causes of medical injury. Add to this the costs of additional supplies, labor, and IV-related complications that can extend hospital stays, and it is easy to see how such an imaging device can be of significant benefit.

Healthcare Informatics

Consider the information-rich environment of a modern hospital. Each moment, the medical staff is inundated with extraordinary amounts of data in the form of alphanumeric displays, graphics, flashing lights, status tones, and alarms from multiple sources, the totality represent-ing the vital parameters and overall physical state of a patient. This information includes heart rate and rhythm monitors, blood pressure readings, respiration rate, oxygen saturation, body temperature, EKG and EEG traces, preoperative and real-time medical imaging products, as well as intravenous fluid and medication rates to name just a few. Given this tsunami of information, it is easy to see how physicians can quickly become overwhelmed. In fact, a compelling argument can be made that the cognitive strain resulting from ever-increasing advances in patient monitoring technologies may actually *increase* the potential of human error.

An equally important problem exists in the form of a physician becoming so fixated on a particular task or procedure that key information, such as a critical change in vital signs, is missed.

This combination of two information management challenges (too much versus too little) is most acute within an operating room where a surgical team must carry out complex invasive procedures while concurrently monitoring sensor data flowing to a variety of displays spread around and above the operating table and often even across the room.

The combination of task and information saturation, as well as the need for increased situational awareness, is strikingly similar to challenges faced by pilots of high-performance fighter aircraft. It also appears to have similar solutions.

VitalStream

California-based Vital Enterprises has developed a software platform known as VitalStream that enables the display and sharing of a complex array of medical sensor and imaging data on several head-mounted augmenting display devices to increase the situational awareness and efficiency of healthcare professionals operating within information-rich, high-skill-high-stakes environments such as an operating room.

As depicted in Figure 16.6, VitalStream can be used with Google Glass, Osterhout Design Group R-7 Smart Glasses (see Chapter 5) and similar devices to enable the display of key data from a variety of point sources directly within the field of view of the user to increase overall situational awareness. Data types enabled for display include vital signs, radiology images, endoscopy and fluoroscopy video, and more.

A powerful feature of the VitalStream platform is known as ZeroTouch capability, which utilizes the accelerometer and gyroscope within the display device to monitor head movements, and thus, enables simple hands-free control of the data presentation and communication capabilities of the system.

VitalStream also leverages the onboard video cameras common with augmenting displays such as Google Glass to record procedures and share imagery with other members of the team via remote PCs, tablets, and so on.

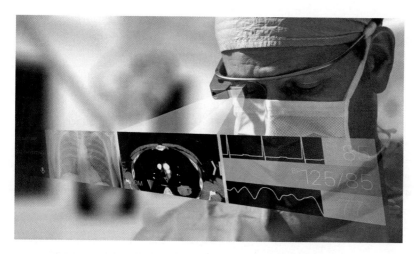

Figure 16.6 The VitalStream software platform combined with displays such as Google Glass can increase situational awareness by placing key medical sensor and imaging data onto the wearer's normal field of view.
Credit: Image courtesy of Vital Enterprise Software, Inc

Quantifiable Benefits

In 2014, the Stanford University School of Medicine carried out a randomized pilot study involving the use of VitalStream and Google Glass to evaluate the effectiveness of streaming a patient's vital signs to an operating surgeon's field of view. Within the study, surgical residents were tasked with performing a relatively routine procedure on dummy simulators during which they were presented with a complication requiring one of two immediate, emergency procedures to be performed: a thoracostomy tube placement (creating a small incision between the ribs and into the chest to drain fluid or air from around the lungs), or a bronchoscopy (inspection of the airways and lungs through a thin viewing instrument called a bronchoscope) (Sullivan, 2014). Within the study, participants carried out the two procedures using both traditional vital-sign monitors as well as the VitalStream/Google Glass method of wireless vital-sign data streaming.

The results of the study were impressive.

In both emergency procedures, live streaming of sensor data to the Google Glass display, and thus, its presence constantly within the surgeons field of view, resulted in participants recognizing critical changes in vital signs earlier than the respective control groups using traditional monitors. In the case of the thoracostomy, Glass users experienced a time to recognition of hypotension (abnormally low blood pressure) 10.5 seconds faster than the control group. In the case of the bronchoscopy, Glass users experienced a time to recognition of critical oxygen desaturation 8.8 seconds faster (Liebert et al., 2014).

Although this application description references only one study, similar results are being achieved across a host of other investigations evaluating the viability of these new displays in high-stress medical scenarios where there is little room for error.

IRIS Vision Aid for Low Vision

The term *low vision* refers to vision impairment characterized by partial sight, such as blurred vision, blind spots, or tunnel vision, but it also includes legal blindness (Vision Council, 2016). Primarily associated with older adults, leading causes of low vision include macular degeneration, diabetic retinopathy, strokes, as well as other medical conditions. Generally, low vision cannot be corrected through the use of glasses, contacts, medications, or surgery. As a result, the estimated 4 to 5 million Americans dealing with the condition often resort to a variety of assistive technologies such as handheld electronic magnifiers, wearable miniature binoculars, variable Loupe magnifier glasses, talking watches, and more.

Recent developments in mobile phone–based immersive displays such as the Samsung GearVR (see Chapter 6) have enabled the development of a variety of new assistive technologies bringing relief to sufferers of low vision. One such product is the IRIS Vision system from California-based Visionize, LLC. Using specially developed software along with the high-resolution display and camera within the mobile device, a magnified "bubble" is placed within the center of the user's field of view such as is shown in Figure 16.7. Because the size of the bubble can be controlled using rocker switches on the side of the display, the user is able to vary the scope of the area being magnified while maintaining the overall context of the scene.

Figure 16.7 The IRIS Vision system uses the camera of a mobile device and specialized software to create high-magnification insets within the wearer's field of view.
Credit: Image courtesy of Prof. Frank Werblin

Developed by scientists from UC Berkeley and Maryland-based Sensics, Inc., the IRIS Vision system clearly demonstrates the ability to keenly identify a widespread problem and bring about a low-cost, highly effective head-mounted display-based solution that can improve the lives of millions.

Conclusion

Virtual and augmented reality hold significant potential in the physical and mental health fields, and fairly clear delineations as to application areas are beginning to emerge. For instance, specialized applications aside, it is difficult to envision regularly occurring instances in the practice of physical medicine where a fully immersive visualization capability is necessary, although the benefits to education are immense, particularly when there is a need to understand the complex interrelationships between various portions of the anatomy. As such, it is highly likely that most practical applications of virtual reality will come in the form of *insilico* training and procedure rehearsal, and then, using fixed displays to enable attention to be focused on a particular worksite. As has been pointed out to me on multiple occasions, surgeons do not like to wear headsets during training if they will not be wearing headsets during actual procedures.

Augmented reality is a different story entirely. Because one of the greatest challenges facing medical practitioners is information accessibility and management (sometimes needing more, sometimes requiring just specific types), the ability to overlay sensor data, medical imaging products, worksite enhancements, and patient records will likely have a profound impact on the quality and efficiency with which medicine is practiced in the coming years.

CHAPTER 17

AEROSPACE AND DEFENSE

Applications for immersive and augmenting display technologies are widespread within the aerospace and defense communities of the United States and most other industrialized nations. From leveraging strengths of the human perceptual system in the control of complex machines such as jet aircraft, to training astronauts and helping refine skill sets and situational awareness of soldiers, virtual and augmented reality systems are having a solid impact on performance and cost efficiency. In this chapter we explore a number of such applications, detailing the benefits gained and some of the challenges still faced.

Flight Simulation and Training

Safely piloting an aircraft is an acquired talent. At the most basic level, it requires dozens of hours of actual flight time, plus classroom study, to develop, demonstrate, and test out on the legally recognized skill set and proficiency level necessary to become a licensed pilot. The more complex the aircraft, the greater the number of hours and specialized training necessary to learn how to safely and effectively handle the increasingly complicated systems.

This training methodology works sufficiently well up until the point that advanced skills are needed, such as flying in formation or aerial refueling. At that point, the training challenges and expense are magnified significantly to include the need for additional aircraft and crews, high-end simulators, and more.

Fused Reality

Systems Technology, Inc. of Hawthorne, California, asked this question: Can we use an actual aircraft as a simulator and get the best of both worlds? The answer is yes. In collaboration with NASA's Armstrong Flight Research Center at Edwards, California, and the National Test Pilot School in Mojave, California, engineers have developed an innovative combination virtual/augmented reality system known as Fused Reality that enables any aircraft to be used as a flying simulator.

As shown in Figure 17.1, the heart of the system is a fully immersive stereoscopic head-mounted display customized to include a centrally mounted video camera. Video signals from this camera are sent to a high-performance notebook computer, which itself is connected to the aircraft avionics data bus. Specialized software algorithms analyze the video signal and determine, quite literally, where the cockpit ends and the windscreen and windows begin. It is into these spaces (the windshield and windows) that computer-generated imagery is placed within the video signal returned to the display and presented to the user.

The orientation of the user's head (roll, pitch, and yaw) is monitored using IMUs built into the display unit. That information, as well as data from the avionics bus such as movement of aircraft controls, airspeed, and heading, is combined to generate and precisely register the computer-generated imagery.

The Fused Reality system provides two primary operating modes. The first, shown in Figure 17.2, provides a real-world view of the interior of the cockpit, but everything seen outside of the windscreen and windows is completely computer generated. Such a capability provides infinite flexibility in the creation of training scenarios. The user could actually be flying high above a barren desert but be presented with a detailed mountain scene within the display. Complicated approaches and precision runway or carrier landings can be practiced thousands of feet in the air. Or, as is depicted in Figure 17.2, complex aerial refueling operations and other formation flying scenarios can be practiced although there are no other aircraft for miles in any direction. It goes without saying that in this operating mode, having a safety pilot in the cockpit is highly recommended.

Figure 17.1 The Fused Reality head-mounted display shown in this image provides the user a combined view of the actual cockpit interior and instruments as well as computer-generated imagery beginning at the windows.
Credit: Image courtesy of NASA

Figure 17.2 One operating mode of the Fused Reality system displays a completely computer-generated virtual environment beyond the edge of the pilot's view of the physical control panel. In this snapshot of an aerial refueling simulation, the pilot attempts to connect a virtual receiver probe into a drogue receptacle extending from the wing of a computer-generated tanker.
Credit: Image courtesy of NASA

The second operating configuration, shown in Figure 17.3, is referred to as "stencil mode." This configuration gives the user a real-world view of both the cockpit interior as well as the scene outside of the aircraft, but with computer-generated objects such as aircraft added into that outside view. Here again, the breadth of potential application scenarios is limitless. Pilots can practice and hone skills at a fraction of the cost, and without the danger, of traditional real-world training missions involving other aircraft and crews. If you collide with a virtual aircraft in these simulations, you simply reset the training application and start again (Merlin, 2015).

In addition, the Fused Reality system holds several other distinct advantages over traditional ground-based simulators used to develop and hone advanced flight skills. Even the most cutting-edge, state-of-the-art, full-motion flight simulators are unable to re-create the internal sensations of g-loading and its subtle vestibular effects, airframe buffet cues, or the feel of energy bleed. By taking the simulator aloft, these important perceptual cues are preserved.

Figure 17.3 This image shows the Fused Reality system operating in stencil mode, within which a computer-generated virtual tanker is displayed over the real scene of the outside world.
Credit: Image courtesy of NASA

Mission Planning and Rehearsal

Simulators and training systems play a critical role in every branch of the U.S. military, as well as the defense forces of most other industrialized nations. These simulators range from large physical systems such as the U.S. Navy's USS Trayer (BST 21), a 210-foot-long Arleigh Burke-class destroyer simulator where recruits are taught to respond to 17 different ship board emergency scenarios, to state-of-the-art, high-fidelity, full-motion flight simulators used by fighter pilots. Every U.S. soldier who deploys to combat zones overseas uses simulators in some aspect of their preparation, with an increasingly heavy reliance on immersive virtual training. As with all simulator methodologies, these systems provide the opportunities to hone skills, rehearse missions, and make mistakes without actual life or death consequence in a safe and cost-effective manner. The next few sections offer an overview of some of these solutions.

Dismounted Soldier Training System

The Dismounted Soldier Training System (DSTS) is a fully immersive virtual reality infantry team training solution specifically designed for the U.S. military. In its basic configuration, the DSTS is a robust, self-contained training system supporting up to nine soldiers, the current size of a standard U.S. Army rifle squad. As shown in Figure 17.4, each soldier is outfitted with a stereoscopic head-mounted display with integrated sensors to track position and orientation of the head, stereo speakers, and microphone for simulation of voice and radio communications, a small backpack containing graphics hardware for generation of display imagery, additional sensors that track movement of the user's body, and an instrumented weapon.

Figure 17.4 This image shows a U.S. Army soldier geared up and participating in a training scenario utilizing the Dismounted Soldier Training System (DSTS).
Credit: Image courtesy of DoD

Each soldier stands on a four-foot diameter rubber pad placed in the center of a 10-foot by 10-foot training area. The feel of the pad beneath the soldier's feet serves to keep each participant in a specific area within the training location. Instead of physically walking, soldiers maneuver their position through a virtual model using simple controls on their weapon. This specific aspect of the systems allows for training to be held in small, multiuse facilities at a fraction of the cost of live exercises.

Specifically designed to enhance squad and team tactics such as movement formations and room-clearing exercises (as opposed to marksmanship skills), the DSTS system provides infinite flexibility in developing training scenarios. The nine-person system is completely portable and can be used anywhere you can find electricity and about 1,600 square feet of space. Hundreds of these systems are in use around the world and are capable of unlimited networking for larger, geographically distributed training exercises (Koester, 2013).

PARASIM Virtual Reality Parachute Simulator

The very idea of humankind being able to step off into space from a great height and descend safely to the ground has been traced as far back as 9th century Chinese civilization. The first recorded design for a parachute by a known individual came from Leonardo da Vinci in 1495. That design consisted of a pyramid-shaped linen canopy held open by a square wooden frame. The first practical parachute and the generally accepted predecessor to modern parachute systems came in 1783 from French physicist Louis-Sebastien Lenormand. His work ultimately led to the first military use of the parachute by artillery observers in tethered observation balloons during World War I. Because the balloons were dangerously idle targets for enemy aircraft, the observers would bail out of the basket as soon as the threat was spotted.

Fast forwarding to the present, the parachute has become an essential tool for most modern armies. Parachutes enable the rapid delivery of large numbers of soldiers, equipment, and supplies into a warzone, and they facilitate the silent, nighttime arrival of small groups of special operations forces directly into the backyard of an enemy. But with all the advances to the science of parachute design and utilization, the activity, by its very nature, remains highly dangerous given the large number of variables and potential fault points. Those whose profession makes regular use of parachutes are in a constant search for new technologies and methodologies that can help mitigate risk.

One of those advances is the PARASIM Virtual Reality Parachute Simulator shown in Figure 17.5, from Systems Technology, Inc. of Hawthorne, California. Initially developed for the U.S. Forest Service to help train smokejumpers (wilderness firefighters) in identifying emergencies in their chutes, the system has gone on to become a vital training tool for all branches of the U.S. military, Special Operations Command, USDA Forest Service, the Bureau of Land Management, and similar organizations worldwide.

The PARASIM system is available in multiple configurations with the selection based on end user needs. For instance, in premeditated static-line and freefall operations, jumpers exit an aircraft and either immediately assume a horizontal orientation until a chute is deployed, or in the case of a static line jump, are relatively quickly moved into a vertical orientation. To support training for these operations, one version of the product includes powered winches, which will automatically transition a user from a horizontal to a vertical orientation once a virtual chute is deployed within a simulation.

Figure 17.5 The PARASIM Virtual Reality Parachute Simulator is used by all branches of the U.S. military as well as other departments and agencies to train personnel in critical airborne operations. *Credit: Image courtesy of Systems Technology, Inc*

Another version of the product is specifically designed to facilitate training in aircrew emergency ejections and bailouts. In most real-world training scenarios, these situations result in immediate canopy deployment, thus eliminating the need for extra rigging in the simulator.

As shown in Figure 17.6, the general configuration of both versions of the system include a stereoscopic head-mounted display (a variable component based on customer specifications), IMU sensors to track orientation of the user's head, and control lines/steering toggles. In the version of the simulator used for premeditated jumps and delayed openings, a Microsoft Kinect sensor (see Chapter 11, "Sensors for Tracking Position, Orientation, and Motion") is used to track hand and arm motions to enable control of the fall through virtual space, just as in an actual jump.

The real magic of this simulator is in the software. PARASIM is a high-fidelity, physics-based jump simulator that includes more than 50 different chute designs, the detailed performance characteristics for which are accurately reproduced within the simulations. This enables high precision training using any chute, under any atmospheric conditions. Designed for training both novice as well as experienced jumpers, the system allows for simulation of malfunctions and emergency procedures, canopy control, development of proper situational awareness, variable landing techniques, and more. The software suite also includes a variety of simulation environments based on real-world locations (STI, 2013a).

Another highly useful feature of PARASIM is the ability to network an unlimited number of systems. In such simulations, all jumpers can see representations of one another, providing an ideal means through which to plan and rehearse group operations.

Figure 17.6 The PARASIM Virtual Reality Parachute Simulator includes a stereoscopic wide field of view (FOV) head-mounted display and sensors to track the orientation of the user's head.
Credit: Image courtesy of DoD

As shown in Figure 17.7, a third variation on the system is available for training jump masters. Using the Fused Reality technology described in the previous section, the system is a mixed-reality application intended to develop and refine the skills necessary to oversee and manage a combat-equipped jump and can be used in combination with groups of PARASIM users (STI, 2013b).

Figure 17.7 The Jump Master variant for the PARASIM system is a mixed reality application enabling in-depth training of jump masters in the management and oversight of airborne operations.
Credit: Image courtesy of Systems Technology, Inc

Dismounted Soldier Situational Awareness

Historically, battlefields have been places of great confusion and uncertainty in situational awareness, making information one of the most valuable commodities to a soldier. Indeed, even the classic guide to combat strategy, Sun Tzu's *Art of War* written in the 6th century B.C., carries the underlying theme that victory on the battlefield comes from a commander's ability to acquire, control, and manipulate information. In modern terms, this means information about enemy location and force strength, information about your own squad members and their locations, as well as information from remote-sensing platforms such as UAVs and other aircraft and satellites. In an ideal situation, and one the armed forces of the United States have been working on for decades, every soldier would act as both a consumer and a producer of information as part of a larger network. Over the past several years, the foundational elements of such a system have begun being deployed.

Nett Warrior

Nett Warrior is an integrated dismounted soldier situational awareness system for use during U.S. Army combat operations. As shown in Figure 17.8, the current implementation of the system utilizes an Android-based smartphone-like handheld/chest-worn device that connects to the soldier's Rifleman Radio for the sharing of position information, text messages, photos, maps, and other data. This secure radio-based connectivity is referred to as the On-The-Move self-forming network.

Figure 17.8 This image shows U.S. Army soldiers using their Android-based Nett Warrior integrated and dismounted situational awareness and mission command systems.
Credit: Image courtesy of DoD

The next phase of the program under active development will add a head-mounted augmented reality display component to the system intended for both day and night tactical applications. This phase of the program is intended to provide networked heads-up situational awareness to further reduce fratricide, as well as increase lethality, survivability, and maneuverability.

An example of tactical information to be displayed within such a device is shown in Figure 17.9. The baseline software for the system, known as ARC4, was developed by Applied Research Associates of Albuquerque, New Mexico, during a six-year collaboration with the Defense Advanced Research Projects Agency (DARPA). The display-agnostic ARC4 software gives users accurate geo-registered icons overlaid on their real-world view. The precision placement of the iconic information will be enabled via a helmet-mounted head tracking/video processing unit. The military version of the interface is intended to provide a common operating picture (COP) for commanders and small-unit teams, including heads-up blue (friendly force) tracking, navigation, target handoff, and nonverbal, non-line-of-sight communication between a team leader and individual warfighters (Applied Research Associates, 2015).

Figure 17.9 This image depicts an example of a dismounted soldier tactical information display enabled using the ARC4 augmented reality software solution developed by Applied Research Associates of Albuquerque, New Mexico.

Credit: Image courtesy of Applied Research Associates, Inc

Advanced Cockpit Avionics

Aircraft have evolved to become some of the most complex and consequential machines created by man. As their size and capability have steadily increased over the years, so too have the challenges involved in their safe operation and effective utilization. In the following sections we look at some of these challenges and the solutions found through the application of virtual and augmented reality-enabling technologies.

Military

The cockpit designs of military aircraft, and in particular fighter jets, have changed significantly over the past several decades. Previously, cockpits were filled with dozens of switches, buttons, and other manual controls, in addition to numerous highly coded dials and gauges providing information on aircraft systems, navigation, weapons status, sensors, and more. Often this information was presented in alphanumeric form (a combination of alphabetic and numeric characters), the totality of which was intended to communicate critical information and help a pilot form a mental image about what was happening outside of the aircraft. This complex mental processing task was over and above the actual job of operating the aircraft and solving problems related to the geometry of flight, aerial combat maneuvering, and tactical engagement. The great challenge with these early designs was that the pilot was forced to spend a significant amount of time with his attention focused inside the cockpit reading dials and gauges or interpreting grainy sensor images instead of looking outside the aircraft where targets and threats were located. The net result was a frequent sense of information overload, high stress, and a loss of situational awareness.

Movement to multifunction displays (small screens surrounded by buttons) within which this same information about aircraft systems, navigation, weapons status, sensors, and so on is logically organized into multiple pages, rather than everything always being visible, helped the information processing task immensely. Similarly, the widespread adoption of HUDs, or heads-up displays—a transparent screen, or combiner, typically mounted on the cockpit dash at eye level—and the conversion of some cockpit avionics information from letters and numbers to a symbolic representation further eased this burden. But here, the major limiting factor is that the pilot must be looking straight ahead to see this information.

At this point, the next logical step in cockpit design was the movement of the information display from the HUD unit to optical elements mounted within, or directly onto the visor of, the pilot's helmet. Such systems allow critical information to be displayed to a pilot regardless of where his head is pointing, further maximizing the amount of time a pilot spends looking outside of the aircraft instead of inside of the cockpit. In many regards, helmet-mounted displays can be considered the first widely deployed augmented reality systems.

To date, dozens of different helmet-mounted displays have been developed for fixed- and rotary-wing aircraft around the world, each of which has served at least one of the following purposes:

- Display targeting, navigation, and aircraft performance data to the pilot.
- Direct high off-boresight (HOBS) air-to-air and air-to-ground weapons.
- Slave onboard sensors such as radar and FLIR.
- Display sensor video.

Figure 17.10 shows two modern, currently deployed helmet-mounted displays in use within fixed- and rotary-wing aircraft.

Figure 17.10 This image shows two head-mounted displays currently in use within U.S military aircraft. On the left is the GENTEX Scorpion Helmet-Mounted Cueing System in use within the A-10 Thunderbolt and the Air National Guard/Air Force Reserve F-16 Block 30/32 Viper aircraft. On the right is the Thales TopOwl Helmet-Mounted Sight and Display that is operational in five major helicopter programs across 16 countries, including the Cobra AH-1Z and Huey UH-1Y.
Credit: Photos courtesy of Thales—a global technology leader for aerospace, transport, defense and security markets. www.thalesgroup.com

It is important to point out that within this application setting, extremely wide FOV displays are actually considered a hindrance and potentially dangerous. The goal is to provide the pilot with essential information from airborne weapons and sensor targeting suites without cluttering the visual field, which could have disastrous consequences.

F-35 Joint Strike Fighter Helmet-Mounted Display System

The most advanced helmet-mounted display system (HMDS) currently in use and representative of the absolute state-of-the-art in capabilities is that which is deployed with the Lockheed Martin F-35 Lightning II Joint Strike Fighter.

Built into the lightweight helmet shown in Figure 17.11 is a $30° \times 40°$ binocular FOV, high-brightness, high-resolution display with integrated digital night vision. A fully integrated day and night flight weapons and sensor data visualization solution, pilots in aircraft equipped with the system have immense capabilities, not the least of which is to aim weapons simply by looking at a target. For night missions, in addition to the cueing of sensors and weapons, the system projects the night vision scene directly onto the interior of the visor, eliminating the need for separate night-vision goggles.

Figure 17.11 This image shows an oblique view of the F-35A Lightning II helmet-mounted display, which provides pilots unparalleled situational awareness, with real-time imagery from six sensor packages mounted around the exterior of the aircraft.
Credit: Image courtesy of DoD

One of the most innovative features of this system is the ability to display a spherical 360° degree view of the world outside of the cockpit as if the airframe were not present, including below and to the sides of the aircraft. Sometimes referred to as a "glass cockpit," this capability is enabled via an electro-optical Distributed Aperture System, which consists of six high-resolution infrared sensors mounted around the F-35 airframe. The overlapping FOV of the six sensors are blended to provide unobstructed spherical (4π steradian) imagery as well as missile and aircraft detection and countermeasure cueing. Figure 17.12 provides an example of the view a pilot would receive within the HMD by combining the infrared scene along with avionics and sensor data.

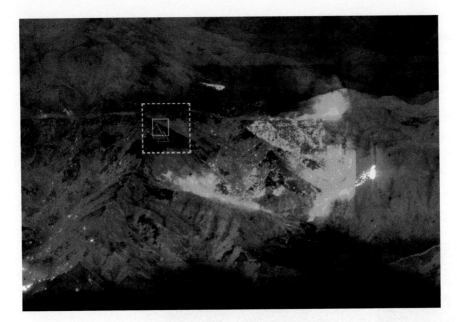

Figure 17.12 The F-35's Distributed Aperture System (DAS) fuses real-time imagery from externally mounted sensors with data provided by onboard avionics systems.
Credit: Image courtesy of S. Aukstakalnis

Commercial Aviation

Pilots within the commercial aviation sector face many of the same information availability and cognitive processing challenges as their military counterparts, but without the added burden of combat maneuvering, weapons targeting and deployment, and so on. In particular, challenges for the commercial aviation sector come in the form of takeoffs and landings in low-visibility conditions such as heavy fog and storms, to potential runway incursions when taxiing under the same conditions. These problems are obviously not new, and although aircraft manufacturers and avionics suppliers have integrated heads-up display technologies into a variety of aircraft, the challenge of the pilot only being able to see the information while facing forward remains. As such, several manufacturers are now introducing head-mounted displays for commercial aircraft as an option to their cockpit avionics suites. One such company is Elbit Systems, Ltd of Haifa, Israel.

Skylens Display

Skylens is the wearable display component of the Elbit Clearvision Enhanced Flight Vision System (EFVS). Clearvision uses multispectral sensors mounted outside of the aircraft to capture terrain and airport lights in darkness and reduced visibility. This data is fused with topology from a global terrain database as well as conformal flight guidance symbology and, typically, projected onto a fold-down HUD providing a high-fidelity view of the outside world even when actual visibility is limited or zero.

The Skylens component provides the pilot with the same information that would normally be displayed in the HUD, but in a head-mounted device. By tracking the pilot's head movements, critical information and symbology can be stabilized and correlated to the real world as the pilot scans the scene, improving the operator's ability to execute precision and nonprecision approaches and reducing the risks of Controlled Flight into Terrain (CFIT) accidents.

The Skylens system itself is a monocular, off-the-visor display, the image source for which is a 1280×1024 monochromatic (green) microdisplay with an effective area of 1024×1024 in a circular area. The system uses triple redundant optical sensors for head tracking.

Civilian

The general aviation sector also faces the same information availability and mental processing challenges as their commercial and military counterparts. Although cockpit avionics in general aviation aircraft have made significant advances over the past decade in enabling the visualization of terrain, navigational aids, hazards, weather, and traffic awareness information on state-of-the-art multifunction displays, here again, accessing the information still requires the pilot to focus attention inside of the cockpit and off the skies. Further, current display technologies still require pilots to mentally convert this complex assortment of 2D information into a 3D mental image of the environment surrounding the aircraft, dramatically increasing the workload and stress levels.

But unlike the military and commercial sectors, general aviation enthusiasts have, until recently, not had viable (or affordable) solutions on the horizon. Fortunately, the confluence of advances in augmented reality software and display hardware, as well as seemingly unrelated initiatives with U.S. and international aviation authorities, is resulting in the development of some amazing alternative information display possibilities for general aviation participants.

In a nutshell, if you want to operate an aircraft in designated U.S. airspaces (Class A, B, C, and parts of D and E) after January 1st, 2020, federal regulations require that your aircraft be equipped with what is known as an ADS-B (Automatic Dependent Surveillance-Broadcast) transponder. This small piece of electronics gear, simply referred to as ADS-B OUT, transmits information about your plane's altitude, airspeed, and GPS-derived location to ground stations, as well as to other aircraft in your vicinity equipped with ADS-B IN receivers. Air traffic controllers and properly equipped aircraft use this information to "see" participating aircraft in real time, with the ultimate goal of improving air traffic management and safety. Typically, the ADS data is shown on a 2D multifunction display within the cockpit.

Aero Glass

Aero Glass, Inc. of San Diego, California, and Budapest, Hungary, is one of several companies developing a means through which to display ADS-B and other instrument data within augmenting head-mounted displays such as the Epson Moverio and Osterhut Design Group (ODG) R-7 (both of which are detailed in Chapter 5, "Augmenting Displays").

As shown in Figure 17.13, the visual effect is the overlay of this information in graphics and symbolic form onto the user's real-world view regardless of the position and orientation of the pilot's head or the aircraft.

Figure 17.13 This image depicts a sample of the aeronautical information that can be displayed using Aero Glass software, an augmented reality head-mounted display and sensor to track position and orientation of the pilot's head.
Credit: Image courtesy of Aero Glass Corporation

As depicted in this image, several of the raw data types shown that would normally be represented in 2D on a multifunction display or map/chart in the pilot's lap actually represent static as well as time-varying 3D phenomena, such as controlled or restricted *volumes* of airspace, multiple airways, and the position and movement of nearby aircraft. By displaying information in a manner that depicts the actual spatial characteristics of the data, as well as its precise position, the pilot is given a greatly increased level of situational awareness and visual understanding about the real environment through which one is flying.

The Aero Glass system consists of a software suite that combines ADS-B and other avionics data, information from sensors measuring the pilot's head position and orientation, and the actual display device.

Space Operations

Some of the most advanced virtual and augmented reality systems and applications found anywhere in the world are located in NASA laboratories spread across the United States in support of manned and unmanned space operations. Significant time, effort, and expense have been put toward developing a host of facilities and tools that are now used to train every U.S. astronaut who travels to space. Most of that training takes place in the Virtual Reality Laboratory (VRL) at NASA's Johnson Space Center in Houston, Texas, a snapshot from which is shown in Figure 17.14.

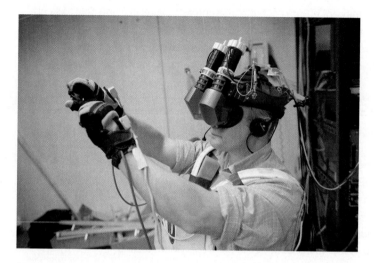

Figure 17.14 This image shows NASA astronaut Michael Fincke using virtual reality hardware in the Space Vehicle Mock-up Facility at NASA's Johnson Space Center.
Credit: Image courtesy of NASA

In addition to years of traditional training and preparation, NASA makes extensive use of immersive virtual reality systems and related technologies to train the astronauts in four primary areas:

- **Extra-Vehicular Activity (EVA) Training**, which prepares the astronauts for space walks and the tasks they will be performing while outside of the International Space Station (ISS).

- **Simplified Aid for EVA Rescue (SAFER) Training**, which teaches the astronauts how to use a small, self-contained propulsive backpack system worn during spacewalks. In the event that an astronaut becomes detached from the ISS or a spacecraft and floats out of reach, SAFER provides a means of self rescue.

- **Robotics Operations**, which teaches astronauts the use of robotic systems such as the Canadarm2.

- **Zero-G Mass Handling**, which simulates zero-g mass characteristics of objects in a microgravity environment. (Remember that while objects in space may be *weightless*, an object's *mass* still presents formidable handling and maneuvering challenges if large enough.)

Project Sidekick

Despite upward of two years of training astronauts undergo prior to space travel, it is impossible to carry out missions without extensive assistance from team members and subject matter experts on the ground. From solving engineering problems to proper operation of onboard experiments, significant effort is put into assisting astronauts in being able to safely and effectively carry out their mission objectives. To this end, NASA is constantly investigating methods with which to render this support beyond standard radio, video, and textual communications. One such investigation underway at the time this book was written is known as Project Sidekick.

Leveraging advances in augmenting display technologies such as those provided by Microsoft's HoloLens (see Chapter 5), the goal of this project is to explore the use of an immersive procedural reference (that is, a manual or guidebook) and remote assistance system developed to provide the crew information and task support whenever it is needed. Based on the concept of a mixed reality setting (combining the physical environment and virtual objects), high-definition holograms displayed within the HoloLens device can be integrated into the astronaut's real-world view within the Space Station, enabling new ways to access and exchange key information and guidance between personnel on orbit and individuals on the ground. Figure 17.15 shows the HoloLens device in pre-deployment testing.

Figure 17.15 This image shows NASA and Microsoft engineers testing Project Sidekick on NASA's Weightless Wonder C9 jet. Project Sidekick will use Microsoft HoloLens to provide virtual aid and ground-based assistance to astronauts working on the International Space Station.
Credit: Image courtesy of NASA

At the time of this writing, the Sidekick system had two basic operating modes: Standalone (a procedural reference system) and Remote Expert:

- **Standalone Mode** gives the astronaut access to an extensive preloaded manual with instructions, procedures, and checklists displayed as holograms that can be placed anywhere the astronaut finds it most convenient.
- **Remote Expert Mode** is a video teleconference capability enabling real-time first person assistance with ground personnel. In operation, the crew member opens a holographic video screen where he can see the flight control team, system expert, or payload developer. Using the HoloLens' built-in camera, the ground crew is able to see the astronaut's work area and offer direct assistance in support of the task objectives.

The Sidekick project is only one of multiple applications for the HoloLens and other head-mounted augmenting displays within various manned and unmanned space programs. Another project referred to as OnSight currently places Earth-based scientists and engineers within a virtual re-creation of the operational environment of the Curiosity Rover on Mars. Using data sent back from the rover, 3D models are generated and displayed within the HoloLens device, enabling scientists to freely explore the area from a first-person perspective, plan new rover operations, and preview the results of past system tasking.

Conclusion

This chapter has only lightly touched on the large number of solid, existing applications for virtual and augmented reality technologies within the aerospace and defense sectors. This advance stage of adoption and utilization in comparison to other areas is due to a variety of reasons, including well-defined, mission-critical needs (which ultimately drives a focused development agenda), budgets that support intensive multiyear research, development and problem-solving efforts, as well as the technology showing demonstrable results.

To this end, it is impossible to quantify the immense breadth and depth of the contributions of the Department of Defense and NASA to the current state of the art in virtual and augmented reality systems. From the start of their separate research and development efforts with these technologies in the 1960s and 1980s respectively and continuing to the present, their support of small businesses and university researchers in this field through product acquisition and grants, collaboration, and the sharing of subject matter knowledge and experts has been, and continues to be, absolutely vital to the field's development. Some of the areas where their contributions are most notable include sensor technologies, user interface design, binaural audio, optical systems, and core research on human perception and performance.

CHAPTER 18

EDUCATION

From helping master core skills required in a variety of vocations, to aiding students in learning abstract concepts in complex fields such as architecture, to experiential learning for children, virtual and augmented reality hold incredible potential in the field of education. In this chapter we explore several existing applications having a proven impact on learning outcomes, and we detail some of the challenges faced in the implementing systems to assist in the educational process.

Tangible Skills Education

One of the earliest and most successful application realms for virtual and augmented reality systems in education is the teaching of specific, tangible, skill sets. From astronauts using immersive systems to practice assembly and repair procedures for the International Space Station, to teaching specific skilled trades, development of such applications and turnkey systems is a straightforward process. In a simplified explanation, these types of applications take on a common pattern: take this virtual tool, carry out this task, and refine your movements and procedures until you are within the required tolerances. Such educational applications are significantly easier to implement than, say, developing systems to teach complex physics and chemistry theories.

In this section we explore two applications where immersive virtual reality systems are used to teach acquired, practiced tangible skills, the outcomes for which can be quantified and analyzed for immediate feedback.

VRTEX 360 Welding Simulator

The education of skilled tradesman invariably requires hundreds, if not thousands, of hours of supervised training and practice to build the skill set and expertise necessary to pass certification exams for a particular field. Often the training is expensive, dangerous, and wasteful. One of the skilled trades most well known for these challenges is that of industrial welding. Students of the craft spend considerable time, effort, and consumable materials practicing a myriad of techniques to consistently turn out a good product.

To make this learning process more efficient and less expensive, Lincoln Electric of Cleveland, Ohio, a multinational manufacturer of welding equipment and products, teamed up with VRSim, Inc. of East Hartford, Connecticut, to develop a high-performance, virtual reality–based welding simulator for use in schools to supplement and enhance traditional methods of training welders.

The VRTEX 360 is a complete welding station trainer designed to simulate a variety of welding processes, including shielded metal arc welding (SMAW), gas metal arc welding (GMAW), pipe welding, multiposition welding, and more. As shown in Figure 18.1, the system is completely immersive and incorporates a head-worn display built into a welding helmet, multiple position sensors, lifelike welding gun and stinger assemblies, adjustable welding stand, and large flat-panel display for system control and instructor viewing of student efforts.

The VRTEX 360 is specifically designed to help educators provide hands-on training that's consistent with standard industry methodology and evaluation criteria, but without the normal issues associated with safety, material waste, and so on. The system features actual machine setup replication and a realistic simulation of a welding puddle, sounds and effects, and utilities to measure and record a student's training results in real time, allowing instructors to identify deficiencies tied to the welder's movement instantly (Lincoln, 2012).

Figure 18.1 The VRTEX 360 Arc Welding Simulator by Lincoln Electric is in use worldwide and includes comprehensive curricula for developing a variety of welding skills.
Credit: Used with permission of Lincoln Electric, Cleveland, OH U.S.A.

A powerful feature of the VRTEX 360 can be found in the realistic behavior of the system's stinger device (a clamp that holds a welding rod during shielded metal arc welding), which retracts into the handpiece simulating the manner in which an electrode melts away during a real welding task, the factors for which vary depending on materials and conditions set for a scenario.

The welding helmet incorporates dual Sony 1280×720 OLED microdisplays and optical assemblies that are adjustable for varied interpupillary distances. The position and orientation of the helmet display and the welder's gun are tracked using magnetic position sensors supplied by Polhemus (see Chapter 11, "Sensors for Tracking Position, Orientation and Motion"). As shown in Figure 18.2, the system provides highly accurate simulations of the welding process and weld puddle dynamics based on a student's hand movements and angle, travel time, and training system settings.

A smaller, easily transportable version of the system is also available for use in a classroom environment, at a recruitment event, and even as an HR screening tool.

In terms of quantifiable benefits, across a number of studies (Stone et al., 2011a, 2011b, 2013), outcomes resulting from the use of immersive virtual reality welding simulators in core skills education have produced results that are statistically and demonstrably significant, in all instances demonstrating skills development equal to or exceeding those of traditionally trained students. In one study (Stone et al., 2011b), those students who received integrated training (50% traditional welding, 50% via simulation) resulted in a 41.6% increase in overall certifications earned over those in the straight traditional welding group.

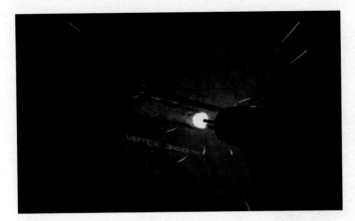

Figure 18.2 The VRTEX Welding Helmet uses an integrated face-mounted display to immerse the student in the virtual environment where they can practice their welding technique.
Credit: Used with permission of Lincoln Electric, Cleveland, OH U.S.A.

Use of the VRTEX simulator is now widely accepted as a viable option for welding education and is used in 141 countries around the world along with comprehensive curricula available in 16 languages.

SimSpray Spray Paint Training System

Spray painting is a technique widely used in industries ranging from aerospace, to automotive, to manufacturing and construction. Far more than simply waving a spray gun around to cover a surface, it is a skilled trade that requires considerable training and expertise to properly apply a variety of paints and industrial coatings at proper thicknesses. Inconsistent applications can mean uneven coatings. Depending on the industry, uneven coatings can result in everything from a lousy finish on an automotive collision repair, to dramatic reductions in aerodynamic efficiency and increased operating costs of high-performance aircraft, to creating a fire or corrosion hazard if an industrial coating is improperly applied. As a case in point, manually applied paints and protective coatings are widely used by NASA in the U.S. space program.

Some of the challenges faced in professional spray paint training include the high expense of environmentally controlled paint booths, excessive setup and prep times for different parts and surfaces (ranging from simple flat-metal surfaces to irregularly shaped objects like a car door or fuselage panel), the cost of raw materials, and potential health hazards. These and other factors pose significant challenges to the amount of knowledge transfer that can actually occur during a training program.

The SimSpray training system developed by VRSim, Inc. of East Hartford, Connecticut, dramatically reduces or eliminates many of these challenges. Designed to augment traditional training methodologies, SimSpray combines physical components such as a custom spray gun with haptic feedback to provide a "kickback" feeling, along with a stereoscopic head-mounted display and position/orientation sensors to immerse trainees in a 3D, simulated environment where they can practice the proper techniques for spray painting and coating.

The full SimSpray system is shown in Figure 18.3. The system incorporates a two-sensor magnetic tracker from Polhemus to precisely monitor the position and orientation of both the spray gun and the Sony HMZ-T1 stereoscopic head-mounted display.

Figure 18.3 The SimSpray training system incorporates the use of a stereoscopic head-mounted display and force feedback cues to provide students a realistic training utility.
Credit: Image courtesy of VRSim, Inc

The SimSpray system comes with a comprehensive set of software utilities to enable a wide selection of painting scenarios, including process choice, parts selection (flat panel, wavy panel, car fender, fuel tank, and so on), and painting environment (booth, shop, bridge). Two versions of the systems are available (standard and industrial) to accommodate varying training needs.

In addition to giving students immediate realistic visual feedback such as is depicted in Figure 18.4, the system also provides instructors with a variety of tools and metrics with which to evaluate a student's learning progress. A utility known as Paintometer calculates totals for actual time spent painting, measures of the paint/coating applied and wasted, number of parts painted, VOC (volatile organic compound) total emissions, and more.

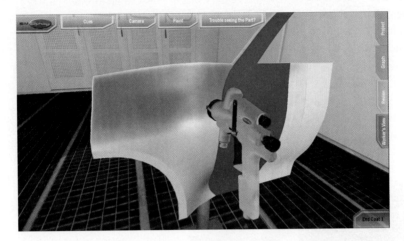

Figure 18.4 When combined with professional instruction, the ability to continually repeat tasks and refine techniques enables students using SimSpray to become more proficient painters.
Credit: Image courtesy of VRSim, Inc

Perhaps most important, SimSpray inverts the traditional training model by maximizing the amount of time a student spends actually pulling the trigger on a paint gun and practicing the skills necessary to correctly carry out a painting or coating task, such as mil build, standoff distance, travel angle and speed, and edge blending. This inversion directly translates into more training repetitions in less time without the added costs of materials, consumables, and waste disposal fees.

Similar to the VRTEX welding simulator detailed earlier, SimSpray is now accepted as a viable training tool and is used at schools across the United States and around the world.

Theory, Knowledge Acquisition, and Concept Formation

In addition to applications in teaching inflexible, practiced skill sets such as those examples in the previous section, augmented and virtual reality also hold significant potential in the teaching of topical theory and concepts. An ideal example is that of architecture and the building sciences.

Architectural Education

The learning task faced by architecture students is immense. On one hand, a key objective in most university programs is the development of skills required to combine concepts of space, form, materials, function, and aesthetics in the design of large, habitable structures. On the other hand, the student must learn to accurately translate and externalize these mental concepts to communicate the ideas and design intent to others. The mechanisms through which this is accomplished typically take the form of plans, sections and elevations, sketches, color renderings, scale models, visualizations, construction documents, and more. The difficulty in combining these tasks is that until the student sees a design physically constructed at scale, there is no means with which to validate a concordance between how the structure was mentally envisioned and what was actually depicted through the tools used to guide construction such as drawings or CAD models. None provides a means for the student to actually experience the structure from the perspective through which it would eventually be used—that is, the inside. What is the impact the space has on a visitor? How does the space appear from different angles and positions? Are windows of an appropriate size and placement for the existing or intended views? This basic visualization and externalization problem has plagued the profession for centuries and extends far beyond a modern academic setting.

Enter VR

From the earliest days that the individual component technologies for fully immersive virtual reality systems were first cobbled together for civilian uses within university research labs, architectural walk-throughs have been a baseline, mainstay application. This is due, in part, to the parallel development of commercially available CAD utilities that greatly facilitated the design of the geometric models that could be imported into a simulation utility. Rare is the architect, or instructor, who does not immediately grasp the significance of the technology and the problems it can solve in their field. Although there are numerous tools available to assist in the visual analysis of an architectural space, immersive systems such as head-mounted displays or computer-assisted virtual environment (CAVE)-like systems are some of the first true solutions for visualizing, communicating, and experiencing design decisions at true scale.

Fast forward to the present. Dozens of university architecture programs across North America, and literally hundreds worldwide, have either established virtual and augmented reality visualization labs or are attempting to integrate the use of immersive displays into the pedagogical flow of the course of study. But along these lines, significant challenges exist.

The value of these systems for spatial analysis, design review, and problem identification are obvious, and there is a growing body of case studies to demonstrate such strengths. (See Chapter 14, "Architecture and Construction.") But from a pedagogical standpoint, how are the outcomes of using immersive and augmenting displays in architectural design *education* actually measured against traditional techniques? What are the mechanisms through which the benefits are quantified? What are the metrics? Should students still be taught all of the more traditional techniques of design representation? If not, which skill sets should be eliminated?

These and many other questions are currently being wrestled with at institutions around the world. Some have initially opted to use the technology to help new entrants firmly develop crucial cognitive abilities such as visual-spatial skills (ability to mentally manipulate 2-and 3-dimensional figures), projection and regeneration of solids, and so on. Often, problems in this area are not rooted in aptitude, but in the method of teaching (Pandey et al., 2015). In this type of application, progress and the impact of this visualization technology can actually be measured with standard testing and outcome comparison with other techniques.

But what about the opinion-driven aspects of design analysis? How do you quantitatively measure the effect of the use of immersive visualization technologies on design ability in a field notorious for differing opinions and tastes? Invariably, many programs rely upon *subjective analysis* of faculty and other students (such as experienced during the design review, also known as the critique, crit, or jury process found in all architectural schools), as well as testimonials and detailed surveys of the students, the preponderance of which are extremely enthusiastic.

Another important question being addressed is when, within a multiyear course of study, the use of these technologies should begin being used as part of the design curriculum. For instance, in researching this chapter, I encountered an anonymous forum post recounting a first-year design studio project within which the instructor's directions were simple: "Design a beautiful cube. Use any tool available in the studio to complete the project." The poster went on to relate how, in using a geometric modeling program and head-mounted display, as opposed to physical materials, he missed out on the insights gained by watching the creativity and work of others in his design studio class. To this student, it represented an "Aha" moment, that there is a proper time and place for the use of the technology. Although this example may be overly simplistic, it cuts to the core of the challenge faced by instructors grappling not only with the question of how to integrate a powerful new technology into the curriculum, but when.

Virtual Overlays

It is not just immersive displays that are disrupting architectural design education. The advent of augmenting displays such as those detailed in Chapter 5, "Augmenting Displays," is also likely to have a transformational impact on the industry. Used in combination with Building Information Modeling (BIM) applications such as Autodesk Revit (described in greater detail in Chapter 14), whole new opportunities are emerging for those in the architectural design profession, but determining how to properly prepare students in their use within professional practice is still being addressed.

As an example, in a partnership between Florida International University (Miami) and Missouri State University (Springfield) , researchers have begun a multidisciplinary investigation into the use of augmenting displays, BIM, and interactive lessons to determine if the combination of these technologies can improve students' problem-solving and collaborative learning skills leading to the design of more sustainable and better-performing buildings. As depicted in Figure 18.5, a portion of the investigation will involve students using augmenting displays to view BIM data overlaid onto their real-world view of buildings on campus.

Figure 18.5 Researchers from Florida International University and Missouri State University will be using augmenting displays to enable students to visualize Building Information Modeling (BIM) data overlaid onto real-world views of structures on campus.
Credit: Image courtesy of Florida International University

The project, Strategies for Learning: Augmented Reality and Collaborative Problem-Solving for Building Sciences, is funded in part with a grant from the National Science Foundation and is intended to explore not only "if" the technologies can improve learning outcomes, but "how" to craft the curriculum to bring about such a result, as well as begin the development of a set of metrics by which such outcomes can be measured and analyzed (NSF, 2015).

Google Expeditions Pioneer Program

The application of virtual reality within a learning environment is not only limited to higher education. The Google Expeditions Pioneer Program is a new immersive learning experience for the K-12 sector that enables teachers to engage their classes in virtual field trips, providing the opportunity for students to gain a deeper understanding of the world beyond the classroom. As shown in Figure 18.6, using low-cost stereoscopic viewers distributed to students, instructors can guide classes on visits to museums, distant geographic locations, and even into space to study the layout and organization of our solar system (Suburu, 2015).

Part of the Google for Education initiative and conducted in partnership with automotive manufacturer Surburu, PBS, educational publisher Houghton Mifflin Harcourt, and others, the goal of the program is to enhance the in-classroom learning experience by applying Google's technologies and resources. As of November 2015, more than 100,000 students in schools around the world have used Google Expeditions in their classes.

Figure 18.6 The Google Expeditions Pioneer Program has enabled more than 100,000 students around the world to use inexpensive virtual reality headsets as part of their school curriculum. *Credit: Image courtesy of Laurie Sullivan via Flickr under a CC 2.0 license*

Schools apply directly to Google for participation in the program. If selected, the company supplies what is referred to as an Expeditions Kit, which contains Android-based ASUS smartphones, display housings such as Google Cardboard or Mattel's View-Master virtual reality viewers, an instructor's tablet, a wireless router to enable the smartphones to operate offline, as well as teaching materials. The system enables instructors to guide up to 50 students on tours of more than 120 locations such as Antarctica, the Acropolis of Athens, the Great Wall of China, and elsewhere, with each of the expeditions including some combination of 360° spherical imagery, videos, and sound. The instructor's tablet enables the teacher to control the expeditions while providing information and facts about the scenes to guide the class.

An important aspect to the deployment of this program is the fact that Google representatives actually visit each school where the technology is deployed to facilitate setup and to provide training for instructors.

Conclusion

It is clear by the application examples provided in this chapter that virtual and augmented reality hold significant potential within the educational arena. But, as in most instances, the technology is only now becoming available in the form of stable commercial offerings. There has been little time for the art and science of teaching methodologies incorporating these technologies to take shape. Few instructors in the plethora of applicable fields have enough personal experience with the technologies to understand how they should be employed to the actual benefit of students or how to harness their strengths to advance pedagogic goals.

Digital innovation in educational environments does not automatically translate into higher quality learning outcomes. As explained by Dr. Kentaro Toyama of the University of Michigan, technology's primary effect is to *amplify human forces*. In education, technologies amplify whatever pedagogical capacity is already there (Toyoma, 2015). In effect, this means that without knowledgeable instructors appropriately familiar with or trained in the use of a new technology, or without carefully adapted curricula, there is little chance for the new technology to amplify outcomes.

As a hypothetical example, enabling a classroom of high school students to randomly fly around models of ancient Greek ruins with smartphone-based stereoscopic viewers might make for an interesting activity, but without a plan or guidance, it could actually end up as more of a distraction than an educational tool. Conversely, guiding the students on a virtual tour where the instructor points out the unique features of Doric, Ionic, and Corinthian columns, or the differences between temples and stoas (a covered walkway or portico), could dramatically enhance the traditional curriculum and the overall retention of knowledge.

Educational psychologist Dr. Richard E. Mayer of the University of California at Santa Barbara has written extensively on the topic of learning, teaching, and assessing using multimedia technologies (Mayer, 1999, 2003, 2005, 2008). Many of his research findings are directly relevant to the application of virtual and augmented reality technologies in educational settings and are highly recommended reading.

CHAPTER 19

INFORMATION CONTROL AND BIG DATA VISUALIZATION

To some, the phrase *Big Data* results in a knowing nod. To others, a roll of the eyes. Regardless of your viewpoint or the hype, Big Data itself poses big problems, and big urgency, for businesses and organizations that need to harness complex datasets in a manner that brings about genuine, usable insights. In this chapter we explore several examples of how groups have leveraged the strengths of immersive virtual reality systems to gain increased understanding from large, often disparate pools of information.

What Is Big Data?

Our physical world contains an incomprehensible amount of digital information, and it is growing at an equally incomprehensible rate. The 2014 IDC/EMC Digital Universe study that quantifies and forecasts the amount of data produced annually indicates that by 2020, the digital universe will grow by a factor of 10—from 4.4 zettabytes to 44 zettabytes. This represents a doubling of the amount every two years (Turner et al., 2014).

Equally impressive is the growing number of sources for this computed data. These include massive retail databases; machine log data; sensors in our environment (the Internet of Things); web traffic; health data; social media sites such as Facebook, Twitter, and Instagram; mobile devices; traditional media; business applications; scientific research projects; utilities and smart grids; and on and on.

Big data is popularly characterized using three defining properties or dimensions known as the 3Vs: volume, velocity, and variety. Volume obviously refers to the amount of data being generated within an enterprise, organization, or research project. Velocity refers to the speed at which the data is being generated. Variety refers to the number of different types of data. According to the 3V characterization model, the great challenges of big data management and analysis stem from the expansion of all three properties, as opposed to just volume alone (Laney, 2001).

With all of this information being generated and stored, the great challenge now is how to carefully exploit the data in a manner enabling the organization or researchers to extract value to increase efficiency, grow profits, or otherwise uncover hidden trends, important features, or interrelationships. The result can aid corporate decision-making (assuming a company understands how to use the resulting data), help defense and intelligence organizations identify emerging threats, determine which ads you are most likely to click on, and provide insights into various science and engineering problems (Cukier, 2010).

This challenge of exploiting big data can be broken down into several areas, including curation (organization and integration of data from multiple sources, annotation, presentation, and preservation), storage, querying, and sharing, all of which directly impacts efficient analysis.

Big Data Analytics and Human Vision

Big data analytics is the process of collecting, organizing, and analyzing large sets of data to better understand the information contained therein. Typically this is carried out using specialized software tools and applications for predictive analytics, data mining, text mining, forecasting, and data optimization (Beal, 2014), the totality of which represents the computational side of the process. But there are aspects to data analytics where humans greatly excel beyond the capabilities of computers, most notably in perceiving and interpreting patterns across multiple variables and groups, identifying anomalies, and interpreting the content of images. This means visualization.

Currently it is standard practice in big data analysis to present results in the form of colorful graphs, charts, plots, and pseudo-volumetric representations based on fundamental cognitive psychology principles such as color and size to denote differences and importance, connections to identify patterns, and similarities. Such output can be highly useful, but it is still limited in terms of what can be effectively communicated because of preset visualization types.

As has been shown throughout this book, the human brain is capable of extraordinary information processing tasks as long as the data is in a form that leverages the strengths of the human perceptual mechanisms. Of these mechanisms, vision is our dominant sense, with roughly a quarter of our brain devoted to processing visual stimuli and which provides the highest-bandwidth perceptual channel into our cognitive systems (Reda et al., 2013). Ideally, developing the tools and methods to more effectively harness this pathway is a major goal.

In the remainder of this chapter we will look at several impressive examples of applying immersive virtual reality to the analysis of big data problems. It is important to point out that unlike general scientific visualization applications for immersive displays (which are widespread), these examples are different in a number of ways.

Foremost, scientific visualization generally refers to analysis of large amounts of data produced by numerical simulation of physical processes. These examples deal with real or measured data, as well as data from multiple sources.

Visualization of Longitudinal Study Data

In 2015, Epic Games (makers of the Unreal 4 gaming engine) and The Wellcome Trust biomedical research charity launched a contest known as the Big Data VR challenge. The goal of the challenge was to develop methods of using immersive virtual reality systems to unlock new ways to manipulate and interrogate the huge data sets that are now generated by many scientific studies and to facilitate greater information understanding (Cowley, 2015).

Competing teams from around the world were paired with live scientific research projects for a four-month period. In the winning effort, two London-based companies, Masters of Pie and Lumacode, Ltd (together known as team LumaPie), were partnered with the University of Bristol's Avon Longitudinal Study of Parents and Children (ALSPAC) titled, "Children of the 90s." Within that study, which has lasted more than 20 years, researchers have intensively tracked a broad selection of variables for more than 14,000 pregnant women, their spouses, and offspring. The variables include diet, lifestyle, socioeconomic status, parent-child contact, BMI, pulse, waist size, weight, and more. Tens of thousands of biological samples were also collected from the participants over the years, including urine, blood, hair, toenails, milk teeth, and DNA. The totality of enormous scientific dataset represents the most detailed study of its kind in the world investigating the environmental and genetic factors that affect a person's health and development (ALSPAC, 2015).

In developing the visualization layout, the application designers leveraged the inherent ability to spread the data out around the user, such as is depicted in Figure 19.1. Data elements were represented by 3D primitives whose size, orientation, color, and position could depict field values with a simple glance, such as an elongated pyramid or spheres textured with heat maps. Those data elements were used to populate circular and arc-shaped DNA-like coils, allowing more data to be represented in a given area than would have been possible on simple straight lines. The coils themselves could be set in motion to rotate around the user, allowing researchers to quickly scan the data far more efficiently just by moving their head rather than scrutinizing spreadsheets of alphanumeric data (Masters of Pie, 2015).

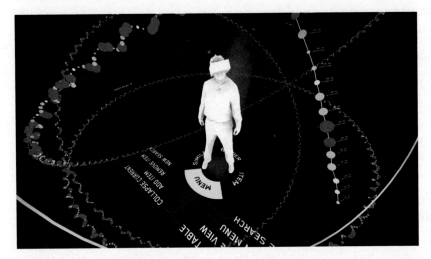

Figure 19.1 This image depicts the information layout of the LumaPie Avon Longitudinal Study of Parents and Children (ALSPAC) data visualization application. Note how the space was effectively utilized by laying out data in a manner that completely surrounds the user.
Credit: Image courtesy of Masters of Pie, Ltd

Filters and modifiers were developed to sort data and facilitate pattern and trend recognition (see Figure 19.2), as well as to easily export the results of a particular study back into raw alphanumeric form for sharing with other researchers. During investigations, the user employs a virtual laser (driven via commercial handheld controllers) to point to specific data elements. When the laser would hit one of the 3D primitives, a label would appear displaying the alphanumeric values of that particular piece of data (Masters of Pie, 2015).

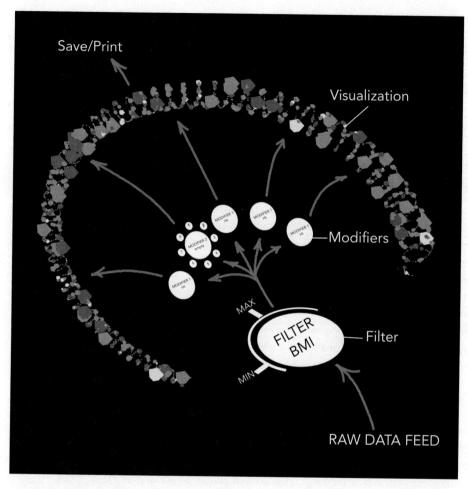

Figure 19.2 This image is an end-to-end data flow diagram detailing filter and modifier functions for the ALSPAC visualization and analytical application.

Credit: Image courtesy of Masters of Pie, Ltd

An interesting aspect to the overall solution was the multiuser system design. While the main user drives a particular investigation and has complete access to all the raw and highly confidential data, a second user, either local or remote, is able to view a filtered version of the specific visualization underway but only the key data relevant to his query, to protect ALSPAC participant privacy. Direct interaction between the two users is facilitated using a live-chat capability (Masters of Pie, 2015).

Results

LumaPie's solution has received rave reviews for its ability to rapidly facilitate discovery of trends and patterns in the data even by untrained analysts. The system is a fully functional immersive virtual environment built from the data itself. Users have full control within the VR space, enabling intuitive interaction and manipulation of the data (Cowley, 2015). The application leverages the unique human ability to quickly recognize patterns in color, size, movement, and 3D spatial position to produce tangible outputs (ALSPAC, 2015).

Visualization of Multidisciplinary Mining Data

The establishment of an underground mining operation is a massive, complicated, and expensive undertaking that generates tremendous amounts of multidisciplinary information. Consider what is involved in just the exploration stage. Everything starts with detailed studies and surface reconnaissance, including aerial photos, aeromagnetic and gravimetric surveys, geological surface mapping, sampling, geochemical studies, and more. Once a deposit of interest is located (referred to as discovery), the next stage is the mapping of underground structures and dimensions of the deposits, as well as the content and distribution of the ore. This is then followed by drilling to further investigate and sample the mineralization in depth. It is only after this extensive analysis that a project then moves into the development and production phases, which themselves produce even greater quantities of data.

Throughout each phase of a mining project, from initial geoscience and exploration to development and production, significant time and expense are invested in attempting to understand exactly what is below the surface, as well as how to safely and cost effectively recover the desired material. Unfortunately, despite many advances in the mining industry, so called "Big Data" in this field is very different from that of other industries. Project data is often deposited in both hard and soft copy formats spread across multiple locations without structure or standards. Additionally, although much of this information describes complex 3D structures and phenomena, it is often represented in two dimensions. This creates significant challenges in performing detailed, integrated evaluations, and it impedes discovery and establishment of relationships between different data types (Suorineni, 2015).

In plain English, the result is highly inefficient data interpretation and less than optimal mining operations.

To facilitate increased understanding of exactly what this varied data represents below the surface, as well as to more accurately plan and execute recovery operations, researchers with the University of New South Wales (UNSW) in Sydney, Australia, are applying immersive visualization technologies as a means of supplementing traditional mining data interpretation, to facilitate mine planning and infrastructure layout.

In one simple example, Figure 19.3 shows the integration of mapping, geophysical (surface and inversion models), drilling, and resource models to help engineers visualize the full potential of deposits within a prospective mining site (Vasak and Suorineni, 2010). As can be inferred from these model images, significantly greater understanding of the overall geometry of the complex underground structures, as well as the location of existing sample drillholes (blue lines on the left), can be acquired by combining multiple datasets and viewing within an immersive, interactive 3D setting. Further, the planning of new drillholes (red lines on the right) to explore the extent of the formation of recoverable materials (blue areas on right) becomes a far more intuitive 3D positioning task compared to making such determinations based on 2D representations.

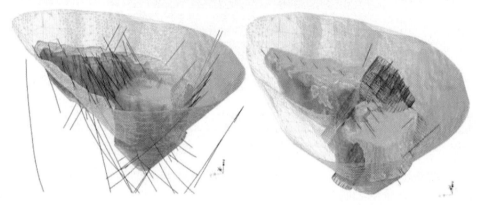

Figure 19.3 This image shows the integration of mapping, geophysical, drilling, and resource models to help engineers more effectively visualize the full potential of ore deposits within a prospective mining site.
Credit: Image courtesy of Fidelis T Suorineni - UNSW Australia

In a more complex example, Figure 19.4 shows a detailed snapshot from UNSW's Block Cave Mining Visualizer, an interactive 3D application designed to allow users to visualize multiple combined datasets associated with the "block cave" underground mining process.

In block cave mining, once a recoverable ore body is identified, a large network of tunnels is dug beneath the ore formation. Large upward-facing funnels are blasted into the rock above these tunnels. Ultimately, the ore formation is then undercut, creating an artificial cavern that fills with rubble as it collapses under its own weight. This broken ore falls into the large rock funnels and then into the tunnels, where it is recovered and transported to the surface.

Of particular note with this visualization application is the fact that, in addition to simultaneously displaying multiple tightly correlated datasets, including those representing geologic formations, numerical stress estimation results, seismic sensor positions, and actual mine development geometry (tunnels, undercuts, and so on), the application allows the playback of actual seismic events and other time-sequenced data (Vantage, 2015).

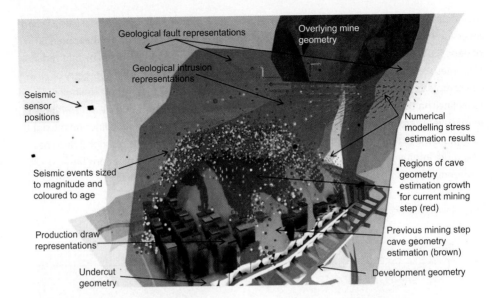

Figure 19.4 This image shows a detailed, multi-dataset model within UNSW's Block Cave Mining Visualizer.

Credit: Image courtesy of Fidelis T Suorineni – UNSW Australia

This application was developed for use with the UNSW's innovative AVIE (Advanced Visualization and Interactive Environment) display shown in Figure 19.5, a custom-designed, standalone, cylindrical silvered screen measuring 10 meters in diameter by 4 meters in height. Active stereo imagery is supplied by six overhead projectors, the display fields for which are seamlessly blended to create a continuous 360° immersive viewing area. Users of the system are given active stereo shutter glasses.

In standard operating mode, real time markerless motion tracking and gesture recognition allows the operator to control movement through the models. The large size of the display together with the application provides a high degree of spatial and temporal context, a compelling sense of immersion as well as ample space for multidisciplinary collaboration.

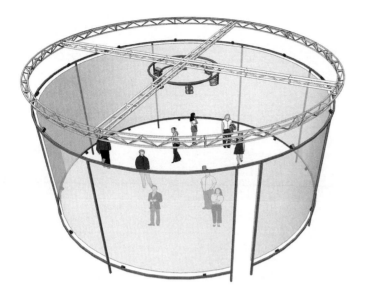

Figure 19.5 This illustration shows the design of the 10-meter diameter 360° AVIE (Advanced Visualization and Interactive Environment) display located at the University of New South Wales (UNSW) in Sydney, Australia.
Credit: Image courtesy of iCinema Centre for Interactive Cinema Research, UNSW Australia

Conclusion

Immersive virtual reality systems appear to hold significant potential as another means through which to conduct Big Data analytics, although this application area is extremely young and filled with questions. Just as there are ongoing struggles encountered in attempting to figure out effective ways to produce useful analytical products based on 2D graphics, charts, and other representations, similar challenges exist with this new medium, albeit with the benefit of an additional dimension and interactivity with which to work. In one sense, this could be considered an expansion of an artist's palette. Specifically, what is the best way to represent data (often abstract, or of high dimensionality, or of great variety and quantity) in a manner that facilitates greater insight and understanding? This is made even more challenging by the fact that in most instances you do not know what you are looking for; otherwise, you would likely be able to automate the search. Could the visual representation be expanded to include an audio or tactile component? The technologies are certainly there. Now all that remains is the creative application.

CHAPTER 20

TELEROBOTICS AND TELEPRESENCE

The enabling technologies of virtual and augmented reality also hold significant promise in telerobotics, telepresence, and the control of semi-autonomous robots and systems from a distance. In this chapter we will explore three such applications, demonstrating use of these technologies in a high-end professional setting down to recent capabilities made available to the general hobbyist.

Defining Telerobotics and Telepresence

The objective of a telerobotic system is to connect humans and robots to reproduce operator actions at a distance (Ferre, 2007). The field is a branch of general robotics, the roots of which can be found in the need to perform work in hazardous or otherwise unreachable environments. The modern foundations of the field can be traced back to the 1950s and 1960s at Argonne National Laboratory and the handling of nuclear waste (Goertz, 1964). Today telerobotics has grown significantly to encompass a large number of fields including explosive ordnance disposal, control of remotely piloted vehicles, undersea exploration, and more.

Telepresence is defined as the experience or perception of presence within a physically remote environment by means of a communication medium (Steuer, 1992). Although in recent years the phrase has been liberally applied to a variety of disparate technologies such as video conferencing, face-to-face mobile chat, and even high-definition television, all the examples we provide in this chapter involve the use of some form of stereoscopic visualization technique, with head-mounted displays as the primary interface in most instances.

Space Applications and Robonaut

The International Space Station (ISS) is an extremely complex microgravity laboratory orbiting the Earth at an altitude of approximately 250 miles. Measuring 357 feet in length (just short of the size of a football field), the internal living volume is larger than a six-bedroom home. Fifty-two computers control the basic functionality of the station. In the U.S. segment alone, 1.5 million lines of software code run on 44 computers communicating via 100 different data networks. Tremendous amounts of information are passed between the different onboard systems and Earth stations. Nearly an acre of solar panels provide 75–90 kilowatts of power to the overall structure. Now think of the time and effort it takes to maintain this basic infrastructure, and this is before you consider the complex collection of experiments and engineering systems.

Early into the Space Shuttle program, NASA recognized the need for a means to assist astronauts in carrying out maintenance projects, experiments, and tasks deemed either too dangerous for crew members or too boring, mundane, and a poor use of an astronaut's time (NASA, 2011). In 1996, the Dexterous Robotics Laboratory at NASA's Johnson Space Center began collaboration with the Defense Advanced Research Projects Agency (DARPA) to develop a robotic assistant to help meet these needs.

The result of these collaborations is NASA's Robonaut, a humanoid robot designed to function autonomously, as well as side by side with humans, carrying out some of these tasks. The newest model, developed by NASA and General Motors, is called Robonaut 2 (R2). As shown in Figure 20.1, the anthropomorphic R2 has a head, torso, arms, and dexterous hands capable of handling and manipulating many of the same tools as an astronaut would use to carry out different tasks. Delivered to the ISS in February 2011 aboard STS-133 (one of the final flights of the Space Shuttle), R2 is the first humanoid robot in space.

Figure 20.1 Robonaut 2 is the next-generation dexterous humanoid robot, developed through a Space Act Agreement by NASA and General Motors. Controlled by an astronaut or ground personnel using a stereoscopic head-mounted display, vest, and specialized gloves, the system is being developed to perform a variety of tasks both inside and outside the International Space Station. *Credit: Image courtesy of NASA*

R2's height is 3 feet, 4 inches (from waist to head) and incorporates more than 350 processors. The system can move at rates up to 7 feet per second. Between the fingers, arms, and head, the system is capable of movement across 42 degrees of freedom.

R2 has two primary operating modes; astronauts can give R2 a task to perform that is carried out autonomously, or the system can be controlled via teleoperation. In the case of the latter, as shown in Figure 20.2, an astronaut on the space station or a member of the ground crew dons a stereoscopic head-mounted display and pair of Cyberglove motion-capture data gloves. (See Chapter 12, "Devices to Enable Navigation and Interaction.") Movement of R2's head, arms, and hands are slaved precisely to those of the human operator.

Figure 20.2 In the International Space Station's Destiny laboratory, NASA astronaut Karen Nyberg wears a stereoscopic head-mounted display and CyberGloves while testing Robonaut 2's capabilities. *Credit: Image courtesy of NASA*

In 2014, R2 received its first pair of legs measuring 9 feet in length to help the system move around the ISS to complete simple tasks. Instead of feet, the robot has clamps that allow it to latch onto objects and maneuver through the interior of the ISS.

Robotic Surgery

Efforts are also underway at developing the techniques and procedures to enable the Robonaut system to eventually be able to carry out basic surgery and medical procedures in case of an emergency. As an example of the emerging capabilities of the system, in 2015 researchers with Houston Methodist Institute for Technology, Innovation & Education (MITIE) used the R2 platform to perform multiple ground-based medical and surgical tasks via teleoperation. These tasks included intubation, assisting during simulated laparoscopic surgery, performing ultra sound guided procedures, and executing a SAGES (Society of American Gastrointestinal and Endoscopic Surgeons) training exercise (Dean and Diftler, 2015).

Of the many challenges that engineers face in fielding an effective robotic helper, and in particular, one that can carry out telemedicine procedures, is the time lag between a human operator's movement or a command and the resulting action of the robotic system. Inside of a lab setting or across town, this time delay is negligible, but between a surgeon or physician on the ground and an orbiting space station, this delay could measure up to several seconds depending on the path the signal has to take (data relay satellites, ground stations, and so on). For deep space travel, these times increase dramatically. As an example, communications with spacecraft operating on Mars could have round-trip delays of up to 31 minutes depending on the planets' relative positions (Dunn, 2015).

As R2 technology matures, NASA is considering the wide variety of additional areas where similar robots could be utilized in the space program, including being sent further away from Earth to test the system in harsher conditions. Ultimately, NASA envisions the potential use of such systems in servicing weather and reconnaissance satellites and eventually paving the way to remote locations such as Mars to be followed by human explorers (NASA, 2014).

Undersea Applications

About 70% of the earth's surface is covered with water. Similar to space, the world's oceans present innumerable opportunities for exploration and discovery, but along with these opportunities come unique challenges and dangers. On one side, robotic submarines, autonomous underwater vehicles (AUVs), and underwater ROVs don't have the dexterity or finesse of human divers. On the other side, human divers are unable to reach certain ocean depths without significant expense and danger. To address these challenges and open the doors to exploration and study of a greater portion of our planet, researchers with Stanford University have developed a highly advanced telerobotic system shown in Figure 20.3 known as OceanOne.

Figure 20.3 The OceanOne highly dexterous robot from Stanford University uses artificial intelligence, haptic feedback systems, and stereo vision to enable human operators to work and explore at remote underwater task sites.
Credit: Image courtesy of Kurt Hickman / Stanford News Service

Designed with the original intent of conducting studies of deep coral reefs in the Red Sea, the highly dexterous OceanOne system measures approximately 5 feet in length and includes two fully articulating arms, a torso, and a head with stereo video cameras capable of motion across two degrees of freedom (DOF). A tail section neatly combines redundant power units, onboard computers, controllers, and a propulsion system made up of eight multidirectional thrusters.

The end effectors of OceanOne's arms include an array of sensors that send force feedback information to human operators located on the surface, enabling the pilot to delicately manipulate objects such as artifacts from shipwrecks, elements of a coral reef, sensors, and other instrumentation.

The system is outfitted with an array of sensors to measure conditions in the water and is able to automatically adjust for currents and turbulence to maintain position (known as station keeping).

The OceanOne system has already proven its capabilities and usefulness during a maiden dive in early 2016. Controlled by human operators on the surface, the system was used to explore *La Lune*, the flagship of King Louis XIV located 100 meters below the surface of the Mediterranean Sea approximately 20 miles off the southern coast of France. It is at this location that the vessel sank in 1664. During the dive, OceanOne was used to recover and return to the surface a delicate vase untouched by human hands for more than 350 years (Carey, 2016).

Terrestrial and Airborne Applications

In many Earth-based applications, experiencing a true sense of presence at a remote task site does not need to cost millions of dollars, nor does it have to take the form of the increasingly laughable model of a pole on wheels with tablet computer on top. The recent introduction of consumer-priced wide field of view (FOV) stereoscopic displays such as Oculus, HTC Vive, and OSVR are opening a host of opportunities for companies large and small to introduce alternative, highly useful, and cost effective remote visualization solutions.

DORA (Dexterous Observational Roving Automaton)

One such system is an immersive teleoperated robotic platform known as DORA (Dexterous Observational Roving Automaton), developed by an early-stage start-up team of student roboticists from the University of Pennsylvania. Sensors in the Oculus display system track the orientation of the operator's head. This data is wirelessly transmitted to the robot's microcontrollers, prompting actuators to move the stereo camera–equipped head to follow the user's movements.

The idea behind DORA is pretty straightforward. As shown in Figure 20.4, the user puts on a stereoscopic head-mounted display, the video signals for which are supplied from the DORA platform. Sensors in the display are used to slave the motion of the DORA system to that of the wearer's head. One of the most impressive features of the system was the original development price of less than $2,000 USD.

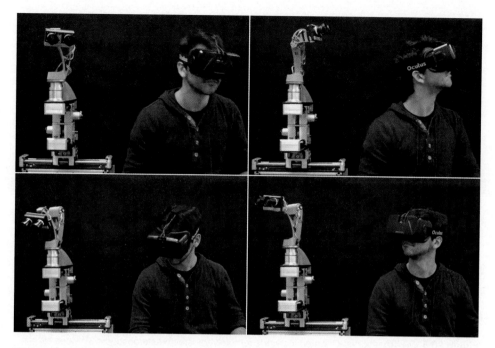

Figure 20.4 The DORA telerobotics platform gives users an immersive view of a remote task site by slaving the movement of stereo cameras to movement of an Oculus display, and thus, the operator's head.
Credit: Image courtesy of Daleroy Sibanda / DORA

The team envisions its first markets to be application settings such as museums for remote tour rentals as well as a tool for use by first responders, disaster relief workers, and combat engineers to enter areas deemed too dangerous for a human operator, but with the added benefit of a variable stereoscopic first-person point of view, something woefully lacking in most current robotics platforms specifically designed for that purpose.

Transporter3D DIY Telepresence System

Despite the relative youth of the availability of consumer-level wide-field-of-view immersive display technologies, systems are already appearing on the market that enable technophiles to rapidly construct their own low-cost, first-person view (FPV) stereoscopic telepresence systems. One such offering of particular note is the Transporter3D system shown in Figure 20.5 from EMR Laboratories of Waterloo, Ontario, Canada.

The Transporter3D is a device that supports use of head-mounted displays by converting remotely transmitted stereoscopic 3D video to real-time output over HDMI that is specifically designed for the Oculus Rift and other HD HMDs. (See Chapter 6, "Fully Immersive Displays.")

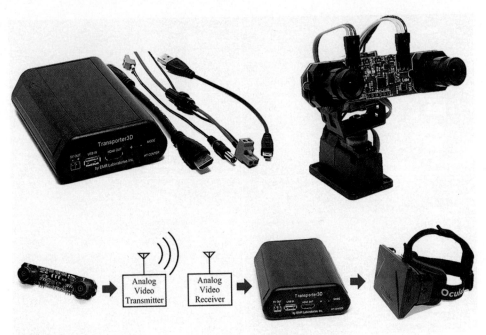

Figure 20.5 The Transporter3D system converts remotely transmitted stereoscopic 3D video to real-time output over HDMI for viewing within stereoscopic head-mounted displays. The system is specifically designed for hobbyists and radio controlled aircraft enthusiasts.
Credit: Image courtesy of EMR Laboratories, Inc

This 3D-Cam FPV camera is capable of both serial 3D (field sequential 3D over a single video transmitter) and parallel 3D (dual channel output), can be used in either 2D or 3D mode, and has remotely adjustable exposure and white balance locking for keeping ground and sky colors true under adverse lighting conditions. The camera lenses are positioned at the mean human inter-ocular distance for correct parallax offsets and ease of viewing. The IPD of the images shown in the Oculus display can also be easily adjusted for precision convergence alignment. Vertical and horizontal alignment of the onscreen images can be varied by the user, as can the aspect ratio of the displayed imagery.

A highly unique feature to this system is support for mounting the 3D-Cam FPV camera on a 3-axis pan/tilt/rollmount such as the FatShark gimbal shown in Figure 20.5. In this configuration, the system allows use of the Oculus IMU-based internal head tracker to slave movement of the camera to the operator's head pan, tilt, and roll motions completely independent of any other controls. Thus, if mounted on an RC aircraft or helicopter, the human operator can swivel his head to look in any direction without impacting the flight of the aircraft.

Conclusion

Telerobotics and telepresence are not new fields, but until recently they have been the realm of defense and university labs due to the traditionally high cost of enabling technologies, and in particular, specialty wide FOV stereoscopic head-mounted displays. The introduction of consumer displays such as Oculus, HTC Vive, and OSVR will likely have a dramatic impact on this field, resulting in the introduction of a host of new systems and applications in the coming few years.

CHAPTER 21

HUMAN FACTORS CONSIDERATIONS

With the surge of new virtual and augmented reality systems and technologies entering the marketplace, it is important to remember that there are a number of aspects to these advanced man-machine interfaces that can have direct implications for health, safety, and overall usability. In this chapter we explore a number of these issues, highlighting known problem areas and steps that can be taken to minimize their impact.

What Are Human Factors?

Human factors is an interdisciplinary field dealing with the application of information and understanding of physical and psychological characteristics about human behavior, abilities, and limitations in the design and evaluation of devices and systems (Chapanis, 2016). Within the fields of virtual and augmented reality, human factors studies extend into four principle areas: manual controllers, tactile and force feedback devices, spatial sound solutions, and visual displays. Each of these primary focus areas is a specialized field in and of itself, but to date, the majority of human factors studies have centered on issues related to visual displays and content, and for good reason. As we have learned throughout this book, the human visual system tells us more about our surroundings than any of the other four senses. Research estimates that 80–85% of our perception, learning, cognition, and activities are mediated through vision (Politzer, 2015).

From an engineering standpoint, our eyes are precision optical instruments, sensors, and transducers. Their design is optimized to gather photons of light in a specific manner and focus that light onto the retinal bed, where it is converted via complex neurochemical processes into electrical impulses encoded with information about stimulus size, color, and movement. The system is delicately balanced and works in close coordination and alignment with a variety of other sensory mechanisms. The totality of this converted stimulus is used by our brain to bring information about our surroundings—real or virtual—to our conscious awareness. As with any precision mechanism, when the functional processes of this system, or its inputs, are altered or even slightly askew, problems arise.

Given the immense complexities of the human visual system and the central role visual displays play in the overall topic of virtual and augmented reality, complications with these functional processes will make up the bulk of this chapter.

Physical Side Effects

When referring to virtual and augmented reality and the use of stereoscopic head-mounted displays, issues regarding user health and welfare are paramount and a growing area of concern as headsets targeting the broader consumer market are now shipping. Some of the most significant areas of uncertainty in reference to mainstream acceptance of these systems are their tendency to cause nausea, eye strain, disorientation, and other forms of discomfort. In fact, some studies report 80–95% of individuals using a stereoscopic head-mounted display experience some combination of these symptoms, with 5–50% severe enough to end participation (Ling et al., 2013). As will be shown, the problem is a combination of the precision and balance of the human perceptual system, shortcomings in the functional properties of the head-mounted displays, and other technical factors, as well as age, gender, and even race.

Comparing Real and Virtual Worlds

Consider the difference between a natural viewing situation and that provided via a modern flat panel-based head-mounted display. In natural viewing, light entering the eyes is the result of reflection off different objects and surfaces. Accommodation and convergence are tightly coupled, with the light patterns ultimately falling on the retinas containing parallax offsets, shading, and a variety of monocular and binocular depth cues. As the observer moves, their head and eyes scan an environment that remains in a fixed position.

With stereoscopic flat panel–based head-mounted displays, things are very different. Light entering the eyes is not the result of natural reflections from all angles, but projections from 2D surfaces (that is, the front of the LCDs or OLED panels) with simulated parallax offsets and depth cues. Absent are the natural perspectives, shading, and infinite depths of field. These projections then pass through any of a variety of optical systems (as well as that of your own eyes) to enable you to focus on the display surface. In the process, distortions and aberrations are introduced to the light field eventually reaching the retina. Depending on the quality and precision of the display, the performance of the computer driving the simulation, update rates from position and orientation sensors, and the care put into designing the simulation, a wide variety of perceptual issues can arise.

Visually Induced Motion Sickness

Some of the most common complaints from users of fully immersive virtual reality systems are dizziness and nausea. This phenomenon is referred to by several names, including simulator sickness, cyber sickness, 'RGB yawn,' and visually induced motion sickness (VIMS). The full range of symptoms regularly reported includes nausea, increased salivation, drowsiness, disorientation, dizziness, headaches, difficulty focusing, blurred vision, and occasionally even vomiting. The onset of these symptoms can take place within minutes and may continue for some time after an immersive experience has concluded (Biocca, 1992; Ebenholtz, 1992; Pausch et al., 1992; Cobb et al., 1999).

Although standard motion sickness and VIMS share some similar symptoms, it is important to highlight the fact that standard motion sickness occurs in the absence of *vection*, which is the illusory visual sensation of self-motion in the absence of physical movement (Fischer and Kornmüller, 1930; Dichgans and Brandt, 1973). A side-by-side comparison of the symptomatology of standard motion sickness and VIMS is shown in Table 21.1.

Table 21.1   Symptomatology of Standard Motion Sickness and VIMS

Motion Sickness	Simulator Sickness/Visually Induced Motion Sickness (VIMS)
Nausea	Nausea
Pale Skin	Queasy StomachIncreased Salivation
Increased Salivation	Increased Sweating
Cold Sweats	Postural Instability
Retching/Vomiting	Pallor
Dizziness	Apathy
Headache	Drowsiness
Fatigue	Disorientation
	Dizziness
	Headaches
	Difficulty Focusing
	Blurred Vision
	Retching /Vomiting

Physiological Factors in VIMS

The current, most widely held theory for these physiological responses and one that has withstood more than 40 years of debate is based on the idea of sensory conflict. First proposed in 1975 in relation to flight simulators (Reason and Brand, 1975), the theory holds that these physiological side effects are a result of the compelling visual sensation of motion without the corresponding vestibular or proprioceptive cues (Stanney and Kennedy, 2009; Groen and Bos 2008; Nichols and Patel, 2002; Reason and Brand, 1975). For clarity, the visual system provides information relating to body orientation with respect to the visual world; the vestibular system offers information relating to linear and angular acceleration and position with respect to gravity; and the kinesthetic or proprioceptive system provides information relating to limb and body position (Barratt and Pool, 2008).

Figure 21.1 perfectly illustrates an application setting for such conflicts to arise. As the driving simulation progresses, the user has a highly compelling visual sensation of self-motion, but none of the other corresponding sensations that would accompany an actual driving experience with the exception of hands on the wheel. The sensory conflict theory also holds that this response can occur when these various cues are in conflict with what would be expected on the basis of previous personal experience. In all cases, the inclusion of vestibular cues in the theory is crucial because individuals with a damaged vestibular system do not experience these side effects.

Figure 21.1 This staged image is intended to illustrate the concept of conflicting sensory input that can ultimately result in nausea and discomfort. This user is experiencing the compelling visual sensation of motion without any of the normal vestibular or proprioceptive cues.
Credit: Image courtesy of Nan Palmero and SuperCar-RoadTrip.fr via Flickr under a CC 2.0 license

Additional theories have been proposed over the years as an explanation for VIMS. One such theory, known as the Ecological Theory, holds that these side effects result from prolonged instability in the control of posture (Riccio and Stoffregen, 1991; Bonnet et al., 2008). Because the sensory conflict theory continues to dominate the scientific literature and general topical discourse, the remainder of this chapter will assume the theory to be correct. However, readers should be firmly aware that the scientific community in no way has a full understanding of this topic (thus the use of the word *theory*). Additional research is ongoing.

Key Technology Factors in VIMS

Latency

A key performance and usability measure for all immersive virtual and augmented reality systems is that of latency, or the time lag between a user's action and the system's response to this action (Papadakis et al., 2011). Latency is a product of the processing, transport, and synchronization delays of key system components. It is well known to be detrimental to a primary factor that detracts from the sense of presence, a user's sense of immersion, physical performance, and comfort level (Meehan et al., 2003; Friston and Steed, 2014). Perhaps most important to this chapter, latency can result in a breakdown between proprioceptive cues of the user and the visual stimuli shown in the display resulting in increased incidence of VIMS (Buker et al., 2012).

Figure 21.2 illustrates the central latency challenge facing system designers. When a user wears a head-mounted display, sensors must continually recalculate the position and orientation of the user's head to account for movement. Those position changes are then sent to the core application, which calculates the individual left- and right-eye scene views to be generated. Only then can the proper scenes be rendered by the graphics engine and the resulting output sent to the display elements within the head-mounted device. The sum of the times involved in these processing steps represents the cumulative base latency measurement, which varies widely depending on the specific position tracker used (inertial, optical, and so on), CPU capabilities, type of display (LCD, OLED, LCOS, and so on), as well as on-scene complexity.

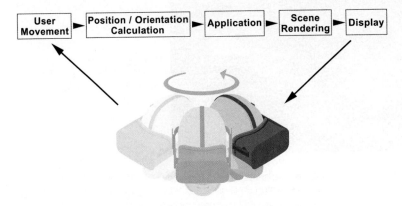

Figure 21.2 This diagram illustrates the central latency challenge faced in supplying an immersive display experience.
Credit:Head illustration by andrewrybalko © 123RF.com

Obviously, the desired goal of hardware designers and manufacturers would be to produce systems capable of zero latency (as is the case human eyesight), but this is not feasible because each step in the processing model requires some measure of time to complete. In short, we will never get to zero latency, but commercial virtual reality systems recently introduced to the market have exceptional baseline capabilities nonetheless. These specifications are summarized in Table 21.2.

Table 21.2   HTC Vive VR, Oculus Rift, and Sony PlayStation VR Comparison Chart[1]

	HTC Vive VR	**Oculus Rift**	**PlayStation VR**
Display Type	AMOLED	AMOLED	AMOLED
Resolution	1080 × 1200 (2 scrn, combd 2160 × 1200)	1080 × 1200 (2 scrn, combd 2160 × 1200)	960 × 1080 (single 1920 × 1080 scrn)
Max Refresh	90 Hz	90 Hz	90 Hz, 120 Hz
Field of View	~ 110 degrees	~ 110 degrees	~ 100
Sensors	Accelerometer, Gyroscope, Front-facing camera, Laser sensor	Accelerometer, Gyroscope, Magnetometer, Tracking Array	Accelerometer, Gyroscope, Magnetometer, PS Eye Tracking

Connections	3-in-1 connector to interface box with HDMI/ display port, USB, and power	HDMI, USB	**VR headset:** HDMI, Aux, Stereo Headphone Jack **Processor unit:** HDMI TV, HDMI PS4, USB, HDMI, Aux
Base Latency	~ 18ms	~ 18ms	~ 18ms

[1] Input/sensors are often run in separate threads so they are not confined to the frame rate. They run as fast as they can independently and are then polled for results at the appropriate time of the pipeline. This helps minimize latency and in some cases even allows other applications (or computers) to handle input calculations.

Incorrect Interpupillary Distance Settings

The distance between the centers of your pupils, known as the interpupillary distance (IPD), varies from person to person, by gender, and even by ethnicity. This measurement is extremely important for all binocular viewing systems ranging from standard eyewear to stereoscopic head-mounted displays.

In the case of regular eyeglasses, if the interpupillary distance measurement is wrong, then the principle axis of each lens will not align with the centers of your eyes, resulting in eyestrain and headaches. In the case of sporting binoculars or stereo microscopes, given the small exit pupils of the eye ports, the devices will be difficult or impossible to use without adjustment.

When it comes to stereoscopic head-mounted displays, proper IPD settings are extremely important for a variety of reasons. As shown in Figure 21.3, poor eye-lens alignment can result in image distortion, the effect of which can also result in eye strain and headaches and may contribute to the overall onset of VIMS (Ames et al., 2005). Incorrect settings can also impact ocular convergence and incorrect perception of the displayed imagery. For instance, when there is a greater-than-normal separation of inputs to the two eyes, the convergence angle to an object being viewed is increased, potentially resulting in the distance to a viewed object appearing shorter and the object appearing closer (Priot et al., 2006).

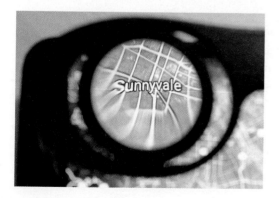

Figure 21.3 This shows an example of the level of image distortion possible with poor eye-lens alignment.
Credit: Photo by S. Aukstakalnis

The mean adult IPD is around 63 mm, with the majority of adults having IPDs in the range 50–75 mm. Some fall into the wider range of 45–80 mm, however. The minimum IPD for children (down to five years old) is around 40 mm (Dodgson, 2004).

Of the three major consumer head-mounted displays available at the time of this book's preparation, two (HTC Vive and Oculus Rift) provide the ability to mechanically adjust IPD settings, moving each eye's lens and screen together as a single assembly. Thus, the lens and screen remain perfectly aligned while allowing for lateral adjustment. In the case of the Sony PlayStation VR system, lenses within the display remain in a fixed position while IPD settings are adjusted through software (which moves the center of each eye's view on the display).

Display Field of View

As discussed in Chapter 3, "The Mechanics of Sight," the combined field of view (FOV) of the human visual system measures approximately 200° horizontal by 130° vertical, with a centered binocular overlap of approximately 120° (Velger, 1998, p. 50). It is generally held that a wide FOV within a head-mounted display is better because it more closely simulates natural viewing and contributes to the user's sense of immersion and presence within the simulation model (Primeau, 2000; Rogers et al., 2003).

Although this may be the case, it is important to point out that some studies suggest a wider FOV may also contribute to or increase the likelihood of VIMS. The basic premise is that a wide FOV display can induce a stronger perception of self-motion (vection) than a display with a restricted FOV (Pausch et al., 1992). Further, because flicker is most efficiently detected at the periphery of the visual field, consideration of refresh rates and luminance is also warranted (Kolasinski 1995).

Another potential contributing factor to the VIMS phenomenon is a discordance between the display field of view (DFOV) and geometric field of view (GFOV), which defines the horizontal and vertical boundaries of the perspective projection scene generated by a graphics engine (Draper et al., 2001).

Optical Distortion of Scene Geometry

Research demonstrates that the pattern of geometric distortion by stereoscopic display optics changes substantially as the observer's eye moves from one position to another. The basic phenomenon of optical distortion is well known and often compensated for by predistortion of the imagery, but these techniques often do not take consider changes in eye position relative to the lens as well as rotation of the eye off a central axis. The net result is incorrect vergence information leading to inaccurate depth judgments and the appearance of geometry shifting position as the user's eyes scans the scene (Jones et al., 2014).

Frame Rate

Also known as refresh rate, this is the speed at which the contents of a frame buffer are displayed onscreen. Frame rate is directly related to flicker, which, at slower speeds, can contribute to the onset of nausea. Flicker above 30 Hz is most noticeable in the periphery of your FOV, but significantly less so in the foveal (or central) vision area (Pausch et al., 1992), thus contributing to issues with extremely wide FOV displays.

Persistence

This is the duration of time each pixel in a display remains lit. One of the effects of high persistence is the blurring and smearing of images which, in addition to contributing to poor image quality, has been associated with increased incidence of nausea and other forms of discomfort. High persistence is a common problem with many LCD-based head-mounted displays, although the shift to OLED/AMOLED flat-panel arrays and their inherently faster pixel-switching speeds reduces this problem.

Susceptibility to VIMS

Published research suggests that susceptibility to motion sickness in general and VIMS in particular is multifaceted, varying with age, ethnicity, gender, and overall health. For instance, the response is seen to be greatest between the ages of 2 and 12 (Stanney et al., 2002), slowing rapidly until about age 21 (Reason and Brand, 1975), and then increasing dramatically after age 50 (Brooks et al., 2010). People of Asiatic descent may be more susceptible than non-Asian counterparts (Barrett, 2004). Chinese women appear to be hyper sensitive to visually induced motion sickness (Stern et al., 1993). Women in general appear to be significantly more susceptible than men (Kennedy and Frank, 1985; Park et al., 2006; Kennedy et al., 1989; Boyd, 2001).

Adaptation

A fascinating aspect of the human perceptual system is the ability of many individuals to adapt to the sensory conflict with repeated exposure, not only to the specific stimuli leading to the condition but also with continued exposure to distorting lenses (Reason and Brand, 1975). Conversely, research also shows that adaptation to immersive virtual environments and a reduction in nausea results in an increase in after effects, including postural instability (Stanney and Salvendy 1998; Kennedy et al., 1997).

Visual Side Effects

There are growing concerns about potentially harmful effects on the visual system from the use of flat panel–based head-mounted displays in general, and stereoscopic systems in particular, due to conflicts introduced into normal sensory input. In this section we review some of what are thought to be the more important of these conflict areas.

Vergence—Accommodation Conflicts

One of the most significant known factors contributing to visual discomfort while viewing stereoscopic 3D displays in general, and in modern flat panel–based stereoscopic head-mounted displays in particular, is the challenge of *vergence-accommodation conflict* (or vergence-accommodation decoupling). As shown in Figure 21.4, vergence is an involuntary function within which the two eyes rotate in opposing directions around the vertical axis to maintain binocular fixation (bifoveal fixation) when shifting attention between objects at varying distances in the visual scene.

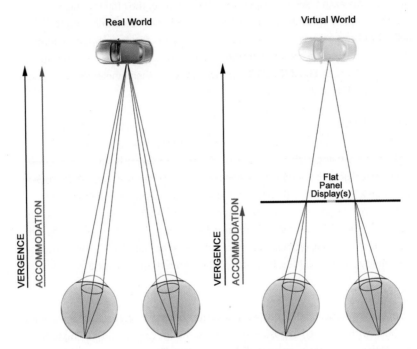

Figure 21.4 This image illustrates vergence-accommodation conflict experienced when wearing a flat panel–based stereoscopic head-mounted display. While focused on the display surface, the eyes are converging on objects at a completely different depth of field.
Credit: Illustration by S. Aukstakalnis

Closely related to vergence is accommodation, which is a change in the focal power (or focus) of the eye lens when shifting attention between objects. As shown in Figure 21.5, focusing on objects nearer the viewer requires convergence and a shorter focal length. Conversely, objects farther away require divergence and a longer focal length. Retinal blur is believed to be the actual visual cue that drives accommodation, or adjustment of the eye's lens, to focus the light reaching the retina (Kramida, 2015).

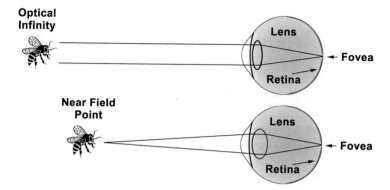

Figure 21.5 This image illustrates variation in lens focal power as one focuses on objects located at different depths of field.
Credit: Illustration by S. Aukstakalnis

Normally, vergence and accommodation are tightly correlated ocular functions that are neurally linked and reflexive (vergence triggers accommodation, and vice versa) (Banks et al., 2013).

Unfortunately with most fully immersive stereoscopic head-mounted displays, your eyes are focused at a fixed distance (on the surface of the flat panel display elements within the HMD) to keep images sharp on the retina, while trying to converge or diverge on objects with varying simulated depths within imagery seen on the display.

Although this decoupling is known to result in eye muscle fatigue and contribute to visually induced motion sickness, the vergence-accommodation conflict can also result in various perceptual errors. For instance, the lack of an appropriate relationship between accommodation and distances to virtual objects is suspected to be an important factor in the lack of size constancy when many monocular cues are absent from the scene (Roland, Gibson, and Ariely, 1998; Wann et al., 1995; Peli, 1995).

Vergence-accommodation conflict is not limited to stereoscopic head-mounted displays. The same effect can also be experienced in large-scale display walls and immersive systems such as the computer-assisted virtual environment (CAVE), which is based on similar display principles (Wann and Mon-Williams, 1997).

Potential Impact

At the time of this book's preparation, there were simply not enough planer head-mounted displays in circulation to understand the full scope of impact from the vergence-accommodation conflict, and in particular, the ramifications from extended use. For instance, could there be a loss of normal sight function after a few hours of continuous use, and if yes, could this impact the ability of someone to, say, safely operate an automobile? What about long-term impact from repeated extended use?

Conclusion

In this chapter, we have explored the primary human factors consideration directly impacting overall usability and enjoyment of virtual and augmented reality systems. It is clear that although issues regarding physical discomfort, eye strain, and lingering after-effects are complex problems, many will be sorted out or eliminated with additional research and as new display technologies enter the marketplace. In fact, it is safe to assume that within the next few years, flat panel–based stereoscopic displays will give way to new technologies that more closely harness the unique capabilities and functionality of the human visual system.

CHAPTER 22

LEGAL AND SOCIAL CONSIDERATIONS

The transition of virtual and augmented reality from specialty systems in research labs and high-end defense applications to the general consumer marketplace is raising profound legal, social, and ethical issues. From product safety to the increasing violence and realism of first-person games and even immersive pornography, the introduction of these technologies into the broader population is certain to have dramatic implications. In this chapter we explore a number of these issues, noting areas of concern and some of the serious challenges faced in the course of their increasingly widespread use.

Legal Considerations

Immersive virtual and augmenting simulation technologies hold significant potential to become both disruptive and transformative influences on many industries. As has been shown throughout this book, the process is already well underway in such application areas as architecture, engineering, defense, and entertainment. But along with such broad-ranging impact undoubtedly comes a new range of liabilities spanning multiple areas due to increased risks of personal injury, property damage due to faulty or harmful products, inadequate warnings, and even crimes committed in virtual space. In this section we will review a number of looming areas of potential liability for hardware and software manufacturers in this industry almost certain to be tested within the U.S. legal system.

Potential Product Liability

Product liability refers to a manufacturer, wholesaler, or retailer (and often all three) being held responsible for putting a dangerous or defective product into the hands of consumers. Given the unique nature of commercially oriented virtual and augmented reality systems, and in particular, head-mounted displays, the ground is fertile for a host of product liability lawsuits. In this regard, there are three types of liability claims: defective design, defective manufacturing, and failure to provide adequate warnings or instructions. Each stands a high probability of being the focus of litigation within the next few years.

Personal Injury/Property Damage

As shown in Figure 22.1, one of the most obvious likely causes for future litigation will be either injury or property damage resulting from the use of fully immersive head-mounted displays. When in use, most, if not all, of a user's visual reference to real-world surroundings is blocked from view.

At the time of this book's preparation, there appear to be two primary design strategies being employed by manufacturers to reduce this risk. The first is incorporation of a front-facing video camera within the display, the output from which can be overlaid onto the virtual world scene to allow the user to detect objects in their path (such as with the Chaperone feature of the HTC Vive display detailed in Chapter 6, "Fully Immersive Displays"). The second is to limit functionality of the system by only tracking changes in orientation of the user's head (roll, pitch, and yaw), but with no provision for position tracking (X, Y, and Z). This strategy would necessitate affecting translation through a virtual model using some form of manual controller, thereby dramatically reducing or eliminating the need for a user to be on his feet.

Figure 22.1 This figure depicts two of the greatest product liability challenges facing fully immersive virtual reality systems.

Credit: Illustration by deimosz © 123RF.com

Simulator Sickness and Other Physical Impacts

Another key scenario likely to lead to future product liability claims will arise out of issues concerning the physiological impact of these systems, and in particular, the tendency for a certain segment of the population to become nauseous when using immersive virtual reality displays.

As covered extensively in Chapter 21, "Human Factors Considerations," it is well known that many immersive head-mounted displays are prone to generate sickness in users under a variety of different circumstances. Often referred to as *simulator sickness*, *cybersickness*, or *visually induced motion sickness* (VIMS), this psychophysiological response to perceptual illusions can produce a range of symptoms including blurred vision, eye strain, fatigue, drowsiness, pallor, cold sweats, disorientation, seizures, and general nausea (Stanney and Kennedy, 2009; Groen and Bos, 2008; Nichols and Patel, 2002; Reason and Brand, 1975). Following the removal of the display, these symptoms can last from several minutes to several hours (Kennedy et al., 2010).

Hardware Issues

While there is much that is understood about the VIMS phenomenon, there are also glaring gaps in our understanding. For example, on the hardware side, it is known that anomalies in optical flow patterns, incorrect interpupilary distances, binocular rivalry, image flicker, and latency can be contributing factors. To this end, inexpensive, poorly designed head-mounted displays rushed out into the marketplace could not only place a company in serious legal jeopardy, but also result in unnecessary physical harm.

There are also questions looming about the impact from conflicts between the fundamental design of these display systems, the natural function of the human eye, and potential negative impact. For instance, the time needed for your eyes to converge (such as when looking at an object approaching you) and the time needed for them to focus (or adjust the amount of light entering the eye, or accommodation) are the same. Your brain normally functions using this tight *vergence-accommodation coupling.*

Unfortunately, with most fully immersive stereoscopic head-mounted displays, your eyes are focused at a fixed distance (on the surface of the flat panel display element) while trying to converge or diverge on objects seen moving toward or away from you. Although this decoupling is known to result in eye muscle fatigue and contribute to the nausea phenomenon described earlier, are there long-term use impacts? Could there be a loss of normal sight function after a few hours of continuous use, and if yes, could this impact the ability of someone to safely operate an automobile? What about long-term impact from repeated and extended use? At this point there is simply not enough published research to answer these questions.

Software Issues

The design of software applications for immersive virtual reality systems holds just as much significance, and potential liability, as the display components. As indicated earlier, the compelling visual sensation of motion without the corresponding vestibular cues can result in VIMS, disorientation, vertigo, and more. This is a content (software) issue. There are also other visual cues and content features for virtual environments that can contribute to this effect. These include models requiring the user to make numerous right-angle turns and other excessive visual stimuli that result in frequent, dramatic head movements, thereby exasperating the disconnect between visual, vestibular, and a range of proprioceptive cues and exasperating the potential onset of VIMS.

Collateral Damage

Games and other applications that require the user of a fully immersive display to be physically punching, swinging a controller, or performing other gesticulating actions are also potential candidates for litigation as a result of collateral damage, both to physical property as well as injury of bystanders or other participants. Consider that in 2008, a $5 million class-action lawsuit was filed against Nintendo by a mother from Littleton, Colorado, claiming that the wrist strap attached to the family Wii controller was "ineffective." The plaintiff alleged that her 52-inch Samsung television was damaged by a Wii controller that flew out of her son's hand while playing virtual bowling.

In addition to potential legal exposure based on claims of product defects, negligence, and breach of warranties, it is almost guaranteed that if this industry grows at even a fraction of the anticipated rate, there will emerge an appropriate body of federal regulations and consumer product safety acts with which to contend.

Distraction

Not to be left out, augmented reality systems pose their own unique set of issues in terms of potential liability claims. Although not fully occluding a user's view, there is the potential for the information displayed within the device, or elements of the device itself, to be distracting enough to lead to potential liability claims.

In just one example, a 2014 study conducted by researchers from the University of Central Florida, the Air Force Research Laboratory, and Ball Aerospace asked 40 individuals in their 20s to drive in a car simulator while using either Google Glass or a smartphone. During the simulator runs, the subjects were interrupted with an emergency brake event. Both the response event and subsequent recovery were analyzed. In the results of this one investigation, Glass-delivered messages served to moderate—but did not eliminate— distracting cognitive demands. A potential passive cost to drivers merely wearing Glass was observed also. Messaging using either device impaired the test subject's driving as compared to driving without multitasking (Sawyer, 2014).

Unknowns

Given the overriding goal of supplementing or replacing various perceptual stimuli, a host of questions remain as to the long-term impact these technologies could have on cognitive processes. For instance, neuroscientists at UCLA have been conducting research on how the use of virtual reality systems affects the brain, with some startling results. In one such investigation, researchers built special treadmills within which lab rats could explore a virtual room. While the rats (with probes wired into their brains) appeared to behave normally, analysis of signals from the hippocampus, a region of the brain involved in mapping an individual's location in space, showed 60% of neurons simply "shut down." Of those that did not shut down, many showed abnormal patterns of activity (Lewis, 2015).

This book is filled with examples of where cognitive processes are aided through the use of virtual and augmenting display technologies within specific applications, but little is known about the potential negative ramifications, if any, from other uses.

Potential Courtroom Applications and Implications

Immersive virtual reality systems also hold dramatic implications for courtroom settings. Consider the following scenarios, one possible at this very moment, and another, certain to be put to use in the not-so-distant future.

Criminal Investigation

It is standard practice with nearly all crime scene investigations for technicians to thoroughly document the area through photography. This includes evidence that, prior to collection, must be carefully photographed to accurately capture its position in relationship to the entire crime scene. These photographs are in addition to video, physical measurements, sketches, charts, hand-written notes, and voice recordings. Along with being used to help solve crimes, the totality of this information is used to present a case or mount a defense in courtroom proceedings.

Now consider the implications of a prosecutor or defense attorney not only presenting traditional evidentiary material, but also guiding a judge, jury, and other members of a court on a first-person trip through high-resolution 3D scans or stereo 360° panoramic photographs of that same crime scene. Instead of the judge and jury attempting to form a mental image of the setting or struggling to visualize spatial and temporal relationships and viewpoints based on traditional evidence, they are able to experience them firsthand through this new medium.

This capability is here now. In addition to systems such as the Matterport camera discussed in Chapter 14, "Architecture and Construction," FARO Technologies of Lake Mary, Florida, has developed a high-precision, high-speed 3D laser scanner for the detailed measurement and documentation of large objects, buildings, and indoor and outdoor spaces with complex geometries, including crime scenes. The FARO Laser Scanner Focus 3D shown in Figure 22.2 uses a fixed laser reflected off of a horizontally rotating angled mirror to capture 976,000 measurement points per second to produce dense point clouds with ±2 mm accuracy, as well as detailed color information. A key feature of this system is the ability to scan outdoors in direct sunlight. Once an area is scanned from multiple viewpoints, well-established software paths allow the scanned data to be easily transferred to any of several simulation utilities or gaming engines for viewing via a stereoscopic head-mounted display.

Figure 22.2 The FARO Laser Scanner Focus 3D (left) is a high-speed 3D laser scanner for the detailed measurement and documentation of large objects, spaces, and buildings. The system produces photorealistic 3D point clouds of complex interior and outdoor spaces. The FARO Freesyle (right) is a handheld device that enables the capture of high-resolution point clouds in smaller spaces, such as the interior of an automobile.

Credit: Images provided by FARO Technologies — www.FARO.com

At the time this book was written, although both 360° panoramic photographic evidence and 3D scans of crime scenes have been used extensively in U.S. and international courts, these applications have been limited to that achievable using standard 2D displays. The recent introduction of immersive stereoscopic displays, including those based on mobile devices (Samsung Gear VR, Google Cardboard, and so on), means it is no longer a question of technical feasibility or cost, but admissibility. In this regard, the keys will be how such evidence is ultimately submitted to the courts, establishing that this new medium and form of evidence is relevant and beneficial to an informed verdict and does not unduly prejudice a jury (Schofield, 2011).

Presentation of Evidence

The second area in courtroom application for these technologies comes in the form of actual crime scene and event *reconstruction*. Unlike novel photographic evidence or the capturing of an actual scene with advanced sensors, computer-generated reconstructions are a different matter entirely. Imagine a jury translating its own first-person viewpoint around a re-creation of an accident or crime scene as an incident unfolds, with the details drawn from forensic analysis, witnesses, and expert testimony. In these instances, the gauntlet that must be traversed for such evidence to be acceptable in U.S. courts will likely be greater. This will be due, in part, to the generally conservative nature of judges in admitting new technologies in the courtroom (Dixon, 2012), as well as attorneys' lack of awareness of the potential these technologies hold.

It is too soon to tell when the first court cases will be taking place using immersive virtual reality in the presentation of evidence, but make no mistake; it will happen. These technologies hold far too much potential to not be utilized. The clarity they can add to efforts at explaining complex, multidimensional phenomena to a lay jury is too great to be held to the side, particularly as our courts become increasingly bogged down with high-tech litigation.

Virtual Worlds Law

To date, companies like Google, Facebook, Sony, Microsoft, HTC, and dozens of smaller firms have invested billions of dollars into the new medium of consumer-oriented virtual reality. Many have stated that the underlying goal is the creation of large online communities similar to existing massively multiplayer online games (MMOGs) or shared virtual worlds such as Second Life, a scene from which is shown in Figure 22.3. Along with the introduction and growth in the use of these online resources come some fascinating legal questions.

Figure 22.3 This figure shows a simple scene from the online virtual community known as Second Life. Such virtual vacation spots can be custom-designed by users or purchased in completed form.
Credit: Image courtesy of Nico Time via Flickr under a CC 2.0 license

For instance, consider a hypothetical virtual clothier where online community participants can acquire outfits for their avatar, or *PersonaForm* (see the following Note). If this virtual clothier is making freely available jackets displaying the famous Gucci logo, does this constitute trademark infringement because the logo is not being used "in commerce"? What if the jackets are sold for some form of virtual currency that itself has no real-world value? Would the jackets be considered a "good" by real-world courts? Could the owners of the servers hosting the virtual community be held liable?

> ### note
>
> **PersonaForm** is a term first coined in the 1990s by futurist Gregory Panos and used to describe a 3D digitized face, expressions, body motion, voice library, and other sampled data gathered from that person by various technological means.

Or consider a situation where real-world currency can be used to purchase units of a virtual currency intended for use within one of one of these online communities. What safeguards will be needed to prevent use of such a system in criminal activity such as money laundering or the movement of monies abroad? It would seem pretty straightforward to have partners in a criminal enterprise open accounts in one of these virtual communities, deposit funds using prepaid credit cards, transfer those funds through the purchase of expensive virtual goods of some type, with those funds eventually withdrawn into another real-world account overseas. What new regulations will need to be put in place to curtail such activity? Will platform owners need to be registered as financial institutions?

How about virtual theft? Consider that rare virtual sculpture you purchased for the living room of your virtual home within an online community. For the sake of argument, let's assume that real-world currency was converted into a virtual currency to acquire that sculpture. If another character within the online community enters that virtual dwelling and steals that sculpture, can the thief be prosecuted in real-world courts?

Although some may find these hypothetical examples far-fetched, law firms around the world, not to mention legislators and regulators, are actively pondering these very questions. It is completely reasonable to expect that as virtual communities grow in popularity in conjunction with the increasing adoption of these technologies, significant changes and additions to existing laws and regulations will likely be implemented.

Moral and Ethical Considerations

Much more than augmented reality, the introduction of immersive virtual reality systems into the broader consumer market is already raising a host of moral and ethical questions, two of which are considered next.

Violent First-Person Games

One of the most obvious areas of concern is the impact commercially available immersive virtual reality systems will have on school-aged children (6–12 years) and adolescents (ages 13–17) and their potential as a contributing risk factor to aggressive behavior when used as part of violent, first-person games.

For some perspective, published research has for many years documented links between violent first-person video games and increased aggressive behavior (Anderson and Bushman, 2001; Bushman and Anderson, 2002; Kirsh, 2003; Funk et al., 2003; Anderson, 2004; Anderson et al., 2007, 2008; Konijn et al., 2007; Möller and Krahé, 2009; Neetu and Shalini, 2016; Milani et al., 2015). More recent research takes things even a step further, showing compelling evidence that using a realistic firearm controller positively impacts (or increases) cognitive aggression (McGloin et al., 2015).

Additionally, a detailed August 2015 report from the American Psychological Association (APA) Task Force on Violent Media clearly states that "research demonstrates a consistent relation between violent video game use and increases in aggressive behavior, aggressive cognitions and aggressive affect, and decreases in prosocial behavior, empathy and sensitivity to aggression" (Appelbaum et al., 2015). Although the report is careful to point out that there is "insufficient research to link violent video game play to *criminal violence*," it does not mean such links do not exist, only that there is "insufficient research."

As would be reasonably expected, some researchers debate these findings (Ferguson, 2013; Ferguson and Dyck, 2012; Salonius-Pasternak and Gelfond, 2005; Grimes et al., 2008; Ferguson et al., 2008; Kutner and Olsen, 2008). Between the two sides, a tepid, often times angry debate exists between gaming industry stakeholders and a host of professional mental health and psychological associations, as well as parental and child protection organizations.

Given the incredibly lucrative marketplace for computer and console-based entertainment, it should be expected that violent, first-person gaming titles will dramatically increase in popularity as existing games are ported to, and new games are specifically developed for, immersive virtual reality systems.

A Free Speech Issue?

In 2005, the California State Legislature passed a bill (AB 1179) that banned the sale of violent video games to individuals under the age of 18. Once the bill was signed into law, several associations of companies that create, publish, distribute, sell, or rent video games filed suit seeking to invalidate the newly enacted law under the First and Fourteenth Amendments of the U.S. Constitution.

The court ruled in favor of the plaintiffs and prevented the enforcement of the law. The next stop was the U.S. Court of Appeals for the Ninth Circuit, which found that violent video games did not constitute "obscenity" under the First Amendment, nor did the state have a compelling interest in preventing psychological or neurological harm to minors allegedly caused by video games.

In 2010, the case (*Brown* v. *Entertainment Merchants Association*, 564 U.S. 08–1448) was argued before the U.S. Supreme Court and essentially focused on one simple question:

> Does the First Amendment bar a state from restricting the sale of violent video games to minors?

In June 2011, the U.S. Supreme Court ruled that the original California law was unconstitutional and that video games do in fact qualify for protection under the First and Fourteenth Amendments, although one of the concurring opinions written by Justice Samuel Alito made very clear that the door is left open for the court to revisit the topic in the future. In the last sentence of this opinion, Justice Alito wrote:

> "If differently framed statutes are enacted by the States or by the Federal Government, we can consider the constitutionality of those laws when cases challenging them are presented to us."

Thus, while it is currently the law of the land to allow even the most violent of video games to be sold to minors, the following question needs to be asked:

> If something is currently considered legal, does this automatically mean it is also moral and ethical?

> The obvious answer to this question is no.

Conclusion

In this chapter we have explored a broad range of the formidable legal and social implications looming in the near future for virtual and augmented reality. In the coming years as these advanced simulation technologies steamroll their way into the broader consumer electronics industry generating billions in revenue for stakeholders, the question of ethics and morality become subjects of great importance, not only for violent content in general, but also for such rapidly emerging applications as immersive pornography. At what point is a line drawn? In this regard, in lieu of codified law, the answers to these questions fall squarely into the lap of content developers. Just as a pen cannot be held up as responsible for spelling errors, the enabling hardware technologies of virtual reality, including stereoscopic head-mounted displays, spatial audio solutions, and tactile and force feedback devices, are merely the mechanisms for delivery of an experience proactively designed by another human being.

CHAPTER 23

THE FUTURE

As relatively new commercial technology offerings, augmented and virtual reality remain messy. Displays are large, cables are everywhere, and people are still getting sick. But changes are rapidly approaching. In this chapter we explore some of the next major steps for key enabling components, highlighting the short- and long-term outlook and directions to be taken and the benefits that the changes will enable.

A Wide-Angle View of Things to Come

Throughout this book we have explored the current state-of-the-art for virtual and augmented reality technologies, highlighting strengths, weaknesses, and technological breakthroughs, along with a host of solid, professional applications demonstrating their true value in helping solve real-world problems, increasing data understanding, and maximizing human efficiency.

Now that consumer versions of these technologies are beginning to enter the marketplace, it will be a fascinating experience to see the manner in which these technologies are leveraged— in particular, beyond gaming and entertainment.

As explained earlier in this book, one sure-fire way to kill virtual reality this time around is bad content or a bad experience. General consumers will not buy into these technologies in any sustainable way without the existence of high-quality, well-thought-out applications that genuinely enhance daily living in some useful manner. On the flip side, development of such apps is an expensive undertaking that is predicated on consumer demand and available hardware platforms. Fortunately, the enthusiasm quotient is high, and both hardware and software manufacturers are hard at work jump-starting the process.

When history books are written a few decades from now, it will be clear that one of the single most influential events underpinning the rise of this field will not be the multi-billion dollar acquisition of a small tech start-up, but the simple introduction of a low-cost DIY viewer called Google Cardboard, along with a baseline Android development toolkit. Practically overnight, this move swept the legs out from under the very notion that immersive virtual experiences required significant computing horsepower, expensive headsets, and a host of external sensors. Suddenly, a mechanism was available through which virtual reality, albeit initially in crude form, could be experienced by anyone with a smartphone, essentially priming a massive pump of intrigue, demand, and application development efforts. Since the initial introduction in the summer of 2014, millions of the fold-up viewers have been shipped, with dozens of knockoffs and higher quality headsets introduced and hundreds of individual apps developed.

Short-Term Outlook

It is abundantly clear that this field is still in the infant stage and current systems represent only the tip of the iceberg of what is to come. In the near term, virtual reality (as opposed to augmented reality) will be the primary driving force for the market and appeal mostly to serious gaming enthusiasts who are eager to immerse themselves in simulated worlds filled with action, challenges, and tests of skill. At the time of this book's preparation, although companies such as Oculus and HTC were the current major players addressing the consumer gaming market, it is highly likely they will soon be eclipsed, or better yet, mowed down, in terms of the number of systems deployed by powerhouses Sony and Microsoft, both of whom have an established user base of tens of millions of existing, VR-ready gaming consoles, associated software titles, and peripherals.

For the moment, PC-based virtual reality systems understandably pose a significant barrier to entry in terms of performance requirements. For example, the initial consumer Oculus system is priced at $599 USD and includes the head-mounted display with built-in headphones and mic, motion sensor, and an Xbox One controller. But this price does not include the high-end PC required to drive the system. In fact, according to industry statistics compiled by game manufacturer Steam, fewer than 5% of U.S. households have a PC with enough graphics processing horsepower necessary to drive the Oculus system. Thus, the $599 USD entry price point realistically increases to approximately $1,500 USD.

In comparison, the Sony PlayStation VR system shown in Figure 23.1 costs $399 and is plug-and-play ready for any of the 30+ million PlayStation 4 systems currently deployed.

Figure 23.1 The Sony PlayStation VR system is on its way to being one of the most widely used fully immersive virtual reality systems available due to its plug-and-play compatibility with more than 30 million existing gaming platforms.
Credit: Image courtesy of Marco Verch via Flickr under a CC 2.0 license

Microsoft has not yet announced a head-mounted display specifically intended for use with the Xbox platform, but the field is young and wide open to a host of participants. For the moment, Microsoft Windows 10 natively supports the Oculus display. Additionally, Xbox One will be able to stream games through Windows 10 to the Oculus device, albeit in "cinema" (nonstereo) mode.

Long-Term Outlook

While the hype and excitement surrounding virtual reality is at a fevered pitch, it must be remembered that potentially harmful health ramifications are still lurking for near-eye stereoscopic 3D displays. Companies may claim they have "solved" the vestibulo-ocular reflex and vergence-accommodation conflicts through software and innovative optical designs, but when you peel back the layers of hype, the fundamental decoupling of the mechanical processes of vergence and accommodation still exist. And herein rest the unknowns. There have simply not been enough of these displays in circulation and use for extended periods of time to enable proper studies to be carried out on the potential health or cognitive impacts. Although users may "adapt" and ultimately move beyond manifestations of physical discomfort and nausea, this does not mean the actual decoupling of the mechanical processes cease.

That said, there are a number of efforts underway to attempt to resolve this issue through innovative redesigns of this type of display. For instance, researchers at Stanford University are attempting to use stacked liquid crystal displays to simulate varying focal depths (Huang et al., 2015). The work holds significant promise but is still years away from being fully understood or commercialized, if ever.

The Shift to Augmented Reality Displays

As explained in Chapters 4 through 6, the fundamental problem necessitating current bulky display form factors ultimately comes down to the image source and optics. To have a wide field of view (FOV) display, you need to use large image sources. At this time, the most cost-effective and accessible options are LCD, Organic Light-Emitting Diode (OLED), and Active Matrix OLED (AMOLED) arrays. To be able to focus on the flat-panel arrays so close to the eyes, the display needs large bulky optics. It is for this and other reasons that over time the industry will likely experience a shift away from flat panel–based fixed-focus head-mounted displays toward some type of dual-purpose augmenting display.

And here is where things get really interesting. Companies such as the highly secretive Magic Leap and their adaptive optics-based light field display technology hold significant promise, as do a myriad of other displays detailed in Chapter 5, "Augmenting Displays." Here again, the ultimate success of such systems will be based on applications and content. To this end, it is unlikely there will be one killer app that drives the industry, but a range of useful tools similar to the way so many are available for smartphones and other mobile computing platforms.

Another key direction the augmented reality display industry will likely take is completely separating the optics from the display. One such system already years in development is known as iOptik from Innovega, Inc of Bellevue, Washington. In this system initially developed for DARPA, the usual magnifying optics are completely removed from the eyewear and are instead integrated into an advanced contact lens, such as shown in Figure 23.2. The Innovega eyewear system is thus composed of two elements: stylish eyeglasses incorporating high-resolution micro-displays or projectors, and the novel iOptik contact lenses that focus and direct photons from the real-world and media onto the wearer's retina. When the projection eyewear is not in use, the innovative design of the contacts allows them to also serve as normal corrective lenses.

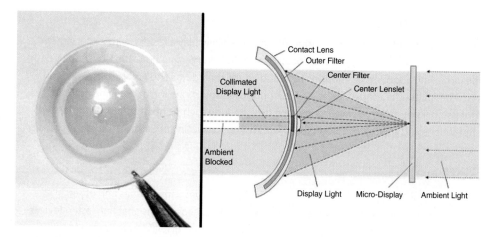

Figure 23.2 The Innovega iOptik system uses a specialized optical element built into a contact lens that allows the wearer to focus on imagery projected onto the spectacles, enabling a high-resolution, wide FOV display.
Credit: Images courtesy of Innovegas, Inc

Does this sound farfetched? Well, get ready, because at the time of this book's preparation, Innovega was nearing completion of nearly nine months of clinical trials and preparing for the final step of requesting and gaining FDA approval. According to principles with Innovega, more than 100 million global consumers already wear contact lenses. This group includes more than 20% of North American 18- to 34-year-olds, a demographic representing the same consumers who are today's drivers of demand for gaming, smartphone, and other media-rich applications. Interestingly, the prevalence of nearsightedness in Asian countries is nearly double that of North America (Innovega, 2014). These statistics point to a potentially massive user base as augmented reality technologies roll out and gain traction in the coming years.

Tactile and Force Feedback Devices

Another key area where significant change can be expected in the long term will be in the area of tactile and force feedback devices. As indicated in Chapter 10, "Tactile and Force Feedback Devices," while current implementations of these technologies generate mostly crude vibro-tacticle sensations, these cues are a major contributor to a sense of presence, immersion, and control. Although it is unlikely there will ever be a means through which to accurately produce the broad range of real-world mechanical stimuli we experience on a daily basis, alternative approaches are already under development, including extra-cutaneous neuro-tactile stimulators. Here, minute, encoded electrical impulses will be used to directly stimulate the afferent nerves connected to mechanoreceptors sitting just below the surface of the skin. Experimental suits have already been developed with this exact capability. Other companies are at work developing similar offerings.

3D Sound

Binaural audio and other spatial sound solutions will likely play a much greater role within this industry in the coming years, particularly with fully immersive simulations. In addition to the increasing adoption of solutions such as binaural recordings and ambisonics, precision software utilities for modeling the acoustics of closed spaces are increasingly being used for professional simulations as well as in game designs. One such company offering impressive applications and capabilities along these lines is Impulsonic, Inc of Carrboro, North Carolina.

Software

The proverbial Achilles heel of this industry is software. From gaming titles and other specific applications employed by end users, to complete ecosystems enabling input devices from company A to work with software from company B, and displays from company C, the continued growth of this field is dependent on quality and interoperable software. The latest and greatest sporty-looking stereoscopic augmenting display is nothing more than an interesting paperweight without applications that solve problems, increase efficiency, or provide engaging, entertaining experiences.

An excellent example of how exclusivity can cause an industry to go askew is in the battle between Oculus VR, LLC, and their fans. At the time of this book's preparation and as is fully their right, Oculus has instituted a digital rights management (DRM) protocol through which it attempts to prevent games developed for and hosted on the Oculus platform from being played on competing systems such as the HTC Vive. This has led to the development of a third-party program known as Revive that bypasses the DRM to enable this cross-platform functionality. Oculus then released a software update that blocks the Revive bypass. And around and around it goes. Caught in the middle are the software developers who see revenue slipping away by being locked to one platform, resulting in piracy and hacks.

Growth pains such as these are not unexpected and in many ways force companies to adapt business models and strategies to ultimately engage an increasingly larger customer base.

Conclusion

Hype is good. Hype motivates, encourages, fosters creative thought, and gets people excited. Hype often lifts the heavy hands of venture capitalists to make investments they would, under other circumstances, never consider. But at some point, the hype needs to be dialed back and the hard work performed, converting the promises to reality and tangible offerings.

For the first time since the virtual reality craze of the 1990s, the enabling technologies underpinning this field are providing sound platforms for developers to begin showing off their best ideas, which hopefully will extend far beyond first-person games, apps that overlay the location of coffee shops in your neighborhood, or enable you to tweet your heart rate and check email while out for a jog. These technologies hold potential for so much more.

APPENDIX A

BIBLIOGRAPHY

This appendix contains citations for all inline references made within this book.

Chapter 1

Caudell, Thomas P., and David W. Mizell. "Augmented Reality: An Application of Heads-Up Display Technology to Manual Manufacturing Processes." In *System Sciences*, 1992. Proceedings of the Twenty-Fifth Hawaii International Conference, Vol. 2, pp. 659–669. IEEE, 1992.

Clarke, Wallace. *British Aircraft Armament: Volume 2: RAF Guns and Gunsights from 1914 to the Present Day*. Patrick Stephens Limited, Somerset, England, 1994.

Dornheim, M. "VTAS Sight Fielded, Shelved in 1970s." *Aviation Week & Space Technology* 143, no. 17 (1995): 52–103.

Grubb, Howard (Sir). "A New Collimating-Telescope Gun-Sight for Large and Small Ordnance." *Scientific Transactions of the Royal Dublin Society*, Vol. VII, pp. 321–330, August 1901.

Lord, Dick. Vlamgat: *The Story of the Mirage F1 in the South African Air Force*. 30° South Publishers, 2008.

Lowood, Henry E. "Virtual Reality." *Encyclopædia Britannica Online*. Accessed March 14, 2016. http://www.britannica.com/technology/virtual-reality.

Newcomb, D., "Eyes On with Heads-Up Display Car Tech." *PC Magazine* (PCmag.com), July 18, 2014.

Nijboer, Donald. *Fighting Cockpits: In the Pilot's Seat of Great Military Aircraft from World War I to Today*. Zenith Press, 2016.

Previc FH, Ercoline WR, eds. *Spatial Disorientation in Aviation, Progress in Astronautics and Aeronautics*, Vol. 203. AIAA 2004: pp. 95–144.

Sutherland, Ivan. "Odysseys in Technology: Research and Fun." Retrieved March 11, 2015 from https://youtu.be/FIMaf4RemOU.

Chapter 2

Jowett, Benjamin. *The Dialogues of Plato, Translated into English with Analyses and Introductions*, Vol. 3. (1901).

Mendell, Henry. "Topoi on Topos: The Development of Aristotle's Concept of Place." *Phronesis* (1987): 206–231.

Slater, Mel, Martin Usoh, and Anthony Steed. "Taking Steps: The Influence of a Walking Technique on Presence in Virtual Reality." *ACM Transactions on Computer-Human Interaction (TOCHI) 2*, no. 3 (1995): 201–219.

"Space." Merriam-Webster.com. Accessed January 15, 2016. http://www.merriam-Webster.com/dictionary/space.

Chapter 3

Anderson, Barton L. "The Role of Partial Occlusion in Stereopsis." *Nature* 367, no. 6461 (1994): 365–368.

Atchison, David A. "Accommodation and Presbyopia." *Ophthalmic and Physiological Optics* 15, no. 4 (1995): 255–272.

Bhola, Rahul. "Binocular Vision." Department of Ophthalmology and Visual Sciences. University of Iowa (2006).

Bower, T. G. R., J. Ma Broughton, and M. K. Moore. "The Coordination of Visual and Tactual Input in Infants." *Perception & Psychophysics* 8, no. 1 (1970): 51–53.

D'Amico, Donald J. "Diseases of the Retina." *New England Journal of Medicine* 331, no. 2 (1994): 95–106.

Delamere, Nicholas A. "Ciliary Body and Ciliary Epithelium." *Advances in Organ Biology* 10 (2005): 127–148.

Dodgson, Neil A. "Variation and Extrema of Human Interpupillary Distance." In *Electronic Imaging* 2004, pp. 36–46. International Society for Optics and Photonics, 2004.

Duane, Alexander. "Normal Values of the Accommodation at All Ages." *Journal of the American Medical Association* 59, no. 12 (1912): 1010–1013.

Ebenholtz, Sheldon M., and David M. Wolfson. "Perceptual Aftereffects of Sustained Convergence." *Perception & Psychophysics* 17, no. 5 (1975): 485–491.

Edgar, Graham K. "Accommodation, Cognition, and Virtual Image Displays: A Review of the Literature." *Displays* 28, no. 2 (2007): 45–59.

FAA. Human Factors Awareness Course. "Visual Displays Lesson Goals: Rod & Cone Sensitivities." Retrieved April 4, 2016 from http://www.hf.faa.gov/Webtraining/VisualDisplays/HumanVisSys2c.htm.

Gibson, Eleanor J., James J. Gibson, Olin W. Smith, and Howard Flock. "Motion Parallax as a Determinant of Perceived Depth." *Journal of Experimental Psychology* 58, no. 1 (1959): 40.

Gillam, Barbara, and Eric Borsting. "The Role of Monocular Regions in Stereoscopic Displays." *Perception* 17, no. 5 (1988): 603–608.

Harris, Julie M., and Laurie M. Wilcox. "The Role of Monocularly Visible Regions in Depth and Surface Perception." *Vision Research* 49, no. 22 (2009): 2666–2685.

Helmholtz, H. von. "Physiological Optics." *Optical Society of America* 3 (1925): 318.

Howard, I. P., and B. J. Rogers. "Perceiving in Depth, Volume 2: Stereoscopic Vision." no. 29. (2012).

Huang, David, Eric A. Swanson, Charles P. Lin, Joel S. Schuman, William G. Stinson, Warren Chang, Michael R. Hee, Thomas Flotte, Kenton Gregory, and Carmen A. Puliafito. "Optical Coherence Tomography." *Science* 254, no. 5035 (1991): 1178–1181.

Hubel, D. "Eye, Brain, and Vision." Harvard Medical School (1995). Retrieved April 4, 2016 from http://hubel.med.harvard.edu/book/bcontex.htm.

Ittelson, William H. "Size as a Cue to Distance: Radial Motion." *The American Journal of Psychology* 64, no. 2 (1951): 188–202.

Jung, Jae-Il, Jong-Ho Lee, In-Yong Shin, J. H. Moon, and Y. S. Ho. "Improved Depth Perception of Single-View Images." *Ecti Transactions on Electrical Eng., Electronics, and Communications* 8 (2010): 164–172.

Khatoon, Naima. *General Psychology*. Pearson Education, 2011, p. 98.

Kolb, Helga, Eduardo Fernandez, and Ralph Nelson. "Facts and Figures Concerning the Human Retina—Webvision: The Organization of the Retina and Visual System." (1995).

Lambooij, Marc, Marten Fortuin, Ingrid Heynderickx, and Wijnand IJsselsteijn. "Visual Discomfort and Visual Fatigue of Stereoscopic Displays: A Review." *Journal of Imaging Science and Technology* 53, no. 3 (2009): 30201-1.

Leigh, R. John, and David S. Zee. *The Neurology of Eye Movements*. Oxford University Press, USA, 2015.

Linkenauger, Sally A., Markus Leyrer, Heinrich H. Bulthoff, and Betty J. Mohler. "Welcome to Wonderland: The Influence of the Size and Shape of a Virtual Hand on the Perceived Size and Shape of Virtual Objects." *PloS one* 8, no. 7 (2013): e68594.

Mather, George. *Foundations of Perception*. Taylor & Francis, 2006.

Mather, George. *Foundations of Sensation and Perception*, Vol. 10, p. 2. Psychology Press, 2009.

Nakayama, Ken, and Shinsuke Shimojo. "Da Vinci Stereopsis: Depth and Subjective Occluding Contours from Unpaired Image Points." *Vision Research* 30, no. 11 (1990): 1811–1825.

Ono, Mika E., Josée Rivest, and Hiroshi Ono. "Depth Perception as a Function of Motion Parallax and Absolute-Distance Information." *Journal of Experimental Psychology: Human Perception and Performance* 12, no. 3 (1986): 331.

Purves, D., G. J. Augustine, D. Fitzpatrick, L. C. Katz, A. S. La Mantia, J. O. McNamara, and S. M. Williams. *Neuroscience,* 2nd edition. Sunderland (MA): Sinauer Associates (2001).

Riggs, L. A., "Vision." In J. W. Kling & L. A. Riggs, eds. *Woodworth and Schlosberg's Experimental Psychology*. 3rd edition. New York: Holt, Rinehart, and Winston (1971).

Slater, Mel, and Martin Usoh. "Simulating Peripheral Vision in Immersive Virtual Environments." *Computers & Graphics* 17, no. 6 (1993): 643–653.

Suri, S., and R. Banerjee. "In Vitro Evaluation of In Situ Gels as Short-Term Vitreous Substitutes." *Journal of Biomedical Materials Research Part A* 79, no. 3 (2006): 650–664.

von Helmholtz, Hermann, and James PC Southall. "Mechanism of Accommodation" (1924).

Wallach, Hans, and D. N. O'Connell. "The Kinetic Depth Effect." *Journal of Experimental Psychology* 45, no. 4 (1953): 205.

Yoonessi, Ahmad, and Curtis L. Baker. "Depth Perception from Dynamic Occlusion in Motion Parallax: Roles of Expansion-Compression Versus Accretion-Deletion." *Journal of Vision* 13, no. 12 (2013): 10.

Chapter 4

Ames, Shelly L., James S. Wolffsohn, and Neville A. McBrien. "The Development of a Symptom Questionnaire for Assessing Virtual Reality Viewing Using a Head-Mounted Display." *Optometry & Vision Science* 82, no. 3 (2005): 168–176.

Barfield, Woodrow, and Thomas A. Furness, eds. *Virtual Environments and Advanced Interface Design.* Oxford University Press, 1995.

Boger, Y. "What Is Binocular Overlap and Why Should You Care?" The VRguy's Blog, May 10, 2013.

Chung, James C., Mark R. Harris, Fredrick P. Brooks, Henry Fuchs, Michael T. Kelley, John Hughes, Ming Ouh-Young, Clement Cheung, Richard L. Holloway, and Michael Pique. "Exploring Virtual Worlds with Head-Mounted Displays." In *OE/LASE* '89, 15–20 January, Los Angeles, CA, pp. 42–52. International Society for Optics and Photonics, 1989.

Conn, Coco, Jaron Lanier, Margaret Minsky, Scott Fisher, and Alison Druin. "Virtual Environments and Interactivity: Windows to the Future." In *ACM SIGGRAPH Computer Graphics*, Vol. 23, no. 5, pp. 7–18. ACM, 1989.

Fisher, Scott S., Michael McGreevy, James Humphries, and Warren Robinett. "Virtual Environment Display System." In *Proceedings of the 1986 Workshop on Interactive 3D Graphics*, pp. 77–87. ACM, 1987.

Melzer, James E. *Head-Mounted Displays: Designing for the User.* McGraw-Hill Professional, 1997.

Meyer-Arendt, Jurgen R. "Radiometry and Photometry: Units and Conversion Factors." *Applied Optics* 7, no. 10 (1968): 2081–2084.

Vikrant R., Bhakta, Jesse Richuso, and Anshul Jain. *DLP Technology for Near Eye Displays.* Texas Instruments White Paper, Literature Number: DLPA051, September 2014.

Chapter 5

Atheer Website. "High Level AiR Glasses Specs." Retrieved April 24, 2016 from http://atheerair.com/shop/.

DAQRI Smart Helmet. (2016). Retrieved April 24, 2016 from http://daqri.com/home/product/daqri-smart-helmet/.

Epson Moverio BT-300 Data Sheet, January 2016.

Google Glass Help, 2014. Retrieved April 24, 2016 from https://support.google.com/glass/answer/3064128?hl=en.

Lumus, DK-50 Development Kit (2016). Retrieved April 24, 2016 from http://lumus-optical.com/#plx_products_section.

Kreylos, O. "HoloLens and Field of View in Augmented Reality." Doc-Ok.org: A Developer's Perspective on Immersive 3D Computer Graphics. August 18, 2015. Retrieved from http://doc-ok.org/?p=1274.

McLellan, Charles. "AR and VR: The Future of Work and Play?" ZDNet, February 1, 2016. Retrieved April 24, 2016 from http://www.zdnet.com/article/ar-and-vr-the-future-of-work-and-play/.

"Microsoft HoloLens: Hardware Details." Microsoft Developer Resources. Windows Development Center. Spring 2016. Retrieved from https://developer.microsoft.com/en-us/windows/holographic/hardware_details.

Nelson, F. "Epson Announces Moverio BT-300 Augmented Reality Glasses, Big Improvements." Tom's Hardware. February 22, 2016. Retrieved April 24, 2016 from http://www.tomshardware.com/news/epson-moverio-augmented-reality,31243.html.

NVIS. "nVisor ST50 Detailed Datasheet." NVIS, Inc. May 30, 2016.

"ODG R-7 Smart Glasses User Guide." Rev 1.1.5. November 2015.

Pandey, Avaneesh. "Google Glass and Drones to Assist Nepal in Fighting Poachers in Protected Areas." *International Business Times*. July 3, 2014.

Seiko Epson. "Epson Announces World's Lightest OLED Binocular See-Through Smart Glasses." The Moverio BT-300, News Release. February 23, 2016. Retrieved April 24, 2016 from http://global.epson.com/newsroom/2016/news_20160223.html.

Surur. "Satya Nadella Re-Targetted HoloLens at Enterprise." MSPowerUser.com. April 5, 2016. Retrieved from http://mspoweruser.com/satya-nadella-targetted-hololens-at-enterprise/.

Vuzix M100. "Smart Glasses Product Data Sheet." January 1, 2016.

Vuzix M300. "Smart Glasses Product Data Sheet." January 1, 2016.

Wagstaff, Keith. "Ready, Aim, Fire! Google Glass-Equipped Rifles Can Shoot Around Corners." NBC News, June 4, 2014.

Chapter 6

Bruce, C. "Oklahoma Air Support Unit Trains on Advanced Combat Simulator." Oklahoma National Guard Office of Public Affairs, May 7, 2014.

Digital Trends. "Spec Comparison: The Rift Is Less Expensive Than the Vive, But Is It a Better Value?" April 5, 2016. Retrieved April 12, 2016 from http://www.digitaltrends.com/virtual-reality/oculus-rift-vs-htc-vive/.

Google. "Cardboard Manufacturer Help: Specifications for Viewer Design." January 1, 2016. Retrieved April 12, 2016 from https://support.google.com/cardboard/manufacturers/answer/6323398?hl=en.

Orland, Kyle. "The Ars VR Headset Showdown—Oculus Rift vs. HTC Vive." ArsTechnica. April 11, 2016. Retrieved April 12, 2016 from http://arstechnica.com/gaming/2016/04/the-ars-vr-headset-showdown-oculus-rift-vs-htc-vive/.

QuantaDyn Corporation. "System Description—Advanced Joint Terminal Attack Controller Training System (AJTS)." (2013). Retrieved from http://www.quantadyn.com/ajts.html.

Samsung. "Gear VR: The Official Samsung Galaxy Site." May 1, 2016. Retrieved May 4, 2016 from http://www.samsung.com/global/galaxy/wearables/gear-vr/.

Shanklin, W. "Oculus Rift vs. HTC Vive." Gizmag. February 29, 2016. Retrieved April 2, 2016 from http://www.gizmag.com/htc-vive-vs-oculus-rift-comparison/42091/.

Chapter 7

Aukstakalnis, Steve, and David Blatner. *Silicon Mirage: The Art and Science of Virtual Reality*. Peachpit Press, 1992.

Cheng, Corey I., and Gregory H. Wakefield. "Introduction to Head-Related Transfer Functions (HRTFs): Representations of HRTFs in Time, Frequency, and Space." In *Audio Engineering Society Convention* 107. Audio Engineering Society, 1999.

Devore, Sasha, Antje Ihlefeld, Kenneth Hancock, Barbara Shinn-Cunningham, and Bertrand Delgutte. "Accurate Sound Localization in Reverberant Environments Is Mediated by Robust Encoding of Spatial Cues in the Auditory Midbrain." *Neuron* 62, no. 1 (2009): 123–134.

Faddis, B. T. "Structural and Functional Anatomy of the Outer and Middle Ear. Clark, William W., and Kevin K. Ohlemiller. *Anatomy and Physiology of Hearing for Audiologists*. Singular Publishing Group, 2008, pp. 93–108.

Fritzsch, Bernd, Israt Jahan, Ning Pan, Jennifer Kersigo, Jeremy Duncan, and Benjamin Kopecky. "Dissecting the Molecular Basis of Organ of Corti Development: Where Are We Now?" *Hearing Research* 276, no. 1 (2011): 16–26.

Gray, Henry, and W. H. Lewis. *Anatomy of the Human Body,* 20th edition. Philadelphia: Lea and Febiger, New York (1918).

Harding, S. (2006, January 1). "Binaural Processing." Retrieved April 1, 2015 from http://perception.inrialpes.fr/~Horaud/POP/TutorialsFEB06/SueHarding.pdf.

Heeger, D. (2006, January 1). "Auditory Pathways and Sound Localization." Retrieved April 1, 2015 from http://www.cns.nyu.edu/~david/courses/perception/lecturenotes/localization/localization.html.

Heffner, Rickye S., and Henry E. Heffner. "Hearing in Large Mammals: Sound-Localization Acuity in Cattle (Bostaurus) and Goats (Capra Hircus)." *Journal of Comparative Psychology* 106, no. 2 (1992): 107.

Katz, Jack. "Clinical Audiology." *Handbook of Clinical Audiology*. Baltimore, Williams & Wilkins (2002): 4.

Letowski, Tomasz R., and Szymon T. Letowski. "Auditory Spatial Perception: Auditory Localization." No. ARL-TR-6016. Army Research Lab Aberdeen Proving Ground MD, 2012.

McAnally, Ken I., and Russell L. Martin. "Sound Localization with Head Movement: Implications for 3-D Audio Displays." *Frontiers in Neuroscience* 8 (2014).

Middlebrooks, John C., and David M. Green. "Sound Localization by Human Listeners." *Annual Review of Psychology* 42, no. 1 (1991): 135–159.

Nave, C. (2012, January 1). "Sensitivity of Human Ear." Retrieved January 1, 2015 from http://hyperphysics.phy-astr.gsu.edu/hbase/sound/earsens.html.

Occupational Safety & Health Administration (OSHA). Noise and Hearing Conservation. Appendix I:B, "Anatomy and Physiology of the Ear" (2013). Retrieved April 12, 2016 from https://www.osha.gov/dts/osta/otm/noise/health_effects/physiology.html.

Perrott, D. R. B. Costantino, and J. Ball. "Discrimination of Moving Events Which Accelerate or Decelerate Over the Listening Interval." *Journal of the Acoustical Society of America* 1993, 93, 1053–1057.

Purves, D., G. J. Augustine, D. Fitzpatrick, et al., eds. "The Inner Ear." *Neuroscience*, 2nd edition. Sunderland (MA): Sinauer Associates; 2001. Available from http://www.ncbi.nlm.nih.gov/books/NBK10946/.

Purves D., G. J. Augustine, D. Fitzpatrick, et al., eds. "Hair Cells and the Mechanoelectrical Transduction of Sound Waves." *Neuroscience*, 2nd edition. Sunderland (MA): Sinauer Associates; 2001. Available from: http://www.ncbi.nlm.nih.gov/books/NBK10867/ [REF 3].

Rash, Clarence E., Michael B. Russo, Tomasz R. Letowski, and Elmar T. Schmeisser. "Helmet-Mounted Displays: Sensation, Perception and Cognition Issues." Army Aeromedical Research Lab, Fort Rucker, AL, 2009.

Richardson, Guy P., Andrei N. Lukashkin, and Ian J. Russell. "The Tectorial Membrane: One Slice of a Complex Cochlear Sandwich." *Current Opinion in Otolaryngology & Head and Neck Surgery 16*, no. 5 (2008): 458.

Schasse, A, C. Tendyck, and R. Martin. "Acoustic Signal Enhancement." Proceedings of IWAENC 2012; International Workshop, September 4–6, 2012, 1–4, ISBN 978-3-8007-3451-1, Aachen, Germany.

Shaw, Edgar AG. "The External Ear." In *Auditory System*, pp. 455–490. Berlin, Heidelberg: Springer, 1974.

Stinson, Michael R., and B. W. Lawton. "Specification of the Geometry of the Human Ear Canal for the Prediction of Sound-Pressure Level Distribution." *The Journal of the Acoustical Society of America* 85, no. 6 (1989): 2492–2503.

Van Wanrooij, Marc M., and A. John Van Opstal. "Contribution of Head Shadow and Pinna Cues to Chronic Monaural Sound Localization." *The Journal of Neuroscience* 24, no. 17 (2004): 4163–4171.

Vetter, Douglas, "How Do the Hammer, Anvil and Stirrup Bones Amplify Sound into the Inner Ear?" *Scientific American*, January 31, 2008.

Wada, Yuji, Norimichi Kitagawa, and Kaoru Noguchi. "Audio-Visual Integration in Temporal Perception." *International Journal of Psychophysiology* 50, no. 1 (2003): 117–124.

Yantis, Steven. *Sensation and Perception*. Palgrave Macmillan, 2013, p. 336.

Chapter 8

Ajdler, Thibaut, Christof Faller, Luciano Sbaiz, and Martin Vetterli. "Interpolation of Head-Related Transfer Functions Considering Acoustics." In *Audio Engineering Society Convention* 118. Audio Engineering Society, 2005.

Anderson, J. Telephone interview, June 18, 2015 (b).

Anderson, J. "FAQ: Where Is the HEAD?!?!" 3Dio. Free Space Binaural Microphone, 2015. Accessed June 17, 2015 at http://3diosound.com/index.php?main_page=gv_faq&faq_item=1.

Anderson, Jeff. "Binaural Audio File Formats." Free Space Instruction Manual. 3Dio, Inc., 2013. Web. 24 June 2015. http://3diosound.com/instructions_binaural_file_formats.php.

Ardito, Carmelo, Maria Francesca Costabile, Antonella De Angeli, and Fabio Pittarello. "Navigation Help in 3D Worlds: Some Empirical Evidences on Use of Sound." *Multimedia Tools and Applications* 33, no. 2 (2007): 201–216.

Arms, Caroline, and Carl Fleischhauer. "Digital Formats: Factors for Sustainability, Functionality, and Quality." In *Archiving Conference*, Vol. 2005, no. 1, pp. 222–227. Society for Imaging Science and Technology, 2005.

Avanzini, Federico, and Paolo Crosato. "Integrating Physically Based Sound Models in a Multimodal Rendering Architecture." *Computer Animation and Virtual Worlds* 17, no. 3–4 (2006): 411–419.

Blattner, Meera M., Georges Grinstein, Ephraim P. Glinert, William Hill, Creon Levit, and Stuart Smith. "Multimedia Environments for Scientists." In *Proceedings of the 2nd Conference on Visualization '91*, pp. 348–353. IEEE Computer Society Press, 1991.

Brungart, Douglas S., and Griffin D. Romigh. "Spectral HRTF Enhancement for Improved Vertical-Polar Auditory Localization." In *Applications of Signal Processing to Audio and Acoustics*, 2009. WASPAA'09. IEEE Workshop, pp. 305–308. IEEE, 2009.

Chandak, Anish, Lakulish Antani, and Dinesh Manocha. "Ipl sdk: Software Development Kit for Efficient Acoustics Simulation." In *INTER-NOISE and NOISE-CON Congress and Conference Proceedings*, Vol. 2012, no. 4, pp. 7938–7949. Institute of Noise Control Engineering, 2012.

de Sousa, Gustavo HM, and Marcelo Queiroz. "Two Approaches for HRTF Interpolation." In *The 12th Brazilian Symposium on Computer Music* (SBCM 2009). 2009.

Dolby Atmos Redefines Your Entertainment Experience. (2015). Retrieved June 8, 2015, from http://www.dolby.com/us/en/brands/dolby-atmos.html.

Ferrington, Gary. "Audio Design: Creating Multi-Sensory Images for the Mind." *Journal of Visual Literacy* 14, no. 1 (1993): 61–67.

Fisher, S. "Virtual Environments, Personal Simulation and Telepresence." *Implementing and Interacting with Real Time Microworlds* (1991).

Fisher, Scott S., Michael McGreevy, James Humphries, and Warren Robinett. "Virtual Environment Display System." In *Proceedings of the 1986 Workshop on Interactive 3D Graphics*, pp. 77–87. ACM, 1987.

Freeland, Fabio P., Luiz WP Biscainho, and Paulo SR Diniz. "Efficient HRTF Interpolation in 3D Moving Sound." In *Audio Engineering Society Conference: 22nd International Conference: Virtual, Synthetic, and Entertainment Audio*. Audio Engineering Society, 2002.

Geil, Fred. "Experiments with Binaural Recording." *The Sound Engineering Magazine*, June 1, 1979, 30–35.

Genuit K., and W. Bray. "Binaural Recording for Headphones and Speakers," *Audio Magazine*, December 1989.

Genuit, Ing Klaus. "Artificial Head with Simplified Mathematical Describable Geometry." *ICA2004*, Kyoto, Japan (2005).

Griesinger, David. "Binaural Techniques for Music Reproduction." In *Audio Engineering Society Conference: 8th International Conference: The Sound of Audio*. Audio Engineering Society, 1990.

International Telegraph and Telephone Consultative Committee (CCITT). "Artificial Head Technique with a New Type of Pinna-Simulator." Interim Meeting, QUESTION: 72/XII COMXII, Federal Republic of Germany, September 1992.

Keyrouz, Fakheredine, and Klaus Diepold. "A New HRTF Interpolation Approach for Fast Synthesis of Dynamic Environmental Interaction." *Journal of the Audio Engineering Society* 56, no. 1/2 (2008): 28–35.

Khosrow-Pour, Mehdi (Ed). *Encyclopedia of Information Science and Technology*, 3rd edition. IGI Global, 2014, p. 6022.

Kistler, Doris J., and Frederic L. Wightman. "A Model of Head-Related Transfer Functions Based on Principal Components Analysis and Minimum-Phase Reconstruction." *The Journal of the Acoustical Society of America* 91, no. 3 (1992): 1637–1647.

Larsson, P., D. Västfjäll, and M. Kleiner. "Ecological Acoustics and the Multi-Modal Perception of Rooms: Real and Unreal Experiences of Auditory-Visual Virtual Environments," In *Proceedings of ICAD*, Helsinki, 2001.

Lombardi, Victor. "Spatialized Audio." *Noise Between Stations*. Music Technology Program, NYU Graduate School of Education, 1 March. 1997. Web. 1 June 2015. http://www.noisebetweenstations.com/personal/essays/audio_on_the_internet/Spatialization.html.

Middlebrooks, John C. "Individual Differences in External-Ear Transfer Functions Reduced by Scaling in Frequency." *The Journal of the Acoustical Society of America* 106, no. 3 (1999): 1480–1492.

PSA Peugeot Citroën. "Sound Spatialisation, Enhancing Safety and Well-Being." (n.d.). Retrieved June 6, 2015, from http://www.psa-peugeot-citroen.com/en/automotive-innovation/innovation-by-psa/sensations-well-being/sound-spatialisation.

Romigh, Griffin D., and Brian D. Simpson. "Do You Hear Where I Hear?: Isolating the Individualized Sound Localization Cues." *Frontiers in Neuroscience* 8 (2014).

Schauer, C., and H-M. Gross. "Model and Application of a Binaural 360 Sound Localization System." In *Neural Networks*, 2001. Proceedings of the IJCNN'01 International Joint Conference, Vol. 2, pp. 1132–1137. IEEE, 2001.

Snow, William B. "Basic Principles of Stereophonic Sound." *Journal of the Society of Motion Picture and Television Engineers* 61, no. 5 (1953): 567–589.

Sontacchi, Alois, Markus Noisternig, Piotr Majdak, and Robert Holdrich. "Subjective Validation of Perception Properties in Binaural Sound Reproduction Systems." In *Audio Engineering Society Conference: 21st International Conference: Architectural Acoustics and Sound Reinforcement.* Audio Engineering Society, 2002.

Taylor, Micah, Anish Chandak, Qi Mo, Christian Lauterbach, Carl Schissler, and Dinesh Manocha. "Guided Multiview Ray Tracing for Fast Auralization." *IEEE Transactions on Visualization and Computer Graphics* 18, no. 11 (2012): 1797–1810.

Vorländer, Michael. *Auralization: Fundamentals of Acoustics, Modelling, Simulation, Algorithms and Acoustic Virtual Reality.* Springer Science & Business Media, 2007.

Wenzel, Elizabeth M., Marianne Arruda, Doris J. Kistler, and Frederic L. Wightman. "Localization Using Nonindividualized Head-Related Transfer Functions." *The Journal of the Acoustical Society of America* 94, no. 1 (1993): 111–123.

Wolfrum, Ed., and S. Aukstakalnis. *The Wolfrum Sessions: Conversations with an Audio Engineering, Electro-Acoustic and Binaural Audio Specialist.* July 2015.

Chapter 9

Adrian E. D, and K. Umrath. "The Impulse Discharge from the Pacinian Corpuscle." *Journal of Physiology* 68 (1929): 139–154.

Barker, Roger A., and Francesca Cicchetti. *Neuroanatomy and Neuroscience at a Glance,* Vol. 85. John Wiley & Sons, 2012.

Barrett, Kim E., and William F. Ganong. *Ganong's Review of Medical Physiology.* New York, London: McGraw-Hill, Medical McGraw-Hill distributor, 2012, p. 150.

Bear, Mark F., Barry W. Connors, and Michael A. Paradiso, eds. *Neuroscience,* Vol. 2. Lippincott: Williams & Wilkins, 2007.

Boundless. "Structure of the Skin: Dermis." *Boundless Anatomy and Physiology,* 21 July 2015. Retrieved 19 August 2015.

Brenner, Michaela, and Vincent J. Hearing. "The Protective Role of Melanin Against UV Damage in Human Skin." *Photochemistry and Photobiology* 84, no. 3 (2008): 539–549.

Burgess, P. R. "Cutaneous Mechanoreceptors." *Handbook of Perception* 52 (2012): 219–249.

Cauna, Nikolajs, and Leonard L. Ross. "The Fine Structure of Meissner's Touch Corpuscles of Human Fingers." *The Journal of Biophysical and Biochemical Cytology* 8, no. 2 (1960): 467–482.

Charkoudian, Nisha. "Skin Blood Flow in Adult Human Thermoregulation: How It Works, When It Does Not, and Why." In *Mayo Clinic Proceedings,* Vol. 78, no. 5, pp. 603–612. Elsevier, 2003.

Dahiya, Ravinder S., Giorgio Metta, Maurizio Valle, and Giulio Sandini. "Tactile Sensing—From Humans to Humanoids." *IEEE Transactions on Robotics* 26, no. 1 (2010): 1–20.

Denda, Mitsuhiro. "Skin Barrier Function as a Self-Organizing System." *Forma* 15, no. 3 (2000): 227–232.

Dillon, Yvonne K., Julie Haynes, and Maciej Henneberg. "The Relationship of the Number of Meissner's Corpuscles to Dermatoglyphic Characters and Finger Size." *Journal of Anatomy* 199, no. 05 (2001): 577–584.

Freinkel, Ruth K., and David T. Woodley, eds. *The Biology of the Skin*. CRC Press, 2001, p. 160.

Gardner, Esther P (May 2010). "Touch." In *Encyclopedia of Life Sciences (ELS)*. John Wiley & Sons, Ltd: Chichester. DOI: 10.1002/9780470015902.a0000219.pub2.

Geffeney, Shana L., and Miriam B. Goodman. "How We Feel: Ion Channel Partnerships That Detect Mechanical Inputs and Give Rise to Touch and Pain Perception." *Neuron* 74, no. 4 (2012): 609–619.

Gentaz, Edouard. "General Characteristics of the Anatomical and Functional Organization of Cutaneous and Haptic Perceptions." *Touching for Knowing* (2003): 17–31.

Gibson, James J. "Observations on Active Touch." *Psychological Review* 69, no. 6 (1962): 477.

Gilman, S. "Joint Position Sense and Vibration Sense: Anatomical Organisation and Assessment." *Journal of Neurology, Neurosurgery & Psychiatry* 73, no. 5 (2002): 473–477.

Grey M. J., J. B. Nielsen, N. Mazzaro, and T. Sinkjaer. "Positive Force Feedback in Human Walking." *Journal of Physiology* 2007; 581(Pt 1):99–105.

Guyton, Arthur C., and John E. Hall. *Pocket Companion to Textbook of Medical Physiology*. Philadelphia: W. B. Saunders, 2001, p. 362.

Helander, Herbert F., and Lars Fändriks. "Surface Area of the Digestive Tract-Revisited." *Scandinavian Journal of Gastroenterology* 49, no. 6 (2014): 681–689.

Huss, A. Joy. "Touch with Care or a Caring Touch." *American Journal of Occupational Therapy* 31, no. 1 (1977): 295–310.

Jablonski, Nina G. *Skin: A Natural History*. Univ of California Press, 2013.

Johansson, Roland S., and Å. B. Vallbo. "Tactile Sensibility in the Human Hand: Relative and Absolute Densities of Four Types of Mechanoreceptive Units in Glabrous Skin." *The Journal of Physiology* 286, no. 1 (1979): 283–300.

Johnson, Kenneth O. "The Roles and Functions of Cutaneous Mechanoreceptors." *Current Opinion in Neurobiology* 11, no. 4 (2001): 455–461.

Kandel, Eric R., James H. Schwartz, and Thomas M. Jessell, eds. *Principles of Neural Science*, Vol. 4. New York: McGraw-Hill, 2000.

Kanitakis, Jean. "Anatomy, Histology and Immunohistochemistry of Normal Human Skin." *European Journal of Dermatology*: EJD 12, no. 4 (2001): 390–399.

Kelly, Edward J., Giorgio Terenghi, A. Hazari, and Mikael Wiberg. "Nerve Fibre and Sensory End Organ Density in the Epidermis and Papillary Dermis of the Human Hand." *British Journal of Plastic Surgery* 58, no. 6 (2005): 774–779.

Klein, Stephen B., and B. Michael Thorne. *Biological Psychology.* Macmillan, 2006.

Knibestöl, M. "Stimulus-Response Functions of Rapidly Adapting Mechanoreceptors in the Human Glabrous Skin Area." *The Journal of Physiology* 232, no. 3 (1973): 427–452.

Kortum, Philip. *HCI Beyond the GUI: Design for Haptic, Speech, Olfactory, and Other Nontraditional Interfaces.* Morgan Kaufmann, 2008.

Madison, Kathi C. "Barrier Function of the Skin: 'la raison d'etre' of the Epidermis." *Journal of Investigative Dermatology* 121, no. 2 (2003): 231–241.

Maksimovic, Srdjan, Masashi Nakatani, Yoshichika Baba, Aislyn M. Nelson, Kara L. Marshall, Scott A. Wellnitz, Pervez Firozi, et al. "Epidermal Merkel Cells Are Mechanosensory Cells That Tune Mammalian Touch Receptors." *Nature* 509, no. 7502 (2014): 617–621.

Mancall, Elliott L., and David G. Brock. *Gray's Clinical Neuroanatomy.* Elsevier Health Sciences, 2011, p. 28.

McCarthy, B. G., S-T. Hsieh, A. Stocks, P. Hauer, C. Macko, D. R. Cornblath, J. W. Griffin, and J. C. McArthur. "Cutaneous Innervation in Sensory Neuropathies Evaluation by Skin Biopsy." *Neurology* 45, no. 10 (1995): 1848–1855.

Mileusnic, M. P., and G. E. Loeb. "Mathematical Models of Proprioceptors. II. Structure and Function of the Golgi Tendon Organ." *Journal of Neurophysiology.* 2006; 96:1789–1802.

Mosby's Medical, Nursing & Allied Health Dictionary, 4 edition. Mosby-Year Book 1994, p. 1285.

Mountcastle, Vernon B. *The Sensory Hand: Neural Mechanisms of Somatic Sensation.* Harvard University Press, 2005.

Muniak, Michael A., Supratim Ray, Steven S. Hsiao, J. Frank Dammann, and Sliman J. Bensmaia. "The Neural Coding of Stimulus Intensity: Linking the Population Response of Mechanoreceptive Afferents with Psychophysical Behavior." *The Journal of Neuroscience* 27, no. 43 (2007): 11687–11699.

Nat'l Institutes of Health (NIH). "Layers of the Skin." National Cancer Institute SEER Training Modules. May 6, 2006. Retrieved August 1, 2015.

Nestle, Frank O., Paola Di Meglio, Jian-Zhong Qin, and Brian J. Nickoloff. "Skin Immune Sentinels in Health and Disease." *Nature Reviews Immunology* 9, no. 10 (2009): 679–691.

Noback, Charles Robert, Norman L. Strominger, Robert J. Demarest, and David A. Ruggiero. *The Human Nervous System: Structure and Function.* No. 744. Springer Science & Business Media, 2005.

Oxford Dictionary Online. Oxford University Press, August 23, 2015.

Ponto, Kevin, Ryan Kimmel, Joe Kohlmann, Aaron Bartholomew, and Robert G. Radwin. "Virtual Exertions: A User Interface Combining Visual Information, Kinesthetics and Biofeedback for Virtual Object Manipulation." In *3D User Interfaces (3DUI),* 2012 IEEE Symposium, pp. 85–88. IEEE, 2012.

Prochazka, A. "Muscle Spindle Function During Normal Movement." *International Review of Physiology* 25 (1980): 47–90.

Proske U., Gandevia S. C. "The Kinesthetic Senses." *Journal of Physiology*. 2009; 17:4139–4146.

Purves, Dale, George J. Augustine, David Fitzpatrick, Lawrence C. Katz, Anthony-Samuel Lamantia, James O. McNamara, and S. Mark Williams. *Neuroscience*, 2nd edition. Sunderland: Sinauer (2001).

Rantala, Jussi, "The Tactile Senses and Haptic Perception, Tampere Unit for Computer." *Human Interaction* (TAUCHI). School of Information Sciences. University of Tampere, Finland, 2013.

Rinzler, Carol Ann. *The Encyclopedia of Cosmetic and Plastic Surgery*. Infobase Publishing, 2009. p. 189.

Sembulingam, K., and Prema Sembulingam. *Essentials of Medical Physiology*. JP Medical Ltd, 2012: 354.

Sherrington C. "On the Proprioceptive System, Especially in Its Reflex Aspects." *Brain* 29 (1906): 467–482.

Tablot, William H., Ian Darian-Smith, and H. Hans. "The Sense of Flutter-Vibration: Comparison of the Human Capacity with Response Patterns of Mechanoreceptive Afferents from the Monkey Hand." PubMed (1968). Retrieved from http://www.ncbi.nlm.nih.gov/pubmed/4972033

Taylor, Lyn. *Neuromuscular Reeducation with Electromyometric Feedback*. Advanced Therapy Institute (2006), 5.

Vallbo, A. B. and R. S. Johansson. "Properties of Cutaneous Mechanoreceptors in the Human Hand Related to Touch Sensation." *Human Neurobiology* 3, 3–14 (1984).

Weinstein, Sidney. "Intensive and Extensive Aspects of Tactile Sensitivity as a Function of Body Part, Sex and Laterality." In *The First Int'l Symposium on the Skin Senses*, 1968.

Chapter 10

Aggelopoulos, Nikolaos C. "Perceptual Inference." *Neuroscience & Biobehavioral Reviews* (2015).

Bobich, L. R., J. P. Warren, J. D. Sweeney, S. I. Helms Tillery, and M. Santello. "Spatial Localization of Electrotactile Stimuli on the Fingertip in Humans." *Somatosensory and Motor Research* 24, no. 6 (2007): 179–188.

Cuthbertson, Anthony. "Haptic Glove for Surgeons Enables Virtual Reality Operations." *International Business Times UK*. October 28, 2015. Accessed November 2, 2015. http://www.ibtimes.co.uk/haptic-glove-surgeons-enables-virtual-reality-operations-1526101.

Danilov, Yuri P., Mitchell E. Tyler, and Kurt A. Kaczmarek. "Vestibular Sensory Substitution Using Tongue Electrotactile Display." In *Human Haptic Perception: Basics and Applications*, pp. 467–480. Birkhäuser Basel, 2008.

Doucet, Barbara M., Amy Lam, and Lisa Griffin. "Neuromuscular Electrical Stimulation for Skeletal Muscle Function." *The Yale Journal of Biology and Medicine* 85, no. 2 (2012): 201.

Higashiyama, Atsuki, and Gary B. Rollman. "Perceived Locus and Intensity of Electrocutaneous Stimulation." *IEEE Transactions on Biomedical Engineering* 38, no. 7 (1991): 679–686.

Kaczmarek, Kurt A., Mitchell E. Tyler, Amy J. Brisben, and Kenneth O. Johnson. "The Afferent Neural Response to Electrotactile Stimuli: Preliminary Results." *IEEE Transactions on Rehabilitation Engineering* 8, no. 2 (2000): 268–270.

Kaczmarek, Kurt, and Steven J. Haase. "Pattern Identification and Perceived Stimulus Quality as a Function of Stimulation Waveform on a Fingertip-Scanned Electrotactile Display." *IEEE Transactions on Neural Systems and Rehabilitation Engineering* 11, no. 1 (2003): 9–16.

Kajimoto, Hiroyuki, Naoki Kawakami, T. Maeda, and S. Tachi. "Electro-Tactile Display with Tactile Primary Color Approach." Graduate School of Information and Technology, The University of Tokyo (2004).

Lake, David A. "Neuromuscular Electrical Stimulation." *Sports Medicine* 13, no. 5 (1992): 320–336.

Menia, Lisa L., and Clayton L. Van Doren. "Independence of Pitch and Loudness of an Electrocutaneous Stimulus for Sensory Feedback." *IEEE Transactions on Rehabilitation Engineering* 2, no. 4 (1994): 197–206.

Monkman, G. J., S. Egersdörfer, A. Meier, H. Böse, M. Baumann, H. Ermert, W. Kahled, and H. Freimuth. "Technologies for Haptic Displays in Teleoperation." *Industrial Robot: An International Journal* 30, no. 6 (2003): 525–530.

Precision Microdrives. "Integration Guide: Haptic Feedback and Vibration Alerting for Handheld Products," 2015.

Raisamo, Roope, and Jukka Raisamo. "Proprioception and Force Feedback" 2007. Retrieved from http://bit.ly/1UvB0MJ .

Robles-De-La-Torre, Gabriel. "International Society for Haptics: Haptic Technology, an Animated Explanation." Isfh. org (2010): 2.

Sheffler, Lynne R., and John Chae. "Neuromuscular Electrical Stimulation in Neurorehabilitation." *Muscle & Nerve* 35, no. 5 (2007): 562–590.

Tang, Hui, and David J. Beebe. "An Oral Tactile Interface for Blind Navigation." *IEEE Transactions on Neural Systems and Rehabilitation Engineering* 14, no. 1 (2006): 116–123.

Van Erp, J. B. F., and B. P. Self. "Introduction to Tactile Displays in Military Environments." *Tactile Displays for Orientation, Navigation and Communication in Air, Sea, and Land Environments* (2008): 1–1.

Woojer, Inc. "Augmented Reality Device Elevates the Listening Experience." Triple Point Newsroom. N.p., October 29, 2014. Web. November 1, 2015. http://pressreleases.triplepointpr.com/2014/10/29/let-the-bass-drop-silent-wearable-subwoofer-begins-shipping/.

Zlotnik, Morris. "Applying Electro-Tactile Display Technology to Fighter Aircraft-Flying with Feeling Again." In *Aerospace and Electronics Conference*, 1988. NAECON 1988. Proceedings of the IEEE 1988 National, pp. 191–197. IEEE, 1988.

Chapter 11

Leap Motion, Inc., "Leap Motion Launches World's Most Accurate 3-D Motion Control Technology for Computing." Press Release, July 22, 2013. Retrieved 11/28/2015 from https://www.leapmotion.com/news/leap-motion-launches-world-s-most-accurate-3-d-motion-control-technology-for-computing.

Shafer, P., and J. Sirven. "Photosensitivity and Seizures." Epilepsy Foundation, Published November 2013. Retrieved on December 3, 2015 from http://www.epilepsy.com/learn/triggers-seizures/photosensitivity-and-seizures.

Silberman, N. and R. Fergus. "Indoor Scene Segmentation Using a Structured Light Sensor." Proceeding of IEEE International Conference on Computer Vision Workshops (ICCV Workshops), New York, NY, USA, November 6–13, 2011; pp. 601–608.

Chapter 12

Chudler, Eric. "Brain Facts and Figures." November 1, 2011: Accessed: Jane 26, 2016 at http://facts.randomhistory.com/human-brain-facts.html.

Crawford, Chris. "The Art of Computer Game Design." Berkeley, CA. Osborne/McGraw-Hill (1984): 2010.

CyberGlove Systems (CGS). "CyberGlove II Product Overview." Published 2015. Retrieved January 26, 2016 from http://www.cyberglovesystems.com/cyberglove-ii/.

Greenemeier, Larry. "Computers Have a Lot to Learn from the Human Brain, Engineers Say." *Scientific American*. March 10, 2009. Retrieved January 26, 2016 from http://blogs.scientificamerican.com/news-blog/computers-have-a-lot-to-learn-from-2009-03-10/.

Juan, Stephen. "The Odd Brain: Mysteries of Our Weird and Wonderful Brains Explained." Andrews McMeel Publishing, 2006.

Kechavarzi, Bobak D., Selma Šabanovic, and Kurt Weisman. "Evaluation of Control Factors Affecting the Operator's Immersion and Performance in Robotic Teleoperation." In *RO-MAN*, 2012 IEEE, pp. 608–613. IEEE, 2012.

Le, Tan. "A Headset That Reads Your Brainwaves." Presentation, TEDGlobal 2010, July 2010. Retrieved January 26, 2016 from https://www.ted.com/talks/tan_le_a_headset_that_reads_your_brainwaves.

Maskeliunas, Rytis, Robertas Damasevicius, Ignas Martisius, and Mindaugas Vasiljevas. "Consumer-Grade EEG Devices: Are They Usable for Control Tasks?" *PeerJ* 4 (2016): e1746.

Monroy, Mary, María Oyarzabal, Manuel Ferre, Alexandre Campos, and Jorge Barrio. "Masterfinger: Multi-Finger Haptic Interface for Collaborative Environments." In Haptics: Perception, Devices and Scenarios, pp. 411–419. Berlin, Heidelberg: Springer, 2008.

Reber, P. "What Is the Memory Capacity of the Human Brain? Paul Reber, Professor of Psychology at Northwestern University, Replies." *Scientific American*, May 1, 2010. Retrieved January 26, 2016 from http://www.scientificamerican.com/article/what-is-the-memory-capacity/.

Turkington, Carol. *The Brain Encyclopedia*. Facts on File, 1996.

Chapter 13

CCP. "CCP Games Introduces Gunjack for Samsung Gear VR: New Arcade Shooter for Mobile Virtual Reality Platform Cements CCP's Leadership in VR Gaming." Press Release, August 3, 2015. https://www.ccpgames.com/news/2015/ccp-games-introduces-gunjack-samsung-gear-vr/.

Jaunt. "Jaunt ONE, The First Professional Quality Camera System Designed to Capture High Quality Cinematic VR Experiences." System Specifications, 2016 (Online). https://www.jauntvr.com/jaunt-one/.

Metz, C. "Inside Mark Zuckerberg's Big Bet That Facebook Can Make VR Social." *WIRED Online*. February 21, 2016. http://www.wired.com/2016/02/mark-zuckerberg-plays-zero-gravity-ping-pong-president-indonesia/.

Olivetti, Justin. "Wizard Online Takes a Stab at a Full Fledged VR MMO, Massively Overpowered." January 6, 2016. http://massivelyop.com/2016/01/06/wizard-online-takes-a-stab-at-a-full-fledged-vr-mmo/.

Opposable VR. "Artist Alix Briskham Talks Tilt Brush on the HTC Vive." November 17, 2015. YouTube Video https://youtu.be/EYY-DZ14i9E.

Ong, Josh. "Paul McCartney and Jaunt Release an Awesome 360-Degree Concert Video for Google Cardboard." *The Next Web* (Online). November 20, 2014. http://thenextweb.com/insider/2014/11/20/paul-mccartney-jaunt-release-awesome-360-degree-concert-video-google-cardboard/.

Simpson, Campbell. "This Is Zero Latency." *The Future of Immersive Gaming*. Gizmodo Australia (Online). August 4, 2015. http://www.gizmodo.com.au/2015/08/this-is-zero-latency-the-future-of-immersive-gaming/.

Chapter 14

Jacobi, J. "4D BIM or Simulation-Based Modeling." Apr, 2011. Structuremag.org. Retrieved November 1, 2015 from http://www.structuremag.org/wp-content/uploads/2014/08/C-InSights-Jacobi-April111.pdf.

McKinney, K., J. Kim, M. Fischer, C. Howard. "Interactive 4D-CAD." In *Proceedings of the Third Congress on Computing in Civil Engineering*, pp. 17–19. ASCE: Anaheim, CA, June 1996.

Mortenson Construction. "Integrated Team Utilizes Advanced Tools and Processes to Deliver the New Pegula Ice Arena." 2014 AIA TAP BIM AWARD Submission, December 2013.

Chapter 15

Ford Motor Company. "Ford Reduces Production Line Injury Rate by 70 Percent for Its More Than 50,000 'Industrial Athletes.'" Media Release, July 16, 2015. Retrieved December 28, 2015 from https://media.ford.com/content/fordmedia/feu/fr/fr/news/2015/07/16/ford-reduces-production-line-injury-rate-by-70-percent.html.

Ford Motor Company. "New Virtual Lab Improves Ford Global Vehicle Quality." Media Release, December 12, 2013. Retrieved December 27, 2015 from https://media.ford.com/content/

fordmedia-mobile/fna/us/en/news/2013/12/12/new-virtual-lab-improves-ford-global-vehicle-quality--engineers-.html.

Merlin, Peter. "Fused Reality: Making the Imagined Seem Real." NASA Center Feature, October 6, 2015. Retrieved from http://www.nasa.gov/centers/armstrong/features/fused_reality.html.

National Academy of Engineering. "NAE Grand Challenges for the 21st Century." August 25, 2015. Retrieved December 29, 2015 from http://www.engineeringchallenges.org/.

Nuclear Advanced Manufacturing Research Center (NAMARC). Nuclear AMRC News. "Modelling the Four-Dimensional Factory." Issue 9, Q4, 2012, p. 5. Retrieved December 27, 2015 from http://namrc.co.uk/wp-content/uploads/2012/10/Nuclear-AMRC-News-Q4.pdf.

PTC Case Study. "BAE Systems Submarine Solutions Brings Virtual Reality to the Manufacturing Floor with Integrated PTC-Virtalis VR Solution." 2007. Retrieved October 20, 2015 from http://images.connect2communities.com/pdf/2293_bae_cs_en_may_22_2007.pdf.

Royal Institute of Naval Architects (RINA). "Type 26 Programme Changes Course to Reflect SDSR Outcomes." *Warship Technology*: 30–31. May 2011.

Virtalis, Case Study. "BAE Systems Submarine Solutions." 2010. Retrieved October 20, 2015 from http://www.virtalis.com/blogs/casestudies/bae-systems-submarine-solutions-3/.

Chapter 16

American Psychological Association (APA). "The Psychological Needs of US Military Service Members and Their Families: A Preliminary Report." Washington, DC: American Psychological Association (2007).

Broyles, James R., Peter Glick, Jianhui Hu, and Yee-Wei Lim. "Cataract Blindness and Simulation-Based Training for Cataract Surgeons" (2012).

DeAngelis, Tori. "PTSD Treatments Grow in Evidence, Effectiveness." *Monitor on Psychology* 39, no. 1 (2008): 40–41.

Difede, Joann, and Hunter G. Hoffman. "Virtual Reality Exposure Therapy for World Trade Center Post-Traumatic Stress Disorder: A Case Report." *Cyberpsychology & Behavior* 5, no. 6 (2002): 529–535.

Difede, JoAnn, Judith Cukor, Nimali Jayasinghe, Ivy Patt, Sharon Jedel, Lisa Spielman, Cezar Giosan, and Hunter G. Hoffman. "Virtual Reality Exposure Therapy for the Treatment of Posttraumatic Stress Disorder Following September 11, 2001." *Journal of Clinical Psychiatry* 68, no. 11 (2007): 1639–1647.

Foa, Edna B., E. A. Hembree, and B. O. Rothbaum. *Prolonged Exposure Therapy for PTSD.* New York: Oxford University (2007).

Forsell, T. "SenseGraphics—Medical Simulators Built on H3DAPI." Proceedings of the 6th Intl Conference on Virtual Learning, Models & Methodologies, Technologies, Software Solutions. Bucharest University Press: October 2011, p. 27.

Frey A. "Success Rates for Peripheral IV Insertion in Children." *Journal of Intravenous Nursing*, Vol. 21, no. 3, May/June 1998.

Gerardi, Maryrose, Barbara Olasov Rothbaum, Kerry Ressler, Mary Heekin, and Albert Rizzo. "Virtual Reality Exposure Therapy Using a Virtual Iraq: Case Report." *Journal of Traumatic Stress* 21, no. 2 (2008): 209.

Harris, M. "Peripheral IV Access Procedures Are Problematic for Nursing." Peripheral IV Success Rates in Adults & Children: Internal Study 2004. Division of Emergency Medicine. Loma Linda University Medical Center: Loma Linda, CA.

Hautzinger, Sarah, and Jean Scandlyn. *Beyond Post-Traumatic Stress: Homefront Struggles with the Wars on Terror.* Left Coast Press, 2013.

HelpMeSee. "2014 Annual Report." 2014d. Retrieved October 12, 2015 from http://helpmesee.org/wp-content/uploads/dlm_uploads/2015/06/HMS_0001_AR_lo-res_spreads.pdf.

HelpMeSee. "Cataract Surgical Training Program." 2014b. Retrieved October 7, 2015 from https://helpmesee.org/the-solution/training-program/.

HelpMeSee. "The Surgery: In Only 5 Minutes, A Life Can Be Transformed." 2014a. Retrieved October 7, 2015 from http://helpmesee.org/the-solution/the-surgery/.

Hoge, C.W., C. A. Castro, S. C. Messer, D. McGurk, D. I. Cotting, and R. L. Koffman (2004). "Combat Duty in Iraq and Afghanistan, Mental Health Problems, and Barriers to Care." *New England Journal of Medicine*, 351(1), 13–22.

Liebert, C., M. Zayed, J. Tran, J. Lau, and O. Aalami. "Novel Use of Google Glass for Vital Sign Monitoring During Simulated Bedside Procedures." Stanford University School of Medicine, 2014. Abstract retrieved October 13, 2015 from https://www.vital.enterprises/assets/downloads/Holman_Abstract_Google_Glass.pdf.

Moog Industrial Group. "Moog Simodont Dental Trainer: First Academic Centre for Dentistry to Adopt the Dental Trainer." March 2011. Video retrieved October 13, 2015 from https://youtu.be/OUnng6phcxw.

Moog, "Help Me See and Moog Demonstrate Cataract Eye Surgery Simulator for Chinese Government. Bill & Melinda Gates Foundation's Grand Challenge Meetings." October 5, 2015. Retrieved October 8, 2015 from http://www.moog.com/news/operating-group-news/2015/helpmesee-moog-demonstrate-cataract-eye-surgery-simulator-for-chinese-government-bill-melinda-gates-foundations-gr-cha/.

Morina, Nexhmedin, Katharina Meyerbröker Hiskeljntema, and Paul MG Emmelkamp. "Can Virtual Reality Exposure Therapy Gains Be Generalized to Real-Life? A Meta-Analysis of Studies Applying Behavioral Assessments." *Behaviour Research and Therapy* 74 (2015): 18–24.

National Eye Institute (NEI). "Facts About Cataract." September 2009. Retrieved October 7, 2015 from https://nei.nih.gov/health/cataract/cataract_facts.

Ogden-Grable H, and G. W. Gill. "Phlebotomy Puncture Juncture Preventing Phlebotomy Errors: Potential for Harming Your Patients." *Laboratory Medicine* 36(7): (2005) 430–433.

Ramchand, Rajeev, Terri Tanielian, Michael P. Fisher, Christine Anne Vaughan, Thomas E. Trail, Caroline Batka, Phoenix Voorhies, Michael Robbins, Eric Robinson and Bonnie Ghosh-Dastidar. "Military Caregivers: Who Are They? And Who Is Supporting Them?" Santa Monica, CA: RAND Corporation, 2014. http://www.rand.org/pubs/research_briefs/RB9764.

Reger, Greg M., and Gregory A. Gahm. "Virtual Reality Exposure Therapy for Active Duty Soldiers." *Journal of Clinical Psychology* 64, no. 8 (2008): 940–946.

Rizzo, Albert, Bruce Sheffield John, Brad Newman, Josh Williams, Arno Hartholt, Clarke Lethin, John Galen Buckwalter. "Virtual Reality as a Tool for Delivering PTSD Exposure Therapy and Stress Resilience Training." *Military Behavioral Health* 1, 2012.

Rizzo, Albert, Bruce John, Brad Newman, Josh Williams, Arno Hartholt, Clarke Lethin, and J. Galen Buckwalter. "Virtual Reality as a Tool for Delivering PTSD Exposure Therapy and Stress Resilience Training." *Military Behavioral Health* 1, no. 1 (2013): 52–58.

Rizzo, Albert, Jarrell Pair, Ken Graap, Brian Manson, Peter J. McNerney, Brenda Wiederhold, Mark Wiederhold, and James Spira. "A Virtual Reality Exposure Therapy Application for Iraq War Military Personnel with Post Traumatic Stress Disorder: From Training to Toy to Treatment." *NATO Security Through Science Series E Human and Societal Dynamics* 6 (2006): 235.

Rizzo, Albert, Judith Cukor, Maryrose Gerardi, Stephanie Alley, Chris Reist, Mike Roy, Barbara O. Rothbaum, and JoAnn Difede. "Virtual Reality Exposure for PTSD Due to Military Combat and Terrorist Attacks." *Journal of Contemporary Psychotherapy* (2015): 1–10.

Rizzo, Albert, Ken Graap, Robert N. Mclay, Karen Perlman, Barbara O. Rothbaum, Greg Reger, Thomas Parsons, JoAnn Difede, and Jarrell Pair. "Virtual Iraq: Initial Case Reports from a VR Exposure Therapy Application for Combat-Related Post Traumatic Stress Disorder." In *Virtual Rehabilitation*, 2007, pp. 124–130. IEEE, 2007.

Singh, Ajay, and Glenn H. Strauss. "High-Fidelity Cataract Surgery Simulation and Third World Blindness." *Surgical Innovation* (2014): 1553350614537120.

Sullivan, M., "Google Glass Makes Doctors Better Surgeons, Stanford Study Shows." *Venture Beat*. September 16, 2014. Retrieved October 13, 2015 from http://venturebeat.com/2014/09/16/docs-performed-surgery-better-wearing-google-glass-stanford-study-shows/.

Tabin G, M. Chen, and L. Espandar. "Cataract Surgery for the Developing World." *Current Opinion in Ophthalmology*, 19 (2008): 55–59.

Virtually Better, Inc. "Telemental Health VR Project: Virtual Iraq Overview" (2008). Retrieved September 2015 from http://www.virtuallybetter.com/af/virtualiraq_overview.html.

Vision Council. "Vision Loss in America: Aging and Low Vision—2015 Low Vision Report." Published 2016. Retrieved May 25, 2016 from https://www.thevisioncouncil.org/sites/default/files/VC_LowVision_Report2015.pdf.

Walsh, G. "Difficult Peripheral Venous Access: Recognizing and Managing the Patient at Risk." *Journal of the Association for Vascular Access* 13(4) (2008): 198–203.

World Health Org (WHO). "Visual Impairment and Blindness Fact Sheet N°282." August 2014a. Retrieved October 7, 2015 from http://www.who.int/mediacentre/factsheets/fs282/en/.

World Health Org (WHO). "Prevention of Blindness and Visual Impairment: Priority Eye Diseases." July 2014b. Retrieved October 7, 2015 from http://www.who.int/blindness/causes/priority/en/index1.html.

Chapter 17

Applied Research Associates. "ARC4: True Augmented Reality." ARC Press Kit, November 2015. Retrieved from https://www.ara.com/sites/default/files/docs/ARC%20PressKit.pdf.

Bymer, Loren. "DSTS: First Immersive Virtual Training System Fielded" (Online). August 1, 2012. https://www.army.mil/article/84728/ DSTS__First_immersive_virtual_training_system_fielded/.

Intelligent Decisions. "Dismounted Soldier Training System Video" (Online), December 9, 2011. http://www.intelligent.net/news/dismounted-soldier-training-system-0812.

Joiner, Stephen. "We Test-Drive the Country's Only Skydiving Simulator: Terminal Velocity Without the Wind Blast. *Air and Space Magazine* (Online), September 2014. http://www .airspacemag.com/articles/we-test-drive-countrys-only-skydiving-simulator-180952398/.

Koester, J. "Virtual Training Opens for the Dismounted Soldier." *NCO Journal*. October 22, 2013.

Merlin, Peter. "Fused Reality: Making the Imagined Seem Real." NASA Armstrong Flight Research Center, September 29, 2015. Accessed online at http://www.nasa.gov/centers/armstrong/ features/fused_reality.html.

"Net Warrior: Mission." *ARMY Magazine* (Online). June 2013. https://www.ausa.org/publications/ armymagazine/archive/2013/06/Documents/Gourley1_June2013.pdf.

STI. "Parasim Version 5—Enhanced Features." YouTube promotional video. June 3, 2013. Retrieved from https://youtu.be/VR6nokbANOw [a].

STI. "FusedReality Jump Master Trainer." YouTube promotional video. June 3, 2013. https:// youtu.be/CZXPLs_Vl3g [b].

Systems Technology, Inc. "Fused Reality: A Technology Platform That Revolutionizes Mixed-Reality Training with a Quantum Leap Beyond Virtual and Augmented Reality." (2016) http://www.fused-reality.com/.

Szondy, David. "NASA Trains Pilots with Fused Reality." Gizmodo (Online). September 30, 2015. http://www.gizmag.com/nasa-fused-reality-train-pilots/39650/.

Zamora, Penny. "Virtual Training Puts the 'Real' in Realistic Environ-ment." (Online). March 4, 2013. https://www.army.mil/article/97582/ Virtual_training_puts_the__real__in_realistic_environment/.

Chapter 18

Lincoln Electric. "Lincoln Electric Launches VRTEX Family of Virtual Reality Training Products." November 2012. Retrieved December 11, 2015 from http://news.thomasnet.com/companystory /lincoln-electric-launches-vrtex-family-of-virtual-reality-training-products-854410.

Mayer, Richard E. "Applying the Science of Learning: Evidence-Based Principles for the Design of Multimedia Instruction." *American Psychologist* 63, no. 8 (2008): 760.

Mayer, Richard E. "Research-Based Principles for the Design of Instructional Messages: The Case of Multimedia Explanations." *Document design* 1, no. 1 (1999): 7–19.

Mayer, Richard E. "The Promise of Multimedia Learning: Using the Same Instructional Design Methods Across Different Media." *Learning and Instruction* 13, no. 2 (2003): 125–139.

Mayer, Richard E., ed. *The Cambridge Handbook of Multimedia Learning*. Cambridge University Press, 2005.

National Science Foundation. Award Abstract #1603648. "Collaborative Research: Strategies for Learning: Augmented Reality and Collaborative Problem-Solving for Building Sciences." published October 27, 2015. Retrieved online December 16, 2015 from http://www.nsf.gov/awardsearch/showAward?AWD_ID=1603648&HistoricalAwards=false.

Pandey, M., V. Luthra, P. G. Yammiyavar, and P. Y. Anita. "Role of Immersive Virtual Reality in Fostering Creativity Among Architecture Students." In *DS79: Proceedings of The Third International Conference on Design Creativity*. Indian Institute of Science, Bangalore, 2015.

Stone, R. T., E. McLaurin, P. Zhong, and K. Watts. "Full Virtual Reality vs. Integrated Virtual Reality Training in Welding." *Welding Journal* 92, no. 6 (2013).

Stone, R. T., K. Watts, and P. Zhong. "Virtual Reality Integrated Welder Training." *Welding Journal* 90, no. 7 (2011a): 136.

Stone, Richard T., Kristopher P. Watts, Peihan Zhong, and Chen-Shuang Wei. "Physical and Cognitive Effects of Virtual Reality Integrated Training." *Human Factors: The Journal of the Human Factors and Ergonomics Society* 53, no. 5 (2011b): 558–572.

Suburu. "Subaru Partners with Google Expeditions to Help Excite, Educate and Engage Students Around the Globe." September 28, 2015. Retrieved online December 16, 2015 from http://www.prnewswire.com/news-releases/subaru-partners-with-google-expeditions-to-help-excite-educate-and-engage-students-around-the-globe-300149943.html.

Toyoma, Kentaro. "Technology Won't Fix America's Neediest Schools." It Makes Bad Education Worse." *Washington Post*. Published June 4, 2016. Retrieved December 16, 2015 from https://www.washingtonpost.com/posteverything/wp/2015/06/04/technology-wont-fix-americas-neediest-schools-it-makes-bad-education-worse/.

Chapter 19

ALSPAC. "Virtual Reality Helps Make Sense of Complex Scientific Data." Press Release July 20, 2015. Retrieved February 19, 2016 from http://www.bristol.ac.uk/alspac/news/2015/vr-big-data-prize.html.

Beal, V. "Webopedia: Big Data Analytics." (2014). Retrieved February 22, 2016 from http://www.webopedia.com/TERM/B/big_data_analytics.html.

Cowley, Dana. "The Wellcome Trust and Epic Games Launch the Big Data VR Challenge." News Release, Epic Games. March 24, 2015. Retrieved February 18, 2016 from https://www.unrealengine.com/news/wellcome-trust-epic-games-launch-ue4-big-data-vr-challenge.

Cukier, Kenneth. "Data, Data Everywhere: A Special Report on Managing Information." *Economist Newspaper*. February 25, 2010. Retrieved February 2016 from http://www.economist.com/node/15557443.

Laney, D. "3-D Data Management: Controlling Data Volume, Variety and Velocity." META Group File 949 (2001).

Masters of Pie. "Project Overview: Winners of the Big Data VR Challenge" (2015). Retrieved February 19, 2016 from http://www.mastersofpie.com/project/winners-of-the-big-data-vr-challenge-set-by-epic-games-wellcome-trust/.

Reda, Khairi, Alessandro Febretti, Aaron Knoll, Jillian Aurisano, Jason Leigh, Andrew Johnson, Michael E. Papka, and Mark Hereld. "Visualizing Large, Heterogeneous Data in Hybrid-Reality Environments." *IEEE Computer Graphics and Applications* 4 (2013): 38–48.

Suorineni, F. T. "The Future of Mega Data in Virtual Reality Environments in Mining Practice." Proceedings of the 24th International Mining Congress and Exhibition of Turkey IMCET15, 2015.

Turner, Vernon, John F. Gantz, David Reinsel, and Stephen Minton. "The Digital Universe of Opportunities: Rich Data and the Increasing Value of the Internet of Things." IDC Analyze the Future (2014).

Vantage Interactive. "Block Cave Mining Visualizer." January 2015. Retrieved February 22, 2016 from http://vantageinteractive.com.au/portfolio-item/bcrm/.

Vasak, P., and F. T. Suorineni. "Extracting More Value from Mine Data Using Virtual Reality and Scientific Visualization Techniques." In *UMaT 1st Mining & Mineral Conference*. University of Mines and Technology. Tarkwa, Ghana, Vol. 4, 2010.

Chapter 20

Carey, B. "Maiden Voyage of Stanford's Humanoid Robotic Diver Recovers Treasures from King Louis XIV's Wrecked Flagship." *Stanford News*. April 27, 2016. Retrieved May 22, 2016 from https://news.stanford.edu/2016/04/27/robotic-diver-recovers-treasures/.

Dean, Marc, and Myron Diftler. "Utilization of the NASA Robonaut as a Surgical Avatar in Telemedicine." (2015).

Dunn, Andrea. NASA Is Laser-Focused on Deep Space Communication." NASA JSC International Space Station Program Science Office. October 6, 2015. Retrieved March 27, 2016 from http://www.nasa.gov/mission_pages/station/research/news/comm_delay_assessment.

Ferre, Manuel, Martin Buss, Rafael Aracil, Claudio Melchiorri, and Carlos Balaguer. "Introduction to Advances in Telerobotics." In *Advances in Telerobotics*, pp. 1–7. Berlin, Heidelberg: Springer, 2007.

Goertz, R. "Manipulator Systems Development at ANL. In *Proceedings of the 12th Conference on Remote Systems Technology*, ANS, pp. 117–136, 1964.

NASA. "Robonaut 2 Getting His Space Legs" (2011). Retrieved from http://www.nasa.gov/mission_pages/station/main/robonaut.html .

Steuer, Jonathan. "Defining Virtual Reality: Dimensions Determining Telepresence." *Journal of Communication* 42, no. 4 (1992): 73–93.

Chapter 21

Ames, Shelly L., James S. Wolffsohn, and Neville A. Mcbrien. "The Development of a Symptom Questionnaire for Assessing Virtual Reality Viewing Using a Head-Mounted Display." *Optometry & Vision Science* 82, no. 3 (2005): 168–176.

Banks, Martin S., Joohwan Kim, and Takashi Shibata. "Insight into Vergence/Accommodation Mismatch." In *SPIE Defense, Security, and Sensing*, pp. 873509–873509. International Society for Optics and Photonics, 2013.

Barratt, Michael R., and Sam Lee Pool, eds. *Principles of Clinical Medicine for Space Flight*. Springer Science & Business Media, 2008.

Barrett, Judy. "Side Effects of Virtual Environments: A Review of the Literature." No. DSTO-TR-1419. Defence Science and Technology Organisation. Canberra (Australia), 2004.

Biocca, Frank. "Will Simulation Sickness Slow Down the Diffusion of Virtual Environment Technology?" *Presence: Teleoperators and Virtual Environments* 1, no. 3 (1992): 334–343.

Bonnet, Cédrick T., Elise Faugloire, Michael A. Riley, Benoît G. Bardy, and Thomas A. Stoffregen. "Self-Induced Motion Sickness and Body Movement During Passive Restraint." *Ecological Psychology* 20, no. 2 (2008): 121–145.

Boyd, D. "Depth Cues in Virtual Reality and the Real World: Understanding Differences in Depth Perception by Studying Shape-from-Shading and Motion Parallax." (Undergraduate honors thesis). Brown University (2001). Retrieved January 8, 2016.

Brooks, J. O., R. R. Goodenough, M. C. Crisler, N. D. Klein, R. L. Alley, B. L. Koon, and R. F. Wills (2010). "Simulator Sickness During Driving Simulation Studies." *Accident Analysis & Prevention* 42: 788–796. doi:10.1016/j.aap.2009.04.013.

Chapanis, A. "Human-Factors Engineering." *Encyclopedia Britannica Online*, s. v. Accessed March 07, 2016 from http://www.britannica.com/topic/human-factors-engineering.

Cobb, Sue V. G., Sarah Nichols, Amanda Ramsey, and John R. Wilson. "Virtual Reality-Induced Symptoms and Effects (VRISE)." *Presence: Teleoperators and Virtual Environments* 8, no. 2 (1999): 169–186.

Dichgans, J., and T. Brandt. "Optokinetic Motion Sickness and Pseudo-Coriolis Effects Induced by Moving Visual Stimuli." *Acta Oto-Laryngologica* 76, no. 1–6 (1973): 339–348.

Dodgson, Neil A. "Variation and Extrema of Human Interpupillary Distance." In *Electronic Imaging* 2004, pp. 36-46. International Society for Optics and Photonics, 2004.

Draper, Mark H., Erik S. Viirre, Thomas A. Furness, and Valerie J. Gawron. "Effects of Image Scale and System Time Delay on Simulator Sickness Within Head-Coupled Virtual Environments." *Human Factors: The Journal of the Human Factors and Ergonomics Society* 43, no. 1 (2001): 129–146.

Ebenholtz, Sheldon M. "Motion Sickness and Oculomotor Systems in Virtual Environments." *Presence: Teleoperators and Virtual Environments* 1, no. 3 (1992): 302–305.

Fischer, M. H., and A. E. Kornmüller. "Optokinetically Induced Motion Perception and Optokinetic Nystagmus." *Journal für Psychologie und Neurologie* 41 (1930): 273–308.

Friston, Sebastian, and Anthony Steed. "Measuring Latency in Virtual Environments." *IEEE Transactions on Visualization and Computer Graphics* 20, no. 4 (2014): 616–625.

Groen, Eric L., and Jelte E. Bos. "Simulator Sickness Depends on Frequency of the Simulator Motion Mismatch: An Observation." *Presence: Teleoperators and Virtual Environments* 17, no. 6 (2008): 584–593.

Jones, Jack A., David M. Krum, and Mark Bolas. "The Effect of Eye Position on the View of Virtual Geometry." *Virtual Reality* (VR), IEEE, 2014.

Kennedy, R. S., M. G. Lilienthal, K. S. Berbaum, D. R. Baltzley, and M. E. McCauley. "Simulator Sickness in US Navy Flight Simulators." *Aviation, Space, and Environmental Medicine* 60, no. 1 (1989): 10–16.

Kennedy, Robert S., D. Susan Lanham, Julie M. Drexler, Catherine J. Massey, and Michael G. Lilienthal. "A Comparison of Cybersickness Incidences, Symptom Profiles, Measurement Techniques, and Suggestions for Further Research." *Presence: Teleoperators and Virtual Environments* 6, no. 6 (1997): 638–644.

Kennedy, Robert Samuel, and Lawrence H. Frank. "A Review of Motion Sickness with Special Reference to Simulator Sickness." Canyon Research Group Inc, Westlake Village CA, 1985.

Kolasinski, Eugenia M. "Simulator Sickness in Virtual Environments." No. ARI-TR-1027. Army Research Inst for the Behavioral and Social Sciences. Alexandria, VA, 1995.

Kramida, Gregory. "Resolving the Vergence-Accommodation Conflict in Head-Mounted Displays" (2015).

Ling, Yun, Harold T. Nefs, Willem-Paul Brinkman, Chao Qu, and Ingrid Heynderickx. "The Relationship Between Individual Characteristics and Experienced Presence." *Computers in Human Behavior* 29, no. 4 (2013): 1519–1530.

Meehan, Michael, Sharif Razzaque, Mary C. Whitton, and Frederick P. Brooks Jr. "Effect of Latency on Presence in Stressful Virtual Environments." In *Virtual Reality*, 2003. Proceedings. IEEE, pp. 141–148. IEEE, 2003.

Nichols, Sarah, and Harshada Patel. "Health and Safety Implications of Virtual Reality: A Review of Empirical Evidence." *Applied Ergonomics* 33, no. 3 (2002): 251–271.

Papadakis, Giorgos, Katerina Mania, and Eftichios Koutroulis. "A System to Measure, Control and Minimize End-to-End Head Tracking Latency in Immersive Simulations." In *Proceedings of the 10th International Conference on Virtual Reality Continuum and Its Applications in Industry*, pp. 581–584. ACM, 2011.

Park, George D., R. Wade Allen, Dary Fiorentino, Theodore J. Rosenthal, and Marcia L. Cook. "Simulator Sickness Scores According to Symptom Susceptibility, Age, and Gender for an Older Driver Assessment Study." In *Proceedings of the Human Factors and Ergonomics Society Annual Meeting*, Vol. 50, no. 26, pp. 2702–2706. Sage Publications, 2006.

Pausch, Randy, Thomas Crea, and Matthew Conway. "A Literature Survey for Virtual Environments: Military Flight Simulator Visual Systems and Simulator Sickness." *Presence: Teleoperators and Virtual Environments* 1, no. 3 (1992): 344–363.

Peli, Eli. "Real Vision and Virtual Reality." *Optics and Photonics News* 6, no. 7 (1995): 28.

Politzer, T. "Vision Is Our Dominant Sense." BrainLineMilitary.org. Retrieved March 19, 2016 from http://www.brainline.org/content/2008/11/vision-our-dominant-sense_pageall.html.

Primeau, Gilles. "Wide-Field-of-View SVGA Sequential Color HMD for Use in Anthropomorphic Telepresence Applications." In *AeroSense* 2000, pp. 11–19. International Society for Optics and Photonics, 2000.

Priot, Anne-Emmanuelle, Sylvain Hourlier, Guillaume Giraudet, Alain Leger, and Corinne Roumes. "Hyperstereopsis in Night Vision Devices: Basic Mechanisms and Impact for Training Requirements." In *Defense and Security Symposium*, pp. 62240N–62240N. International Society for Optics and Photonics, 2006.

Reason, James T., and Joseph John Brand. *Motion Sickness*. Academic Press, 1975.

Riccio, Gary E., and Thomas A. Stoffregen. "An Ecological Theory of Motion Sickness and Postural Instability." *Ecological Psychology* 3, no. 3 (1991): 195–240.

Rogers, Steven P., Charles N. Asbury, and Zoltan P. Szoboszlay. "Enhanced Flight Symbology for Wide-Field-of-View Helmet-Mounted Displays." In *AeroSense* 2003, pp. 321–332. International Society for Optics and Photonics, 2003.

Rolland, Jannick P., William Gibson, and Dan Ariely. "Towards Quantifying Depth and Size Perception in Virtual Environments." *Presence: Teleoperators and Virtual Environments* 4, no. 1 (1995): 24–49.

Stanney, Kay, and Gavriel Salvendy. "Aftereffects and sense of presence in virtual environments: Formulation of a research and development agenda." *International Journal of Human-Computer Interaction* 10, no. 2 (1998): 135-187.

Stanney, K. M., and R. S. Kennedy (2009). "Simulation Sickness." In D. A. Vincenzi, J. A. Wise, M. Mouloua, and P. A. Hancock eds. *Human Factors in Simulation and Training*. Boca Raton: CRC Press.

Stanney, Kay M., Kelly S. Kingdon, David Graeber, and Robert S. Kennedy. "Human Performance in Immersive Virtual Environments: Effects of Exposure Duration, User Control, and Scene Complexity." *Human Performance* 15, no. 4 (2002): 339–366.

Stern, Robert M., Senqi Hu, Ree LeBlanc, and Kenneth L. Koch. "Chinese Hyper-Susceptibility to Vection-Induced Motion Sickness." *Aviation, Space, and Environmental Medicine* 64, no. 9 Pt 1 (1993): 827–830.

Timothy J. Buker, Dennis A. Vincenzi, and John E. Deaton. "The Effect of Apparent Latency on Simulator Sickness While Using a See-Through Helmet-Mounted Display: Reducing Apparent Latency with Predictive Compensation." *Human Factors: The Journal of the Human Factors and Ergonomics Society*, 54(2): 235–249, January 2012.

Velger, Mordekhai. "Helmet-Mounted Displays and Sights." Norwood, MA: Artech House Publishers, 1998.

Wann, John P., and Mark Mon-Williams. "Health Issues with Virtual Reality Displays: What We Do Know and What We Don't." ACM SIGGRAPH *Computer Graphics* 31, no. 2 (1997): 53–57.

Wann, John P., Simon Rushton, and Mark Mon-Williams. "Natural Problems for Stereoscopic Depth Perception in Virtual Environments." *Vision Research* 35, no. 19 (1995): 2731–2736.

Chapter 22

Anderson, Craig A. "An Update on the Effects of Playing Violent Video Games." *Journal of adolescence* 27, no. 1 (2004): 113–122.

Anderson, Craig A., Akira Sakamoto, Douglas A. Gentile, Nobuko Ihori, Akiko Shibuya, Shintaro Yukawa, Mayumi Naito, and Kumiko Kobayashi. "Longitudinal Effects of Violent Video Games on Aggression in Japan and the United States." *Pediatrics* 122, no. 5 (2008): e1067–e1072.

Anderson, Craig A., and Brad J. Bushman. "Effects of Violent Video Games on Aggressive Behavior, Aggressive Cognition, Aggressive Affect, Physiological Arousal, and Prosocial Behavior: A Meta-Analytic Review of the Scientific Literature." *Psychological Science* 12, no. 5 (2001): 353–359.

Anderson, Craig A., Douglas A. Gentile, and Katherine E. Buckley. *Violent Video Game Effects on Children and Adolescents*, Vol. 10. New York: Oxford University Press, 2007.

Appelbaum, M., S. Calvert, K. Dodge, S. Graham, G. H. Hall, S. Hamby, and L. Hedges. "2015 Resolution on Violence in Video Games and Interactive Media." American Psychological Association Task Force Report. August 2015.

Bushman, Brad J., and Craig A. Anderson. "Violent Video Games and Hostile Expectations: A Test of the General Aggression Model." *Personality and Social Psychology Bulletin* 28, no. 12 (2002): 1679–1686.

Dixon, B. "The Evolution of a High-Technology Courtroom." National Center for State Courts. *Future Trends in State Courts* (2012), 1 (6), 28–32. Retrieved on February 25, 2016 from http://ncsc.contentdm.oclc.org/cdm/ref/collection/tech/id/769.

Ferguson, Christopher J. "Violent Video Games and the Supreme Court: Lessons for the Scientific Community in the Wake of Brown v. Entertainment Merchants Association." *American Psychologist* 68, no. 2 (2013): 57.

Ferguson, Christopher J., and Dominic Dyck. "Paradigm Change in Aggression Research: The Time Has Come to Retire the General Aggression Model." *Aggression and Violent Behavior* 17, no. 3 (2012): 220–228.

Ferguson, Christopher J., Stephanie M. Rueda, Amanda M. Cruz, Diana E. Ferguson, Stacey Fritz, and Shawn M. Smith. "Violent Video Games and Aggression: Causal Relationship or Byproduct of Family Violence and Intrinsic Violence Motivation?" *Criminal Justice & Behavior* 35 (2008): 311–332. Web. 10 August 2011.

Funk, Jeanne B., Debra D. Buchman, Jennifer Jenks, and Heidi Bechtoldt. "Playing Violent Video Games, Desensitization, and Moral Evaluation in Children." *Journal of Applied Developmental Psychology* 24, no. 4 (2003): 413–436.

Grimes, Tom, James A. Anderson, and Lori Bergen. *Media Violence and Aggression: Science and Ideology.* Sage, 2008.

Groen, Eric L., and Jelte E. Bos. "Simulator Sickness Depends on Frequency of the Simulator Motion Mismatch: An Observation." *Presence* 17, no. 6 (2008): 584–593.

Kennedy, Robert S., Julie Drexler, and Robert C. Kennedy. "Research in visually induced motion sickness." *Applied Ergonomics* 41, no. 4 (2010): 494-503.

Kirsh, Steven J. "The Effects of Violent Video Games on Adolescents: The Overlooked Influence of Development." *Aggression and Violent Behavior* 8, no. 4 (2003): 377–389.

Konijn, Elly A., Marije Nije Bijvank, and Brad J. Bushman. "I Wish I Were a Warrior: The Role of Wishful Identification in the Effects of Violent Video Games on Aggression in Adolescent Boys." *Developmental Psychology* 43, no. 4 (2007): 1038.

Kutner, Lawrence, Ph.D. and Cheryl K. Olson, scD. *Grand Theft Childhood: The Surprising Truth About Video Games and What Parents Can Do.* New York: Simon & Schuster, 2008.

Lewis, Tanya. Samsung Gear VR. "Virtual Reality Tech May Have Nasty Side Effects." *LiveScience,* February 03, 2015. Retrieved February 29, 2016 from http://www.livescience.com/49669-virtual-reality-health-effects.html.

McGloin, Rory, Kirstie M. Farrar, and Joshua Fishlock. "Triple Whammy! Violent Games and Violent Controllers: Investigating the Use of Realistic Gun Controllers on Perceptions of Realism, Immersion, and Outcome Aggression." *Journal of Communication* 65, no. 2 (2015): 280–299.

McGloin, Rory, Kirstie Farrar, and Marina Krcmar. "Video Games, Immersion, and Cognitive Aggression: Does the Controller Matter?" *Media Psychology* 16, no. 1 (2013): 65–87.

Milani, Luca, Elena Camisasca, Simona CS Caravita, Chiara Ionio, Sarah Miragoli, and Paola Di Blasio. "Violent Video Games and Children's Aggressive Behaviors." SAGE Open 5, no. 3 (2015): 2158244015599428.

Möller, Ingrid, and Barbara Krahé. "Exposure to Violent Video Games and Aggression in German Adolescents: A Longitudinal Analysis." *Aggressive Behavior* 35, no. 1 (2009): 75–89.

Neetu, Singh, and Agarwal Shalini. "Negative Effect of Violent Video Game Across Gender." *International Journal of Research* 3, no. 01 (2016): 706–710.

Nichols, Sarah, and Harshada Patel. "Health and Safety Implications of Virtual Reality: A Review of Empirical Evidence." *Applied Ergonomics* 33, no. 3 (2002): 251–271.

Reason, James T., and Joseph John Brand. *Motion Sickness.* Academic Press, 1975.

Salonius-Pasternak, Dorothy E., and Holly S. Gelfond. "The Next Level of Research on Electronic Play: Potential Benefits and Contextual Influences for Children and Adolescents." *Human Technology: An Interdisciplinary Journal on Humans in ICT Environments* 1, no. 1 (2005): 5–22.

Sawyer, Ben D., Victor S. Finomore, Andres A. Calvo, and Peter A. Hancock. "Google Glass: A Driver Distraction Cause or Cure?" *Human Factors: The Journal of the Human Factors and Ergonomics Society* (2014): 0018720814555723.

Schofield, Damian. Chapter 10: "Virtual Evidence in the Courtroom." *The Handbook of Research on Practices and Outcomes in Virtual Worlds and Environments* (2011). Publisher: IGI Global, eds. Harrison Yang, Stephen Yuen, pp. 200–216.

Stanney, K. M., and R. S. Kennedy (2009). "Simulation Sickness." In D. A. Vincenzi, J. A. Wise, M. Mouloua, and P. A. Hancock eds. *Human Factors in Simulation and Training*. Boca Raton: CRC Press.

Chapter 23

Huang, Fu-Chung, David Luebke, and Gordon Wetzstein. "The Light Field Stereoscope." ACM SIGGRAPH Emerging Technologies (2015): 24.

Innovega. 2014 CES. "Innovega Staff Wear Mega-Pixel Panoramic Eyeglasses." Press Release. January 6, 2014. Retrieved March 21, 2016 from http://innovega-inc.com/press_ces_2014.php.

RESOURCES

Throughout this book we have highlighted dozens of products and companies in such categories as visual displays, spatial audio solutions, tactile and force feedback devices, position/orientation sensors, and more. Within this appendix we consolidated a list of these and other suppliers by category. Also included is a section listing a variety of DIY resources for those inclined to develop their system and a list of product trademarks.

Product Manufacturers

This book has highlighted or otherwise made reference to dozens of hardware devices and software utilities spanning each of the core enabling technologies of augmented and virtual reality systems. These and other manufacturers of similar offerings are listed next.

Augmenting Head-Mounted Displays

- **NVIS (Multiple)**—http://www.nvisinc.com/
- **AtheerAiR Glasses**—http://atheerair.com/
- **Epson Moverio (Multiple)**—http://www.epson.com
- **DAQRI Smart Helmet**—http://daqri.com
- **Microsoft HoloLens**—https://www.microsoft.com/microsoft-hololens
- **Vuzix (Multiple)**—http://www.vuzix.com
- **ODG R-7 (Multiple)**—http://www.osterhoutgroup.com
- **Lumus (Multiple)**—http://lumus-optical.com/
- **SONY SmartEyeglass**—http://developer.sonymobile.com/products/smarteyeglass/
- **Laster Wave**—http://www.laster.fr/
- **Optinvent (Multiple)**—http://www.optinvent.com/
- **Recon Instruments (Multiple)**—http://www.reconinstruments.com
- **Telepathy Japan Inc.**—http://www.telepathywalker.com
- **SKULLY Systems**—http://www.skully.com/
- **Penny AB**—http://www.penny.se/

Fully Immersive Head-Mounted Displays

- **HTC Vive**—https://www.htcvive.com/us/
- **Sony PlayStation VR**—https://www.playstation.com/psvr
- **OSVR (Open-Source VR Development Kit)**—http://www.osvr.org/
- **Oculus Rift CV1**—https://www.oculus.com/
- **Sensics** (Multiple)—http://sensics.com
- **VE Union Claire**—http://vrunion.com/
- **Star VR**—http://www.starvr.com/

Mobile Device-Based Headsets

- **Samsung GearVR**—http://www.samsung.com/us/explore/gear-vr/
- **SmokeVR**—http://smokevr.net/
- **Wearality**—http://www.wearality.com/

- **Free Fly VR**—https://www.freeflyvr.com/
- **Zeiss VR One**—http://www.zeiss.co.uk
- **Yay3D VR Viewer**—http://www.yay3d.com/
- **Homido**—http://www.homido.com/
- **VisusVR**—https://www.visusvr.com/
- **SeeBright**—http://seebright.com/
- **VRVana**—https://www.vrvana.com
- **Meta**—https://www.metavision.com/

Caves, Coves, and Cubes

- **Mechdyne Corporation**—https://www.mechdyne.com
- **Visbox, Inc**—http://www.visbox.com/products/cave/
- **Christie Digital**—https://www.christiedigital.com/
- **Virtalis Ltd**—http://www.virtalis.com/
- **EON Reality**—http://www.eonreality.com/
- **WorldViz**—http://www.worldviz.com/
- **TechViz**—http://www.techviz.net

Dome Displays

- **Virtual Immersion**—http://vorteximmersion.com/
- **3D Perception**—http://3d-perception.com/
- **7th Sense**—http://www.7thsensedesign.com

AR Software for Business and Enterprise

- **Augmate**—http://www.augmate.com/
- **Augment**—http://www.augment.com/
- **DIOTA**—http://www.diota.com/
- **CurvSurf**—http://www.curvsurf.com/
- **iQagent**—http://iqagent.com/
- **Cimagine**—http://cimagine.com/
- **Infinity Augmented Reality**—http://www.infinityar.com/
- **Scope AR**—http://www.scopear.com/
- **Production AR**—http://productionar.com/

- **Pikkart**—http://www.pikkart.com/
- **NGRAIN**—http://www.ngrain.com/
- **Optech4D**—http://optech4d.com/
- **Vuforia**—https://www.vuforia.com/
- **WOWEmotions**—http://wowemotions.com/
- **Yetzer Studio**—http://www.yetzerstudio.com/
- **Vivid Works**—http://www.vividworks.com/
- **VanGogh Imaging**—http://www.vangoghimaging.com/
- **ViewAR**—http://www.viewar.com/
- **Virtuality NS**—http://virtuality-ns.com/

Binaural Recording Systems

- **HEAD Acoustics**—http://www.head-acoustics.de/eng/
- **Georg Neumann GmbH**—https://www.neumann.com/
- **G.R.A.S. Sound & Vibration A/S**—http://kemar.us/
- **3diosound**—http://3diosound.com/
- **Roland Corporation**—http://www.rolandus.com/
- **VisiSonics Corporation**—http://visisonics.com/

Acoustic Modeling Software

- **Impulsonic**—https://www.impulsonic.com/
- **Acoustics By Design**—http://www.acousticsbydesign.com
- **CATT-Acoustic**—http://www.catt.se/
- **Olive Tree Lab**—http://www.olivetreelab.com/Room
- **ODEON**—http://www.odeon.dk/
- **EASE**—http://ease.afmg.eu/
- **CadnaR**—http://scantekinc.com
- **iSimpa**—http://i-simpa.ifsttar.fr/

Tactile and Force Feedback Devices

- **NeuroDigital Technologies/GloveOne**—https://www.gloveonevr.com/
- **Tesla Studios/TeslaSuit DK1**—http://www.teslastudios.co.uk/
- **StudioFeed USA LLC/The SubPac**—http://thesubpac.com
- **Woojer, Ltd.**—http://www.woojer.com/

- **Clark Synthesis**—http://clarksynthesis.com/
- **CyberGlove Systems, LLC**—http://www.cyberglovesystems.com/
- **Geomagic Touch**—http://www.geomagic.com
- **Immersion Corp**—http://www.immersion.com/
- **Haption SA**—http://www.haption.com/

Sensors for Tracking Position and Orientation

- **NaturalPoint**—http://naturalpoint.com/
- **OptiTrack**—https://www.optitrack.com/
- **Advanced Realtime Tracking**—http://www.ar-tracking.com/
- **PS-Tech**—http://www.ps-tech.com/
- **Leap Motion**—https://www.leapmotion.com/
- **Microsoft Kinect**—http://www.microsoftstore.com
- **Intel RealSense**—https://software.intel.com/en-us/realsense/home
- **Polhemus**—http://polhemus.com/
- **Sixense**—http://sixense.com/
- **InterSense**—http://www.intersense.com/
- **PhaseSpace**—http://www.phasespace.com/
- **Perception Neuron**—https://neuronmocap.com

Stereo 360 Cameras

- **Panocam**—http://www.panocam3d.com/
- **iZugar**—http://izugar.com/
- **360 Heros**—http://www.360heros.com
- **Vuze**—http://vuze.camera/
- **HumanEyes Technologies Ltd**—http://www.humaneyes.com/
- **Jaunt**—https://www.jauntvr.com/
- **Next VR**—http://www.nextvr.com/

DIY Resources

Are you interested in tinkering away with your own home brew VR development project? A host of do-it-yourself resources are available online to get curious tinkerers up and running in no time. Most of the following resources are available at no cost or at most, a modest fee.

FOV2GO Stereoscopic Viewer

Two years before Google Cardboard there was FOV2GO, a DIY stereoscopic viewer for mobile devices developed by the Mixed Reality Lab at the University of Southern California's Institute for Creative Technologies. The FOV2GO is made out of foam board and a pair of inexpensive plastic lenses. Several designs are available to accommodate different smartphone models.

A variety of additional free resources are available, including detailed plans for other stereoscopic viewers, software and scripts, middleware, product modifications, and more.

The hardware and software on their site is available at no cost to individuals, nonprofit educational, and research institutions (including U.S. government entities), although they are flexible in their arrangements with those envisioning commercial applications.

USC Mixed Reality Lab DIY Resources—http://projects.ict.usc.edu/mxr/diy/

Google Cardboard

Google has placed all Cardboard viewer specifications in the public domain and is encouraging everyone to take advantage, including commercial interests. The Manufacture Kit includes technical specifications and drawings for lenses, conductive strips, die-cut lines, and more, plus manufacturing tolerances and material specifications. It also includes production templates, best practices, a viewer profile generator, guidance for quality assurance, first article inspections, and production scaling procedures.

Google Cardboard Main Site—https://www.google.com/get/cardboard/manufacturers/

PC-Driven Stereoscopic Displays

In addition to these inexpensive smartphone-based displays, there are dozens of PC-driven DIY head-mounted display projects to be found on the Internet simply by performing searches using the phrases "DIY head-mounted display" and "DIY HMD."

Misc Software and Utilities

If you are building your own stereoscopic head-mounted display, you also need to be able to track, at a minimum, the orientation of your head. If your headset is driven by a smartphone, most applications will make use of accelerometers within that device. For PC-driven displays, there are free utilities available for tracking both position (X, Y, and Z) and orientation (roll, pitch, and yaw) of the user's head.

FreeTrack Motion Tracking Software

FreeTrack is an optical motion tracking application for Microsoft Windows. Available at no cost and released under the GNU General Public License, the primary purpose of the package is to enable inexpensive head tracking in computer games and simulations across six degrees of freedom (6DOF). Using a webcam or other video capture device, the software enables tracking of infrared LEDs or retroreflective points mounted on objects and illuminated via an infrared light source.

FreeTrack Motion Tracking Software—http://www.free-track.net/english/

Game Conversion Software

Next, software utilities are available that will automatically convert games and other applications into stereo 3D when connected to a compatible 3D display device.

TriDef 3D

TriDef 3D enables any standard DirectX 9/10/11 PC games to be run in 3D mode by generating separate left and right eye viewpoints. This software is not free but available for a modest fee.

TriDef 3D—http://tridef.com

Game Streaming Utilities

There are also software utilities available enabling games and applications running on your PC to be accessed from the mobile device inside of your DIY headset.

Splashtop

Splashtop is an audio and video streaming utility that allows you to see and control your computer from another device. This includes graphics-intensive 3D PC applications and games. The software is free for use on a local area network, such as within your home, school, or business. Free for most devices. There is a nominal charge for the iPad and iPhone versions.

Splashtop—http://www.splashtop.com

Kainy

Kainy is another audio and video streaming utility that allows you to see and control your computer from another device. This includes graphics-intensive 3D PC applications and games. The software supports most types of devices and is either ad-based or ad-free for a modest fee.

Kainy—http://www.kainy.com

Software Ecosystems

One surefire way to impede growth of the AR/VR industry is for hardware and software manufacturers to limit their operability. Efforts spearheaded by Razer, Inc and Sensics Corporation have resulted in the release of a professionally developed, highly robust software platform designed to set an open standard for virtual reality input devices, games, and output to enable the development of a cohesive VR ecosystem.

Open-Source Virtual Reality

Open-Source Virtual Reality (OSVR) is a widely used, highly robust open source software ecosystem that allows virtual reality developers to detect, configure, and operate virtual reality devices across a wide range of operating systems. It is provided under the Apache 2.0 license.

OSVR—http://www.osvr.org

Prescription and Protective Lenses for VR Headsets

Individuals who are dependent on prescription glasses face considerable challenges when using modern stereoscopic head-mounted displays. In most instances, there is simply not enough eye relief available to accommodate the use of corrective lenses without severe discomfort or the potential for damaging the optics of both the HMD and the user's spectacles. Thankfully, adapters for prescription lenses are now available for the most popular commercially available VR HMDs.

VR Lens LabStuttgart, Germany
https://vr-lens-lab.com/

Rochester Optical
Rochester, New York
http://rochesteroptical.com

Hygienic VR Headset Covers

An emerging problem with head-mounted displays is the rapid development of unsanitary conditions within facial padding, particularly when the display devices are shared among multiple users. Fortunately, washable after-market covers are available for the most popular commercially available displays that fit snugly over the normal padding, thus ensuring a more sanitary condition is maintained.

VR Cover
Bangkok, Thailand
https://vrcover.com

Audio Resources

Individuals and organizations interested in carrying out their own research and development efforts in the area of binaural audio (see Chapter 8, "Audio Displays") have access to high-quality head-related transfer function (HRTF) databases at no cost.

CIPIC HRTF Database

A public-domain collection of high-spatial-resolution HRTF measurements for 45 different subjects measured at 25 different azimuths and 50 different elevations (1250 directions) at approximately 5° angular increments. Also includes measurements for the KEMAR mannequin with both small and large pinnae.

Center for Image Processing and Integrated Computing (CIPIC)
University of California, Davis
http://interface.cipic.ucdavis.edu/sound/hrtf.html

Listen HRTF Database

The Listen collection is a public-domain database of high-spatial-resolution HRTF measurements for 46 different subjects.

Institut de Rechercheet Coordination Acoustique/Musique
Paris, France
http://recherche.ircam.fr/equipes/salles/listen/index.html

MIT Media Lab KEMAR HRTF Database

The MIT collection is a public-domain database of HRTF measurements for a KEMAR dummy head. There were 710 different positions sampled at elevations ranging from −40 degrees to +90 degrees.

Media Lab

Massachusetts Institute of Technology
Cambridge, Massachusetts
http://sound.media.mit.edu/resources/KEMAR.html

Trademark and Copyright Information

3Dio and FreeSpace are registered trademarks or trademarks of 3DIO, LLC.

AachenHEAD and HEAD Acoustics are registered trademarks or trademarks of HEAD Acoustics GmbH.

ActiveCube is a registered trademark or trademark of Virtalis, LTD.

Advanced Joint Terminal Attack Controller (JTAC) Training System is a registered trademark or trademark of Quantadyn Corporation.

Aero Glass is a registered trademark or trademark of Aero Glass LLC.

Android is a registered trademark or trademark of Google, Inc.

Apple and QuickTime are registered trademarks or trademarks of Apple, Inc.

ARC4 is a registered trademark or trademark of Applied Research Associates, Inc.

Atheer and AiRare registered trademarks or trademarks of Atheer, Inc.

Auro-3D is a registered trademark or trademark of Auro Technologies NV.

Autodesk 3ds MAX, AutoCAD, and Maya are registered trademarks or trademarks of Autodesk, Inc.

BAE Systems is a registered trademark or trademark of BAE Systems plc.

Barco is a registered trademark or trademark of the Barco group.

Bluetooth is a registered trademark or trademark of Bluetooth SIG, Inc.

CATIA is a registered trademark or trademark of Dassault Systèmes.

CAVE and CAVE2 are registered trademarks or trademarks of the University of Illinois Board of Trustees.

Cinemizer is a registered trademark or trademark of Carl Zeiss.

CyberGlove and CyberGrasp are registered trademarks or trademarks of CyberGlove Systems, LLC.

DAQRI, Smart Helmet and 4D Studio are registered trademarks or trademarks of DAQRI, LLC.

DLP is a registered trademark or trademark of Texas Instruments.

Dolby Atmos is a registered trademark or trademark of Dolby Laboratories, Inc.

DORA is a registered trademark or trademark of Dora Platform.

DTS:X is a registered trademark or trademark of DTS, Inc.

Emotiv and EPOC are registered trademarks or trademarks of Emotiv Systems, Inc.

Epson is a registered trademark or trademark of Seiko Epson Corporation.

Eve, Gunjack and Valkyrie are registered trademarks or trademarks of CCP Games.

Evena and Eyes-On are registered trademarks or trademarks of Evena Medical, Inc.

Facebook is a registered trademark or trademark of Facebook, Inc.

Simodont is a registered trademark or trademark of Moog B.V.

SimSpray and Paintometer are registered trademarks or trademarks of VRSim, Inc.

SmokeVR is a registered trademark or trademark of PhaseSpace Inc.

SONY is a registered trademark or trademark of Sony Corporation.

SteamVR is a registered trademark or trademark of Valve Corporation.

SteelSeries is a registered trademark or trademark of SteelSeries ApS.

SubPac is a registered trademark or trademark of Studiofeed Ltd.

TeslaSuit is a registered trademark or trademark of Tesla Studios.

The terms HDMI and HDMI High-Definition Multimedia Interface are trademarks or registered trademarks of HDMI Licensing LLC.

TopOwl is a registered trademark or trademark of Thales Avionics S.A.

Transporter3D is a registered trademark or trademark of EMR Laboratories.

Unity is a registered trademark or trademark of Unity Technologies ApS

Unreal is a registered trademark or trademark of Epic Games.

View-Master is a registered trademark or trademark of Mattel, Inc.

Virtually Better is a registered trademark or trademark of Virtually Better, Inc.

Virtuix and Virtuix Omni are registered trademarks or trademarks of Virtuix Holdings, Inc.

VRTEX is a registered trademark or trademark of The Lincoln Electric Company.

Vuze is a registered trademark or trademark of HumanEyes Technologies Ltd.

Vuzix is a registered trademark or trademark of Vuzix Corporation.

Wizard Online is a trademark or registered trademark of Mahir Ozer.

Woojer is a registered trademark or trademark of Woojer LTD.

ZeroTouch and VitalStream are registered trademarks or trademarks of Vital Enterprises.

INDEX

REGISTER YOUR PRODUCT at informit.com/register
Access Additional Benefits and SAVE 35% on Your Next Purchase

- Download available product updates.

- Access bonus material when applicable.

- Receive exclusive offers on new editions and related products.
  (Just check the box to hear from us when setting up your account.)

- Get a coupon for 35% for your next purchase, valid for 30 days. Your code will
  be available in your InformIT cart. (You will also find it in the Manage Codes
  section of your account page.)

Registration benefits vary by product. Benefits will be listed on your account page
under Registered Products.

InformIT.com–The Trusted Technology Learning Source

InformIT is the online home of information technology brands at Pearson, the world's foremost
education company. At InformIT.com you can

- Shop our books, eBooks, software, and video training.
- Take advantage of our special offers and promotions (informit.com/promotions).
- Sign up for special offers and content newsletters (informit.com/newsletters).
- Read free articles and blogs by information technology experts.
- Access thousands of free chapters and video lessons.

Connect with InformIT–Visit informit.com/community
Learn about InformIT community events and programs.

informIT.com
the trusted technology learning source

Addison-Wesley · Cisco Press · IBM Press · Microsoft Press · Pearson IT Certification · Prentice Hall · Que · Sams · VMware Press

ALWAYS LEARNING   PEARSON